Lotsis Ko



Χαρά

# INTRODUCTION TO GREEK LAW

# Introduction to Greek Law

Edited
by

Konstantinos D. Kerameus
*Professor of Law*
*Athens University*

Phaedon J. Kozyris
*Professor of Law*
*Ohio State University*

KLUWER LAW AND TAXATION PUBLISHERS
Deventer • Antwerp
London • Frankfurt • Boston • New York

SAKKOULAS • Athens

Distribution in the U.S.A. and Canada
Kluwer Law and Taxation Publishers
101 Philip Drive
Norwell, Massachusetts 02061

**Library of Congress Cataloging-in-Publication Data**

Introduction to Greek Law/edited by Konstantinos D. Kerameus, Phaedon J. Kozyris.
p. cm.
Bibliography: p.
Includes index.
ISBN 9065443266
1. Law – Greece. I. Kerameus, Konstantinos D. II. Kozyris, Phaedon J. (Phaedon John)
KKE68.I57 1987
349.495 – dc19
[344.95] 87-20602

CIP

D/1988/2664/5
ISBN 90 6544 3266 (Kluwer)
ISBN 960-232-000-1 (Sakkoulas: for distribution in Greece only)

# Preface

Greek law traces its roots to very ancient times and its main body is inextricably intertwined with the Roman-Byzantine tradition for reasons of history, geography, culture, and language. The civil law system in Europe continues the same tradition and the law of Modern Greece, highly and extensively codified, has been influenced, in many ways, by German, French and Swiss prototypes and by the grand masters of continental legal science.

This is the first time that a comprehensive, albeit summary, text on Greek law appears in English or, for that matter, in any language other than Greek. The need for it has become even more apparent now that Greece is a member of the European Communities and legal intercourse across the borders has unfolded as a matter of everyday life.

Our project brings together some of the best authorities on Greek law in Greece and in the United States. As editors, we have chosen not to force on them specific formulae of exposition or style. Some texts follow very closely the codes which govern their respective fields while others highlight only the main points, concentrating on the comparative law aspects and on differences with the corresponding concepts in the Anglo-American system. Basic bibliography, selected by the authors themselves, accompanies each contribution. Additional references are also, in some instances, to be found in the form of footnotes. The book states the law of Greece as of January 1, 1988.

The chapters were written by their authors in English and it was they who put them in final form following the comments of the editors. Some attempt was made to conform the terminology and spelling to the American rather than to the English usage. The biographical data of the authors appear at the beginning of the volume.

We take this opportunity to express our gratitude to the authors for their efforts, their collaboration and their patience with our editorial interference. Thanks are also due to Professors T. Ansay and Don Wallace Jr., the general editors of the series, and to Dr. D. Bos, Mr. A. van der Veen Vonk and Ms. A. de Visser of Kluwer Law and Taxation Publishers for their help and understanding during the various stages of the project. Finally, we would like to state our appreciation for the hard and effective work done by Mr. Panageotis Tridimas, a lawyer doing graduate work in England, in compiling the two indexes. The index of Greek words was then expanded thanks to the assistance of Ms. C. Gana, Ms. M. Papasaranti and Mr. G. Trantas, graduate students in Athens; the latter also provided extensive help during proofreading.

The editors wish to dedicate this volume to the memory of Dimitrios I. Evrigenis, a mentor, colleague and friend who suddenly passed away while work was still in progress. A firm believer in the value of comparative law, he deeply and permanently contributed to transnational legal studies in Greece through his writings, teaching and organizational activities as professor at the University of Thessaloniki, Judge of the European Court of Human Rights in Strasbourg and member of the European Parliament. What is more, Dimitrios Evrigenis had a profound knowledge and understanding of the Anglo-American system. An attempt to promote communication beyond systematic differences and historical deviations seems to touch the heart of his intellectual heritage.

February 1, 1988

*Konstantinos D. Kerameus* *Phaedon John Kozyris*

# Abbreviations

In this table appear only the abbreviations which are actually used in the book; for a list of the current Greek legal periodicals and other materials, see below, Ch. 2. References to numbers without further specification mean the articles of the code or other comprehensive enactment mainly dealt with in the respective chapter. The Latin numerals following that number denote paragraphs, and the Arabic numerals following thereafter denote subparagraphs; thus, 417 II 2 denotes the second subparagraph of the second paragraph of article 417, and 454.1 denotes the first subparagraph of article 454 consisting of one paragraph only. To avoid repetition, the use of the masculine pronoun includes the feminine, unless otherwise indicated by the context.

| | |
|---|---|
| A.D. | *Anno Domini* |
| AP | Greek Supreme Court in civil and criminal matters |
| art(s). | article(s) |
| B.C. | before Christ |
| BGB | (West) German Civil Code |
| B/L | bill of lading |
| C.C. | Civil Code |
| C.C. Proc. | Code of Civil Procedure |
| C. Crim. Proc. | Code of Criminal Procedure |
| cf. | *confer* (compare) |
| Ch. | Chapter |
| CIF | cost, insurance and freight |
| Com. C. | Commercial Code |
| Const. | Constitution |
| C. Pr. Mar. L. | Code of Private Maritime Law |
| D.P. | administrative district court |

| | |
|---|---|
| drs. | drachmas |
| ed. | edited, edition, editor |
| EDKA | Review of Social Security Law |
| EEC | European Economic Community |
| EEN | Ephimeris Hellinon Nomikon = Journal of Greek Jurists |
| E. Eur. Koin. | Epitheorisi Europaikon Koinotiton |
| EFTA | European Free Trade Association |
| e.g. | *exempli gratia* (for example) |
| etc. | *et cetera* (and so forth) |
| fasc. | fascicule |
| ff | following |
| Harm. | Harmenopoulos |
| ICSID | Convention on the Settlement of Investment Disputes Between States and Nationals of Other States |
| id. | *idem* (the same) |
| i.e. | *id est* (that is) |
| IKA | Social Insurance Organization |
| ILO | International Labour Organization |
| in f. | *in fine* (at the end) |
| Int'l Bus. Law | International Business Law |
| IOU | I owe you |
| L. | Law |
| L.D. | Law Decree |
| L. & Pol. in Int'l Bus. | Law and Policy in International Business |
| lit. | *littera* (letter) |
| MT | metric ton |
| n. | note |
| N.L. | Necessity Law |
| no(s). | number(s) |
| NoB | Nomiko Vima = Law Tribune |

| | |
|---|---|
| OAED | Organization for the Employment and the Insurance of Workmen |
| OECD | Organization for Economic Cooperation and Development |
| p. | page |
| para(s). | paragraph(s) |
| P.C. | Penal Code |
| P.D. | Presidential Decree |
| P/N | promissory note |
| R.D. | Royal Decree |
| Rev. int'le dr. comp. | Revue internationale de droit comparé |
| R. Hell. D.I. | Revue hellénique de droit international |
| S.Ct. | Supreme Court Reporter |
| SE | Greek Council of State |
| spa | resort with mineral springs |
| sq. km. | square kilometer |
| S.S.C. | Greek Supreme Special Court |
| t.o.t. | turnover tax |
| Tul. L. Rev. | Tulane Law Review |
| TV | television |
| UNO | United Nations Organization |
| U.S. | United States; United States Supreme Court Reports |
| V.A.T. | value-added tax |
| vol(s). | volume(s) |

# List of Contributors

1. *Phoebus Chr. Christodoulou*

Professor of Law, Athens School of Economics and Business.

B.Sc. (Comm.), Athens 1957; J.D., Athens 1962; Ph.D. in Law, Hamburg 1968; Habilitation in Civil Law, Athens 1974; former Associate Professor of Civil Law, University of Athens (1981–1983); Attorney at Law, member of the Piraeus Bar. Subjects: Contracts, Professional Liability, Corporations, Admiralty, Insurance, Comparative Law, Jurisprudence.

Address: 59 El. Venizelou Ave., N. Smyrni, 17123 Athens, Greece (tels. 9332–850, 8950–606).

2. *Prodromos D. Dagtoglou*

Professor of Law, University of Athens.

J.D., Athens 1952; Ph.D. in Law, Heidelberg 1959; Attorney at Law, Athens; Honorary Professor at the University of Regensburg and Honorary Lecturer at the University College, University of London. Former Professor of Law at the University of Heidelberg (1967–1968) and Regensburg (1968–1976), Visiting Fellow at All Souls College, Oxford (1972–1973), Visiting Professor at the University College at Buckingham (1973–1977), Research Scholar at Berkeley (1978), Visiting Professor at the University of Burgundy (Dijon, 1987). Subjects: Constitutional Law, Administrative Law, European Community Law.

Address: 33 Hippocratous St., 10680 Athens, Greece (tel.: 3629–065).

3. *Nicholas A. Deloukas*

Professor of Law, Emeritus, University of Athens.

J.D., Athens 1934; Ph.D. in Law, Hamburg 1940; Professor of Law, Thessaloniki (1958–1972); Professor of Law, Athens (1972–1979); Attorney at Law, Athens. Subjects: Commercial Law, Maritime Law, Comparative Law, Insurance, Private Law, Economic Law, International Law, Conflict of Laws, Public Law, International Transactions.

Address: 19 Voulgaroctonou St., Politeia, 14563 Athens, Greece (tel.: 3625–990).

4. *John C. Dryllerakis*

Attorney at Law, Athens; J.D., Athens 1960; Chief Legal Counsel, Shell Hellas; formerly General Counsel of the Exxon affiliates in Greece. Specializes in Business, Tax and Investment Laws and has authored many books and articles on related subjects.

Address: 4 Pindarou St., 10671 Athens, Greece (tels.: 3604–735, 3628–159; telex: 216129; fax: 3644–218).

5. *Anastasia Grammaticaki-Alexiou*

Assistant Professor of Law, University of Thessaloniki.

J.D., Thessaloniki 1970; Ph.D. in Law, Thessaloniki 1980; Attorney at Law practicing in Thessaloniki with Voutyras, Zannas and Associates. Subjects: Conflict of Laws, Comparative Law, European Community Law, International Transactions.

Address: 47 Polytechneiou St., 54625 Thessaloniki, Greece (tels.: 992–997, 540–613, 942–943).

6. *Alexandros G. Karakatsanis*

Professor of Law, University of Athens.

J.D., Athens 1954; Ph.D. in Law, Munich University 1962; Professor of Labor Law, Athens University School of Law 1975; member of the Athens Bar. Subjects: Labor Law, Social Security Law.

Address: 2 Chanioti St., Palaio Psychico, 15452 Athens, Greece (tel.: 6715–702).

7. *Konstantinos D. Kerameus*

Professor of Law, University of Athens.

J.D., Thessaloniki 1960; Ph.D. in Law, Free University of Berlin 1962; Professor of Civil Procedure in Thessaloniki (1971–1982), since then in Athens; practiced law in Thessaloniki, since 1983 member of the Athens Bar. Visiting Professor Berlin, Hamburg (1978, 1982, 1987), Louisiana State U. (1974, 1986), Ohio State U. (1979), Tulane (1981, 1984). Subjects: Civil Procedure, Organization of Courts, International Procedural Law, Comparative Law, International Business Transactions.

Address: 52 Stratigou Kallari St., Palaio Psychico, 15452 Athens, Greece (tels.: 6473–793, 3620–222).

8. *Phaedon John Kozyris*

Professor of Law, The Ohio State University.

J.D., Thessaloniki 1954; M. Comp. L., U. Chicago 1955; J.D., Cornell 1960;

S.J.D., U. Pa. 1984; practiced law 1960–1969 with Cahill, Gordon, Reindel & Ohl, New York City and Paris. Visiting Professor at various U.S. and European Universities. Member of Board of Editors, American Journal of Comparative Law. Principal areas of concentration: Conflicts, Corporations, Corporate Finance, European Community Law, Comparative Law, Legal Philosophy, International Trade and Investment.

Address: 1659 N. High Street, Columbus, OH 43210, USA (tels.: 614–292–0701, 488–2585).

9. *Konstantinos D. Kremalis*

Associate Professor of Law, University of Athens.

J.D., Athens 1970; Ph.D. in Law, Athens 1976; practices law in Athens. Subjects: Social Security Law, Labor Law, EEC Social Security Law.

Address: 7 Makedonias St., Filothei, 15237 Athens, Greece (tels.: 643–1387, 682–4868).

10. *Dionysios D. Spinellis*

Professor of Law, Panteios School of Political Science.

J.D., Athens 1954; Ph.D. in Law, Munich 1962; Special Adviser, Greek Ministry of Justice, Athens (1982–1986). Subjects: Penal Law and Procedure, Criminal Policy.

Address: 1 Myrsinis St., Kifissia, 14562 Athens, Greece (tel.: 801–2985).

11. *Symeon C. Symeonides*

Professor of Law, Louisiana State University.

LL.B. (Private Law, 1972), LL.B. (Public Law, 1973), University of Thessaloniki; LL.M. (1974), S.J.D. (1980), Harvard University; Reporter, Conflicts Law Revision, Louisiana State Law Institute. Teaching Subjects: Conflict of Laws, Civil Law Property, Introduction to Civil Law.

Address: L.S.U. Law Center, Baton Rouge, Louisiana 70803 U.S.A. (tel.: 504–388–8701).

12. *Athanassios N. Yiannopoulos*

W.R. Irby Professor of Law, Tulane University.

J.D., Thessaloniki 1950; M. Comp. L., U. Chicago 1954; LL.M., U. California (Berkeley) 1955; S.J.D., U. California (Berkeley) 1956; Ph.D. in Law, Cologne 1961. Subjects: Admiralty, Property, Conflict of Laws.

Address: Tulane Law School, Tulane, New Orleans, Louisiana 70118, U.S.A. (tel.: 504–865–5984).

# Table of Contents


| | | |
|---|---|---|
| PREFACE | | v |
| ABBREVIATIONS | | vii |
| LIST OF CONTRIBUTORS | | xi |
| Chapter 1. | HISTORICAL DEVELOPMENT | 1 |
| | Athanassios N. Yiannopoulos | |
| | I. INTRODUCTION | 1 |
| | II. ANCIENT GREEK LAW | 1 |
| | A. Early Law | 1 |
| | B. The Era of the Lawgivers | 2 |
| | C. Classical Law | 2 |
| | III. HELLENISTIC, BYZANTINE, AND POST-BYZANTINE LAW | 4 |
| | A. Hellenistic Law | 4 |
| | B. Byzantine Law | 5 |
| | C. Post-Byzantine Law | 6 |
| | IV. MODERN GREEK LAW | 7 |
| | A. Constitutional History | 7 |
| | B. Codification of Civil Law | 8 |
| | Bibliography | 10 |
| Chapter 2. | SOURCES AND MATERIALS | 13 |
| | Anastasia Grammaticaki-Alexiou | |
| | I. LEGISLATION | 13 |
| | II. CUSTOM | 14 |
| | III. JUDICIAL DECISIONS | 15 |
| | IV. WORKS OF LEGAL SCHOLARS | 15 |
| | V. MATERIALS | 16 |
| | Basic Bibliography | 18 |
| Chapter 3. | CONSTITUTIONAL AND ADMINISTRATIVE LAW | 19 |
| | Prodromos D. Dagtoglou | |
| | I. THE CONSTITUTION | 19 |

A. The New Constitution 19
B. Amendments – Emergency Law 19
C. Constitution and International Law 20
D. Constitution and European Communities – The Accession of Greece 20

II. STRUCTURE AND DISTRIBUTION OF STATE POWERS 21
A. System of Government 21
1. Republic 21
2. Democracy 21
3. Representative Democracy 21
4. Parliamentary Democracy 21
5. Rule of Law 22
6. Welfare State 22
B. Distribution of State Power 22
1. Separation of Powers – Links Between the Legislative and Executive Branches 22
2. Shift of the Political Power Center Under the 1975 Constitution – The 1986 Amendment 23
3. Legislation 23
4. Finance 25
5. Executive 25
6. Judiciary 25
C. State and Church 27

III. THE MAIN ORGANS OF STATE 27
A. Parliament 27
1. Composition and Election 27
2. Political Parties 28
3. Legal Status of Members of Parliament 29
4. Legislation and Parliamentary Control 29
5. Dissolution of Parliament 30
B. The President of the Republic 30
C. The Government 30
1. Constitutional Status 30
2. Composition 31
3. Cabinet Committees 31

IV. ADMINISTRATION 32
A. Central Government 32
1. Ministries – Ministers – Ministers of State 32
2. Regional Authorities 33
B. Local Government 34
1. Decentralization – Local Government – Corporations – Towns and Villages 34

2. Local and Central Government Matters 34
3. Organization 35
4. Finance 35
5. State Supervision 36
C. Specialized Self-Government 36
1. Legal Persons of Public Law 36
2. Public Corporations 36
D. General Principles of Administrative Action 37
1. Legality of Public Administration 37
2. Discretionary Power 37
3. Administrative Acts 38
4. Reasons for Decisions and Right to Hearing 38
5. Void and Voidable Administrative Acts 38
6. Revocability of Administrative Acts 38
7. Administrative Contracts 39
8. State Liability 39
9. Expropriation 40
V. CONTROL OF PUBLIC ADMINISTRATION AND JUDICIAL REVIEW 40
A. Administrative Self-Control 40
1. Hierarchical Control 41
2. Formal Petitions 41
3. Administrative Supervision 41
4. Financial Control 41
B. Parliamentary Control 42
C. Judicial Control 42
1. Administrative Courts – Judicial Review as a General Rule 42
2. Remedies Before the Council of State – The 'Application for Annulment' 42
VI. HUMAN RIGHTS 44
A. The Protection of Human Rights 44
1. The Constitutional Protection 44
2. Protection by the European Convention of Human Rights and Fundamental Freedoms and Other Conventions 44
B. Main Problems Relating to the Protection of Human Rights in the New Constitution 44
1. From an Individualistic to a Humanistic Orientation 44
2. Conflict and Synthesis: Private Ownership and Private Economic Activity 45
3. Summary 46

C. Judicial Protection 46
Selected Bibliography 47

Chapter 4. THE GENERAL PRINCIPLES OF THE CIVIL LAW 49
Symeon C. Symeonides
I. INTRODUCTION: SCOPE AND FUNCTION OF BOOK I OF THE CIVIL CODE 49
II. NATURAL PERSONS 49
A. Personality or Capacity to Hold Rights 49
B. Commencement and Termination of Personality 50
C. Absentia 50
D. Domicile 51
E. Protection of Personality 52
III. LEGAL OR JURIDICAL PERSONS 52
A. Categories of Legal Persons 52
B. Some General Principles of the Law of Legal Persons 53
1. Formal Requirements 53
2. Personality 53
3. Seat 54
4. Liability for Juridical Acts 54
5. Non-Contractual and Delictual Liability 54
IV. RIGHTS 55
A. Meaning 55
B. Abuse of Rights 55
C. 'Deactivation' of Rights 56
D. Self-help, Self-defense, Emergency 56
V. JURIDICAL ACTS 57
A. Definition 57
B. Capacity 57
C. Vices of Consent 58
D. Form 59
E. Formation of Contracts 60
F. Consideration and Cause 61
G. Content of Juridical Acts 62
H. Nullities 62
I. Interpretation 63
VI. TERMS AND CONDITIONS 63
VII. REPRESENTATION AND PROCURATION 64
A. Introduction 64
B. Express, Implied, and Apparent Authority 64
C. Undisclosed and Partially Disclosed Agency 65
VIII. PRESCRIPTION AND PEREMPTION 66
A. Clarification of Terms 66
1. Prescription 66

2. Acquisitive Prescription and Prescription of Non-Use 66
3. Peremption 66
B. General Principles of Prescription 66
1. Commencement 66
2. Suspension 67
3. Interruption 67
4. Extension, Reduction, Renunciation 68
5. Accrual 68
Bibliography 68

Chapter 5. LAW OF OBLIGATIONS 71
Phoebus Chr. Christodoulou 71
I. GENERAL PRINCIPLES 71
A. Obligation – The Sources of Obligation 71
B. Obligation to Perform in General 72
1. Performance in Good Faith 72
2. Rules Relating to Particular Kinds of Performance 72
3. Part-performance 73
4. Performance by Third Partics 74
5. Place for Performance 74
6. Time for Performance 74
7. Responsibility for One's Own Conduct 74
8. Responsibility for Employees 75
C. Contractual Obligations 75
D. Two-sided Contracts 76
E. Non-performance of Obligations 76
1. Claim to Performance in Kind 76
2. Impossibility 77
3. Delay 78
4. Other Cases of Breach of Contract 79
5. Default of the Creditor 79
F. Contractual Rescission 80
G. Earnest and Penalty Clause 80
1. Earnest 80
2. Penalty Clause 80
H. Contract for the Benefit of Third Parties – Contract Burdening Third Parties 81
I. Extinction of Obligations 81
1. Fulfillment 82
2. Set-off 82
J. Assignment of Claims 83
K. Assumption of Debt 83
L. Joint and Several Obligations 84
II. SPECIFIC CONTRACTS 85
A. Sale and Exchange 85

B. Lease 87
C. Contract for Services 89
D. Contract for Work 90
E. Mandate 91
F. Loan 92
G. Guaranty 93
H. Abstract Promise or Acknowledgment of Debt 94
1. Concept and Validity 94
2. Effect on the Burden of Proof 94
3. Formal Requirements 94
III. UNJUST ENRICHMENT 95
A. Scope of Application 95
B. Defenses 95
C. Directness of Transfer 95
D. Extent of Liability in Restitution 95
IV. UNLAWFUL ACTS (TORTS, DELICTS) 95
A. The Area of Tort Law 95
B. The Elements of Tort Liability 96
C. Defamatory Rumors 96
D. Unlawfulness 96
E. Culpability 96
F. Strict Liability 97
1. Exceptions to the Fault Principle 97
2. Reversing the Burden of Proof 97
G. Joint Tortfeasors 97
H. Personal Injury and Death 97
I. Consequences of Tort Liability: Remedies 97
1. Relief Other than Compensation 97
2. Compensation and Satisfaction 98
3. Prescription 98
Bibliography 98

Chapter 6. PROPERTY 101
Athanassios N. Yiannopoulos
I. INTRODUCTION 101
II. THINGS 102
A. Object and Thing 102
B. Movables and Immovables – Component Parts and Accessories 103
C. Fungibles 104
D. Consumables 104
E. Things 'Out of Commerce' 105
F. Fruits and Profits 105
III. POSSESSION 106
IV. OWNERSHIP 106

A. Acquisition of Ownership 108
B. Original Acquisition 108
C. Derivative Acquisition 109
D. Protection of Ownership 109
V. PREDIAL AND PERSONAL SERVITUDES 111
VI. RECORDATION 111
VII. REAL SECURITY RIGHTS 112

Chapter 7. REGIONAL AND URBAN PLANNING AND ZONING 115
Anastasia Grammaticaki-Alexiou
I. INTRODUCTION 115
II. THE CONSTITUTIONAL FRAME OF REGIONAL AND URBAN PLANNING 115
III. FORMS OF PLANNING RULES 116
IV. THE PROTECTION OF REGIONAL AND URBAN PLANNING 116
V. THE ORGANS OF REGIONAL AND URBAN PLANNING 117
VI. PLANNING LEGISLATION 117
VII. BUILDING REGULATIONS 119
VIII. ILLEGAL BUILDING ACTIVITY 120
Basic Bibliography 121

Chapter 8. FAMILY LAW 123
Anastasia Grammaticaki-Alexiou
I. INTRODUCTION 123
II. MARRIAGE 124
A. Engagement to Marry 124
B. Essential Requisites of Marriage, Requirements and Impediments 125
C. The Celebration of Marriage 125
D. Nullity of Marriage 126
E. Personal Effects of Marriage 126
F. Matrimonial Property 127
G. Interruption of Marital Life 129
III. DIVORCE 129
A. Grounds 129
B. Procedure 130
C. Effects of Divorce 130
IV. PARENT AND CHILD 131
A. Establishment of Parentage 131
B. Children Born Out of Wedlock 132
V. ADOPTION 132
A. The Legal Situation 132
B. Conditions 133

C. Effects 133
VI. LEGAL EFFECTS OF PARENTAGE 134
A. Name, Domicile, and Nationality of a Child 134
B. Obligation for Mutual Assistance and Affection 134
C. Support and Maintenance Obligations 134
VII. PROTECTION OF MINORS AND OF PERSONS INCAPABLE OF ADMINISTERING THEIR OWN ESTATES 135
A. Parental Care and Custody 135
B. Guardianship of Minors 136
C. Guardianship of Interdicted Persons 136
D. Curatorship of Absent Persons 137
E. Judicial Supervision 137
Selected Bibliography 137

Chapter 9. THE LAW OF SUCCESSION 139
Anastasia Grammaticaki-Alexiou
I. INTRODUCTION 139
II. SUCCESSION IN GENERAL 140
A. Opening of Succession – Acceptance by Heirs 140
B. Acceptance Under the Benefit of Inventory 140
C. Renunciation of Succession 140
D. Unworthiness of Heir 141
E. Vacant Succession 141
F. Certificate of Inheritance 141
G. Action for the Delivery of Possession of Assets of the Estate 142
H. Methods by Which Successors, Other than Heirs, Are Established 142
1. Legacy 142
2. Fideicommissum 142
3. Modus 142
4. Donation Mortis Causa 143
5. Agreements of Inheritance 143
III. INTESTATE SUCCESSION 143
A. Classes of Intestate Heirs 143
B. Accretion 144
C. Collation 144
IV. TESTAMENTARY SUCCESSION 144
A. Capacity to Make a Will 144
B. Form of Wills 145

C. Ordinary Wills 145
1. Holographic Wills 145
2. Public Wills 145
3. Mystic (Secret) Wills 146
D. Extraordinary Wills 146
1. Testaments Made at Sea 146
2. Military Testaments 147
3. Testaments During Blockade 147
E. Contents of Testamentary Dispositions 147
F. Validity of Wills 147
G. Substitution of Testamentary Heir 148
H. Revocation of Wills 148
I. Publication of Wills 149
J. The Executor of the Will 149
V. FORCED HEIRSHIP 150
A. Forced Heirs 150
B. The Legitimate Portion and Its Protection 150
VI. DISINHERISON 150
VII. RELATIONS OF THE HEIR WITH THE SUCCESSION CREDITORS, HIS COHEIRS AND THIRD PERSONS 151
A. Judicial Liquidation of Succession 151
B. Community Among Heirs 151
C. Sale of the Estate 152
Basic Bibliography 152

Chapter 10. COMMERCIAL LAW 153
Nicholas A. Deloukas
I. INTRODUCTORY REMARKS AND GENERAL PROVISIONS 153
II. BANKRUPTCY LAW 154
III. COMMERCIAL PAPERS 156
A. Bills of Exchange and Promissory Notes 156
1. Bills of Exchange 156
2. Promissory Notes 159
B. Checks 160
C. Commercial Money Orders 161
D. Commercial IOU's 162
E. Warehouse Receipts 163
IV. INDUSTRIAL PROPERTY 163
A. Unfair Competition 163
B. Trade Names and Trade Marks 164
1. Trade Names 164
2. Distinctive Titles 165
3. Distinctive Signs 165

4. Protection 165
5. Trade Marks 166
C. Indications of Source (Appellations of Origin) 167
D. Patents 168
E. Utility Models and Industrial Designs 169
V. INTELLECTUAL PROPERTY 169
VI. ANTITRUST LAW 172
VII. BANKING LAW 174
A. The Banking System 174
B. Private Banking Law 175
1. Deposits of Cash and Securities 175
2. Inalienable Deposits 176
3. Joint Accounts 176
4. Documentary Credit Contracts 176
5. Chattel Mortgage 177
6. Bank Hypothecary Mortgages on Realties 178
VIII. PRIVATE INSURANCE LAW 179
A. General Provisions 179
B. Insurance Against Property Loss or Damage 179
C. Specific Instances of Property Loss and Damage Insurance 181
D. Life Insurance 182
E. Inspection of the Insurance Business 182
Bibliography 184

Chapter 11. BUSINESS ASSOCIATIONS 187
Phaedon John Kozyris
I. INTRODUCTION 187
II. CORPORATION 188
A. Formation 188
B. Charter 189
C. Capital 190
D. Meetings of Shareholders 191
1. Convocation 191
2. Quorum, Voting 191
3. Authority 192
E. Board of Directors and Officers 192
F. Special Protection of Minority Shareholders 194
G. Dividends 194
H. Statutory Auditors and Financial Statements 194
I. Consolidation, Transformation, Division, Dissolution, Liquidation 195
III. CLOSE CORPORATION 196

A. Formation and Charter 197
B. Capital 197
C. Meetings of Members 197
D. Management and Interested Transactions 198
E. Distribution of Profits 198
F. Retirement of Members – Dissolution, Liquidation, Merger, Transformation 198
IV. GENERAL PARTNERSHIP 199
V. LIMITED PARTNERSHIP 200
VI. SILENT PARTNERSHIP 200
VII. CIVIL PARTNERSHIP 201
Bibliography 202

Chapter 12. ADMIRALTY AND PRIVATE MARITIME LAW 205
Nicholas A. Deloukas
I. INTRODUCTION 205
II. THE CODE OF PRIVATE MARITIME LAW 205
A. Ships and Their Ownership 205
B. Co-ownership of Ships 206
C. The Master 207
D. The Crew 208
E. Shipowner's Liability 209
F. Affreightment 210
1. General Provisions 210
2. Obligations of the Owner 211
3. Liability of the Owner 212
4. Charterer's Obligations 213
5. Rescission of Contract – Impossibility of Performance 213
6. The Bill of Lading 213
7. Carriage of Passengers 214
G. Fiduciary Transfer of Ownership of a Ship as Security 214
H. Mortgage of Ships 215
1. Simple Mortgage 215
2. Preferred Mortgage 215
I. Maritime Privileges (Liens) 215
J. Arrest and Foreclosure on Ships 216
K. General Average and Contribution 216
L. Collision of Ships 217
M. Maritime Assistance and Salvage 218
N. Limitation of Actions 218
Basic Bibliography 219

Chapter 13. LABOR LAW 221
Alexandros G. Karakatsanis

I. INTRODUCTION 221
II. EMPLOYMENT LAW 222
A. The Contract of Employment 222
1. Working Hours 222
2. Welfare, Health and Safety, Injury at Work 222
3. Leaves 223
4. Wages 223
B. Termination of Employment – Job Security 223
1. Contract of Definite Duration 224
2. Contract of Indefinite Term 224
III. COLLECTIVE LABOR LAW 224
A. Trade Unions 224
B. Collective Bargaining and Collective Agreements (L. 3239/1955, as Amended) 225
C. Arbitration 226
D. Strikes 226
Basic Bibliography 227

Chapter 14. SOCIAL INSURANCE LAW 229
Konstantinos D. Kremalis
I. INTRODUCTION 229
II. ORGANIZATION AND ADMINISTRATION OF SOCIAL INSURANCE 230
A. Multiplicity of Social Insurance Systems 230
B. Self-Governance of Social Insurance Institutions 230
III. FINANCING OF SOCIAL INSURANCE 231
A. Insurance Contributions 231
B. Social Sources and State Economic Support 232
IV. SOCIAL INSURANCE BENEFITS 233
A. Important Characteristics 233
B. Prerequisites of Insurance Benefits 233
C. Types of Insurance Benefits 234

Chapter 15. JUDICIAL ORGANIZATION AND CIVIL PROCEDURE 237
Konstantinos D. Kerameus
I. INTRODUCTION 237
II. JUDICIAL ORGANIZATION 238
A. Principles 238
B. Ordinary Civil Courts 239
C. Ordinary Administrative Courts 239

D. Judicial Independence 240
E. Judicial Staff 240
III. JURISDICTION AND COMPETENCE 241
A. Definitions 241
B. Subject Matter Competence 241
C. Territorial Competence 242
D. Exclusive Jurisdictions 242
E. Concurrent Jurisdictions 243
F. Prorogation 243
G. Review of Jurisdictional Issues 243
IV. PARTIES AND TYPES OF ACTIONS 244
A. Capacity and Standing to Sue 244
B. Types of Actions 245
V. PROCEDURAL PRINCIPLES 246
A. The Dominant Position of the Parties 246
B. Concentration on the First Hearing 247
C. Oral and Written Proceedings 247
D. Good Faith and Morals 247
VI. ORDINARY PROCEEDINGS IN FIRST INSTANCE 247
A. Commencement of the Action 247
B. Contents of the Complaint 248
C. Pleadings 248
D. Defenses and Counterclaim 249
E. Default 249
F. Attempt at Conciliation 249
G. Court Costs and Legal Aid 250
VII. EVIDENCE 250
A. Ordering Evidence 250
B. Subject Matter of Proof 251
C. Burden of Proof 251
D. Means of Proof 251
E. Documentary Evidence 252
F. Administration of Evidence 253
G. Evaluation of Evidence 253
VIII. APPEALS 253
A. Function and Distinctions of the Methods of Appeal 253
B. Reopening of Default 254
C. Regular Appeal 255
D. Reopening of Contested Judgments 255
E. Cassation 256
IX. EFFECTS OF JUDGMENTS 257
A. Drafting and Contents of Judgments 257
B. Binding Effects of Judgments 257
C. Claim and Issue Preclusion 258

D. Preclusion with Respect to Non-Parties 258
E. Time Limits of Res Judicata 259
X. SPECIAL PROCEEDINGS AND PROVISIONAL REMEDIES 259
A. Function of Special Proceedings 259
B. Groups of Special Proceedings 259
C. Common Procedural Features 260
D. Provisional Remedies 260
XI. NON-CONTENTIOUS PROCEEDINGS 261
A. Doctrinal Foundation 261
B. Examples of Non-Contentious Matters 262
C. Procedural Features 262
XII. ARBITRATION 263
A. Legislative Status 263
B. Arbitration Agreement 263
C. Arbitral Procedure 263
D. Authority of Arbitrators 264
E. Control by the Ordinary Courts 264
XIII. ENFORCEMENT PROCEEDINGS 265
A. Enforceable Instruments 265
B. Creditor's Initiative and Control by the Court 265
C. Execution with Respect to Specific Performance 266
D. Execution to Satisfy a Money Claim 266
Bibliographical Note 267

Chapter 16. CONFLICT OF LAWS, NATIONALITY, INTERNATIONAL JURISDICTION AND RECOGNITION AND ENFORCEMENT OF JUDGMENTS AND AWARDS 271
Phaedon John Kozyris
I. CONFLICT OF LAWS 271
A. Introduction 271
B. Obligations 271
1. Contracts 271
2. Torts 273
C. Property 274
D. Domestic Relations 274
E. Descent and Distribution 275
F. Legal Entities, Corporations 276
G. Maritime Law 277
H. General Matters 277
1. Renvoi 277
2. Public Policy 277
3. Statutes of Limitation 278
4. Nationality, Habitual Residence, Residence 278

5. Proof of Foreign Law 278
6. Status of Aliens 279
II. GREEK NATIONALITY 279
A. Acquisition 279
B. Loss 280
C. Reacquisition 280
III. INTERNATIONAL JURISDICTION OF THE GREEK COURTS 280
IV. RECOGNITION AND ENFORCEMENT OF FOREIGN JUDGMENTS AND AWARDS 282
Bibliography 284

Chapter 17. TAX LAW AND INVESTMENT INCENTIVES 287
John C. Dryllerakis
I. INTRODUCTION 287
II. INCOME TAXATION 287
A. General Principles 287
B. Taxation of Natural Persons 290
C. Taxation of Legal Entities 290
1. Corporations 290
2. Dividends 291
3. Cooperatives 291
4. General Partnerships 291
5. Reform 291
D. Bilateral Treaties for Avoidance of Double Taxation 291
III. OTHER DIRECT TAXES 292
A. Gift, Succession and Lottery Gains Taxation 292
B. Property Tax 292
C. Taxation of Ships and Shipping Enterprises 292
D. Capital Gain Tax 293
IV. INDIRECT TAXATION 293
A. Transaction Taxes 293
1. Value-Added Tax 293
2. Stamp Tax 294
3. Turnover Tax 294
4. Banking Tax and Capital Concentration Tax 294
B. Sales Taxes 295
C. Transfer Tax 295
D. Import Duties and Taxes 295
E. Other Taxes 296
V. MUNICIPAL TAXES AND TAXES IN FAVOR OF THIRD PARTIES 296
A. Municipal Taxes 296
B. Taxes in Favor of Third Parties 296

VI. ENFORCEMENT OF TAX LAWS – PENALTIES – LITIGATION 297
VII. INVESTMENT INCENTIVES 297
A. General 297
B. Development Regions and Qualifying Investments 298
C. Capital Aid and Loan Subsidy 298
D. Requirements for Capital Aids 299
E. Reduced Tax Rates 299
F. Tax-Free Reserves – Accelerated and Free Depreciation 299
G. Other Investment Incentives 300
Bibliography 301

Chapter 18. CRIMINAL LAW AND PROCEDURE 303
Dionysios D. Spinellis
I. HISTORICAL DEVELOPMENT AND SOURCES 303
II. SUBSTANTIVE CRIMINAL LAW 303
A. General Principles 303
1. The Two Functions of Criminal Law 303
2. The 'Nullum Crimen, Nulla Poena Sine Lege' Principle 304
B. The Structure of the Criminal Offense 305
1. The Definition and Elements of an Offense 305
2. An Act or Omission 305
3. An Outline of the Method of Analysis 305
4. Justification 306
5. Imputability and Guilt 307
6. The Elements of Imputability 307
(a) Capacity to Appreciate and Conform 307
(b) Mental Culpability 308
(c) Human Possibility to Comply with the Law 309
7. Grounds for Non-Punishment 310
C. Special Forms of Crime 310
1. Attempt 311
2. Accomplices 311
D. Penal Sanctions 311
1. Penalties 312
2. Measures of Security 312
3. Sentencing 313
E. Special Part 314
1. Homicide 314

2. Abortion 314
3. Bodily Injury 315
4. Torture 315
5. Theft 316
6. Embezzlement 316
7. Fraud 316

III. CRIMINAL PROCEDURE 316
A. Institutions 317
1. The Criminal Courts 317
2. The Public Prosecutor's Office 317
B. Persons Involved in Criminal Proceedings 318
1. The Judiciary 318
2. The Parties 318
(a) The Defendant 318
(b) The Civil Claimant 319
(c) The Third Party with Civil Liability 319
C. Outline of the Procedure 319
1. The Stages and the Principles 319
2. The Pretrial Stage 320
3. Procedure Before the Judicial Councils 321
4. The Main Proceedings 321
(a) The Preparatory Stage 321
(b) The Trial 321
(c) Appeals 322
(d) Double Jeopardy 322

Basic Bibliography 323

Index 325

Index of Greek Words 381

# Chapter 1
# Historical Development

*Athanassios N. Yiannopoulos**

## I. Introduction

Greek law and legal thought have a history of more than 3,000 years and constitute a still-living tradition. A brief introduction into this Greek legal tradition may be facilitated by distinguishing five great periods roughly corresponding with landmarks in the political and national history of Hellenism. These are: an ancient Greek period, up to the time Greece became a Roman province; a Hellenistic period, up to the foundation of the Byzantine empire; a Byzantine period, up to the fall of Constantinople; a post-Byzantine period, up to the Greek revolution of 1821 (the War of Greek Independence); and a modern period, from 1821 on.

## II. Ancient Greek Law

### *A. Early Law*

All information we have with regard to early Greek law is based on extralegal sources, such as mythology and epic poetry. Homer's Iliad and Odyssey contain scattered but most valuable information as to the main features of the prevailing legal order which was of tribal origin, primitive, and ill-defined. Law issued from kindred groups and from the tribal government, the king, the elders and the assemblies of the people. Tribal law, and the law of the early city-states as well, consisted of customary rules preserved by popular memory and considered to be immutable. Gods had laid down the fundamental ordinances but did not withhold their hands: from Zeus there came to every king, so Homer recites, the dooms (θεμιστές) according to which he settled disputes. Primitive legal institutions were confused with religious ideas and social customs, and the legal image that emerges is that of a patriarchal society governed by aristocratic rulers.

*W.R. Irby Professor of Law, Tulane University.

## *B. The Era of the Lawgivers*

From about the middle of the seventh century B.C., and until the end of the sixth century B.C., a great movement for codification swept the Greek world, which resulted in the acquisition by most city-states of elaborate written statutes, and even comprehensive codes, establishing substantive rules and procedures for the administration of justice. This legislation was the work of famous lawgivers. Lycurgus of Sparta (650 B.C.) may be a legendary personality but Dracon (621 B.C.) and Solon (594 B.C.) of Athens, Zaleukus of Locris Epizephyrii in South Italy, Charondas of Catana in Sicily, Philolaos of Thebes, Pheidon of Corinth, and the anonymous redactors of the laws of Gortyn in Crete have all lived and legislated for their cities and fellow citizens. The era of the lawgivers spans a period of about 150 years, during which citizens scored victories against absolutist rulers and paved the way toward democracy. The legal systems that emerged in the Greek world as a result of this legislative process became the first formally and substantively rational legal systems that flourished on the Continent.

## *C. Classical Law*

From the fifth century onwards, law was regarded in the Greek world as of human rather than divine origin. Religious ideas remained strong but the institutions of public as well as private law reflect secular ideas of justice, liberty, autonomy, and autarchy. During the classical period, Greek law and legal thought reached maturity. From among the various fields of private law, one may dwell on well-defined institutions of the law of persons, the law of family, the law of property, the law of conventional and delictual obligations, and the law of successions. All fields of law were permeated by the uniquely Greek ideas of contractual freedom, publicity of transactions, and reliance on written documents.

Apart from the fields of law that were proper to each city-state, there was a commercial law that was the true 'common law' of the Greek commonwealth. This law governed the relations of all Greek merchants, traders and sailors from the cities on the coast of the Black Sea to the extremities of the Mediterranean basin. Under this law, all persons, citizens and aliens, had equal rights. The commercial law contained branches of maritime law, including carriage of goods, banking law and procedures for the settlement of disputes. Its character was cosmopolitan; rapidity of transactions, absence of formalities, and evenhanded administration of justice were paramount. Among the substantive institutions of that law, which deserve special mention, are: the maritime loan, agency, and the use of the abstract document. Commercial law was administered as universal law by arbitrators and by special courts sitting in most maritime cities, including Athens, Rhodos, Syracuse, and Marseilles.

The law of the classical period, however, never developed into a systematic discipline. There was no class of professional lawyers in classical Greece performing the function of the Roman *iuris consulti*. There were λογογράφοι and συνήγοροι (speech-writers and orators) who represented parties before the lay courts and had practical familiarity with the laws of the city; but their main concern was to secure a favorable verdict from the mass juries rather than analyze the legal system and develop its institutions. There were also philosophers who were mainly concerned with the ideal of justice, the sources and function of law; for them, positive law was just a temporal expression of the reality of life in a city-state. Legal philosophy and comparative law have their origins in the works of Plato, Aristotle and Theophrastus, but the origin of systematic elaboration on a legal system is to be found in the works of the Roman jurisconsults.

One of the best studied judicial systems of the classical era is that of Athens. In the fourth century B.C., there were numerous courts in Athens, consisting of either lay judges sitting alone or of jurors sitting in panels of 200 to 6,000 men, presided over by a magistrate. The jurisdiction of each court was determined according to the sum claimed and the object of litigation. The bulk of civil litigation came before the *Forty Archons*, a judicial body elected each year by lot from among all the citizens, sitting in panels of four. Suits involving more than ten drachmas were assigned to a public arbitrator, elected from the official list made each year by the Forty Archons. The arbitrator's duty was to make an effort to effect a settlement. If he failed, he had the power to proceed and render judgment on the merits on the basis of all available evidence. His decision, however, was subject to appeal.

The appeal, at the instance of the losing party, was tried by a jury presided over by one of the Archons. All testimonial evidence, reduced to writing, had to be submitted at least one day before the hearing, and, as a rule, no additional evidence could be introduced. Witnesses were sworn in civil matters only when the other party demanded it. However, they were not too trustworthy; money frequently induced them to perjury. In one notorious case, fifteen witnesses testified under oath to the death of a woman who was subsequently brought to the court in perfect health!

Both public and private litigation ordinarily began with a formal summons to the defendant to present himself before the competent court on a specified date. Before the smaller panels of judges or jurors, litigants ordinarily handled their claims alone; but when a case was presented before a large panel, litigants could, with the permission of that jury, have other persons assist them or even act on their behalf. Attorney's fees were considered to be contrary to equality, as offering an advantage to the rich, and were forbidden by law. Attorneys, however, were frequently hired in practice, whether directly or indirectly, and the law does not appear to have been enforced.

The laws were inscribed on wood or marble in the royal portico where the Chief Archon had his office and were recorded in the *Metroon* where they were easily accessible to all. Moreover, publicity was secured by the constitutional requirement that all proposed laws and amendments should be adequately published, and by the participation of most citizens in the annual court of revision. Athenian tribunals were not bound by precedents. Consequently, an Athenian counsel or litigant was not expected to familiarize himself with the recorded body of case law. However, as no judge or juror could fail to be impressed by a precedent, even if he were at liberty to disregard it, cases were frequently cited in court. Demosthenes not only cited cases in his speeches, but he also sought to distinguish adverse precedents.

In private suits, each party paid his own court fees. In case the plaintiff failed to receive in his favor at least one-fifth of the votes cast, he was bound to pay to the state one-sixth of the amount of the damages he had claimed. This proved to be a strong deterrent of frivolous claims and 'strike' suits.

Judgments were executed by the aggrieved creditors themselves. Litigants who refused to satisfy a judgment could be disenfranchized by administrative action.

Athenians were fond of litigation and regarded it as a pleasant pastime. In Aristophanes' comedies, there are humorous descriptions of ancient trials, such as the trial of the dog-seizer in the Wasps; in another comedy, a map of Greece is shown to Socrates but the great philosopher cannot be convinced that the chart pictures Greece, for he can nowhere see a jury in session!

## III. Hellenistic, Byzantine, and Post-Byzantine Law

### *A. Hellenistic Law*

In world history, the Hellenistic period begins with the death of Alexander the Great in 323 B.C. and the founding of the Hellenistic monarchies by his Macedonian successors and ends with the absorption of these monarchies into the Roman Empire. The year 30 B.C. is generally considered to mark the end of the period, when Egypt came under the Roman rule. In terms of legal history, however, the landmarks differ.

In Greece, Greek law continued to exist and apply to the relations of the indigenous populations at least until the year 146 B.C., when Corinth, the last remaining free city, was destroyed by the Romans, and possibly until the year 212 A.D., when Roman law was made applicable to the relations of most inhabitants of the Roman Empire. In the Hellenistic monarchies, a body of *Hellenistic law* applied to the Greek and hellenized inhabitants of Egypt, Palestine, Syria, Asia Minor, and other countries of the ancient Near East. This law was essentially of Greek origin and a part of the Greek civilization that the Macedonians disseminated. It was a 'common law' of all the Greek–speaking people, the very people who spoke and developed the 'common' (κοινή) language from a variety of ethnic dialects. The private Hellenistic law appears to be universal, despite certain influences from local sources; however, it was otherwise in the fields of public law where the local influences were much more pronounced. Knowledge of Hellenistic law is derived from legal as well as extra-legal sources. *Papyri*, parchments, and inscriptions on which contracts, petitions, and records of lawsuits are reported, abound and continue to be the object of intense study.

For centuries, Roman law, Greek law and Hellenistic law lived and grew side by side. The principle of 'personality' of the law was a fundamental precept of most ancient systems of law, including Greek law, Roman law and Hellenistic law. Thus, Greek law governed the relations of the subject Greek populations in Greece while Roman law applied to the legal relations of Roman citizens in Greece. In the Hellenistic monarchies, however, the principle of personality was gradually displaced by a freedom of choice: everybody was allowed to choose the system of law he wished to be governed by. Quite routinely, the language used by the parties in a legal document determined the applicable law. These conditions prevailed well into the second century A.D. In the year 212, however, the celebrated *Constitutio Antoniniana* of Emperor Caracalla granted Roman citizenship to practically all inhabitants of the vast empire, and thus, theoretically, Roman law became applicable to the relations of all citizens, regardless of ethnic extraction.

The following centuries witnessed a struggle between native laws and imperial Roman law; and though Roman law finally prevailed and was able to displace Greek law and Hellenistic law in the official administration of justice, the victory was not achieved without compromise. The strict and inflexible Roman law had by that time been deeply influenced by Greek philosophical and legal thought and had become a Roman-Greek law, a *Ius Greco-Romanum*. The Justinian legislation of the sixth century that concluded this development was predominantly the product of the Hellenic eastern provinces of the empire and largely reflected the work of the law schools of Constantinople and Beirut.

## *B. Byzantine Law*

In spite of Justinian's prohibition of scientific elaboration on his monumental legislation, Greek translations, *indices* and *paratitla*, which were permitted, offered an opportunity for comment and scientific treatment and contributed to a further Hellenization of early Byzantine law. Moreover, the *Novellae* of Justinian, written mostly in Greek, those of his successors, written entirely in Greek, and the iconoclastic legislation of the Isaurian dynasty in the 8th century, were rooted in an unofficial Greek law which continued to live as custom. Direct connection with the Greek legal tradition was particularly apparent in the *Ecloga* (A.D. 740) of Emperor Leo III and in three collections titled Soldier's, Farmer's and Sea Law, attributed to the same emperor. The Isaurian legislation, though later repealed as heretic, continued to influence all further Byzantine legislation.

The same trend – a return to Greek sources – is apparent in the legislative efforts of the Macedonian dynasty (9th and 10th centuries). The *Procheiros Nomos* and the *Epanagoge* of Basil I, while designed to substitute for the repealed Isaurian legislation, in effect preserved its very substance. Finally, the *Basilica* of Leo the Wise, the most important Byzantine recodification of the Justinian legislation, as well as the *Eparchikon Biblion*, dealing with guilds and associations, and several Novellae of the same emperor and of his successors resulted in a complete Hellenization of the law.

The foundation of the new law school of Constantinople by Constantine IX in 1045 gave new impetus to legal studies. In the following centuries several collections of considerable legal significance appeared, such as the *Epitome Legum*, *Ecloga Privata*, *Synopsis Basilicorun*, *Peira* (a collection of judicial precedents) and several *Canones*, *Nomocanones* and *Syntagmata*, dealing with the canon law of the Greek Orthodox Church. The *Hexabiblos* of Harmenopoulos, compiled by a local judge in Thessaloniki in 1345, was one of the last Byzantine collections. Byzantine law, representing a fusion of Roman tradition, Christian ethics and Greek legal thought, exercised a deep influence on the legal systems of most eastern European and Balkan countries.

In Byzantine law, attention was focused on equity, not as a distinct set of rules separate from those of a strict law, but as a built-in humanization of the whole legal system. In this spirit, old modes of procedure were simplified and freed of the excessive formalism that characterized the Roman actions, and substantive rules of law were altered in line with the teachings of Greek philosophy and Christian ethics. The new spirit affected all branches of private law. In the law of persons, a new measure of protection was accorded to minors and other incompetents. In the law of family, the institution of marriage acquired a prominent position, and the previously unlimited authority of the husband over his wife and children was curbed. In the law of property, protection was accorded to the small agricultural owner and the serf, and the idea of family ownership of property found fertile ground for development. In the field of the law of successions, the law governing intestacy was streamlined, and the idea of a forced share took hold. Finally, in the field of the law of obligations, the subjective element of liability, that is fault, was stressed, and a debtor was accorded relief against unscrupulous or greedy creditors.

## C. *Post-Byzantine Law*

The fall of Constantinople in 1453 and the conquest of the Byzantine empire by the Turks mark the beginning of a fourth period in the history of Greek law. Byzantine law did not become extinct but continued to regulate private relations among the Greeks. And, perhaps as a unique phenomenon in legal history, the law of a subjugated people not only was retained in force but also was allowed to expand and to become the subject of further elaboration. Several reasons may account for this development. The religious character of Turkish law limited its application to controversies among Muslim subjects; and the Turkish judge (*khadi*), who was originally entrusted with the administration of justice among all subjects, was supposed to apply personal Christian law in controversies among Christians. Thus Byzantine law was formally kept in force. Further, the Turkish sultans granted a number of privileges and a large measure of self-government, which was exercised by elected or appointed local authorities and by the church. The Patriarch of Constantinople was accorded the status of head of a nation, and gradually the patriarchate and the several *metropoleis* in the provinces became administrative and cultural centres of

Hellenism. Because of growing nationalistic tendencies and because of the practices of the Turkish judges, who were naturally inclined to extend the application of Turkish law even to controversies among Christians, Greeks would go to local authorities and to the church for settlement of their disputes rather than to the *khadi*. In the course of the centuries, the jurisdiction of the local authorities and of the church, which was originally in the nature of arbitration, became clearly judicial and was extended from the fields of family law and succession to those of obligations and criminal law. It was in this way that an incipient system of courts emerged with the local authorities in the lower level, bishop's courts in the *metropoleis* functioning as courts of appeal, and the Patriarch's Synod in Constantinople acting as the court of last resort.

Local authorities and ecclesiastical courts applied Byzantine law as it had been epitomized in several synoptical collections, such as the Hexabiblos of Harmenopoulos, which was most frequently used. At the same time, several local customs had emerged that were given the force of law by the courts and that in some instances, as in the islands of the Aegean sea, were codified. By local custom and through scientific elaboration, new institutions emerged which brought the Byzantine law into line with western European developments. Thus, direct agency became possible and contractual transactions were freed of most formal requirements; and the law of partnership and other associations, as well as the law of banking and exchange, became modernized.

Apart from collections of local customs and some synodical circulars regulating questions of family law and successions, the written sources of Greek law during the post-Byzantine period are scanty. Of extraordinary significance in this regard are the codes of the Danube principalities that were governed by Greek envoys of the Sultan. All such codes were written in the Greek language and reproduced Byzantine law par excellence. The Constitution of Alexander Ypsilantis (1780), the Code of Wallachia of John Caratzas (1818), the Code of Moldavia of Callimachis (1817), and the syntagma of Michael Photinopoulos (1765), a summary of the Basilica in modern Greek, are among the first codifications in western Europe.

## IV. Modern Greek Law

### *A. Constitutional History*

The Greek revolution of 1821 marks the beginning of a new era in the history of Greek law. The first revolutionary assembly adopted in Epidaurus (Jan. 1, 1822) a liberal and democratic constitution modelled on the French Declaration of the Rights of Man. A second constitution (Astros, 1823) established a powerful parliament, and a third constitution (Troizena, 1827), while still in principle liberal and democratic, vested all executive functions in a single man, the Governor, Ioannis Capodistrias. Capodistrias, a native of the Ionian Islands and a former cabinet minister of the Russian Tsar, dissolved the parliament and governed Greece with the assistance of an appointed consultative senate until his assassination in 1831. His death threw Greece into anarchy and chaos, and order was re-established only with the arrival of young King Otho (1833). Greece was governed for a while by a regency council, and then after Otho's majority, by the king himself as an absolute monarch. A successful revolution in 1844 compelled the king to grant a constitution along the lines of the French charter of 1830, which made Greece a constitutional monarchy. Another revolution in 1862 overthrew Otho, and two years later a new democratic constitution was proclaimed by King George I. This constitution recognized the sovereignty of the people and vested all legislative authority in the parliament and the king. For the first time, universal male suffrage by secret ballot was guaranteed. As a result of a bloodless and peaceful revolution, the 1864 constitution was revised in 1911. During and following World War I, the revised constitution was suspended a number of times and finally was replaced in 1927 by a constitution which abolished kingship. The monarchy, however, was restored in 1935 and the 1911 constitution was reintroduced to be quickly rendered inoperative during the Metaxas dictatorship (1936–1941). Following World War II, a new constitutional revision was undertaken. It resulted in the adoption of the 1952 constitution which was another version of the 1911 constitution.

A *coup d'état* in 1967 resulted in the establishment of a military dictatorship, vital provisions of the Constitution were suspended and absolutism reigned. In July 1974, the tragedy in Cyprus precipitated the fall of the dictatorship. Democratic institutions were quickly restored, a national plebiscite confirmed Greece's regime as that of a parliamentary Republic with a strong presidency, and an elected Parliament voted on a new Constitution (1975) that is still the one in force. A constitutional amendment was adopted in 1985 and became effective in 1986, which has significantly reduced the power of the President in favor of the Parliament and the Prime Minister.

## *B. Codification of Civil Law*

Recognizing an uninterrupted legal tradition, the first two revolutionary constitutions designated 'the law of our ever-memorable Byzantine Emperors' as the main source of Greek civil law. In the 1827 constitution, however, a wish was expressed that all future codes should be based on French models. The influence of French doctrine and legislation in Greece may actually be traced to the years preceding the revolution, at a time when parts of the French commercial code of 1804 had been translated into Greek and were in use among Greek merchants, and to a Greek criminal code of 1823 based on that of France. In spite of the constitutional wish, the adoption of French models was confined to these two codes, and the Code Napoléon, though seriously considered, did not become a Greek civil code. Governor Capodistrias, clearly disregarding the constitutional directive, designated the Byzantine laws as the source of Greek civil law and in 1830 announced his plan for collecting and classifying them in an orderly fashion. This work was never accomplished.

Under King Otho four major codes, based on French and Bavarian models, were drafted by the Bavarian lawyer G. L. Maurer, a member of the regency council. Of these, the one dealing with civil procedure, as amended by subsequent acts, remained in force until 1968, when it was replaced by a new Code of Civil Procedure; the second on the organization of justice is still partly in force. The other two, the penal code and the code of criminal procedure, had already been replaced by modern codes in 1951. Maurer did not draft a civil code. An adherent of the historical school of jurisprudence, he believed that native institutions and ideas of law should prevail at least with regard to civil law, and, accordingly, started collecting local customs and current interpretations of Byzantine laws that were regarded as manifesting the spirit of the people. This project was interrupted by his dismissal from the regency council in 1835.

Subsequently, a royal decree of 1835 declared that 'the civil laws of the Byzantine emperors contained in the Hexabiblos of Harmenopoulos shall remain in force till the promulgation of the civil code whose drafting we have already ordered' and that 'customs, sanctioned by long and uninterrupted use or by judicial decisions, shall have the force of law wherever they prevail.' This decree became the cornerstone in the edifice of civil law in Greece and profoundly influenced the path of the law during the next hundred years. Perhaps because of inadequacies in Harmenopoulos' compilation, the scarcity of copies of the Hexabiblos, and the increasing elaboration of Roman law by the Pandectists in Germany, the Greek courts adopted a broad interpretation of the decree. Thus the entire Byzantine legislation from Justinian's time up to the dissolution of the empire, contained not only in the Hexabiblos but in any collection, was reintroduced in modern Greece. For this purpose, the work of the German Pandectists was not only useful but almost necessary. And Greek legal thought, which had been oriented almost exclusively toward France, became increasingly oriented toward Germany. Indeed, by the end of the century the redaction of the German civil code seemed to set a pattern for future codification. But at the same time the Greek jurists developed a more critical attitude and proceeded to new legislative efforts by evaluating achievements in western continental countries.

In accord with the decree of 1835, a committee was appointed to draft a new civil code. Although the final objective of the committee was not realized, its preparatory work resulted in important legislation in the field of civil law, including a comprehensive statute entitled 'Civil Law' in 1856. This contained a variety of provisions, including rules on conflict of laws, rules pertaining to the validity and nonretroactivity of the law, and regulations involving registration of births, marriages and deaths. A draft civil code of 1874, based on French, Italian and Saxon models, was not adopted, partly because of constitutional difficulties.

In the meanwhile, Greek legislation had been introduced in 1866 into the Ionian Islands; later, in 1882, into the newly liberated provinces of Thessaly and Epirus; and, in 1914, into the islands of the Aegean, Crete and Macedonia. However, special provision was made regarding the Ionian civil code (1841), the civil code of Samos (1899), the civil code of Crete (1904) and the code of civil procedure of Crete (1880), which were allowed to remain in force. This situation gave rise to a conflict of local laws and increased the urge for a new civil code that would apply throughout the state.

After another attempt at codification failed in 1922, a new five-member committee was appointed to the task in 1930. This committee published a series of drafts up to 1937, and in the following year professor G. Balis of Athens University was appointed to co-ordinate these. His project was successful and resulted in the passage of the Civil Code of 1940. The backbone of this code was Byzantine law, the national Greek tradition dressed in modern clothes. Far from being a revolutionary codification, it reproduced to a large extent law that was already in force, developed by judicial decisions and scholarly elaboration. The comparative method was also widely used, and an attempt was made to modernize and systematize the law by employing legislative techniques tested in other modern continental codes.

The 1940 Code was scheduled to become effective July 1, 1941. At that time, however, Greece had been overrun by the Axis forces. After the liberation of the country a new committee was appointed to make a final revision of the code, and a revised version was put into effect in 1945. Subsequently, this revision was repealed and the original 1940 Code given the force of law retroactively from February 23, 1946. By the introductory law of the code, all local pre-existing codes and customs were abrogated. The Civil Code, along with other legislation, was introduced in the Dodecanese Islands after their liberation in 1948.

## Bibliography

### *On ancient Greek law*

R. Dareste, B. Hassoullier and T. Reinach, *Recueil des inscriptions juridiques grecques* (1891–1904).
L. Beauchet, *Histoire du droit privé de la République Athénienne*, 4 vols. (1897).
J. H. Lipsius, *Das Attische Recht und Rechtsverfahren* (1905–15).
P. Vinogradoff, *Outlines of Historical Jurisprudence*, vol. II (1922).
R. J. Bonner, *Lawyers and Litigants in Ancient Athens* (1927).
G. M. Calhoun, *The Growth of Criminal Law in Ancient Greece* (1927).
R. J. Bonner and G. Smith, *The Administration of Justice From Homer to Aristotle*, 2 vols. (1930–35).
G. M. Calhoun, *Introduction to Greek Legal Science* (1944).
A. Verdross, *Grundlinien der antiken Rechts- und Staatsphilosophie* (1948).
U. E. Paoli, *Studi di diritto attico* (1930).
E. Wolf, *Griechisches Rechtsdenken*, 3 vols. (1950–56).
J. W. Jones, *The Law and Legal Theory of the Greeks* (1956).
A. R. W. Harrison, *The Law of Athens*, vol. I: *Family and Property* (1968).

*On Hellenistic, Byzantine, and Post-Byzantine law.*

J. A. B. Mortreuil, *Histoire du droit byzantin*, 3 vols. (1843–46).
L. Mitteis, *Reichsrecht und Volksrecht in den östlichen Provinzen des römischen Kaiserreiches* (1891).
K. E. Zachariae von Lingenthal, *Geschichte des griechischrömischen Rechts*, 3d ed. (1892; reprint 1955).
C. Lobingier, The Continuity of Roman Law in the Past, *4 Tul. L. Rev.* 341–369 (1930).
A. H. M. Jones, *The Greek City From Alexander to Justinian* (1940).
P. Zepos, *Greek Law* (1949).
R. Taubenschlag, *The Law of Greco-Roman Eygpt in the Light of the Papyri, 332 B.C.-640 A.D.*, 2d ed. (1955).
E. Seidl, *Ptolemäische Rechtsgeschichte*, 2d ed. (1962).
D. Seremetis, *Sources of Byzantine Law* (1976) (in Greek).

*On the history of the law of the modern Greek State (in Greek)*

D. Papoulias, *Greek Civil Law in its Historical Evolution* (1912).
G. Petropoulos, *The Greek Contribution to the Study of the History of Law* (1949).
P. Zepos, *The Modern Greek Science of Civil Law* (1954).
N. Pantazopoulos, *Georg Ludwig von Maurer: The Total Influence of European Prototypes on Greek Legislation* (1968).
N. Pantazopoulos, *The Law Adopted by the Greek Revolution of 1821 and the Greek Jurists*, 2d ed. (1972).
N. Pantazopoulos, *History of Greek Law: Historical Introduction to the Sources of Greek Law*, vol. I (1973).
N. Pantazopoulos, *History of Greek Law: From The Formal Tradition to The Civil Code*, vol. II (1973).
Pantazopoulos' studies have been republished in four volumes by the University of Thessaloniki Law School (Thessaloniki, 1986).

# Chapter 2
# Sources and Materials

*Anastasia Grammaticaki-Alexiou**

The formal statement as to the sources of law is contained in article 1 of the Civil Code, which defines them as being legislation and custom. This statement seems to rather oversimplify the actual situation. It does not take account of some other sources of law, which may have no formal value but they are nonetheless quite influential. Such sources are judicial decisions and legal writing. The Greek judge or lawyer, in deciding a case or advising a client, will not only take into consideration the existing legislative provisions or, if the case may be, customs, but also those 'informal' sources of law.

## I. Legislation

The Greek legal system, as the other legal systems of the Romano-Germanic family of law, is permeated by the idea that the mission of law is accomplished best by reliance upon enacted law. Although article 1 of the Civil Code does not give any priority to legislation, the latter is by far the most important source of law. This tendency seems to be in agreement with democratic principles as well as with the broadening role of the state in all sectors of social life. It also obeys to the principle of separation of powers: the legislature is exclusively responsible for the law-making process. Besides, it appears as the answer to the exigency of clarity, precision and certainty required by the contemporary complex of social relations.

According to the Constitution, the legislative powers are exercised by the Parliament and the President of the Republic. The executive may enact legal rules only on the basis of a formal statutory delegation of power. The provisions of law emanating from the legislative process exist in the form of hierarchy. At the top of this hierarchy stands the Constitution and its provisions take precedence over all other laws. Next comes ordinary legislation, either in the form of codifications or in the form of statutes. Statutes are either substantive or formal, depending on whether one examines their content or their form. For example, the budget appears in the form of a statute but it does not contain legal

*Assistant Professor of Law, University of Thessaloniki.

rules. It is therefore a formal, but not a substantive, statute. On the other hand, substantive statutes emanate not only from Parliament but from other authorities as well, especially from the President of the Republic in the form of decrees and from cabinet ministers in the form of decisions taken by virtue of authorization by Parliament. Only substantive statutes may constitute sources of law and only their violation is subject to review by the Supreme Court.

Enacted law obeys to certain basic principles. Its rules have no retroactive effect unless otherwise provided by the legislator. They may be repealed by a posterior rule of law of the same or higher rank but never by a rule of lesser rank. The repeal may be explicit or implicit. Provisions of the Constitution cannot be repealed by a statute, and those of a law cannot be repealed by presidential decree. A law contrary to the Constitution is invalid and the courts are required not to apply it. Specific provisions or statutes prevail over general ones.

Based on the idea that there is one sphere of relations between those who govern and another one among private individuals, Greek law is divided into public and private.

Some laws of ordinary legislation of either public or private nature appear in the form of codes, that is extensive compilations gathering and organizing systematically the regulation of special subjects. The most important codifications in Greek law are the following: Civil Code, Commercial Code, Penal Code, Code of Civil Procedure, Code of Criminal Procedure, Code of Private Maritime Law, Military Penal Code. More specific subjects are treated in the Code on Civil Servants, the Code of Greek Nationality, the Agricultural Code, the Forest Code, the Code on Customs, the Code on Stamp Tax, the Code on Practicing Attorneys and the Code on Notaries.

The Greek Constitution declares in article 28 that the 'generally accepted' rules of international law as well as international treaties ratified by Greece are an integral part of Greek law and that they prevail over any contrary rule. Evidently the generally accepted rules of international law constitute a direct source of internal law, while the international treaties are an indirect one, since they become part of the Greek legal system only after ratification.

As a result of the Greek accession to the European Communities, EEC law has become part of the legal system. Besides the rules of primary sources of Community law (Treaties, Annexes and Protocols) which prevail over internal law, secondary Community legislation, especially regulations, is directly applicable in member states and, consequently, in Greece.

## II. Custom

Although custom is far from having the primordial importance of enacted law, article 1 of the Civil Code places it on the same level with legislation, by naming it a source of law. This attitude has been probably influenced by the idea that custom is an infrastructure upon which the law is built, and is created directly by society without the formalities required for the promulgation and enactment of legislation.

Notwithstanding the apparent equality of custom and enacted law, the actual situation is somewhat different since custom may be considered a primary source of law, but according to article 2 II of L.D. 7/10.5.1946, it cannot abolish statutory law. Thus, the role of the custom *adversus legem* is not accepted. The role of the custom *secundum legem* is potentially considerable, because it can help in the clarification of the ideas of the legislator. The codifications and the *de facto* primacy of legislation do not leave much space to the role of custom *praeter legem.*

## III. Judicial Decisions

The creative role of judicial decisions is usually hidden behind the veil of 'interpretation' of legislation. It is not formally admitted that judges may create rules of law; on the contrary, it is stressed that the task of law-making belongs to the legislator and to the governmental or administrative authorities which complete his work by delegation. Consequently, judicial decisions are not considered a source of law and the courts are not bound by judicial precedent unlike what happens in the Anglo-American system.

The non-binding character of judicial precedent does not imply that the courts frequently deviate from their prior practice manifested in a string of decisions. Lower courts, although not technically bound by the decisions of higher courts, usually conform to them. In this respect the judicial precedents, especially those of the Supreme Court, play an important role and may also create customary law.

Furthermore, when a statute uses general concepts, such as 'important cause' or 'inadequately large', or incorporates general clauses, such as 'good morals' and 'good faith' which must be interpreted in order to fit an individual case, the judge necessarily is invited to fill the gaps of the legislation.

## IV. Works of Legal Scholars

Doctrine does not constitute a source of law in the formal sense but a realistic approach brings forward its great importance in the creation and application of laws. It creates the ideas that influence the legislator and establishes the methods by which legal rules will be interpreted. When a judge is formulating his opinion, he usually needs the support of doctrine. Court decisions often cite the names of legal scholars, whose opinions have been taken into consideration.

Doctrine appears in the form of commentaries, treatises, manuals, monographs or articles and comments on judicial decisions published in legal periodicals.

## V. Materials

A. Statutory law must first be published in the Official Gazette. Then it is also published in various private collections appearing on a monthly or yearly basis. The best known private collections of legislation are the following:

- Code of the Law Tribune (Κώδικας Νομικού Βήματος, Kodikas Nomikou Vimatos)
- Code of Laws (Κώδιξ Νόμων-Ζαχαρόπουλος, Kodix Nomon-Zacharopoulos)
- Continuous Code of Legislation (Διαρκής Κώδιξ Νομοθεσίας-Ραπτάρχης, Diarkis Kodix Nomothesias-Raptarchis)
- Continuous Indexes of Cases and Legislation (Διαρκή Ευρετήρια Νομολογίας και Νομοθεσίας, Diarki Euretiria Nomologias kai Nomothesias)
- Bulletin of Motoring Legislation and Cases (Δελτίο Αυτοκινητικής Νομοθεσίας και Νομολογίας, Deltio Autokinitikis Nomothesias kai Nomologias)
- Bulletin of Labor Legislation (Δελτίον Εργατικής Νομοθεσίας, Deltion Ergatikis Nomothesias)
- Bulletin of Construction Legislation and Cases (Δελτίον Δομικής Νομοθεσίας και Νομολογίας, Deltion Domikis Nomothesias kai Nomologias)
- Construction Information (Domiki Enimerosis)
- Code of Tax Legislation and Cases (Κώδιξ Φορολογικής Νομοθεσίας και Νομολογίας, Kodix Forologikis Nomothesias kai Nomologias)
- Code of Taxation and Stamps (Κώδιξ Φορολογίας Εισοδήματος, Κύκλου Εργασιών, Τελών Χαρτοσήμου, Kodix Forologias Eisodimatos, Kyklou Ergasion, Telon Chartosimou)
- Continuous Interpretative Code of Labor Legislation (Διαρκής Ερμηνευτικός Κώδιξ Εργατικής Νομοθεσίας, Diarkis Ermineutikos Kodix Ergatikis Nomothesias)
- Code of the Review of Labor Law (Λώδικας Επιθεωρήσεως Νργατικού Δικαίου, Kodikas Epitheoriseos Ergatikou Dikaiou)
- Pandect of Penal Law (Πανδέκτης Ποινικού Δίκαίου, Pandektis Poinikou Dikaiou)

As is apparent from the respective titles, some of these collections include cases as well. Statutes are published therein either in chronological order or in an arrangement by subject matter. Formal statutes and delegated legislation are usually mixed up with no separated parts of the publication devoted to each category. The most frequent use is made of the Code of the Law Tribume, which is published by the Athens Bar.

B. There are no official collections or reports of judicial decisions in Greece, with the exception of the Council of State which publishes for every year, but with a certain delay, several volumes containing either its opinions of the year in full or extensive indexes with substantial syllabi. Legal periodicals publish a large number of decisions of all courts in all branches of law. Some periodicals specialize in certain subjects only. Cases are cited by the name of the court, their number and year; numbering starts afresh every year for every court. Most legal periodicals publish the names of the judges, usually of the presiding judge and the judge rapporteur, and of the attorneys, as well as a brief summary of the decision. The best known legal periodicals are the following:

- Administrative Justice (Διοικητική Δικαιοσύνη, Dioikitiki Dikaiosyni)
- Archives of Cases (Αρχείο Νομολογίας, Archeio Nomologias)
- Basic Cases (Βασική Νομολογία, Vasiki Nomologia), which is a compilation of all decisions of the Supreme Court in civil matters since 1967
- Bulletin of Tax Legislation (Δελτίο Φορολογικής Νομοθεσίας, Delito Forologikis Nomothesias)
- Criminal Chronicles (Ποινικά Χρονικά, Poinika Chronika)
- Trial (Δίκη, Diki)
- Greek Justice (Ελληνική Δικαιοσύνη, Helliniki Dikaiosyni)
- Greek Review of European Law (Ελληνική Επιθεώρηση Ευρωπαϊκού Δικαίου, Helliniki Epitheorisi Europaikou Dikaiou)
- Harmenopoulos (Αρμενόπουλος)
- Cases (Νομολογία, Nomologia)
- Journal of Greek Jurists (Εφημερίς Ελλήνων Νομικών, Ephimeris Hellinon Nomikon)
- Law Tribune (Νομικό Βήμα, Nomiko Vima)
- Law and Politics (Δίκαιο και Πολιτική, Dikaio kai Politiki)
- Review of Commercial Law (Επιθεώρησις του Εμπορικού Δικαίου, Epitheorisis tou Emporikou Dikaiou)
- Review of Cases (Επιθεώρηση Νομολογίας, Epitheorisi Nomologias)
- Review of Labor Law (Επιθεώρησις Εργατικού Δικαίου, Epitheorisis Ergatikou Dikaiou)
- Review of Maritime Law (Επιθεώρηση Ναυτιλιακού Δικαίου, Epitheorisi Nautiliakou Dikaiou)
- Review of Public Law and Administrative Law (Επιθεώρησις Δημοσίου Δικαίου και Διοικητικού Δικαίου, Epitheorisis Dimosiou Dikaiou kai Dioikitikou Dikaiou)
- Review of Social Security Law (Επιθεώρησις Δικαίου Κοινωνικής Ασφαλίσεως, Epitheorisis Dikaiou Koinonikis Asphaliseos)
- Review of Traffic Law (Επιθεώρησις Συγκοινωνιακού Δικαίου, Epitheorisis Synkoinoniakou Dikaiou)
- Review of Multistory Building Law (Επιθεώρηση Δικαίου Πολυκατοικίας, Epitheorisi Dikaiou Polykatoikias)
- Revue Hellénique de Droit International, published by the Greek Institute of International and Foreign Law only in foreign languages (French, English, German)
- The Constitution (Το Σύνταγμα, To Syntagma)

Basic information on legislation and cases may also be found in the *Law Lexicon* (Λεξικόν Νομικής, Lexikon Nomikis), published in 15 volumes (1959–1973).

As far as commentaries are concerned, the most important one is the *Interpretation of the Civil Code* (Ερμηνεία του Αστικού Κώδικος-ΕρμΑΚ) which has not been completed yet. A more modern commentary is A. Georgiadis and M. Stathopoulos, *Civil Code* (Αστικός Κώδιζ, Astikos Kodix) in six volumes (1978–1985) with probably three more to appear.

Greek legal bibliography is quite rich. However, legal scholars who do not know the Greek language can hardly have access to it.

There is no comprehensive or survey work on modern Greek law and very little writing of any kind in English. Professor P. Zepos' *Greek Law* (Athens 1949) contains three lectures on Greek law and tradition and on the Civil Code as well as a basic bibliography. See, also, P. Zepos, The Greek Legal System, *R. Hell. D.I.* 1–13 (1961). The Civil Code was only recently translated into English with some degree of success and published by C. Taliadouros (1982, with 1983 supplement); *An Outline of the Greek Civil Law* was published by A. Iatrou (Athens, 1986). There exist, however, two good translations of the original text of the Civil Code into French by P. Mamopoulos (1956, 2d ed. 1982) and into German by D. Gogos (1951). A translation of the original text of the Code of Civil Procedure into German was published by G. Baumgärtel and G. Rammos (1969). A two-volume *Greek-English and English-Greek Dictionary of Legal Terms* (Kivotos 1970), compiled by G. Perris, is sometimes helpful but should be used with caution because of omissions and inaccuracies. A more recent attempt is G. Tragakis, H. Caratzas and H. Zombola, *An English-Greek and Greek-English Dictionary of Law Terms* (1986). The chapter on Greece in the *International Encyclopedia of Comparative Law* (1978), originally by Professor Ch. Fragistas, is excellent and its bibliography extensive, but extremely abbreviated. The chapter on the 'Legal System of Greece' by I. Vekris in the *Modern Legal Systems Encyclopedia* (1985) contains some useful current information on the Greek system of government. The 'Greece' *Law Digest* in Martindale and Hubbell (1987), compressed into a dictionary of terms, is carefully written but elliptical and can be misleading. The *World Legal Encyclopedia*, a publication of Facts on File, plans to include a chapter on Greece in its forthcoming edition.

## Basic Bibliography
(in Greek)

G. Balis, *General Principles of Civil Law*, 8th ed. (1961) 4–16.

A. Georgiadis and M. Stathopoulos, *Civil Code*, vol. I: *General Principles* (1978) 1–5.

N. Papantoniou, *General Principles of Civil Law*, 3d ed. (1983) 21–50.

A. Papachristou, *General Principles of Civil Law* (1987) 3–24.

G. Tambakis, Statute and Custom in the Civil Code, *EEN* (1975) 653–666.

K. Tsatsos, *The Problem of the Sources of Law* (1941).

An article in English by K.D. Kerameus and G.D. Kremlis on 'The Application of Community Law in Greece 1981–1987' is forthcoming in the 1988 Spring issue of the *Common Market Law Review*.

# Chapter 3
# Constitutional and Administrative Law

*Prodromos D. Dagtoglou**

## I. The Constitution

### *A. The New Constitution*

The present Constitution (Σύνταγμα, Syntagma) of Greece was adopted by a specially empowered Parliament on June 7, 1975, within a year after the fall of a seven-year military dictatorship.

The Constitution of 1975, which replaced the constitution of 1952, contains a mixture of traditional and more modern provisions based in part on the experience of the dictatorship. Despite its many defects, such as repetitiveness, excessive and uneven detail, and lack of precision, this Constitution is nevertheless an improvement compared to its predecessor. It stands closer to the daily realities of politics and administration, guarantees a more complete judicial protection of the individual, and provides for a more effective and efficient functioning of government.

### *B. Amendments – Emergency Law*

The Constitution is 'rigid' in the sense that, first, it may not be amended within the term of one parliament and through the ordinary legislative procedure; and second, certain constitutional provisions may not be amended at all. These provisions pertain to the form of government as a 'republican, parliamentary democracy' and the sovereignty of the people, the respect for human dignity, the principle of equality, the free access to public offices, the prohibition of titles of nobility, the free development of personality, personal freedom, freedom of religion and separation of powers.

The remaining provisions may be amended in a two-phase procedure: Parliament states first the need for amendment and specifies the provisions to be amended in two resolutions taken by a three-fifth majority (180) of the total number of the members of parliament (300) in two ballots held at least one month apart. The next parliament decides on the amendments, during its first

*Professor of Law, Athens University.

session, by an absolute majority (151) of the total number of its members (art. 110 Const.). This procedure is considerably simpler than those of previous constitutions which were never observed.

The first amendment of the Constitution was completed on March 6, 1986 and affected, totally or partly, articles 32, 35, 37, 38, 39, 41, 42, 43, 44, 47 and 48. The amendment consisted mainly in transferring most of the President's powers, not merely the ceremonial ones, to the Government and, effectively, to the Prime Minister.

In case of emergency, the Government may propose to Parliament or, if Parliament cannot be convened in time, to the President of the Republic to suspend temporarily several constitutional provisions (art. 48 Const.; see below, Section II B 1). Prior to the amendment, this power belonged to the President alone. Only the Cabinet's or the Prime Minister's countersignature was required.

### C. *Constitution and International Law*

The Constitution is particularly open towards international law. Article 2 II proclaims that 'Greece, adhering to the generally acknowledged rules of international law, pursues the strengthening of peace and of justice and the development of friendly relations between peoples and states'. More importantly, article 28 I provides that 'the generally accepted rules of international law, as well as international treaties, as from their ratification by statute and from their coming into force under the conditions of each of them, shall constitute an integral part of Greek domestic law and shall prevail over any contrary statutory provision. The rules of international law and international treaties shall be applied to aliens only on the condition of reciprocity.'

Thus, in the hierarchy of the Greek legal rules, the 'generally accepted rules of international law' and the international treaties ratified by Greece rank between the Constitution and the acts of parliament.

### D. *Constitution and European Communities – The Accession of Greece*

The Constitution takes an even more important step. On certain formal and substantive conditions, it is possible (a) to accept that powers under the Greek Constitution will be exercised by institutions of international organizations (art. 28 II); and (b) to restrict the exercise of national sovereignty (art. 28 III). In this way Greece's accession to, and membership in the European Communities has been made constitutionally possible.

The Treaty of Accession was signed on May 28, 1979, and ratified on June 29, 1979 by the Greek Parliament with a majority of 193 votes out of 300. Greece became a member of the European Communities on January 1, 1981. The main transition period expired on December 31, 1985. The remaining transition periods expired on December 31, 1987.

## II. Structure and Distribution of State Powers

### *A. System of Government*

The Constitution provides that Greece is a 'presidential parliamentary democracy' (art. 1 I). More particularly:

1. Greece is a republic (art. 1 I). Monarchy had already been abolished by the referendum of December 8, 1974. The Constitution declares that Greece is a 'presidential democracy' and bars the restoration of monarchy (art. 110 I). As the word 'republic' is unknown in the Greek language, and the Greek word 'democracy' (δημοκρατία, dimocratia) means both 'democracy' and 'republic', the Constitution speaks of 'presidential democracy' in the sense of 'republican democracy' and in contrast to the 'crowned democracy' of the previous constitution of 1952 (art. 21 I).

2. Greece is a democracy (art. 1 I). Its system of government is based on popular sovereignty (art. 1 II), equality (arts. 4 and 22 I), personal and political freedom (arts. 4 ff), free political parties (art. 29) and therefore a multi-party system, free and regular parliamentary and local government elections (arts. 51 and 102 II), separation of powers (art. 26) and an independent judiciary (art. 87), government accountable both to Parliament (arts. 84–86) and to the courts (arts. 20 I, 95).

3. Greece is a representative democracy (art. 51 II). No state power is directly exercised by the people themselves, but through elected and freely acting representatives (arts. 51 and 61 I) or by the officials they elect, mainly the President of the Republic, or approve, mainly the government. By way of exception, the President of the Republic may by decree order a referendum on 'crucial national issues' (art. 44 II; see also L. 350/1975).

4. Greece is a parliamentary democracy (art. 1 I). The parliamentary system was introduced in Greece more than a century ago. The Constitution provides (a) for the appointment as Prime Minister of the leader of the majority party in Parliament, or, if there is no majority party, of the leader of a party who can form a government enjoying the Parliament's confidence (art. 37); (b) for the dependence of Government on the Parliament's vote of confidence (arts. 37, 38, 84); (c) for parliamentary control (art. 70 VI); and (d) for the right or duty of the President to dissolve Parliament (arts. 32 IV, 37, 38, 41; see below, Section III A 5). In practice, Parliament's position has weakened considerably since the 1982 abolition of the voter's right to choose individual parliamentary condidates from the list submitted by each party. Before the recent amendment, the President could dismiss the Government without a parliamentary vote of censure, and could dissolve Parliament without the Government's proposal. He also had extensive emergency powers. However, none of these powers had ever been activated. It can be reasonably argued that the original text of the

Constitution presented a considerable aberration from the classical parliamentary system in favor of the President. However, the amended constitution (see below, Section II B 2) weakens not only the President, but also Parliament by creating a very strong government under a particularly powerful Prime Minister whose control of the system of selection and election of parliamentary candidates may easily be translated into control over the political career of the majority party representatives.

5. Greece is a state under the rule of law (κράτος δικαίου, kratos dikaiou). The Constitution protects the dignity of the person (art. 2 I) and entrenches human rights (arts. 4–25). The Constitution also provides for the separation of powers and the rule of law over state powers, in particular the prevalence of the Constitution over Parliament; authorizes a limited judicial review of acts of parliament; subjects public administration to the rule of law and judicial review; and guarantees the independence of the judiciary and the citizen's access to the courts (arts. 20 I, 26, 49, 50, 87–100).

6. Greece is a welfare state (κοινωνικό κράτος, koinoniko kratos). The present constitution is more socially oriented than its predecessor. It provides for social restrictions on human rights (arts. 25 III, IV, 17 I, 106 II); protects the family, motherhood, childhood and youth, the weak or poor members of society; proclaims the right to work; and provides for social security (arts. 21 and 22; see below, Ch. 14).

### *B. Distribution of State Power*

#### 1. Separation of Powers – Links Between the Legislative and Executive Branches

The Constitution divides state authority in the three traditional powers ('functions') and assigns each of them to different state organs (art. 26). However, this division does not lead to a real segregation (separation) of powers. Only the judiciary is genuinely separated from the other state powers, but even there significant exceptions exist: the government appoints the heads of the three higher courts, and can also assign administrative duties to judges (arts. 89 III and 90 V).

Between the legislative and executive branches there exist several links. They refer, first, to the parliamentary system, that is the government's origin in political parties and Parliament, the government's dependence on Parliament's confidence, parliamentary control of government, and the executive's right to dissolve Parliament. They refer further to the executive's legislation enacted under authorization by Parliament (delegated legislation). In urgent cases and in case of emergency, the executive can also legislate without the Parliament's (prior) authorization, but subject to its subsequent approval (arts. 44 I, 48 V). Unless Parliament authorizes their extension, these emergency measures expire, in case of war with its end, and in other cases fifteen days after the proclamation of the emergency measures. The links between the legislative and executive branches are particularly discernible in the dual nature of the President of the Republic who shares the legislative function with Parliament and the executive function with Government (arts. 26 I, II).

## 2. Shift of the Political Power Center Under the 1975 Constitution – The 1986 Amendment

Prior to the amendment of the Constitution, the dual office of the President, manifested in his power to dismiss the Government (art. 38 II) and to dissolve Parliament (art. 41 I) and his wide emergency powers (art. 48), represented a considerable shift of the political power centre from the Government and the Prime Minister towards the President. In practice, however, this shift remained on paper and never actually affected the working of the parliamentary system. Nevertheless, the Socialist Government began in the spring of 1985 and completed in March 1986 the process of amending the Constitution and transferring virtually all presidential powers to the Government and, particularly, to the Prime Minister. At the same time, the Parliament's majority remains dependent on their leader's and Prime Minister's favor, with the resulting weakness of Parliament. Thus, the old political bicentrism has been transformed into a governmental monocentrism of power.

## 3. Legislation

Legislation is in the main assigned to Parliament. Within the limits of the Constitution (especially those drawn by the provisions on human rights), the Parliament is subject to no constraints regarding what and how to legislate.

Under the Constitution, the legislative power is exercised by Parliament and the President of the Republic. In normal cases the powers of the President are confined to promulgating and publishing the acts of parliament. Although he has the considerable right of referring a bill back to Parliament, in which case the bill must receive the favorable vote of a majority of the total number of its members (art. 42), no president has as yet made use of this right. The President may only issue decrees containing legal rules on the basis (a) of a statutory (specific) delegation which must state its subject, aim and limits, or (b) of a (newly introduced) *loi-cadre* (arts. 43, 78 V).

Delegation is allowed except where the Constitution requires a 'formal law', that is, an act of parliament, instead of simply a 'law' which may also be any statutory instrument. As a rule, such 'formal laws' are needed for the imposition of taxes (art. 78), but also in many important areas, including the 'exercise and protection of individual rights' where the Constitution requires Parliament to pass a law *in pleno*, i.e., not in one of its two sections (art. 72 I). However, in practice this rule is not strictly complied with and the courts are very lenient.

The most important form of delegated legislation is the presidential decree (προεδρικό διάταγμα, proedriko diatagma), based on specific statutory delegation and issued on a ministerial proposal. Presidential decrees are required to be submitted in draft form to the Council of State which examines their legality and drafting accuracy.

Parliament may also delegate legislative power to other organs of the executive, e.g., ministers, but only with regard to matters of a specialized, local, technical, or detailed nature. However, ministers (particularly the Minister of Finance) often introduce statutory instruments without previous delegation, but with the clause that the instruments concerned 'shall be ratified by act of parliament'. This (retroactive) ratification invariably follows, albeit sometimes many years later. The courts have not objected to this obviously unconstitutional practice.

In urgent cases, the President's powers are wider: on proposal of the Cabinet he is allowed to issue 'legislative acts' without statutory delegation. These acts must be submitted to Parliament's approval within forty days of their adoption or of the Parliament's convocation. However, only their future force, not their past application, depends on this approval, even in case they were not submitted at all to Parliament (art. 44 I). The President has repeatedly used his powers to issue 'urgent' decrees, although manifestly no urgent case existed. These decrees are invariably approved by Parliament and any inquiry as to their 'urgency' is viewed by courts as being of 'political' nature and, therefore, not justiciable.

Prior to the 1986 amendment, the President had very wide, though temporary powers in case of emergency (art. 48). In case of external or internal dangers, he could issue a decree countersigned by the ministers or, in some cases, the Prime Minister, and suspending several constitutional provisions, he could apply the Emergency Act (L. 566/1977) and set up emergency courts. The President was empowered, on the same conditions, to take 'all administrative and legislative measures needed to meet the situation and to restore, as soon as possible, the constitutional order'. This presidential power depended neither on the previous permission nor the subsequent approval of Parliament. However, except for emergency decrees issued in case of war which may remain in force until the termination of the war, all other such decrees remain in force for only thirty days, unless extended by Parliament.

The 1986 amendment assigned the power to declare the state of emergency to Parliament or, if it cannot be convened, to the President. However, in both cases the Government's proposal is needed. In light of the fact that, under the amendment, the Government no longer depends on the President's confidence (in addition to parliamentary confidence), and that the amendment replaced the Cabinet's or Prime Minister's countersignature with the Government's proposal, the weakening of the President's position is considerable. In addition, the emergency measures now need Parliament's approval within fifteen days from their enactment.

## 4. Finance

In public finance, decisive powers are assigned to Parliament. Taxes may be levied only by an act of parliament, which may not have a retroactive effect beyond the previous fiscal year. This act must state the taxable object, the tax rate, and the tax abatements and exemptions. By way of exception a presidential decree, based on a *loi-cadre*, suffices in customs and currency matters, as well as 'within the framework of the country's international relations to economic organizations' (art. 78). Only Parliament itself may add to the state budget, or grant salaries, pensions, subsidies or remunerations (arts. 80 I, 78 IV). However, this constitutional rule is circumvented by the practice of ministerial decrees 'ratified' retroactively by Parliament (see above, Section II B 3).

Parliament votes on the annual budget and confirms the financial statement and the general balance sheet of the state (art. 79 I–VII). Parliament also approves plans on economic and social development (art. 79 VIII; see also L. 503/1976, as amended by L. 747/1978).

## 5. Executive

The executive power is exercised by the President and the Government. In normal cases, the Government is the main executive organ with every decision of the President requiring the countersignature of the appropriate minister (art. 35 I). The powers granted the President by the original Constitution, to summon the Cabinet under his chairmanship, to address messages to the nation, or to call a referendum on 'crucial national issues,' have been abolished or considerably weakened by the 1986 amendment. However, the President may still, without ministerial countersignature, appoint the Prime Minister, dismiss the Government, and dissolve the Parliament under certain circumstances (arts. 35 II, 38 II).

For the President's emergency powers which are now effectively transferred to Government, see above under 3. For the central and local government, ministers, and other authorities, see below, Section IV A–C.

## 6. Judiciary

Judicial power is exercised by the courts of law (arts. 26 III and 87 I). Judicial independence (on which see below, Ch. 15, Section II D) is the basis for the judicial review of the constitutionality of laws and of the constitutionality and legality of statutory instruments. However, while unlawful and unconstitutional (individual) administrative acts and statutory instruments other than acts of parliament may be declared null and void by the administrative courts (art. 95), unconstitutional acts of parliament may only be denied application by the courts – indeed the courts are bound by the Constitution not to apply laws the contents of which are contrary to the Constitution (art. 93 IV). Only the (new)

Supreme Special Court can annul an act of parliament on the ground of unconstitutionality (see below, under the same number).

The law provides in a general manner for the powers of the different courts. No one may be deprived against his will of the judge assigned to him by law, and judicial committees and extraordinary courts (not to be confused with the emergency courts of art. 48 I) are prohibited (art. 8).

There are administrative, civil, and criminal courts of law (art. 93 I). The Council of State (Συμβούλιο της Επικρατείας, Symvoulio tis Epikrateias) was established in 1928 after the model of the French *Conseil d'Etat*, and is the supreme administrative court (art. 95). Except for its advisory function with regard to delegated legislation (see above, Section II B 3), the Council of State is primarily (unlike perhaps its French prototype) a court of law. It is an administrative court of first and last instance with jurisdiction over applications for review ('petitions for annulment') of administrative acts for violations of law or abuse of discretionary power. Its powers, organization and procedure are prescribed by Laws 170/1973, 702/1977 and 1406/1983 and Presidential Decrees 752/1978 and 1218/1981. It is also the supreme court which decides final appeals against judgments of the lower administrative courts. These courts are of first and of second instance. When the law provides for a full ('substantive') judicial review on grounds both of law and equity, this so-called 'substantive' administrative dispute is assigned to the 'ordinary administrative courts' of first and, on appeal (but sometimes directly), of second instance (see mainly L. 702/1977 and 1406/1983). The organization and procedure of these courts are regulated by Laws 3845/1958 and 4125/1960 and Presidential Decree 341/1978.

The civil courts adjudicate all 'private disputes' (disputes between individuals) as well as cases of non-contentious proceedings (art. 94 IV; see below, Ch. 15, Sections II B, III and XI). Final appeals on points of law, both in civil and criminal cases, are decided by the Supreme Civil Court (Άρειος Πάγος, Areios Pagos; see below, Ch. 15, Sections II B, VIII E).

The Auditors' Court (Ελεγκτικό Συνέδριο, Elengtiko Synedrio) is both a court of law and an independent administrative authority responsible for deciding on pensions and for auditing public accounts (art. 98).

Next to the three supreme courts described above, the Constitution provides also for a special court for suits on miscarriage of justice (art. 99), and a special court to hear charges against ministers and against the President (arts. 86, 47 II, 49). They are both courts *ad hoc* and decide in the first and last instance. Their organization and procedure are provided for by Laws 693/1977 and 802/1971.

The Constitution also sets up the Supreme Special Court (Ανώτατο Ειδικό Δικαστήριο, Anotato Eidiko Dikastirio; art. 100 and L. 345/1976). Its jurisdiction includes review of parliamentary elections and referenda; review of the substantive constitutionality or interpretation of provisions of acts of parliament in case of disagreement between the supreme courts; and the resolution of disputes concerning the qualification of a rule of international law as a 'generally accepted rule' within the meaning of article 28 I. This *ad hoc* court is a constitutional court of limited jurisdiction. A statutory provision declared to be unconstitutional by this court is null and void from the pronouncement of the judgment, or from the time stated in the judgment. This judgment is binding *erga omnes*. Together with the judgments of administrative courts annulling (individual) administrative acts and statutory instruments other than acts of parliament (see art. 50 I L.D. 170/1973), this is the only instance where Greek law recognizes something akin to the doctrine of *stare decisis* (for the doctrine of *res judicata*, see below, Ch. 15, Sections II D in f. and IX).

Court proceedings are, as a rule, public, but the judges deliberate *in camera*. Judicial decisions must contain a statement of their reasons, may include dissenting opinions, and must be pronounced at a public hearing (art. 93 II, III). They are known by the name of the court which rendered them, a serial number, and the year (for example Council of State 235/1985).

### *C. State and Church*

The relations between state and church in Greece are *sui generis*. There is neither an 'established Church' nor a complete separation of church and state. The language in article 3 I of the Constitution that 'the prevailing religion in Greece is that of the Eastern Orthodox Church of Christ' is understood not to imply predominance over other religions or churches. No high public official need be a member of the Orthodox Church. It is true that the President of the Republic (art. 33 II) must take an oath 'in the Name of the Holy, Consubstantial and Indivisible Trinity' (a traditional preamble of all Greek constitutions), and this means that the President must be a Christian. However, it does not mean that he has to be an Orthodox, as most Christian denominations accept the Trinity. Furthermore, unlike the king under the constitution of 1952 (art. 43 III), the President does not swear 'to protect the predominant religion of the Greeks'. While article 1 of the constitution of 1952 prohibited proselytism and any other interference with the predominant religion, article 13 II 3 of the present Constitution prohibits proselytism in general. Aside from stating as a matter of fact that nearly all Greeks belong to the Orthodox Church, the term 'prevailing religion in Greece' reflects the tradition under which the Constitution guarantees the dogmatic unity of the Greek Orthodox Church with the Oecumenical Patriarchate in Constantinople, but also its autocephalous character (self-government). The statutory charter of the Church of Greece, provided for in article 3 I of the Constitution, was enacted in its present form as Law 590/1977.

## III. The Main Organs of State

### *A. Parliament*

#### 1. Composition and Election

Parliament consists of one chamber with between two hundred and three hundred (traditionally 300) members, elected for a term of four years in a direct, general and secret ballot (art. 51 I, III). Every citizen who has completed his eighteenth year is entitled to vote (art. I. L. 1224/1981). Every voter who has completed his twenty-fifth year is eligible to run (art. 55 I). Civil servants (but not university professors) and soldiers, mayors, and chairmen of public corporations must resign before they submit their candidacy (art. 56 I, II). Moreover, civil servants and officers of public corporations may not be candidates in the constituencies where they served for more than three months in the three years before the elections (art. 56 III).

The Constitution allows Parliament to decide on the electoral system (art. 54 I). The Parliamentary Elections Act of 1985 (see the codification of all provisions concerning parliamentary elections in P.D. 152/1985) establishes a so-called 'enforced proportional representation' which, despite its name, strongly favors the two major parties. The law establishes fifty-six constituencies with several representatives each. Up to 1/20 of all representatives (in fact now only twelve members) are elected not by a local constituency but by the whole country; these seats are divided among the political parties according to their national poll results and in the priority of the lists of names they had submitted for the election (art. 54 III).

This 'list system' has been extended by Law 1303/1982 to all fifty-six constituencies, so that the voter can only choose a party, but not individual candidates from that party. The candidates are elected according to the position of their name on the party list for their constituency.

The Constitution contains a long list of parliamentary ineligibilities (art. 56) and incompatibilities (art. 57). Disputes about the elections are adjudicated by the Supreme Special Court which functions as an electoral court as well (art. 100 I Const., arts. 6, 24–34 L. 345/1976; see above, Section II B 6).

## 2. Political Parties

The main participants in the parliamentary elections are the political parties rather than independent individuals. The Constitution guarantees the citizen's freedom to establish and to join a political party (art. 29 I), and provides that the 'organization and activity of political parties must serve the free functioning of democratic government'. Law 54/1974, adopted soon after the fall of the dictatorship, required that political parties submit a declaration that they oppose the violent pursuit of power or the overthrow of the free democratic system of government (art. 1 II). However, these provisions have not been implemented. Thus, all parties are free in Greece; there are no prohibited parties. The Constitution does not provide for the possibility of a prohibition of political parties.

In the Parliament itself, status and strength of political parties are in many ways relevant (arts. 37 II, 38, 68 III, 73 IV). The leader of the party with the majority of parliamentary seats is appointed Prime Minister (art. 37 II). In the absence of a majority party, the leader of the relatively largest party, and subsequently the leaders of the second and third largest parties are asked to form the government (art. 37 III). The abolition of the voter's right to choose between candidates of the same party and its replacement by the general introduction of the 'list system' (L. 1303/1982), have strengthened considerably the power of the party leadership. Moreover, Greek political parties generally lack the democratic structure that would provide an adequate system of checks and balances.

A new law provides for public subsidies to political parties (L. 1443/1984). During the period immediately preceding parliamentary elections, political parties are allocated television time proportionate to their parliamentary strength. Greek broadcasting, unlike the free Greek press, is otherwise completely subservient to the party in power, which thus monopolizes the important influence television can exercise on the electorate (L. 1730/1987).

## 3. Legal Status of Members of Parliament

The legal status of members of Parliament is the subject of a series of traditional constitutional provisions (arts. 59–63) on taking oath of office, free mandate, indemnity, immunity, compensation, etc. The same is true for the provisions on the organization and working of Parliament, duration of Parliament, rules of procedure, presidium of Parliament, public sittings, quorum and majority, meeting of Parliament, investigation committees and petitions (arts. 64–69). Parliament can sit not only *in pleno* but also in two sections (art. 70 II). However, the list of important subject matters which have to be dealt with by the plenum is so long (art. 72 I), that the sections have the choice between confining to less important matters and infringing the Constitution.

## 4. Legislation and Parliamentary Control

Legislation procedure follows traditional patterns. The proposal for a new statute may originate either in Parliament or in the Government; the latter is the rule. Bills of financial nature can only be introduced by the Government.

A bill is first discussed by a parliamentary committee (art. 74 II). Then Parliament debates and votes, first on the principle of the bill, then article by article, and then on the bill as a whole. These debates and votes take place without interruption (arts. 76 I and 80 I of the Standing Orders) unless one third of the total number of the representatives requests otherwise (art. 76 II). For statutes it considers to be urgent or of particular importance, the Government may also initiate a summary legislative procedure (art. 76 IV, V). Codes or statutes codifying existing provisions or re-enacting repealed laws (with the exception of tax laws) are voted as a whole only, provided they were prepared by a commission set up by statute (art. 76 VI, VII). Within a month of approval by Parliament, statutes are promulgated by the President and published in part A of the Official Gazette (art. 42 I). Statutes and other legislative instruments are known by their number and the year of publication (e.g., L. 1406/1983).

### 5. Dissolution of Parliament

Parliament may, and in some cases must, be dissolved by the President before the end of its term. The wide powers granted the President by the Constitution to dissolve Parliament were either abolished altogether or transformed into duties by the 1986 amendment, with sole exception the President's discretionary power to dissolve Parliament without governmental countersignature (art. 35 II c) 'if two governments had resigned or were voted down by Parliament and its composition does not ensure stability of government' (art. 41 I).

All other cases of dissolution of Parliament are *obligatory* for the President. Thus the President *must* dissolve Parliament (a) if exploratory mandates to form a government enjoying Parliament's confidence, or an all-parliamentary-party government have been unsuccessful (arts. 37 III, 38 I); (b) if the government, although enjoying Parliament's confidence, requests its dissolution in order to renew the people's mandate in view of particularly important national questions (art. 41 II); (c) if Parliament has failed to elect a new President in three ballots (arts. 32 IV, 41 V). In cases (a) and (c) no countersignature is needed (art. 35 II). The new Parliament cannot be dissolved again within a year save in the cases of articles 37 III and 41 I (art. 41 IV).

## *B. The President of the Republic*

The President is elected by Parliament rather than by direct popular vote. To be eligible for the presidency, a person must be at least forty years old; a descendant of a Greek father; a Greek citizen for at least five years; and legally entitled to vote. He is eligible for reelection only once (arts. 31, 30 V). Although elected by Parliament (art. 32), the President is not politically accountable to it or to the people. He may be deposed only for high treason or for intentional violation of the Constitution and only upon criminal impeachment proceedings originating from within Parliament and conducted before the special court for charges against ministers (arts. 49 I, 86; L. 265/1976).

## *C. The Government*

### 1. Constitutional Status

The executive power is entrusted to both the President and the Government (art. 26 II). However, the country's general policy is determined by the Government alone (art. 82 I). The cabinet ministers are jointly accountable to Parliament for the Government's general policy and cannot be relieved from this responsibility by the President's mandate (art. 85). Moreover, as a rule, the decisions of the President must be countersigned by the appropriate minister (art. 35).

Thus the Government depends on Parliament's confidence (art. 84 I). Within fifteen days of the swearing in of the Prime Minister, the Government must, and at any other time may, ask Parliament for a vote of confidence. Parliament may, on its own initiative, withdraw its confidence from the Government as a whole, or from a particular minister. However, the Constitution provides for procedural rules which make it difficult to withdraw confidence recklessly (arts. 84 II ff; cf. also art. 41 I). Once Parliament withdraws its confidence from the Government, the President dismisses the Prime Minister (art. 38 I). This applies *mutatis mutandis* to the minister who lost Parliament's confidence.

## 2. Composition

The composition and function of the Cabinet and the Government are regulated by Law 1558/1985. The Government (κυβέρνηση, kyvernisi, also known as the Council of Ministers) consists of the Prime Minister (πρωθυπουργός, prothypourgos) and the ministers (υπουργοί, ypourgoi), each of whom is in charge of a particular ministry. One or more ministers may be appointed as deputy prime minister(s). The Constitution also mentions deputy ministers and ministers without portfolio. The latters' scope of powers is determined by the Prime Minister, the others' by presidential decree at the Prime Minister's proposal. Below the ministers there are 'vice-ministers' (υφυπουργοί, yphypourgoi), that is ministers of state or junior ministers who, under the Constitution, may be members of the Government, but under Law 1558/1985 are not. Law 1558/1985 provides for one to two junior ministers in almost every ministry. The scope of their work is jointly determined by the Prime Minister and the appropriate minister. Ministers are appointed and dismissed by the President at the Prime Minister's proposal (art. 37 I).

Law 1558/1985 has considerably strengthened the already strong position of the Prime Minister who is now an all-powerful figure. After the 1986 constitutional amendment, the Greek Prime Minister seems to wield more power than any other western head of government, whether president or prime minister.

## 3. Cabinet Committees

Cabinet committees are set up from within the Government. The most important among them are the following four established by statute (L. 1558/1985):

(*a*) The very important five-member Government Council (so-called ΚΥΣΥΜ, KYSYM), chaired by the Prime Minister and acting within the framework of the Cabinet's decisions and directions, decides on subjects of general importance, takes the necessary measures for implementing the Government's policy, and monitors and coordinates the implementation of its own and the Government's decisions by the ministers and other government authorities.

(*b*) The nine-member Government Council on Foreign Policy and National Defense (so-called ΚΥΣΕΑ, KYSEA), chaired by the Prime Minister, is responsible for foreign and defense policy as well as intelligence and public order. It also selects the leadership of the armed forces.

(*c*) The five-member High Council for Economic Policy (so-called ΑΣΟΠ, ASOP), chaired by the Prime Minister, decides, within the framework of the decisions of the Government and the Government Council, all important questions of economic policy, takes the necessary measures for implementing the Government's economic plan, and coordinates the implementation of its decisions.

(*d*) The six-member Prices and Income Committee is chaired by the Minister of National Economy. Within the decisions taken by the Government, the Government Council, and the High Council for Economic Policy, this committee adopts measures regarding prices and incomes, and follows and supervises their implementation.

## IV. Administration

### *A. Central Government*

#### 1. Ministries – Ministers – Ministers of State

The government in the sense of administration (διοίκηση, dioikisi), is divided into central (direct state or government administration) and local (decentralized administration). The central government is divided into departments: ministries. The Constitution provides neither for the number nor for the scope of the ministries. This is done by Law 1558/1985 that provides for nineteen ministries in the following order of precedence which is rather arbitrary and reflects partly the political importance of the present incumbents. Minister to the Prime Minister; Interior and Public Order; Foreign Affairs; National Defense; National Economy; Health, Welfare and Social Security; Justice; National Education and Religions; Culture; Finance; Northern Greece; Aegean; Agriculture; Environment, Country Planning and Public Works; Labor; Industry, Energy and Technology; Commerce; Transport and Communications; Merchant Marine. The Prime Minister may change the names of ministries and their order of precedence. Every ministry is divided into directorates, sections, etc. (the 'general directorates' were abolished by L. 1232/1982). The law also provides for a considerable number of self-contained authorities (general secretariats) directly answerable to the appropriate minister. At the top of each ministry there is a minister and sometimes up to three deputy or vice-ministers or ministers of state.

A minister combines two functions: he is a member of the Cabinet and thus responsible for its 'general policy' (collective ministerial responsibility); he is also the head of all authorities of his ministry, its main paymaster, and the chief decision-maker. His responsibilities are determined by law (art. 83 I Const.).

Each minister is also the disciplinary superior of all civil servants of his ministry, including those of the self-contained general secretariats. However, he himself is not a civil servant and is not subject to anyone's disciplinary authority; he is only politically accountable to Parliament, which may withdraw its confidence to him (art. 84 II), and to the Prime Minister on whose proposal the President appoints and dismisses the members of the government and the ministers of state (art. 37 I). Ministers are also subject to civil and criminal responsibility under article 86 of the Constitution and Law 802/1971.

In each ministry there is a secretary general acting as a political permanent secretary. In addition, general secretaries are in charge of the twelve general secretariats (see above).

A novelty of the new law are the special secretaries who are political appointees and administrative heads of the ministry or part thereof. In fact, they replace the old general directors, the highest rank of civil service which has been abolished by Law 1232/1982.

## 2. Regional Authorities

Under article 101 of the Constitution, government authorities are 'decentralized'. This means that the regional authorities, although appointed and supervised by the central government, are entrusted with considerable decision-making powers within their region called 'νομός' (prefecture, nomos). The whole country, with the exception of Mount Athos with its monastic community (art. 105 Const.), is divided into fifty-one *nomoi.*

A *nomos* is both a geographical division and an administrative unit. It is also a voting district, with the exception of the *nomoi* of Attica and Thessaloniki which are divided into five and two such districts (art. 1 P.D. 152/1985). With the exception of the Ministry of Northern Greece and the recently established Ministry of the Aegean, all regional authorities are integrated in *nomoi.* The administrative head of the *nomos* is the nomarch (νομάρχης, nomarchis). The nomarch has a *sui generis* position in the Greek administrative system. Not only is he the head of the *nomos*, but he is also the government's representative in the *nomos.* In these two qualities he ensures the implementation of the law, has precedence over all civil and military authorities in the *nomos*, and is superior to all civil authorities of the *nomos*, except the law courts.

According to Law 1235/1983, the nomarchs are political appointees, appointed and dismissed by presidential decree at the proposal of the Minister of the Interior after decision of the Cabinet. The Constitution confers on them 'general decisive powers on matters of their region' (art. 101 III). Central administrative authorities are entrusted with the general direction, the coordination and the control of the regional authorities. Law 3200/1955 assigned to the nomarchs a system of decision-making and controlling powers. However, under Law 1232/1982, many of these decisions are now exercised by a *nomos* council consisting of representatives of the central and local governments. The nomarch's advisory powers on local government have been mostly confined by P.D. 22/1982 to *ex post facto* supervision regarding the legality of actions (see below, Section IV B 1, 5).

The control exercised on the nomarch by the ministers is also mainly concerned with the legality of his actions, but the recent return of the fully political nomarch made him open to political influence and direction, even more than his predecessors.

## *B. Local Government*

### 1. Decentralization – Local Government – Corporations – Towns and Villages

Under article 102 I of the Constitution, the administration of local affairs belongs to the local government corporations (principle of decentralization). The Constitution provides for two levels of local government, but the actual creation of the second level is left to the discretion of Parliament which has not made use of it yet. The local government corporations are legal persons of public law. They are independent in their own administration (art. 102 II), but not 'autonomous', that is they cannot issue their own by-laws unless authorized by statute. The Constitution (art. 43 II) permits delegation only if it relates to 'specialized matters or matters of local interest or of a technical or detailed character'. The current Local Government Code (L. 1065/1980, as amended by L. 1270/1982 and 1416/1984 and P.D. 22/1982) provides in article 26 (in combination with arts. 83 III and 95 III) that the town or village council may issue by-laws on a considerable number of matters, e.g., markets, pavements, water and sewage systems, parks, cemeteries, etc. However, these by-laws are subject to the nomarch's approval.

Since 1912, local government corporations are divided into town municipalities, and village communities. 'Town' (δήμος, dimos) is every *nomos* capital, as well as every town with more than 10,000 inhabitants. But there are exceptions, e.g., every spa is a 'town', so that the number of 'towns' is disproportionately large. The same is true with the village communities (κοινότητες, koinotites): every 'separate' community with a population of 1,000 and sufficient means to finance its administration may be recognized as a municipality upon application by at least three quarters of its inhabitants. These conditions are stricter in several points than the ones provided in the previous Local Government Code. In any event, the mountainous and insular character of Greece, and the desertion of the countryside, make it very difficult to create municipalities which are both cohesive and viable.

### 2. Local and Central Government Matters

The Constitution entrusts the local government with the administration of all local matters (art. 102 I). The list of the local government's 'exclusive tasks' (art.

23 Local Government Code) – that is to the exclusion of central government – is neither definitive nor exhaustive. However, the actual authority of the local government may suffer from the fact that the line between national and local affairs is not always clear, and, consequently, this line is ultimately drawn by Parliament. This fact, coupled with the chronic financial inadequacy of most municipalities, explains the weak position of local government in the Greek administration. In addition to their 'exclusive tasks', local government corporations share with the central government 'concurrent' powers regarding matters such as tourism, hospitals, old age homes, theatres, within limits defined by central government.

In some cases provided by law, local authorities act as agents of the central government.

## 3. Organization

The organization of village communities is simpler than that of towns and municipalities. Depending on population, a village council consists of seven to ten members, including the chairman. All councillors are elected in a general election every fourth year, simultaneously throughout the country. The leading candidate of the successful list is appointed as chairman of the council.

A town is governed by the town council, the town committee, and the mayor. The town council is elected in a general election every fourth year, and consists of eleven to forty one councillors according to population. The town committee consists of the mayor and two to six councillors. The leading candidate of the successful list is appointed as mayor. In large towns there are deputy mayors as well. The general decision-making power belongs to the council. The other local authorities have only specific powers, that is only powers expressly conferred to them by statute. The mayor and the chairman of the village council propose and implement the council's decisions, are superiors of the municipal employees and paymasters of the municipality. The town council has certain preparatory, controlling and decision-making powers, especially with regard to the budget. In urgent cases the mayor may act alone, subject to the council's approval.

## 4. Finance

Under article 102 VI of the Constitution, the state ensures that local government has the necessary financial means for the discharge of its functions. The law distinguishes between ordinary and extraordinary expenditures on one hand, and obligatory and non-obligatory on the other. All expenditures must be included in the yearly municipal budget which is decided by the village or town council and audited by the nomarch. The nomarch enters obligatory expenditures in the budget, if they were not included, and raises revenue accordingly. His decision may be challenged before the Council of State.

### 5. State Supervision

Local government corporations are independent from the central government. But, they are subject to state supervision (so-called 'administrative supervision') which, however, may not frustrate their 'initiative and free activity' (art. 102 V). State supervision is in principle confined to the legality and only exceptionally to the expediency of municipal activity. State supervision may be either 'preventive' (especially with regard to finances) or 'repressive' (*ex post facto*); it is exercised, as a rule, by the nomarch, and in exceptional cases by the Minister of the Interior, or the Finance Minister.

Every municipal voter and every affected person has standing to initiate state supervision by the nomarch to proceed and to challenge decisions of local authorities before the administrative courts. Greek law also provides for the 'disciplinary liability' of the elected local government officers which may lead up to the forfeiture of their office. Disciplinary liability is activated either automatically, in the cases provided by law (e.g., in case of certain criminal sentences) or, as a rule, after the approval by a committee consisting in its majority of judges (art. 102 V).

## *C. Specialized Self-Government*

While local government has general functions within a certain geographical area, there are self-governing bodies with specialized functions. These are mainly the legal persons of public law and the public corporations.

### 1. Legal Persons of Public Law

These are either self-governing bodies discharging state functions, such as universities and social security funds, or professional self-governing funds, such as bar or medical associations. The latter bodies are administratively and financially almost totally autonomous.

### 2. Public Corporations

Public corporations abound in Greece. Most of them belong to the state, and some to the municipalities. Previously private companies with special 'concessions' (e.g., electricity or water supply companies) were succeeded by public corporations (public enterprises). In recent years it has become common to transform administrative units (e.g., mail, telecommunications, broadcasting) which were parts of the central government or legal persons of public law into corporations of private law, in which the state is the only shareholder. New government bodies are also organized from the outset as 'public corporations'. While it may be explained by the disadvantages, especially bureaucracy, of public administration and public auditing, this development raises some questions about the binding rules of public law: May the state escape the limitations imposed by human rights and (administrative) judicial review by transforming parts of its organization into 'commercial' companies?

Since the Council of State judicially reviews only decisions of bodies belonging to the public administration *stricto sensu*, any application challenging decisions of such 'public' corporations is inadmissible. The result is that judicial review is thus steadily losing its practical importance.

## *D. General Principles of Administrative Action*

### 1. Legality of Public Administration

The decision-making procedure to be followed by Greek public authorities is not codified, but derived from principles of law developed by legal doctrine and judicial decisions now partly incorporated in the Constitution. The principle of the legality of public administration results from the wider principle of the rule of law. It is also based on article 50 of the Constitution: 'The President has only the powers expressly allocated to him by the Constitution and the laws compatible with it'. This provision originates in the Belgian constitution of 1831 and is repeated in every Greek constitution since 1864. It does not only bind the President (previously the king) but the executive in general (cf. also art. 83). The legality of administration covers constitutionality as well. This is deduced from the supreme position of the Constitution in the hierarchy of legal rules, and also from the fundamental duty of allegiance of the public servants to the Constitution (art. 103 I; cf. art. 120 II, IV). However, before the 1975 Constitution, the Council of State recognized the existence of an emergency law prevailing over positive law and drawing its legitimacy from public interest. Since the new Constitution provides for special powers and procedures in emergency cases (art. 48), an extra-constitutional law has no longer any democratic legitimacy or practical justification.

With the exception of the cases regarding the emergency law and expanding the scope of public interest, the Council of State has adhered to the strict view that administrative action not based on a statute is not lawful (see, e.g., judgment 1603/1964).

### 2. Discretionary Power

Administrative authorities always have discretionary power unless the law provides otherwise (see judgment 97/1929 and many later judgments of the Council of State). The limits of discretionary powers are drawn by the prohibition of abuse of discretion (*détournement de pouvoir*). In addition to the limits provided in each particular law, there are also general limitations derived from general principles of law, or directly from the Constitution. The Council of

State often speaks of the principles of 'fair administration,' the priority of public interest, equality, and impartiality of public administration. The principles of proportionality and of legitimate expectation have also been recognized in some judgments.

### 3. Administrative Acts

Following French administrative law, Greek law includes under 'administrative act' not only decisions addressed to individuals (individual administrative acts) but also statutory instruments containing legal rules (though not administrative contracts). However, the differences between these two administrative activities are considerable and numerous, so that a distinction should be made in the terminology as well.

It is important to define what is understood under 'administrative act', since an 'application for annulment' is admissible only if it challenges the validity of an administrative act. Applying organizational rather than functional criteria, the Council of State considers as administrative acts only those issued by a central or local government authority. In view of the fact that, as mentioned above (Section IV C 2), in the last three decades an increasing number of government authorities or self-governing administrative units have been re-organized into commercial companies with the state as the only shareholder, the Council of State's insistence that only government authorities' decisions can be considered as 'administrative acts' has been criticized as too formalistic.

### 4. Reasons for Decisions and Right to Hearing

The Council of State has insisted on the requirement that individual administrative acts affecting interests of their addressees must state their reasons. Article 20 II of the Constitution guarantees the right to a hearing of persons affected by administrative action before the authorities come to a decision. The Council of State construes this obligation in a restrictive manner.

### 5. Void and Voidable Administrative Acts

The distinction between void and voidable administrative acts, while known in legal doctrine, is of no great relevance in the cases. The Council of State considers voidability as the rule. There is no statutory list of the instances in which an administrative act is void.

### 6. Revocability of Administrative Acts

An unlawful administrative act affecting a person adversely may always be revoked, and in some cases it must be revoked. If an unlawful decision addressed to an individual is beneficial to him, it may be revoked only within 'reasonable time', unless the addressee had caused the unlawfulness himself, or the revocation is necessary for reasons of public policy. Law 261/1968 provides that 'reasonable time' may not be shorter than five years, and that revocation has 'no consequences' for the state. It is doubtful whether this drastic exclusion of state liability is compatible with article 20 I of the Constitution, which guarantees the right of access to courts.

A lawful administrative act addressed to individuals and adversely affecting them may always be revoked. A lawful act which is beneficial to them may only be revoked if it, or the law, includes a revocability clause, or if revocation is needed in the public interest.

## 7. Administrative Contracts

Greek law recognizes administrative contracts as a special category of contracts, and allocates disputes arising out of them to the administrative courts (L. 1406/1983). Reluctant though Greek authorities are in concluding administrative contracts (instead of issuing unilateral administrative acts), many and important matters between public authorities and individuals are dealt with through administrative contracts. As with administrative acts, the criterion applied by the courts is organizational, not functional: to qualify as administrative, a contract must be a 'contract with the central or local government' as a party. However, contracts with organizations operating in the public interest, e.g., public corporations, may also qualify as 'administrative contracts' (AP 727/1969).

The provisions of the Civil Code regarding the law of contract apply by analogy to administrative contracts. A number of administrative contracts are subject to 'approval' by administrative act; the most important administrative contracts must be 'ratified' by statute. Neither 'approval' nor 'ratification' change the contract's legal nature, or the nature of the claims based on it. In case of an unforeseeable change of circumstances, the administrative contract may be adjusted or rescinded by the courts under Civil Code article 388, subject always to the public interest. Influenced by French doctrine, the Greek courts adhere to the principle of mutability (*mutabilité*) of administrative contracts, which allows the unilateral alteration or termination of such contracts by an act of parliament and without compensation. This doctrine is, however, not compatible with the broader scope of compulsory purchase under the new Constitution.

## 8. State Liability

Under Greek law, state liability for damage caused by public servants is direct, primary, and strict. It exists, as a rule, only for unlawful damage. Under articles 105 and 106 of the Introductory Law to the Civil Code, when typical activities of public authorities are concerned, it suffices that the law is (objectively) infringed, and it is not necessary to prove the (subjective) fault of a particular public servant as well. The state is liable only if the infringed legal rule is not meant to serve mainly the public interest.

Personal liability of the public servant exists only towards the state, and only when the public servant's conduct was intentional or grossly negligent and caused positive damage, not a mere loss of profits. As of June 1985, state liability disputes belong to the jurisdiction of the administrative rather than the civil courts (L. 1406/1983).

### 9. Expropriation

The Greek courts limit the constitutional protection of property (art. 17) to real rights in property, movable or immovable – they do not include rights *in personam*. Since expropriation requiring compensation is limited to cases in which rights *in rem* are interfered with, the infringement of rights *in personam* without the award of compensation is deemed constitutional. Not least because of this limited protection of private property, the Constitution of 1952 included a special clause guaranteeing foreign investments in Greece (art. 107).

The decisions of the courts restricting the protection of private property to rights *in rem* is, however, hardly compatible with the new Constitution which adopted provisions about the taking of a company (as such, not only of its real property) or the compulsory participation of the state in a company (art. 106 III-V). The new Constitution proclaims, on the other hand, the social commitment of property (art. 17 I; cf. arts. 18, 24, 117 III, IV), and authorizes legislation on planning and environment. Taking of property is only permitted if it serves the public good, is based on an act of parliament or another statutory instrument, and includes full compensation, determined by the civil courts and paid for before the transfer of property. The procedure is regulated by Law 797/1971.

## V. Control of Public Administration and Judicial Review

Greek public administration is subject to a threefold control, exercised by the administrative authorities (administrative self-control), Parliament (parliamentary control), and the courts (judicial review).

### *A. Administrative Self-Control*

There are different kinds of control exercised by administrative authorities or agencies on other administrative authorities or agencies. The 'hierarchical control' is exercised by the 'superior' on the 'inferior' agency or authority within the central or local government or public corporation. Sometimes the law provides for special control organs independent of the administrative hierarchy, to decide on formal petitions. On the other hand, the control exercised by the central government on local government (or specialized self-governing public corporations) is called 'administrative supervision'. Finally, financial control is an important form of administrative control.

## 1. Hierarchical Control

The hierarchical relationship between superior and inferior authorities leads to the controlling power of the former over the latter; it is called 'hierarchical control'. All administrative organs are subject to this control with the exception of the President, the Prime Minister, the ministers and the junior ministers, as well as of committees (which are not incorporated in the organ hierarchy) and most tax agencies. These agencies are only subject to judicial review. The hierarchical control encompasses the lawfulness of the inferior's conduct (control of legality), but may also extend to the advisability of such conduct (control of advisability). The delineation of the scope of control is not always easy in practice.

## 2. Formal Petitions

Control may be initiated by exercising the general right to petition public authorities (art. 10 Const.; L. 796/1971). If the law allows within a time-limit a formal petition leading to a substantive examination, such petition, being similar to an action before a court, is called 'action-like petition' (ενδικοφανής προσφυγή, endikophanis prosfygi). It cannot lead to a *reformatio in peius*, and must precede the application for judicial review (application for annulment) before the Council of State (art. 45 II L. 170/1973).

## 3. Administrative Supervision

The control of central government over self-government is restricted to legality control and only exceptionally extends to the advisability of action. While a dispute before the courts between administrative authorities is not admissible, the opposite is true, in principle, as between the central government's supervisory authority (minister or nomarch) and the supervised self-governing body.

## 4. Financial Control

Financial control applies to public expenses and receipts and is exercised by the appropriate minister or nomarch, the Minister of Finance and the Auditors'

Court. In the latter case, financial control takes place under guarantees of judicial independence.

### *B. Parliamentary Control*

Parliamentary control is one of Parliament's most important tasks. Since Parliament has no power over the civil servants, its control is addressed to the government as a whole or to a particular minister, both of which depend on Parliament's confidence. The minister is politically responsible for the conduct of the civil servants of his ministry, as well as – in the framework of administrative supervision – for the conduct of self-governing bodies even if organized and acting under forms of private law. Parliamentary control is exercised *in pleno* at least twice a week (art. 70 VI).

### *C. Judicial Control*

#### 1. Administrative Courts – Judicial Review as a General Rule

Judicial control of public administration was entrusted in Greece to special administrative courts since the first years after the establishment of the modern Greek State. These courts were the Auditors' Court (1833), the Council of State, and the district and appellate courts (1838). However, since the administrative courts were then associated with King Otho's absolutism, they were abolished by the constitution of 1844 which introduced the system of a unitary judiciary. This system was preserved in principle in the constitutions of 1864, 1911, and 1927.

The Constitution now provides for a fully developed system of administrative courts next to the ordinary civil courts, and in addition for the Supreme Special Court entrusted with some of the tasks of a constitutional court (see above, Section II B 6). Article 20 I of the Constitution includes an important new provision. It reads as follows: 'Every one shall be entitled to legal protection by the courts and may plead before them his position on his rights or interests, as specified by law'. It is true that this general guarantee of judicial protection brings no radical change to the law, since every administrative act could be challenged before the Council of State under prior law as well. However, exceptions from this rule, based particularly on the doctrine of the so-called 'government acts' (state acts), which can also be found in Law 170/1973 on the Council of State (art. 45 VI) can no longer be reconciled with article 20 I.

#### 2. Remedies Before the Council of State – The 'Application for Annulment'

Remedies before the Council of State are the 'application for annulment' of an administrative decision (individual administrative act or statutory instrument), the appeal on points of law against judgments of lower administrative courts, and the application for substantive judicial review in cases referred to the Council of State by the Constitution or a statute.

The application for annulment is the main remedy before the Council of State. This remedy is patterned after the model of the French *recours pour excès de pouvoir*, and may challenge both administrative action and inaction. In the latter case, what is challenged is the implied decision of refusal which is to be inferred after a certain time from the silence on the matter.

The application for annulment is admissible on the following conditions:

(*a*) that it is addressed against an individual administrative or a statutory instrument (but not an act of parliament);

(*b*) that no other judicial remedy is available, or the available ones have been exhausted;

(*c*) that a formal complaint before the administrative authorities, specifically required for by law, has already been filed but not answered for at least three months; if the complaint has been dismissed *expressis verbis* the dismissing decision may be challenged;

(*d*) that in cases of unlawful failure to act, the authority concerned has been called upon to act and the complaint has been left unanswered for at least three months; if the complaint has been dismissed *expressis verbis* the dismissing decision may be challenged;

(*e*) that the proceedings have been instituted within sixty days of the notification of the act to the plaintiff, or of its publication if the law provides for it, or, in the absence thereof, of the day on which the act came to the knowledge of the petitioner, or in case of failure to act, of the expiry of the three-month period after the authority had been called upon to act; and

(*f*) that the petitioner was either the addressee of the contested administrative act, or was affected in his legal (legally relevant) interests by it or by the failure to take it.

The application for annulment may assert lack of competence, infringement of an essential procedural requirement, substantive violation of the law, or abuse of discretionary power. If one of these 'grounds' is substantiated, the application is well founded. The application for annulment has no suspensive effect. However, a judicial committee may order suspension, if it considers that circumstances invoked by the petitioner or the appropriate minister so require.

A judgment for the petitioner declares the contested decision to be null and void *erga omnes*. However, dismissal of the petition does not bar other persons from challenging the same act. Whether favorable or not, a judgment has the force of *res judicata*, but courts and administrative authorities are only bound by annulling judgments. If the judgment declares a failure to act to be unlawful, it remands the case to the appropriate administrative authority for the necessary measures. The authorities are obligated to take the measures called for by the judgment, or to refrain from any action declared to be unlawful (art. 95 V Const.; art. 50 IV L. 170/1973). A violation of this obligation may lead to disciplinary or even criminal sanctions against the responsible person and may establish state liability.

# VI. Human Rights

## *A. The Protection of Human Rights*

### 1. The Constitutional Protection

In its first part (art. 2 I), the Constitution assigns to the state the primary obligation to respect and protect the value of the human being. In its second part (arts. 4–25), the Constitution defines and protects the individual and social rights, such as the rights of equality; free development of personality; personal freedom; life and corporal integrity; free movement; right to the judge prescribed by law; sanctuary of home; right to petition; right to assembly; right to associate; freedom of religion; freedom of opinion and press; freedom of art, science, research and teaching; self-government of universities; protection of property; secrecy of letters and other correspondence; right to judicial protection; protection of the family, marriage, motherhood, childhood, families with many children, poor and homeless; right to work; trade union freedom; and right to strike. Fundamental rights such as the free establishment of political parties and the right to belong to them (art. 29) are also protected in other parts of the Constitution.

### 2. Protection by the European Convention of Human Rights and Fundamental Freedoms and Other Conventions

Human rights are also protected by the European Convention for the Protection of Human Rights and Fundamental Freedoms of November 4, 1950, and its Protocols. Greece ratified the Convention and its First ('Additional') Protocol in 1953 (L. 2329/1953) and again, after the restoration of democracy, in 1974 (L.D. 53/1974). Greece also ratified Protocols 2, 3, 5 and 7 (L. 215/1974, 1705/1987) and has signed but not yet ratified Protocols 6 and 8. Thus, the Convention and the ratified Protocols have become 'an integral part of domestic Greek law' and 'prevail over any contrary statutory provision' (see above, Section I C). Greece has not yet signed Protocol 4 of the Convention. Greece has also ratified the European Social Charter of October 18, 1961 (L. 1426/1984), and acceded to the UN International Covenant on Economic, Social and Cultural Rights (L. 1532/1985), but not yet to the UN Covenant on Civil and Political Rights of December 16, 1966.

## *B. Main Problems Relating to the Protection of Human Rights in the New Constitution*

### 1. From an Individualistic to a Humanistic Orientation

It is not possible here to analyze each particular human right. The following remarks relate to the general structure and the new features of the protection of human rights in the new Constitution. Although it places the human being in the centre, this Constitution adopts a less individualistic philosophy than its predecessor of 1952. The humanistic orientation of the present Constitution is expressed mainly in the new non-amendable provision of article 2 I which reads as follows: 'The state has the fundamental duty to respect and protect the dignity of man'. Article 7 II, also new, prohibits the infringement of the dignity of man and provides for its punishment by law. 'Man' is not just an abstract notion, nor does it relate to the anonymous 'people' only, but encompasses also the concrete individual. However, while the Constitution protects human dignity, it also rejects through a series of provisions the individualistic orientation which was typical of the 1952 Constitution. For the first time, the Constitution includes a provision prohibiting the abuse of rights (art. 25 III) which must be understood as human rights. Article 25 IV also provides that 'the state has the right to demand from all citizens to fulfill the duty of social and national solidarity'.

## 2. Conflict and Synthesis: Private Ownership and Private Economic Activity

The Constitution rejects the purely individualistic view of human rights in favor of a socially oriented view. Experience teaches that a legal order which subordinates the individual to the will of the whole, sooner or later ends up sacrificing man to the state. For this reason, the Greek Constitution aims to a synthesis that puts forward the humanistic element and rejects an individualistic orientation. Paragraphs 1 and 2 of article 25 speak of the 'rights of man as an individual and as a member of society'; 'the recognition and the protection of ... human rights by the state is oriented towards the accomplishment of social progress in freedom and justice'. The Constitution does not substitute the individual to the community. However, in the areas where conflict is likely, the Constitution restricts the rights of the individual in favor of human dignity and the general interest.

The areas where this conflict is most likely are private ownership and private economic activity, both of which are protected by the Constitution. Private economic activity is protected expressly (art. 5 I) for the first time and without the possibility of an amendment (art. 110 I). However, the Constitution also emphasizes the limitations of these rights. According to article 17 I, 'the rights which result from private ownership may not be exercised at the expense of the general interest'. Moreover, the Constitution establishes (art. 24), also for the first time, a series of restrictions in favor of the natural and cultural environment, and urban and rural planning. The new Constitution expands both the content of the protected 'ownership' and the possibilities of state intervention as illustrated by the provisions about expropriation of firms or compulsory participation of the state in them. For the first time the Constitution recognizes expressly the social content of ownership by limiting the owner's powers (e.g., arts. 18, 24 I, 117 III), and by imposing duties to tolerate the so-called 'statutory social restraints', that is, government regulations which may be burdensome or economically damaging, but socially necessary (e.g., arts. 17 VII, 24 III).

In general, the new Constitution emphasizes the social role of ownership by limiting the framework within which protection is provided. This restriction of the individualistic element results either from direct provisions of the Constitution, or, usually, from constitutionally authorized statutory provisions. The scope of the constitutional protection of ownership is thus being considerably limited and may be limited even further by the legislature whenever permitted by the Constitution (e.g., art. 25 IV).

The protection of private economic activity is viewed as an incident of the right to develop one's personality. However, this protection may not exceed the limits set by the rights of others, the Constitution, or the *boni mores* (art. 5 I). Article 106 II is equally important and reflects the same rejection of individualism. Under this provision, 'private economic initiative shall not be permitted to develop at the expense of freedom and human dignity or to the detriment of the national economy'.

### 3. Summary

In the area of human rights the Constitution of 1975 differs in two main respects from its predecessor. First, because of the experience during the dictatorship, the Constitution guarantees explicitly human dignity, and emphasizes the rights of man vis-à-vis the state; second, influenced by the social trends of our time, the Constitution provides expressly for the social restraints of human rights, and in particular of private ownership and economic freedom. Both the guarantee and the social restraints of human rights are legally binding. This applies also to the principle of equality, as unanimously accepted by the legal doctrine and the courts.

## *C. Judicial Protection*

The legally binding force of human rights manifests itself in their judicial protection. Greek courts have the power to review the constitutionality of laws as well as the constitutionality and legality of secondary legislation. Legal rules and individual administrative acts issued by administrative authorities may be annulled by the administrative courts on the ground of 'violation of law' (art. 95 I); 'violation of law' includes also the infringement of the Constitution.

Acts of parliament may not be challenged directly, but their unconstitutionality may be asserted before the courts and may lead to their non-application. Under the Constitution (art. 87 II), judges are 'in no way required to obey provisions enacted in abolition of the Constitution.' Even in an ordinary case, 'the courts are obligated not to apply a law the contents of which are contrary to the Constitution' (art. 93 IV). However, the courts may not annul such law. Greek law does not recognize a general duty to refer the question of constitutionality to a supreme court. The new Supreme Special Court (see above, Section II B 6) has no 'monopoly' of declaring a law unconstitutional. This court is empowered to adjudicate 'disputes on the substantive constitutionality or the meaning of provisions of a formal law', but only if 'contradictory judgments of the Council of State, the Areios Pagos, or the Auditors' Court have been issued' (art. 100 I).

Under article 46 of the European Convention for the Protection of Human Rights and Fundamental Freedoms, Greece has recognized (as of January 30, 1979) for three years, which have been since extended, the jurisdiction of the European Court of Human Rights. On November 20, 1985, Greece also recognized for three years the right to individual petition to the European Commission of Human Rights, under article 25 of the Convention.

## Selected Bibliography
(in languages other than Greek)

N. Alivizatos, *Les institutions politiques de la Grèce à travers les crises 1922–1974* (L.G.D.J., Paris 1979).

P. Dagtoglou, Die Verfassungsentwicklung in Griechenland von der Einführung der geltenden Verfassung bis zum Tode König Pauls, *JöR* N.F. 14 (1965) 381–408.

P. Dagtoglou, Verfassung und Verwaltung, in: K. D. Grothusen (ed.), *Südosteuropahandbuch*, vol. III: *Griechenland* (Göttingen, 1980).

P. Dagtoglou, Die griechische Verfassung von 1975. Eine Einführung, *JöR* N.F. 32 (1983) 355–394.

P. Dagtoglou, Die Verfassungsgerichtsbarkeit in Griechenland, in: C. Starck/ A. Weber (ed.), *Verfassungsgerichtsbarkeit in Westeuropa* (Baden-Baden, 1986).

J. Iliopoulos-Strangas, Grundrechtsschutz in Griechenland, *JöR* N.F. 32 (1983) 395–442.

N. Kaltsogia-Tournaviti, Greece: The Struggle for Democracy. Constitutional and Political Evolutions since 1964, *JöR* N.F. 32 (1983) 297–354.

A. Pantélis, *Les grands problèmes de la Constitution hellénique* (Paris, 1979).

G. Papadimitriou, Die Grundrechte der neuen griechischen Verfassung, *EuGRZ* 1976. 150–155.

E. Spiliotopoulos, Judicial Review of Legislative Acts in Greece, 56 *Temple Law Quarterly* 463–502 (1983).

Ph. Spyropoulos, *Die Beziehungen zwischen Staat und Kirche in Griechenland* (Athens, 1981).

# Chapter 4
# The General Principles of the Civil Law

*Symeon C. Symeonides**

## I. Introduction: Scope and Function of Book I of the Civil Code

Like the German Civil Code, but unlike most other continental civil codes, the Greek Civil Code devotes the first of its five books to what it calls the general principles of the civil law. Among them are provisions about natural and juridical persons; capacity to hold rights and to enter into juridical acts; formal and substantive validity of juridical acts; terms and conditions; representation and authority; consent and ratification; prescription and peremption; and abuse of rights, self-help and self-defense. Unless displaced or contradicted by more specific rules provided elsewhere in the Code or in other statutes, these general principles pervade the entire Civil Code, and, for that matter, the entire private law, including commercial law. While it enhances systematization and helps avoid repetition, this organizational feature may often be a trap for a common-law lawyer who is not accustomed to working with continental civil codes. One must be especially wary not to expect to find all, or even most, rules regulating a given transaction in a single place in the Civil Code. For instance, in a case involving the sale of a movable, one may have to look in Book III (e.g., arts. 1034–1040 dealing with transfer of ownership), Book II (e.g., arts. 513–572 dealing with the contract of sale), as well as Book I (e.g., arts. 127–200 dealing with juridical acts in general).

## II. Natural Persons (φυσικά πρόσωπα, physika prosopa)

### *A. Personality or Capacity to Hold Rights* (προσωπικότητα, ικανότητα δικαίου, prosopikotita, ikanotita dikaiou)

According to article 34 of the Civil Code, 'every human being is capable of being the subject of rights and duties'. This capacity, the same as the German *Rechtsfähigkeit*, is distinguished from the capacity to enter into juridical acts

*Professor of Law, Louisiana State University Law School.

(*Geschäftsfähigkeit*, see below, Section V B), and the capacity to be accountable for torts (*Zurechnungsfähigkeit*). While all natural persons, regardless of age or other personal qualities, are capable of holding rights and being subject to duties, not all of them are capable of entering into juridical acts or capable of being legally at fault for purposes of delictual responsibility. For example, a five-year old child is capable of inheriting and is charged with a duty of respect to his parents, but he can neither contract without their consent nor can he be held personally accountable for his torts.

### B. *Commencement and Termination of Personality*

Personality commences with live birth and ceases with death (art. 35), and only with death. However, a child in his mother's womb is capable of acquiring inheritance and other rights accruing during gestation, provided he is later born alive (art. 36). While there is no presumption that one has been born alive, there is also no requirement as in the French Civil Code that he be born 'capable of living.' It suffices that the person has lived for moments after birth. While the proof of death is regulated in detail by special statutes and the rules of evidence provided in the codes of Civil and Criminal Procedure, the Civil Code considers as proven the death of a person whose body has not been recovered, 'if he disappeared under conditions rendering his death certain' (art. 38), e.g., in an airplane crash. However, unlike the French and like all other continental civil codes, the Greek Civil Code abolished the age-and-sex-based presumptions of survivorship of the Roman law for determining the order of death of several persons. Article 38 establishes a rebuttable presumption of simultaneous death if 'it cannot be proven that the one has survived the other.' Among other things, this means that none of these 'simultaneously' deceased persons inherits from the other and that their estates devolve respectively to the heirs next in line. Unlike the presumption of §20 of the BGB (later replaced by §11 of the Missing Persons Law of 1939), which applied only when the deceased persons had succumbed to 'a common danger,' the presumption of article 38 applies even if the deceased persons have not perished in the same incident, provided that the time of their respective deaths cannot otherwise be established.

### C. *Absentia* (αφάνεια, aphaneia)

A person whose death is 'strongly probable,' either because he disappeared while in mortal danger, or because he has been absent for 'a long time' without any news having been received of him, may be declared an absentee (art. 40) by the competent court, under procedures provided in articles 42–44, and articles 783–785 of the Code of Civil Procedure. Any persons whose rights depend on the death of the missing person, such as his heirs, spouse, or creditors, has standing to seek the declaration of absentia. But the petition is inadmissible, unless filed after the lapse of a year from the last moment of the mortal danger, or after five years from the last time any news had been received of the missing person (art. 41).

Unless otherwise provided by law (see, e.g., art. 1446 for divorce), the judicial declaration of absentia produces the same effects that would result 'if the death [of the absentee] had been proven' (art. 48). It produces a legal presumption of death, both as to its occurrence and its time. Thus, as of the time specified in the judgment, persons whose rights depend on the death of the absentee, such as his heirs, legatees, or creditors, may exercise these rights subject to an obligation to provide security for a term of ten years (art. 49). This presumption may, as to the occurrence of the death, be rebutted by the reappearance of the absentee (art. 50) or by a subsequent judgment revoking the declaration of absentia (art. 46). As to the time of the death, the above presumption is rebutted by a judgment establishing an earlier or later time (art. 46).

### D. *Domicile* (κατοικία, katoikia)

Like most legal systems, Greek law distinguishes between domicile and residence, but, unlike many other systems, attributes little legal significance to residence as such, independent of domicile. Domicile is defined by article 51 as 'the place where one has his principal and permanent establishment.' Doctrine and judicial decisions describe the two ingredients of domicile as the *corpus*, i.e., the physical residence or 'establishment' at a given place, and the *animus*, i.e., the intent to have that place as one's principal and permanent establishment. Residence is the first of these ingredients, that is, the *corpus* unaccompanied by the *animus*. Since, factually as well as legally, residence is included in domicile, in all cases where the domicile can be determined, residence is absorbed thereby and does not have any independent significance, except in rare cases in the law of criminal procedure. However, residence becomes significant as the residual nexus in all cases where the domicile of a person cannot be determined. In such cases residence is deemed by law the equivalent of domicile (art. 53).

A domicile is retained until a new one is acquired (art. 52). But, unlike other systems, Greek law does not recognize multiple simultaneous domiciles (art. 51). The only exception is provided in the same article for persons engaging in a trade or profession who, aside from their general domicile, may have a 'special domicile' at the place where they carry out their trade or profession.

While the determination of a person's domicile is normally a factual question to be decided by the judge from the totality of the circumstances, the domicile of certain classes of persons at a given place is fixed by operation of law (legal domicile). Thus, public servants have, by law, a domicile at the place where they are supposed to render their services (art. 54), and minors have the domicile of their parents or the parent who has the custody of them. When both parents have custody but are domiciled at different places, the minor has the domicile of the parent with whom the minor usually resides. Minors under guardianship and persons under interdiction have the domicile of their guardian (art. 56). Until recently, the wife had by law the same domicile as her husband, and could not acquire a separate domicile except when she was not required to follow the husband (art. 55). However, the pertinent article was repealed following the 1975 Constitution which established, more categorically than in the past, the equality of sexes (L. 1329/1983; see below, Ch. 8, Section I).

### *E. Protection of Personality*

After the Swiss Civil Code, the Greek Civil Code was the first continental civil code to recognize an all-inclusive, comprehensive right of personality of natural persons, and to accord it the protection of the civil law (art. 57). This protection overlaps with, but also goes beyond, the protection of the criminal law, since it encompasses compensation for the victim. It also goes beyond the protection of constitutional law which, strictly speaking, protects the person from state rather than from private intrusion. Purposefully, the Code does not define the exact perimeters of the concept of personality, thus allowing expansion of the concept as the fabric and mores of society change. It is generally said that personality encompasses all the tangible and intangible elements which constitute one's physical, emotional, intellectual, moral, and social existence.

The Code grants a general action for the protection of one's personality against any 'unlawful' intrusion, invasion, or infringement (art. 57). The action is available even against a defendant who is not, or is incapable of being, at fault, and may result in a prohibitory or mandatory injunction. If at fault, the defendant may be forced to pay monetary compensation or make other reparation for moral damage (art. 59) and may be sued under general tort law for patrimonial damage. A similar action is available for the protection of the memory of a deceased person. Special protection is provided for a person's name by article 58 which is interpreted to extend to juridical persons as well.

Rights of intellectual and industrial property are protected in Greece by a dense network of special statutes and international conventions signed and ratified by Greece. Among the latter are the Bern Convention for the Protection of Literary and Artistic Products of 1886 as revised in Brussels in 1948 and expanded in Paris in 1971. For industrial property, Greece has acceded to the pertinent convention of Paris-Brussels-Washington-Hague-London. In addition, article 60 grants a general action for the protection of the products of one's intellect. The conditions for and the content of the action are the same as those of the action for the protection of one's name.

## III. Legal or Juridical Persons (νομικά πρόσωπα, nomika prosopa)

### *A. Categories of Legal Persons*

Greek law distinguishes between legal persons of public law and of private law. Doctrine and the courts have developed the intermediate category of legal persons of mixed character for entities that do not fall neatly into either category. Legal persons of public law are established by the state for the promotion of a public, governmental or quasi-governmental, purpose. As their name suggests, these legal persons are governed by the rules of public law and only in default thereof by the rules of private law. The same is true for the legal persons of mixed character who, although organized as private corporations, are devoted to a public purpose, or a purpose in which the state has a great interest. Examples of this latter kind are the public utilities, communications, and major transportation companies. The legal persons of private law are devoted to a private purpose, whether for profit or not, and are regulated by private law. They are subdivided into commercial or business associations regulated by the commercial law (see below, Ch. 11) and non-commercial legal persons regulated by the Civil Code. Articles 741–785 regulate the civil, i.e., non-commercial, partnership, an unincorporated association which, when pursuing an economic purpose, may, under certain conditions (art. 784), be accorded legal personality (see below, Ch. 11). Articles 78–126 deal with three legal entities not devoted to the pursuit of profit: associations (78–107), foundations (108–121), and fund-raising committees (122–126). Due to their limited interest to the foreign lawyer and to space limitations, these entities are not discussed here. This section presents briefly some of the general principles of the law of legal persons provided for in articles 61–77 of the Civil Code. Unless displaced by more specific rules provided elsewhere, these principles apply to all legal persons, including business associations and, to a lesser extent, legal persons of public law and of mixed character.

## B. *Some General Principles of the Law of Legal Persons*

### 1. Formal Requirements

A legal person cannot be established orally in Greece. Article 63 mandates that the agreement for the formation of the entity and for its internal organization and outward operation (καταστατικό, katastatiko) referred to hereafter as 'charter') must be in writing, under penalty of nullity (art. 159.1). Special provisions impose additional formalities, such as notarial act, for particular legal persons, and recordation in the public records or publication in special bulletins or in the newspapers for all legal persons.

### 2. Personality

When the requirements for its valid formation have been met, the legal person comes into existence and is accorded juridical personality. This means that it acquires the capacity to be the subject of rights and duties, to own property, to sue and be sued in its own name, to enter into juridical acts, and generally to be treated as a person in the eyes of the law. Naturally, this does not extend to activities or legal relations that presuppose the qualities of a natural person. (art. 62).

### 3. Seat

The seat of the legal person is at the place designated by the charter, and in default thereof at the place where its central administration is located (art. 64). While it is disputed whether a legal person may have multiple general seats, a 'special seat' in addition to the general seat is clearly permissible under art. 51.3 (see above, Section II D), applicable here by analogy.

### 4. Liability for Juridical Acts

The legal person is bound by juridical acts (below, Section V A) entered into by the persons entrusted by the charter with the management of its affairs, provided that they have acted within the limits of their authority (art. 70). Their authority is expressly or impliedly prescribed in the charter which is publicly recorded or otherwise publicized and is assertible against third parties (art. 68) regardless of their good or bad faith. By analogical application of the rules of representation (arts. 211–235, see below, Section VII) and mandate (arts. 713–729, below, Ch. 5, Section II E), a legal person may also be bound by other juridical acts provided they were otherwise authorized and performed either by the above named persons or by any other authorized agents or employees (art. 68.2).

### 5. Non-Contractual and Delictual Liability

Article 71 provides that 'the legal person is liable for the acts or omissions of its representative organs . . . in the performance of their delegated duties . . . The individual organ who is at fault is also liable in solido.' By virtue of other articles (e.g., arts. 334, 922) the legal person is also liable for the acts of its non-representative organs, such as servants or other subordinates, while acting within the course of their duties. However, unlike the liability of articles 334 and 922 which is liability for someone else's acts, the liability of article 71 is liability for one's own acts. This is so, because the 'representative organs' of article 71 are generally understood to encompass only those persons, such as the chairman or members of the board, or the managing partner, who are authorized by the charter to act for the legal entity. According to the prevailing, so-called 'organic theory,' these organs do not merely represent but *are* the entity. Consequently, the liability of the entity for their acts is not secondary or derivative but rather primary, and attaches even if the organ was not at fault, so long as the act or omission has given rise to an obligation for damages. When the organ is at fault, he is solidarily liable (i.e., for the whole amount) to the victim, and is subject to an action for indemnity by the entity which discharges the obligation to the victim.

The liability of the legal person attaches even if the organ violated, exceeded, or abused his duties, as long as he was acting 'in the performance' of these duties. It is disputed whether the entity will be liable for the acts of the organ committed merely 'on the occasion' of the performance of his duties. A typical hornbook example is that, while the entity will be liable for the misrepresentation and fraud perpetrated during negotiations on the other party by its own chairman, the entity will not be liable for the chairman's forgery of the other party's signature.

## IV. Rights (δικαιώματα, dikaiomata)

### A. *Meaning*

The Greek work δικαίωμα (dikaioma) is literally translated as right, and has the same meaning as the French term *droit subjectif* or the German *subjektives Recht*, a meaning, however, that is not defined in the Civil Code. The prevailing definition in Greece seems to be the one suggested by Enneccerus, with slight modifications made by nearly every Greek author. Right is defined as the power granted by law for the vindication of legally recognized interests. All standard treatises on General Principles contain extensive discussion of rights, and their classification, exercise and protection. This discussion usually precedes the discussion of persons, and always the discussion of juridical acts, and is indicative of the Greek lawyer's preoccupation with rights, rather than remedies or actions as his common-law or Roman-law colleague respectively. Unfortunately, space limitations do not permit even a brief presentation of that interesting but mostly pedagogical discussion. Instead, what follows is a short explanation of some aspects of the exercise of rights expressly provided in the Civil Code.

### B. *Abuse of Rights* (κατάχρηση δικαιώματος, katachrisi dikaiomatos)

Unlike the French, and like the German, Austrian, and Swiss civil codes, the Greek Civil Code has codified expressly the doctrine of abuse of rights, originally developed by the French courts in the middle of the nineteenth century. Article 281 provides that '[t]he exercise of a right is prohibited when it manifestly exceeds the limits dictated by good faith, or good morals, or the social or economic purpose of the right.' This formulation of the doctrine is broader than that of §226 of the BGB (already expanded by German jurisprudence) which considers unlawful the exercise of a right when 'its purpose can only be to cause damage to another,' and is more concrete and categorical than that of article 2 of the Swiss Civil Code which merely 'does not sanction the manifest abuse of rights.' A provision parallel to article 281 is now found in article 25 III of the Greek Constitution of 1975, applicable apparently to matters of public law.

In order to be abusive, and thus prohibited under article 281, the exercise of the right must 'manifestly' exceed the limits dictated by the deliberately vague concepts of good faith, good morals, or the social and economic purpose for which the right was granted in the first place. These limits are determined judicially on the basis of objective considerations. The personal motives of the obligee, although material, are not determinative. According to established jurisprudence, all private rights, patrimonial, extrapatrimonial, or facultative, are subject to the limitations of article 281, including rights derived from juridical acts or from rules of public order, and extending into areas outside the civil law. Article 281 is itself a rule of public order that cannot be derogated from by contrary agreement. It is disputed whether the abusive exercise of a right may be taken into account *ex officio* by the court, but it may be raised by the affected party at any stage of the proceedings, provided the supporting facts were pleaded timely. The abusive exercise of a right is not merely 'not sanctioned,' but is 'prohibited.' This means that if the abusive exercise of the right took the form of a juridical act, the act will be void. Otherwise, it may give rise to an action for injunction and potentially to a claim for compensation.

### *C. 'Deactivation' of Rights* (αποδυνάμωση, apodynamosi)

Influenced by German authorities, and based on article 281 and the general principle of good faith (art. 288) which pervades the doctrine of abuse of rights, Greek courts have developed the parallel doctrine of 'deactivation' of rights, which resembles the common law doctrine of latches or equitable estoppel. A right may 'lose its force,' if the obligee fails to exercise it for an inordinately long (though shorter than the applicable prescription) time, under conditions that have led the obligor reasonably to believe that the right has been renounced or would not be exercised, and when the enforcement of the right would render severely onerous the condition of the obligor. All private rights, including the non-prescriptible ones, are subject to 'deactivation'.

### *D. Self-help, Self-defense, Emergency*

The Civil Code permits self-help and self-defense under narrowly defined circumstances. According to article 282, the obligee may use self-help only when the delay in obtaining public assistance would render significantly more difficult or impossible the realization of his claim. If these conditions are not met, or if he used excessive force, he is liable for compensation (art. 283).

Self-defense is permitted for protecting oneself or another from a present actual attack (art. 284). The destruction of things belonging to another is not unlawful, if it became necessary in order to ward off a present danger threatening a disproportionate damage to the actor or another (art. 285).

However, the actor is liable for compensation if he had himself caused the danger. In all other cases he may still be required to provide compensation, but he has an indemnity action against the person who benefited (art. 286).

## V. Juridical acts (δικαιοπραξίες, dikaiopraxies)

### *A. Definition*

If the concept of right is the 'last of abstractions', the concept of juridical acts is the second to last. A juridical act is an act by which a person declares his will to produce certain legal consequences consisting of acquiring, altering, transfering or terminating rights or legal relations, and which act is recognized by law as producing such consequences. Obviously, it is a concept broader than contract or agreement or even the term 'declaration of will' (δήλωση βουλήσεως, dilosi vouliseos) which the Code often uses interchangeably with juridical acts. While some juridical acts, especially unilateral ones, consist of nothing but a declaration of will, others contain more than one declaration and/or some additional operative facts. Moreover, not every declaration produces legal consequences, but only the ones so intended by the declarant and to which the law attaches such consequences. Articles 127 to 200 establish the general principles which, unless displaced by more specific rules contained in the other four books of the Civil Code, apply to all juridical acts, be they unilateral or bilateral, *inter vivos* or *causa mortis*, onerous or gratuitous, abstract or causal, dispositive or non-dispositive, and so forth.

### *B. Capacity* (ικανότητα, ikanotita)

Greek law distinguishes between persons with full, limited, or no capacity at all to enter into juridical acts. All persons above the age of 18 have full capacity (art. 127), unless they fall into any of the classes of persons with limited or no capacity described below.

The following persons are absolutely incapable of entering into any juridical act and may only act through their legal representatives, such as tutors, curators, or guardians: a) minors below the age of ten (art. 128); b) persons interdicted because of a permanent mental or physical infirmity that renders them unable to take care of themselves (arts. 128, 1686); and c) persons incarcerated for felony during their incarceration (arts. 128, 1700), for juridical acts other than testaments (art. 1719). Declarations of will made by or to these persons are absolutely null (arts. 130, 170), regardless of whether or not the attempted juridical act would be beneficial to the incapable. The nullity may be invoked by either party, as well as by third parties who have an interest in doing so. Also absolutely null are the declarations of will made by, or to, a person who at the time was 'not conscious of what he was doing or, due to mental illness, was deprived of the use of reason' (arts. 131, 171). Typical examples are heavy drunkenness or intoxication, extremely high fever, or temporary mental illness. The resulting nullity of the attempted juridical act may be invoked by either party, or by any third party with an interest in doing so. However, article 132 protects the other party who, without fault of his own, was reasonably unaware of the incapacity, by requiring the temporarily incapable party to make reparation, if the damage produced thereby cannot be otherwise covered. Article 171 accords similar protection in cases where the declaration of will was made to, rather than by, the temporarily incapable person.

The following persons have limited capacity: (a) minors above the age of ten (art. 129); and (b) persons placed under judicial guardianship (art. 129) because of mental illness, physical handicap, spendthriftness, habitual drunkenness, or chemical dependency (arts. 1691, 1705). Minors above ten are incapable of entering into juridical acts (art. 133), except those expressly provided in articles 134–137 and under the conditions specified therein. Persons under judicial supervision, on the other hand, are generally capable of entering into all juridical acts, except certain acts enumerated in article 1707, for which the consent of the guardian or the competent court is necessary. Without such consent the juridical act is 'relatively null,' which means that the nullity may be invoked only by the supervisor and the person under supervision or his successors (art. 1709). Although the majority of doctrinal writers support a similar treatment for juridical acts attempted by minors without consent, the courts, based on articles 133 and 172, treat such acts as absolutely rather than relatively null.

### *C. Vices of Consent*

Articles 140-157 deal with what in other systems are usually known as vices of consent: mistake, fraud, and duress or threat. However, because the term consent usually presupposes a contract or other bilateral juridical act, and because the above mentioned articles are applicable to all juridical acts including the unilateral ones, the Code uses the term defects of the 'declaration of will' (δήλωση βουλήσεως, dilosi vouliseos). A declaration of will is defective when it is the result of error, or is procured by fraud or threat.

While all types of fraud may vitiate consent, only a 'substantial' mistake (art. 140), or a threat that is 'unlawful or against good morals' (art. 150) produce that result. Furthermore, the threat must be of the kind which, under the circumstances, instills fear in a sane person and poses a serious and immediate danger to the life, physical integrity, liberty, honor, or patrimony of the declarant or of persons closely related to him (art. 151).

A mistake is 'substantial' when it affects a point of such importance to the juridical act that the declarant would not have attempted it, had he known of the true state of affairs (art. 141), Aside from the marriage contract (where only a mistake as to the identity of one spouse would vitiate the consent of the other), a mistake as to the qualities of a person or a thing is deemed important enough to vitiate the declaration, if, according to the agreement of the parties, the conventional usages, or the principle of good faith, such qualities are so essential to the juridical act that the declarant would not have attempted it had he known of the true situation (art. 142). On the other hand, a mistake pertaining exclusively to the motives of the declarant is not substantial (art. 143), except when the law provides otherwise (see, e.g., arts. 1784–1786 for wills).

The juridical act resulting from a declaration of will based on a vice of consent is voidable, and may be rescinded only judicially at the instance of the declarant or his heirs (arts. 140, 147, 150, 154). When the vice consists of mistake or fraud, rescission is precluded if the other party accepts the declaration as intended by the declarant (arts. 144, 148). In the case of mistake, rescission is also precluded when it is contrary to good faith (art. 144).

The party who obtains rescission on grounds of his own mistake is liable for the loss sustained thereby by others, unless they knew or should have known of the error (art. 145). The award of damages cannot exceed the amount the other party would have received if the juridical act were valid. The party whose declaration was procured by fraud or threat may, in addition to his rescission rights, be entitled to compensation under the general tort provisions (arts. 149, 152). Such compensation may be due even if he chooses to accept the juridical act as is. The right to demand rescission is extinguished by express or tacit renunciation (art. 156), or by the lapse of two years from the juridical act (art. 157). If the vice of consent was a continuous one, the two-year period commences upon the end of the vice, but rescission cannot be demanded after the lapse of twenty years from the juridical act.

Unlike mistake, fraud, or threat, which are defects of the will of the declarant, simulation (εικονικότητα, eikonikotita) involves a situation where, although the will of the declarant is not defective, the declaration of it, knowingly and deliberately, does not correspond to the intent of the declarant, as when he makes a declaration jokingly, or "for appearances only" (art. 138). A simulated juridical act is void, but the nullity may not be asserted against parties who were reasonably unaware of it (art. 139). A juridical act concealed under the simulated act may be valid, if the parties so intended and the act meets the other legal requirements (art. 138).

### *D. Form*

As a general matter, juridical acts must be executed in a certain form only when the law expressly so requires (art. 158) or the parties have so provided (art. 159). The instances where the law does require a particular form cannot be enumerated here, but the types of form known to Greek law are simple writing, i.e., an instrument under a private signature; notarial act; and various kinds of affidavits before public authorities. Except for holographic wills, the text of the act need not be in the handwriting of the declarant, as long as he affixes his signature at the end of the document (art. 160). For bearer instruments issued in great numbers, the signature of the issuer may be affixed by mechanical means (art. 163). In contracts required to be in writing, the signature of both parties must be placed on the same document, but, when multiple originals are issued, it suffices if the signature of one party appears in the original retained by the other (art. 160). When the contract must be executed in notarial form, the offer and the acceptance may be executed in separate documents (art. 161).

A juridical act not executed in the form prescribed by law is void, unless the law provides otherwise (art. 159). The nullity is an absolute one, and may be invoked by either party or by the court on its own motion. Except when the law provides otherwise, as in the case of manual gifts, the nullity cannot be cured retroactively by subsequent performance or other events short of re-execution of the act in the prescribed form (art. 183). In contrast, the failure to observe a form imposed by the parties rather than by law results in nullity only 'in cases of doubt' (art. 159), i.e., when the intent of the parties to that effect is unclear. Even then, the nullity may be cured by subsequent performance.

## *E. Formation of Contracts* (συμβάσεις, symvaseis)

The Greek terms for offer (πρόταση, protasi) and acceptance (αποδοχή, apodochi) have the same meaning as in the common law, but the applicable rules differ in many respects. An offer, an acceptance, and generally any declaration of will, become binding only upon receipt by the addressee (arts. 167, 192), rather than upon dispatch, and may be revoked without any limitation prior to or contemporaneously with receipt (art. 167). The addressee need not receive personally the declaration or knowledge of its contents, as long as the declaration has reached his sphere of control. The validity or effect of an offer is not affected by the death or incapacitation of the offeror or the offeree following dispatch (arts. 169, 188). Upon receipt of the offer, the offeror is bound not to revoke it until the offeree has had a reasonable time to accept it (art. 185), unless the offeror has reserved the right to revoke at an earlier time, or revocation is justified by the nature of the contract or the circumstances of the case (art. 186). The offer expires when it is rejected or not timely accepted by the offeree (art. 187).

To be effective, the acceptance of the offer must be received by the offeree within the prescribed time, or, if no time has been fixed, within the time in which, under the circumstances, the offeror is obligated to wait for the acceptance (art. 189). Nevertheless, an acceptance dispatched timely but received late is effective, unless the offeror immediately notifies the offeree to the contrary (art. 190). A later acceptance as well as a qualified one is deemed as a rejection of the offer and operates as a new offer (art. 191). The contract (*symvasi*) is concluded the moment the acceptance is received by the offeror (art. 192). However, depending on the content of the offer, the conventional usages, and the special circumstances of the case, the contract may be concluded upon dispatch of the acceptance (art. 193) or upon the execution of the notarial act containing the acceptance (art. 194). Absent a contrary intent, the contract is not completed unless there is agreement on all points (art. 195).

The general principle of good faith binds the parties even during the negotiating stage. Article 197 provides that the parties must deal with each other according to the dictates of good faith and conventional mores. Any damage caused in violation of this duty (*culpa in contrahendo*) must be compensated for by the party at fault, even if the contract is not eventually concluded (art. 198).

### *F. Consideration and Cause*

The common law lawyer familiar with civil law systems would not expect to find here any discussion of consideration as an element in the formation of contracts, for the simple reason that consideration as such is unknown to the civil law. Yet, what the common law accomplishes through the doctrine of consideration, the civil law accomplishes through other means, one of which is the theory of *cause* (αιτία, aitia) Simplistically stated, the difference between the two systems on this issue is that, while the common law focuses on what the promisor receives in return for his promise, the civil law focuses on the purpose for which the promisor makes his promise. Cause, therefore, is the reason or purpose for which the promisor obligates himself. This purpose should not be confused with the ultimate motives of the promisor, which are in principle irrelevant in the eyes of the law.

The role and importance of cause varies from one civil law system to the other. For example, cause plays a dominant role in the French Civil Code, as manifested in article 1108 of that Code, which elevates the existence, lawfulness, and validity of the underlying cause into an indispensable foundation for all contracts, and in the French system's general hostility towards non-causal or 'abstract' juridical acts. On the other hand, like the German, the Greek Civil Code does not contain a general rule requiring a cause for all juridical acts. Again, however, what the French code accomplishes through article 1108, the Greek code accomplishes through articles 174–178 which render void all juridical acts whose content is unlawful or immoral, and through the articles on unjust enrichment (arts. 904 ff.) which authorize the recovery of a payment made 'without a lawful cause.' It is from these provisions that Greek authors derive the rule that, as a general matter, cause is an essential element for the validity and enforceability of obligations, and that most juridical acts are 'causal.'

However, unlike the French and like the German, the Greek Civil Code recognizes expressly juridical acts which are detached from their underlying cause, either by operation of law or by the will of the parties. Examples of such acts in the Greek civil, as distinguished from commercial, law are the transfer of movables (art. 1034), the assumption or forgiveness of debts (art. 471, 454), the assignment of claims (art. 455), and the so-called abstract promise or acknowledgment of debts (art. 873). These acts are known as abstract or non-causal juridical acts. Their difference from the causal juridical acts is not that they are entered into without a cause, but rather that their validity and enforceability are independent from the underlying cause. In practical terms, this means that the obligee recovers without having to prove the existence and validity of the cause.

However, if a cause is lacking, or is unlawful or immoral, the obligor is protected through the provisions on unjust enrichment (see below, Ch. 5, Section III).

### G. *Content of Juridical Acts*

A juridical act which is otherwise valid but whose content contravenes a prohibitory provision of law is void, unless a lesser sanction is provided by law (art. 174). An act of alienation prohibited by law or by judicial decision is void. If the prohibition is intended for the protection of certain persons, only they may invoke the nullity (arts. 175, 176). Unless otherwise provided by law, a juridical act restricting the alienation of an alienable right is valid only to the extent of binding the person and does not affect the validity of the alienation (art. 177).

Also void are juridical acts that are contrary to good morals (art. 178). Article 179 mentions two such examples; juridical acts that unduly restrict the liberty of the individual, and acts in which one party exploits the need, feebleness, or inexperience of the other in order to gain benefits that are obviously disproportionate to his own performance (unconscionability). An impressive body of 'case-law', which cannot be recounted here, has been developed around these two open-ended articles.

### H. *Nullities*

As the preceeding discussion indicates, Greek law distinguishes between void and voidable juridical acts. A further category of 'non-existent' juridical acts has practical significance only in the law of marriage (see below, Ch. 8).

Juridical acts that are void produce no legal effects and need not be judicially declared null. The right to invoke the nullity of a void juridical act is not subject to prescription or peremption, although it may be subject to 'deactivation' (see above, Section IV C). Void acts are divided into absolutely void and relatively void, depending on who may invoke the nullity. The first category encompasses acts, such as those contrary to good morals, or which contravene a provision of law designed for the protection of the public interest. This nullity may be invoked by anybody with an interest in doing so, as well as by the court on its own motion. With only minor exceptions, an absolutely void juridical act may not be cured by subsequent events. Even its subsequent ratification does not operate retroactively, although it may impose a personal obligation on the parties to perform as if the original act was valid *ab initio* (art. 183).

The category of relatively null juridical acts encompasses acts which violate rules designed for the protection of a private interest. This nullity may be invoked at any time, but only by the parties for whose protection the violated rule was intended, their heirs, assignees and creditors. Until the nullity is invoked, or if the right to do so is renounced expressly or tacitly, the act produces its legal effects.

Voidable are the juridical acts that are based on a vice of consent (see above, Section V C). These acts produce all their legal effects, unless rescinded by a judicial decision. Only the victim and his heirs have standing to demand rescission. A judicially rescinded juridical act is treated as void *ab initio*, which means its effects are erased retroactively. As in the case of void juridical acts, third parties in good faith are protected only when the law so provides.

### *I. Interpretation*

In addition to a number of special rules scattered throughout the Civil Code, Book I contains two important general rules of interpretation of juridical acts. The first one applies to all juridical acts, and requires the judge to search for the true intent of the parties without undue attachment to the words used (art. 173). The second rule applies primarily to contracts, and requires that they be 'interpreted as dictated by good faith, taking account of conventional mores.' The two rules together strike a good balance between subjective and objective criteria which have been rendered more concrete by a voluminous body of cases.

## VI. Terms and Conditions

The Greek terms for condition (αίρεση, airesi) and term (προθεσμία, prothesmia) have the same meaning as in all other civil law systems as well as in the common law. A condition is suspensive (αναβλητική, anavlitiki) when it delays the effects of a juridical act until the occurrence of a future and uncertain event (art. 201). The condition is resolutory (διαλυτική, dialytiki) when its fulfillment, that is, the occurrence of the future and uncertain event, terminates the effects of the juridical act (art. 202). When the occurrence of the future event is certain, although the time of it may not be, the juridical act is subject to a term which may be suspensive or resolutory. Terms are governed by the same rules as conditions, applicable by analogy (art. 210).

A condition that is incomprehensible, contradictory, unlawful, or immoral renders the juridical act void (for exceptions with regard to wills, see, e.g., art. 1794) A suspensive condition that is impossible also renders the juridical act void. An impossible resolutory condition has no effect (art. 208).

During the pendency of the condition the parties must refrain from acts that would impair or destroy the right subject to the condition. Breach of this duty renders the violator liable for damages that are collectible only upon fulfillment of the condition (art. 204). If the violation consisted in the alienation of the object of the transaction, the alienation becomes *ipso facto* void upon fulfillment of the condition (206). A condition is deemed fulfilled if, in a manner inconsistent with good faith, its fulfillment is prevented by the party who would be adversely affected by its fulfillment. Conversely, the condition is deemed unfulfilled, if, in a manner contrary to good faith, its fulfillment was caused by the party who would benefit thereby (art. 207).

## VII. Representation and Procuration

### *A. Introduction*

Greek law on this subject is more abstract and systematic than, and in many respects different from, either the common law or French law. Under the general concept of representation (αντιπροσώπευση, antiprosopeusi), Greek law treats together all situations where a declaration of will by or to one person binds or benefits directly another person, regardless of whether the underlying relationship is imposed by law (legal representation), is created by contract (voluntary representation) or results from extracontractual conduct of the parties. Also, Greek law distinguishes sharply between, and treats separately, the external aspects of this relationship *vis-à-vis* third parties, and the internal relationship between the principal and his representative. The internal relationship may be created by law or judicial decision, such as the relation between a minor and the custodian parent, or the interdict and his guardian; or it may be based on a contract such as mandate, partnership, or hiring of services. These relationships are regulated in detail in other parts of the Civil Code, notably Books II and IV. The external relationship is regulated in Book I, articles 211–235, and is the only one discussed here. Finally, a significant substantive difference between the common law and Greek law is the failure of the latter to recognize the notion of undisclosed agency, and its rather grudging recognition of partially disclosed agency and apparent authority. These differences are explained below.

### *B. Express, Implied, and Apparent Authority*

The Greek term for procuration or power of attorney (πληρεξουσιότητα, plirexousiotita) signifies both the juridical act by which a person confers representative authority to another, and the authority conferred thereby (art. 216). The procuration which is given directly to the representative is either express or implied and is subject to no special formalities, except when the authorized act is required by law to conform to a certain form. In that case the procuration must be clothed with the same form (art. 217). The procuration may also be given to the third party with whom the representative is authorized to transact (external procuration, art. 217). Again it may be given expressly or impliedly, such as when the principal appoints a person in a certain position from which third parties may reasonably infer that the appointed person has the authority to transact business on behalf of the principal. This is called 'tacit procuration' by Greek commentators, and comes close to the common-law notion of apparent authority or agency by estoppel. Although not expressly recognized by the Civil Code, this notion is grounded by academic writers on the doctrine of abuse of rights (art. 281, see above, Section IV B). In common law language, this means that the principal is estopped from asserting the lack of authority on which third parties in good faith have relied to their detriment.

Aside from these instances, however, the principal is not bound by juridical acts entered into in his name by another without or in excess of his authority, unless the principal has ratified them (art. 229). Until the principal does so, the third party is free to withdraw from the contract (art. 230). If neither of the two occurs, the third party who was reasonably not aware of the lack of authority may at his option demand from the 'representative' either performance of the contract or damages. If the representative was also not aware of his lack of authority, the third party's remedies are confined to damages (art. 231).

Juridical acts entered into by the representative after the termination of the procuration bind the principal only if neither the representative nor the third party knew or should have known of the termination (art. 224). If the representative knew of the termination, the principal is not bound to perform but may be liable for reasonable compensation to a third party in good faith, if the principal could have easily notified him of the termination of authority (art. 225).

### *C. Undisclosed and Partially Disclosed Agency*

Article 211 requires that, in order for the principal to be bound for the juridical acts of his representative, the latter must have acted 'in the name' of the principal, that is, to have disclosed to the third party both the existence and the identity of the principal. The disclosure may be express or tacit, i.e., it may be 'indicated from the surrounding circumstances' (tacit representation, art. 211). The courts have subsumed under the concept of tacit representation what is known in common-law systems as partially disclosed agency, that is, the situation where the agent reveals the existence but not the identity of the principal. However, outside the area of commercial law, neither the courts nor the academic authors have as yet recognized the concept of undisclosed agency. The seemingly similar notion of 'indirect representation' is in fact no representation at all, since the effects of the juridical act of the so-called representative, who acts in his own name, flow directly to him rather than to his undisclosed principal. The 'representative' merely incurs a personal obligation to convey these effects to the principal through a separate juridical act which, although enforcible by an action for specific performance, is often not an effective remedy for the principal. His interests may be protected only if the representative had signed in advance a so-called 'assignment of future interests.' More importantly, however, in the 'indirect representation,' no relation is created between the undisclosed principal and the third party. Even after the identity of the principal is revealed, neither he nor the third party has direct recourse against the other. The third party's only recourse is against the representative.

## VIII. Prescription and Peremption

### *A. Clarification of Terms*

#### 1. Prescription

What is known in the common law world as limitation of actions is called prescription in the civil law world and παραγραφή (paragraphi) in Greek. According to article 247, it is not the right that prescribes, but rather only the claim (αξίωση, axiosi), that is, the right to demand from another, judicially or extrajudicially, a performance consisting of an act or omission.

#### 2. Acquisitive Prescription and Prescription of Non-Use

What is known elsewhere as acquisitive prescription, – a mode of acquiring ownership or other real rights by adverse possession for a period of time – is called χρησικτησία (chrisiktisia) in Greek and is regulated in Book III of the Civil Code (see below, Ch. 6). The same is true for the prescription of non-use (αχρησία, achrisia), that is, a mode of extinction of real rights other than ownership as a result of failure to exercise them for a period of time.

#### 3. Peremption

Greek law recognizes a fourth kind of time limitation called αποσβεστική προθεσμία (aposvestiki prothesmia). It may be translated in English as peremption or forfeiture, and is a period of time fixed by law or by the parties for the existence of the right (art. 279). Unless exercised within the period, the right itself, not only the action, is extinguished. No natural obligation subsists. Whether a particular time limitation is in the nature of peremption rather than prescription is a matter of interpretation of the pertinent statutory provision. Fortunately, the process is facilitated by the Greek legislator's skillful use of signal-words. The practical difference between peremption and prescription is that peremption may not be renounced, and is taken into account *ex officio* by the court (art. 280). For the rest, peremption is governed by the rules of prescription applicable by analogy (art. 279).

### *B. General Principles of Prescription*

#### 1. Commencement

As a general matter, prescription commences from the day the claim may be judicially pursued (art. 251). However, this rule is subject to many exceptions for specific types of claims (see, e.g., arts. 252–254). Prescription accrues upon the expiration of the last day of the period and, if that day is a legal holiday, then upon the expiration of the next working day (art. 242).

### 2. Suspension

Prescription is suspended or tolled: between spouses during marriage even if the marriage is later declared null; between parents and children during their minority; between guardians and interdicts during the guardianship; with regard to the claims by servants against their masters during the period of service, but no longer than fifteen years (art. 256). Greek law also recognizes, though in limited form, the doctrine of *contra non valentem agere non currit prescriptio*. Article 255 provides that, if, during the last six months of the prescriptive period, the obligee is prevented from pursuing his claim through fraud of the obligor or because of *force majeure*, the prescription is suspended for as long as the impediment lasts. In all the above situations, the period of suspension does not count towards accrual of prescription. Upon termination of the period of suspension, prescription commences to run again but is not completed before the lapse of six months thereafter (art. 257).

The following are situations in which, strictly speaking, prescription is prolonged rather than suspended: (a) prescription runs against persons with limited or no capacity to enter into juridical acts, however, if these persons also have no capacity to sue and do not have a tutor, guardian, or curator, prescription is not completed before six months from the acquisition of full capacity or the appointment of a tutor, guardian or curator (art. 258); and (b) claims by or against a succession do not prescribe before six months from the day the heir was put into possession, or an administrator was appointed (art. 259).

### 3. Interruption

The two major modes of interruption are: the acknowledgment of the obligation by the obligor; and the filing of the action by the obligee (arts. 260, 261). Other modes of interruption are provided for in articles 264–269. Acknowledgment may be express or tacit, and is subject to no special form. Under article 216 of the Code of Civil Procedure (see below, Ch. 15, Section VI A) the filing of the action is not complete until process is served. Consequently, prescription is interrupted as of that moment. This interruption is deemed never to have occurred if the plaintiff abandoned the action, or the action was dismissed on grounds not on the merits. However, the plaintiff may retroactively regain the lost interruption by refiling the action within six months (art. 263).

When prescription is interrupted, the time that has run before is not counted. Prescription commences to run anew from the last day of the interruption (art. 270).

### 4. Extension, Reduction, Renunciation

Prescription may be validly renounced only after accrual (art. 276), but not before. Because the rules of prescription are *ius cogens*, Greek law considers void any juridical act purporting to exclude, shorten, or prolong prescription, or to make its terms more or less onerous (art. 275). The only exception made to this important rule by Greek jurisprudence pertains to warranty clauses in contracts of sale, by which the seller warrants the product for a time longer than the applicable prescriptive period.

### 5. Accrual

Upon accrual of prescription, the obligor may refuse performance. However, because a natural obligation survives the accrual of prescription, payment by the obligor is not considered as payment of a thing not due. Consequently, the obligor may not demand the return of the payment. For the same reasons, a written acknowledgment of a prescribed debt, or the giving of security after accrual is enforceable (art. 272).

Unlike peremption (art. 280), prescription may not be supplied by the court on its own motion (art. 277), but must be pleaded by the obligor. If he failed to do so, or if he renounced prescription, his creditors or anybody with an interest in doing so may plead prescription on his behalf (art. 278).

The general prescriptive period is twenty years (art. 249). However, this prescription applies only when the law does not provide otherwise, that is, unless the claim is imprescriptible (see art. 248) or is subject to a shorter prescription (see art. 250 containing a long list of claims subject to a five-year prescription).

## Bibliography

The following are standard treatises on the General Principles of the Greek Civil Code. All of them are in Greek.

G. Balis, *General Principles of the Civil Law*, 8th ed. (1961).
D. Dimitrakakis, *General Principles of the Civil Code*, 2d ed. (1961).
K. Fourkiotis, *General Principles According to the Civil Code*, 3d ed. (1952).
A. Gazis, *General Principles of the Civil Law*, 5 fasc. (1970–1974).
G. Mantzoufas, *General Principles of the Civil Law*, fasc. 1, 2d ed. (1954), fasc. 2 (1957).
N. Papantoniou, *General Principles of the Civil Law*, 3d ed. (1983).
K. Simantiras, *General Principles of the Civil Law*, 3d ed. (1980).
J. Spyridakis, *General Principles* (1987).
J. Spyridakis & E. Perakis, *General Principles of the Civil Law*, 2d ed. (1978).
A. Toussis, *General Principles of the Civil Law*, 2d ed. (1978).

The following are article-by-article commentaries in Greek on Book I of the Civil Code dealing with General Principles.

A. Georgiadis and M. Stathopoulos, *Civil Code, Article-by-Article Interpretation: General Principles* (1978).
*Ermineia tou Astikou Kodikos (ErmAK)* by various authors (1952–1974).
A. Papachristou, *General Principles of the Civil Code. Interpretation by Article* (1979).
G. Vallindas, *Civil Code. General Principles* (1946).
D. Yiannopoulos, *General Principles. Interpretation by Article*, vols. I–II (1948).

# Chapter 5
# Law of Obligations

*Phoebus Chr. Christodoulou**

## I. General Principles

### *A. Obligation – The Sources of Obligation*

1. The Greek law of obligations (ενοχικό δίκαιο, enochiko dikaio) covers contracts in general, specific contracts, *negotiorum gestio*, community, torts, and unjust enrichment. The making of a contract creates a duty to perform; the commission of a tort creates a liability to pay reparations; unjust enrichment creates an obligation to make restitution. The Greek legal system assumes, by abstraction and generalization, that all these obligations have certain common elements and that contract, delict and unjust enrichment are the main sources of obligation.

2. The law is, thus, constructed upon a framework of rights and legal relations, whereby obligation (ενοχή, enochi) is the fundamental category. It is defined as a legal bond by which a person (the debtor) is compelled to render performance (παροχή, parochi) to another (the creditor) (art. 287 C.C.). The effect of an obligation is that the creditor is entitled to claim performance from the debtor. Performance may also consist in refraining from acting.

3. The concept of obligation comprises not only the owing of a debt, or a performance, but also the liability for not paying, or not discharging it (ευθύνη, euthyni). Thus, in case of non-performance, a creditor has in the first place the right to bring an action for performance and to obtain a judgment ordering the debtor to fulfill it. In last resort, the debtor's liability entails the possibility of execution on his property and, exceptionally, on his person, pursuant to articles 904 to 1054 of the Code of Civil Procedure (see below, Ch. 15, Section XIII).

4. An obligation is a personal, not a real, right. The creditor can in principle pursue only the particular person of the debtor who has come under an obligation to him.

*Professor of Law, Athens School of Economics and Business.

## B. *Obligation to Perform in General*

### 1. Performance in Good Faith

The debtor is bound to perform in accordance with the requirements of good faith (καλή πίστη, kali pisti), also giving consideration to business usage (art. 288). Good faith is, thus, considered as the source of collateral duties and obligations which are implied in law.

### 2. Rules Relating to Particular Kinds of Performance

(*a*) If a person owes a thing which is not particular but described only by class (παροχή κατά γένος, parochi kata genos), there arises the problem of identifying the particular thing which must be given in performance. The choice belongs, in case of doubt, to the debtor (art. 289 I). The debtor is not bound to furnish things among the best of the class nor is he entitled to furnish things among the worst of the class (art. 289 II). If the debtor, for the purpose of performance, separates from the class a particular thing, his obligation is limited to that thing only after the creditor has been in default in acceptance, or after the debtor has, at the request of the creditor, delivered the thing to be dispatched to a place other than the place of performance (art. 290).

(*b*) The Civil Code does not contain provisions relating to the national currency. Nevertheless, several separate enactments prescribe a system of exchange and other restrictions for the purpose of protecting the national currency. Thus, pursuant to article 4 I of Law 362/1945, agreements to pay a sum of money in favor of persons having their domicile in Greece should be expressed in drachmas. However, several special laws permit promises in money to be expressed in foreign currency. For such exceptional cases, where the debt is payable within the country, the Civil Code provides that, subject to an agreement to the contrary, the debtor has the right to make payment in drachmas at the current exchange rate (art. 291). During default, the creditor is entitled to interest. If it is the creditor who is in default, the debtor shall not bear the burden of any supervening increase in the value of the foreign currency (art. 292).

(*c*) As regards interest (τόκος, tokos), the Civil Code adopts a theory of rate regulation. (i) It provides that the rate of legal interest shall be fixed and that ceilings for the maximum finance charge shall be set by separate statutes (art. 293).[1] Any agreement relating to interest exceeding the legal ceiling shall

1. By resolutions nos. 145/1979 and 193/1979 of the Council of Ministers, issued under the authorization contained in art. 15 V of L. 876/1976, the annual rate of legal interest has been fixed at 25%. The same resolution no. 145/1979 sets the ceiling of contractual rate of interest at 23%. This ceiling refers in fact to the maximum annual finance charge since, pursuant to art. 293 I 2 C.C., commissions and other recompense agreed upon or paid in addition to interest are, for the purpose of rate regulation, deemed to constitute part of the interest. Separate statutes regulate the rate of interest for loans and deposits by commercial or other banks, whereby a

be void with regard to the excess interest only (art. 294). (ii) Moratory interest is due as damages for default in money debts. It functions as a statutory preestimate of the creditor's loss. A claim for further positive damage is not excluded (art. 345); cf. below, Section II F 2. (iii) An agreement that arrears of interest shall again bear interest is valid only if it refers to interest arrears of at least one year, and it is concluded after the expiration of the year. Saving banks, credit institutions and banks may provide in their articles of association, or agree in advance, that uncollected interest on deposits shall be considered as a new interest-bearing deposit (art. 296).[2]

(*d*) A person who is obligated to pay reparations (αποζημίωση, apozimiosi) shall use money (art. 297 I). Nevertheless, the court may, taking into consideration special circumstances, order restitution to be made in kind in so far as this is not contrary to the interest of the creditor (art. 297 II). (i) The reparations shall include the decrease in the existing property of the creditor (θετική ζημία, thetiki zimia, positive damage) as well as lost profits (διαφυγόν κέρδος, diaphygon kerdos). Profit is deemed to have been lost which could probably have been expected in the ordinary course of events or according to the special circumstances, especially in the light of preparations and arrangements made (art. 298). (ii) For non-pecuniary damage, reparations in money shall be due only in the cases provided for in the law (art. 299). (iii) If any fault of the injured party has contributed to causing the damage or to the extent of the damage, the court may deny or reduce the amount of reparations. This applies also where the injured party omitted to avert or mitigate the damage. This rule shall also apply to the fault of persons for whom the injured party is responsible (art. 300).

(*e*) Whoever has the management of an affair belonging, in whole or in part, to another and involving receipts and payments is obligated to render an account (art. 303). Whoever is obligated to deliver a mass of objects or to give information about such a mass, e.g., about its contents, shall provide an inventory (art. 304).

(*f*) Alternative obligations. If two or several acts of performance are due, of which only one may be demanded, in case of doubt the right to choose belongs to the debtor (art. 305). The choice is made by declaration to the other party (art. 306). The effect of the choice is that the obligation is limited to the performance chosen, which becomes then the only performance due (art. 307). If one of the acts of performance becomes impossible, the obligation is limited to the other acts of performance (art. 310).

### 3. Part-performance

A debtor is not entitled to make part-performance (art. 316).

variety of rate ceilings has developed on an *ad hoc* basis. Unless some other rate is specified by agreement or regulation, the annual rate of interest due for debts of the government shall not exceed 6% pursuant to art. 21 of the Decree of 26.6/10.7.1944.

2. Arts. 110 to 112 of the Introductory Law to the C.C., and art. 8(b) of L. 1083/1980 provide for further exceptions to the restrictions relating to compounding interest.

4. Performance by Third Parties

Performance may be made through third party unless the creditor has an interest in the performance by the debtor himself (art. 317). But the creditor is not bound to refuse the performance offered by a third party only because the debtor objects (art. 318). If the creditor levies execution upon an object belonging to the debtor, any person who through the execution incurs the danger of losing a right in the object or the possession of the object is entitled to satisfy the creditor, in which case the creditor's claim is transferred to him (art. 319).

5. Place for Performance

If a place for performance is neither fixed nor can be deduced from the circumstances, performance shall be effected at the place where the debtor had his residence at the time the obligation arose. If the obligation arose in the course of the debtor's business, his place of business is substituted for his residence (art. 320). If performance consists in the payment of money, the debtor is bound to make payment at the residence of the creditor at the time of the payment. If the claim arose in the course of the creditor's business, his place of business is substituted for his residence (art. 321).

6. Time for Performance

If a time for performance is neither fixed nor may be deduced from the circumstances, the creditor may demand performance at once and the debtor may perform his part at once (art. 323). If a time is fixed, it is to be presumed, in case of doubt, that this is done in favor of the debtor. Therefore the creditor may not demand the performance before that time; the debtor may however perform earlier. But he is not then entitled to deduction of discount interest, unless either the law or the juridical act provide otherwise (art. 324). If the debtor has a matured claim against the creditor arising from the same legal relationship upon which his own obligation is based, he may, unless a contrary intention appears from the relationship, refuse to make the performance due by him until the performance due to him is made (art. 325); cf. below, under E 1 (a).

7. Responsibility for One's Own Conduct

(*a*) A debtor is responsible, unless it is otherwise provided, for any shortfall in the performance of his obligation resulting from wilful misconduct (δόλος, dolos) or negligence (αμέλεια, ameleia) imputable to him or to his legal representatives. A person who does not exercise ordinary care, as normally required in conducting business, acts negligently (art. 330). Liability thus depends on fault. With reference to imputability, the exceptions in the provisions of articles 915 to 918 apply (art. 331; see below, Section IV E).

(*b*) A debtor may not be exempted in advance from responsibility for wilful misconduct or for gross negligence. Any agreement to the contrary is void. Void is also any agreement excluding in advance a debtor's responsibility even for slight negligence, if the creditor is an employee of the debtor, or if the responsibility arises from the conducting of an enterprise for which prior concession by the competent authority was granted to the debtor (art. 332).

### 8. Responsibility for Employees

A debtor is responsible for the fault of the person whom he employs in performing his obligation to the same extent as for his own fault. However, such responsibility may in principle be limited or excluded in advance, subject to the exceptions mentioned above under 7 (*b*) (art. 334).

## *C. Contractual Obligations*

The Civil Code places many rules of contract law, including those dealing with the formation of contract (arts. 192 ff), in Book I (General Principles) in the context of the concept of juridical act (arts. 127 ff.; see above, Ch. 4, Section V). In Book II (Obligations), we find rules relating to some prerequisites for and limits to the creation of obligations by juridical act and to the effect of existing contracts. Fundamental is the rule that for the creation of an obligation by juridical act, as well as for any modification of the substance of an obligation, a contract is necessary unless otherwise provided by law (art. 361). This rule is considered by legal writers as expressing the principles of private autonomy and of freedom of contract. These principles are subject to certain limitations.

1. Freedom of contract is limited by (a) state intervention aiming at the regulation of the economy, and (b) the idea of protecting the weaker party where there is striking inequality of bargaining power between the contracting parties. The Civil Code itself contains certain special restrictions. For example, contracts whereby one party binds himself to assign his future property or to charge it with a usufruct, as well as contracts concerning the estate of a still living person are void (arts. 366, 368). The exceptions to the general principle of informality in the making of contracts also operate to limit party autonomy (art. 158). Thus, contracts concerning the creation or the transfer or the modification or the extinction of real rights on a piece of land must be in notarial form (art. 369). The same is true of a contract assigning all present property or a fraction thereof (art. 367).

2. If the performance of a party is to be determined by one of the contracting parties, it is to be presumed that the determination is to be made in an equitable manner. If the determination is inequitable or if it is delayed it is

made by the court (art. 371). A contract whereby the determination of a performance has been left to the absolute discretion of one of the contracting parties (but not of a third party) shall be void (arts. 372, 373).

### *D. Two-sided Contracts*[3]

The rules governing two-sided contracts (αμφοτεροβαρείς συμβάσεις, amphoterovareis symvaseis), i.e. contracts containing mutual promises as contrasted to one-sided or unilateral contracts (e.g., those containing a promise to make gift), constitute applications of the idea of mutually dependent promises. In fact, they mainly prescribe the legal consequences of a disturbance in the performance due by one of the parties upon the obligation of the other party to counter-performance. In particular, they refer to the excuses for non-performance because of failure of counter-performance (arts. 374–378); to impossibility of performance (arts. 380–382); to delay in performance (arts. 383–385); to the collapse of the basis of the transaction (art. 388); to installments contracts (art. 386); and to the availability of the remedy of discretionary equitable compensation for non-performance, in addition to rescission, in cases where the law prescribes rescission as remedy for impossibility or default in the performance of a two-sided contract (art. 387). These rules will be dealt with in connection with the problems of non-performance of obligations (below, under E).

### *E. Non-performance of Obligations*

In article 330 (see above, under B 7), the Civil Code develops a unitary concept of non-performance of obligations. However, it contemplates in general terms only two categories of non-performance which it regulates in detail: impossibility of performance and delay. Other possible defects in performance are treated in the context of certain specific contractual regimes such as sale, contract for work and lease. Before dealing with the modalities of non-performance, it is useful to say a few words about the claim of performance and its enforcement.

#### 1. Claim to Performance in Kind

(*a*) The primary legal remedy for non-performance is a claim to performance in kind. It is of the very essence of an obligation that it is actionable in this sense. But a party to a two-sided contract may refuse to perform his part until the other party has performed or has properly tendered his own part, unless the former party is bound to perform his part first (art. 374). If one party brings an

3. They are also called reciprocal, mutual, bilateral, or synallagmatic contracts.

action for the performance due to him, the other party's right to refuse performance until counter-performance has been made, has the effect that judgment is to be delivered against the other party for contemporaneous performance (art. 378).

(*b*) A judgment ordering the debtor to perform his obligation can be rendered only if performance is still possible; otherwise, the creditor may bring only an action for damages (see below, under 2 (*a*)). What if the creditor does not know or cannot prove that performance by the debtor is impossible? The legislator assumes that in such a case the creditor will normally bring an action for performance, as he is always entitled to. Article 339 of the Civil Code provides that a creditor who has obtained a final judgment ordering performance may fix a time within which performance by the debtor must be forthcoming, with a declaration that he refuses to accept performance after the expiration of the period. Thereafter, the plaintiff may forthwith institute a claim for damages.

## 2. Impossibility

Unlike the German Civil Code (paras. 306 ff), the Greek Civil Code treats both initial and subsequent impossibility of performance (αδυναμία παροχής, adynamia parochis) in the same way. The important question is who is to blame for this. If it is the debtor, he is liable to pay damages (arts. 335 to 336, 362 to 365, 382); if it is the creditor, the debtor is freed and may even be able to demand what was promised to him (art. 381 I); if neither party is responsible for the impossibility of performance, both are freed from obligation (arts. 336, 363, 380).

(*a*) The general rule is that the debtor who fails to perform is liable unless he proves that he was not responsible for the impossibility of performance. Each party must answer for lack of due care on his part or on the part of those who were assisting him to perform (arts. 330, 334). For initial impossibility or illegality of performance, the debtor is freed from any obligation only if he proves that he, without fault, did not know of the impossibility (art. 363) or the illegality (art. 365) of the performance.

(*b*) An important qualification to this general rule applies to debts described by class (see above, Section I B 2 (*a*)). According to article 290, the debtor's obligation is not limited to a particular thing until he has placed the creditor in default. Therefore, until that time, he is not freed from his duty to perform even if he and his assistants are entirely blameless unless the entire genus to which the object of the obligation appertained has been destroyed. So, in practical terms, the effect of a debt described by class is that the debtor guarantees his ability to supply goods of the promised class when the time for delivery arrives.

(*c*) *The problem of altered circumstances.* Greek courts and legal writers accept the doctrine that a debtor might exceptionally be released from an obligation which it was not wholly impossible to perform if, as the result of an unforeseeable event, performance would involve quite exceptional financial or moral hardships which went beyond the call of duty (e.g., AP 93/1967, NoB 15

(1967) 791). Exceptional hardship might thus be treated as impossibility for which the debtor is not answerable. Pursuant to article 388 of the Civil Code, this doctrine is qualified as regards two-sided contracts. Article 388 reads in part as follows:

'If the circumstances on which the parties, having regard to good faith and to business usage, mainly based a two-sided contract, subsequently changed for extraordinary and unforeseeable reasons, and if, as a result of this change, fulfillment of the obligation, taking into account the counter-obligation, became inordinately onerous for the debtor, the latter may request the court to reduce his obligation at its discretion to a suitable extent, or to rescind the whole of the contract or the part not carried out'.

In this way, the courts are entrusted with the sweeping power not only to rescind the contract but also to let the contractual relationship continue while modifying the terms of the contract to adjust them to the changed circumstances.

(*d*) The Civil Code contains provisions authorizing unilateral termination for cause of long-term agreements such as leases, partnership agreements and employment contracts. Such termination for cause is possible by notice before the end of the agreed-upon term. Code provisions of this kind ordinarily refer to particular types of contracts. However, legal writers have developed and the courts have adopted the broad principle that all long-term contractual relationships may be terminated by either party before the end of the agreed-upon period of the contract if substantial reasons can be shown which justify such premature termination.

## 3. Delay

If the promise is capable of performance but has not been performed in a timely manner, two questions arise: (a) whether the creditor can demand compensation for the damage which the delay has caused him, and (b) whether he can withdraw from the contract and refuse to accept late performance.

(*a*) A claim for damages for lateness in performance may be brought only if the debtor is in 'default' (υπερημερία οφειλέτη, yperimeria opheileti). In order to put the debtor in default after performance has fallen due, the creditor must make a protest (art. 340); this starts the default running unless the debtor can prove that the lateness of performance is attributable to a circumstance for which he is not responsible (art. 342). If the contract fixes a date for performance, a protest is not necessary to put the debtor in default (art. 341).

(*b*) Although putting the debtor in default gives the creditor a claim for damages for delay, it does not in principle free him from the duty to accept performance, late though it is. If the creditor does not desire the performance because of the default, he may refuse it and demand reparations for non-performance (art. 343 II). In a two-sided contract, the creditor may rescind the contract or claim damages for non-performance only if he fixes a period during which the defaulting debtor must complete performance and states that he will refuse to accept after the expiry of that period (art. 383). No such period need be fixed if the delay has deprived the eventual performance of any interest for the creditor (art. 385). In a two-sided contract, neither protest nor a fixed period is required if it was agreed that the performance was to be made exclusively at a fixed time or exclusively within a fixed period. It is then to be inferred that the creditor shall be entitled to rescind by the mere reason of delay, no matter whether the debtor is at fault (art. 401).

## 4. Other Cases of Breach of Contract

Everyday life reveals a variety of situations of non-performance of obligation or of breach of contract which do not fit comfortably within the categories of impossibility and delay, e.g., defective performance, violation of contract duties other than a principal contract obligation, culpable breach of contract duties of care causing personal injury or property damage to the other party.

(*a*) In such cases, the courts have had no hesitation in recognizing that the complaining party was aggrieved and is entitled to seek an appropriate form of relief. This effect derives from a general principle which legal writers found not merely on article 330 but on the whole complex of rules concerning impossibility of performance and delay. According to this principle, a debtor is responsible for any, even a partial, defect in the performance of his obligation and for any violation of contract duty which results from wilful misconduct or negligence imputable to him or his legal representatives or the persons he employs in performing his obligation.

(*b*) As regards the forms of relief, the courts apply by analogy the provisions relating to impossibility and delay. In this respect, the distinction between material and non-material breach is quite important. Material is a breach which imperils the whole purpose of the transaction in such a way that the innocent party cannot be expected to continue with the contract and to perform his own obligation under it. The innocent party is then entitled to withdraw from the contract, or claim damages for non-performance of the whole contract, as under articles 383 to 387 I. A minor breach gives to the aggrieved party the right merely to demand reparations for the damage resulting therefrom.

## 5. Default of the Creditor

(*a*) A creditor is in default if he does not accept the performance tendered to him (υπερημερία δανειστή, ypeřimeria daneisti). The tender must be effective and appropriate (art. 349). If the cooperation of the creditor is necessary, the creditor shall be in default if, although invited by the debtor, he does not perform the necessary act (art. 351). If the debtor is bound to perform his part only upon counter-performance by the creditor, the creditor is in default if, though prepared to accept the performance tendered, he does not offer the required counter-performance (art. 353). If the time of performance is not fixed, the creditor is not in default by reason of the fact that he is temporarily prevented from accepting the offered performance unless the debtor has given him notice of his intended performance a reasonable time beforehand (art. 354).

(*b*) Effects of creditor's default: (i) The default of the creditor in itself does not, as a rule, relieve the debtor of his obligations; he must remain able and willing to perform. (ii) The debtor has the alternative of making a public deposit of the thing owed or its value (arts. 427–429, 431). (iii) During the default of the creditor, the debtor is not responsible for slight negligence (art. 355) and does not have to pay interest on a money obligation. The debtor is entitled to demand compensation for any additional expenses he has been obliged to incur for the ineffective tender of performance and for the safekeeping and maintenance of the object which is due (art. 358).

## *F. Contractual Rescission*

Apart from rescission (υπαναχώρηση, ypanachorisi) which is provided for by law as a remedy for non-performance (as, e.g., in arts. 382–387), it is permissible in a two-sided contract for a party to reserve to himself the right of rescission (arts. 389–401). The effect of rescission is that the mutual obligations arising from the contract are extinguished and the parties are obligated to return to each other whatever they received pursuant to the provisions related to unjust enrichment (art. 389). If such restitution is, for any reason whatsoever, no more possible, the right of rescission is barred (arts. 391–394). Rescission is effected by declaration to the other party (art. 390). The same rules apply by analogy to 'legal' rescission (art. 387 II).

## *G. Earnest and Penalty Clause*

### 1. Earnest

If, upon entering into a contract, something is given as earnest (αρραβών, arravon), this is deemed to have been given to cover the loss resulting from the non-performance of the contract (art. 402). If the giver is responsible for the non-performance, the holder of the earnest is entitled to retain it. If the holder is responsible for the non-performance, he is bound to pay back double the earnest received. Liability for further damages is not excluded (art. 403). On performance of the contract, the earnest is, wherever possible, to be deducted from the price or, if this is not possible, to be returned.

### 2. Penalty Clause

A contract may contain a stipulation providing for the payment of a fixed amount of money or for a performance other than the payment of money by the debtor in the event of his default (ποινική ρήτρα, poiniki ritra).

(*a*) If performance of the principal obligation becomes impossible as a result of an event for which the debtor is not responsible, liability to pay the penalty is discharged. But the penalty shall be due even if the creditor has not suffered any loss (art. 405).

(*b*) A contract with a penalty clause does not create an alternative obligation. Thus, the debtor may not discharge himself by paying the penalty instead of performing his principal obligation. However, a contract might be expressed in such a way as to give the debtor clearly the option of either performing or withdrawing from the contract on payment of a forfeit (art. 398).

(*c*) If the debtor has promised the penalty in the event of his not fulfilling his obligation, the creditor may demand the forfeited penalty in lieu of fulfillment. The forfeited penalty is then deemed as the minimum amount of the damage, further damages not being excluded (art. 406).

(*d*) If the debtor has promised the penalty in the event of his not performing his obligation in the proper manner, especially not in due time, the creditor may demand the forfeited penalty in addition to the performance, further damages not being excluded (art. 407).

(*e*) If the penalty agreed upon is disproportionately high, it may be reduced to a proper level by court decision. Any agreement to the contrary is not valid (art. 409).

### *H. Contract for the Benefit of Third Parties – Contract Burdening Third Parties*

In principle, a contract creates rights and duties only for and against the immediate parties to it.

1. A contract may, however, stipulate performance for the benefit of a third party, so that the promisee may demand performance in favor of the third party (σύμβαση υπέρ τρίτου, symvasi yper tritou; art. 410). Nevertheless, the third party does not acquire the right to directly demand performance from the promisor unless the parties so intended or unless such effect is deduced from the nature and the purpose of the contract (art. 411). If the third party declares to the promisor that he will exercise the right acquired under the contract, the promisee cannot release the promisor from his obligation (art. 412). Defenses arising from the contract are available to the promisor even against the third party (art. 414).
2. A person who by contract promises to another that a third party will furnish a performance is, unless a different conclusion can be deduced from the contract, liable to the promisee if the third party refuses to perform (art. 415).

### *I. Extinction of Obligations* (απόσβεση ενοχών, aposvesi enochon)

Under this heading, the Civil Code provides in Book II, chapter 9, six ways in which an obligation may be discharged: fulfillment (arts. 416–426), deposit (arts. 427–435), novation (arts. 436–439), set-off (arts. 440–452), merger (art. 453), and release (art. 454).

1. Fulfillment

(*a*) Obligation is not an end in itself; it is the legal means to the end of attaining performance. Therefore, effecting to the creditor the performance owed (καταβολή, katavoli) is the normal way of discharging an obligation (arts. 416, 417 I). Performance to be valid as fulfillment should be the performance due. If the creditor has accepted as fulfillment an act of performance offered as fulfillment, the burden of proof is upon him if he asserts that the act of performance had not been appropriate (art. 418).

(*b*) The creditor is not bound to accept in lieu of fulfillment another performance than the one due. If he accepts such a performance, however, the obligation is extinguished (art. 419). If the debtor, for the purpose of satisfying the creditor, assumes a new obligation toward him, it is not to be presumed that he assumes the obligation in lieu of fulfillment unless there is a clear indication to the contrary (art. 421).

(*c*) If the debtor owes several debts to the creditor, the debtor is entitled, on effecting the performance, to specify the debt which is discharged. If the debtor makes no specification, the sequence in which the effected performance shall be applied to each one of the existing debts is provided in the law (arts. 422–423).

(*d*) On effecting the performance, the debtor is entitled to demand from the creditor, at the debtor's cost, a written acknowledgment of receipt and, in the case of total fulfillment, also to demand the return of the document of indebtedness. From such return the discharge of the debt is presumed (art. 424).

2. Set-off

(*a*) If two persons mutually owe acts of performance which are of the same kind, either party may set off his claim against the claim of the other party as soon as he can demand the performance due to him and effect the performance due by him (συμψηφισμός, sympsiphismos; arts. 440, 324. 1). A creditor who has granted to his debtor a period of grace is not prevented thereby from setting off his claim (art. 445). Prescription does not exclude set-off if the claim barred had not prescribed at the time at which the two claims coexisted (art. 443). The set-off is made by declaration to the other party. The declaration is ineffective if made subject to any condition or limitation (art. 444).

(*b*) The effect of the set-off is that the mutual claims, insofar as they cover each other, are deemed to have expired as from the moment they coexisted (arts. 440, 441).

(*c*) The guarantor may set-off the claim of the debtor against the creditor, but the debtor may not set-off a claim of the guarantor against the creditor (art. 447).

(*d*) Set-off is not permissible against a claim which is not subject to attachment (art. 451) or against a claim arising from a wilful delict (art. 450).

## *J. Assignment of Claims*

A claim is, in principle, transferable. The transfer is effected by means of a contract of assignment (εκχώρηση, ekchorisi).

1. Under article 455, the claim passes to the assignee by the contract of assignment without any requirement that the debtor consents. As against the debtor and other third parties, however, the assignee becomes entitled to the claim only when either he or the assignor so notifies the debtor (art. 460). The debtor who pays the assignor without knowing of the assignment is discharged (art. 461).

2. Greek law treats the assignment of a claim as a conveyance: defects in the underlying obligational transaction do not affect the validity of the transfer.

3. The debtor has towards the assignee all the obligations which he had towards the assignor (art. 462). The debtor may assert against the assignee all defenses which, at the time of the notification to him of the assignment, were in existence against the assignor (art. 463).

4. The assignor is not liable towards the assignee for the solvency of the debtor (art. 468). He is only liable, in principle, for the non-existence of the claim (art. 467).

## *K. Assumption of Debt*

1. (*a*) A third party may, by agreement with the creditor, assume the debtor's debt, which has the effect of releasing the debtor. The creditor may thereafter enforce his claim only against such party (αναδοχή χρέους, anadochi chreous, assumption of debt *stricto sensu*; art. 471). For this legal effect to be achieved, a clear indication of intention is required.

(*b*) In the absence of such indication of intention, the debtor is not released but an additional obligation arises so that the creditor may enforce his claim also against the third party (art. 477). This means that the debtor and the third party are joint debtors within the meaning of article 481, that is to say they are liable jointly and severally (see below, under L; AP 42/1969, NoB 17 (1969) 550).

(*c*) A promise, however, by a third party to the debtor that the former will pay the latter's debt does not, in case of doubt, give to the creditor any right against the promisor (art. 478).

(*d*) If by agreement a person takes over another's entire property or enterprise, any creditor of the latter may, after the conclusion of the contract, enforce his then existing claims against such successor up to the value of the assets of the property transferred. The liability of the former owner continues to exist (art. 479).

2. In case of an assumption of debt *stricto sensu*, the person assuming the debt has the same obligations towards the creditor as the former debtor (art. 472). He may raise against the creditor all defenses arising from the legal relationship between the creditor and the former debtor but he may not set off a claim belonging to the former debtor (art. 473).

3. Rights accessory to the claim continue to exist after the assumption. However, guaranties, pledges and mortgages are maintained only with the consent of the guarantor or the person to whom the object pledged or mortgaged belongs (art. 475).

### *L. Joint and Several Obligations*

The several obligation, the joint and several obligation (ενοχή εις ολόκληρον, enochi eis olokliron) and the joint (or entire) obligation are the possible forms of construction utilized by the Civil Code in the case of plurality of parties to an obligation.

1. The principle is that by divisible performance, in case of doubt, the obligation is only several (art. 480).

2. Liability is joint and several when several persons owe the same performance in such a manner that each is liable to effect the whole performance but the creditor is entitled to demand the performance only once (art. 481). The creditor may demand the performance at his option from any one of the debtors, in whole or in part. Until the whole performance has been effected all of the debtors remain bound (art. 482).

(*a*) Fulfillment of the obligation by one co-debtor is effective as towards the creditor in favor of the other debtors. The same applies to any act or performance in lieu of fulfillment, to deposit and to set-off (art. 483), to creditor's default towards one co-debtor (art. 485) and, under certain circumstances, to release agreed upon between the creditor and one co-debtor (art. 484). Other facts are in principle effective in favor of, and as against, only the co-debtor to whom they particularly refer (art. 486).

(*b*) As between themselves, co-debtors are liable in equal shares, unless the relationship indicates otherwise. If the contribution due from one of the co-debtors can not be obtained from him, the deficiency shall be borne by the other debtors who, as towards the co-debtor who has paid, are bound to make up the difference (art. 487).

3. A claim is joint and several if several creditors are entitled to demand the same act of performance in such manner that each can demand the whole performance though the debtor is bound to perform only once (art. 489).

(*a*) The debtor is entitled at his option to perform in favor of any one of the creditors so long as one of the creditors has not brought an action for the performance (art. 490).

(*b*) In case of fulfillment or extinction of the obligation towards one of the creditors, the rights of the other creditors against the debtor are extinguished. Default on the part of one co-creditor is effective also against the other creditors (art. 491).

(*c*) As among themselves, co-creditors are entitled to equal shares, unless there is indication to a different effect (art. 493).

4. If an indivisible performance is owed to several creditors and so long as by virtue of the law or the contract the rights of the latter are not joint and

several, the debtor may perform only in favor of all jointly and each creditor may demand the performance only in favor of all. A fact which affects only one creditor is effective neither in favor of, nor against, the other creditors (art. 495).

## II. Specific Contracts

In the portion of the Civil Code dealing with particular kinds of obligations (Book II, chapters 13 ff, arts. 496 ff), the most frequently encountered types of contracts are specifically regulated. The Civil Code does not attempt an exhaustive listing of contracts. Neither does the validity of any contract depend on its falling within any recognizable category. The parties may, in fact, agree between themselves to fashion their contractual relationship differently. Freedom of contract results thus in a great variety of non-typical contracts and particularly of mixed contracts. The need to furnish non-typical contracts with an apparatus of implied terms poses delicate problems of construction. In construing a contract, courts take into consideration the intention of the parties. Article 200 of the Civil Code requires that construction be 'in accordance with good faith, taking account of business usage'. Provisions governing particular contracts may, under certain circumstances, be applied by analogy to non-typical contracts.

The Code treats the types of particular contracts in a sequence which does not have the character of a logical arrangement. A systematic arrangement, preferred by several legal writers, is to group the different categories of particular contracts according to their economic or practical function. A brief survey of the code articles relating to sale and exchange, lease, contract for services, contract for work, mandate, loan, guaranty and abstract promise or acknowledgment of debt will be made; with respect to partnership see below, Ch. 11. These relations more or less exhaust the common civil transactions. The Civil Code contains provisions also on the following relations: donation (arts. 496–512), usufructuary lease (arts. 619–647), broker's contract (arts. 703–708), reward (arts. 709–712), *negotiorum gestio* (arts. 730–740), community (arts. 785–805), gratuitous loan for use (arts. 810–821), deposit (arts. 822–833), liability of innkeepers (arts. 834–839), annuity (arts. 840–843), gaming and betting (arts. 844–846), compromise (arts. 871–872), order to pay or deliver (arts. 876–887), bearer bonds (arts. 888–900), production of things and documents (arts. 901–903), and defrauding of creditors (arts. 939–946).

### *A. Sale and Exchange*

By the contract of sale (πώληση, polisi), the seller is bound to transfer ownership of the thing sold or to transfer the right sold and to deliver the thing to the purchaser, and the purchaser is bound to pay the price agreed upon (art. 513).

1. The contract of sale is the archetype of two-sided contracts. Things,

rights, any asset or group of assets may be the object of a sale. The price is expressed in terms of money. If, instead of money, another thing is owed, then the contract is not a contract of sale but of exchange (ανταλλαγή, antallagi). The provisions relating to sale apply by analogy, each of the parties being deemed to be the seller with reference to the performance owed by him and to be the buyer with reference to the performance claimed by him (arts. 573, 562).

2. (*a*) The seller is bound to transfer to the purchaser the thing or right sold free from rights enforceable by third parties against the purchaser (art. 514). If there are any such defects of title at the time of sale, the purchaser has all the rights which, in a two-sided contract, belong to the creditor in case the debtor is in default (arts. 516, 380 ff).

(*b*) (i) If, when the risk passes to the purchaser, what is sold is not free from defects destroying or significantly diminishing its value or fitness for its ordinary use, or the use provided for in the contract, or if, at that time, it lacks the promised qualities, the purchaser is entitled to demand either annulment of the sale (cancellation) or reduction of the price. At the time of the purchase, if a promised quality was absent or if what was sold was not free from a defect, and the seller had or ought to have had knowledge thereof, the purchaser may demand compensation for non-performance instead of cancellation or reduction (arts. 534–553). (ii) If the thing or right sold is described by class, the purchaser may demand, instead of cancellation or reduction, that one free from defect be delivered to him (art. 559). However, when the risk passes to the purchaser, if a promised quality is absent, or if the seller has fraudulently concealed a defect, the purchaser may demand compensation for non-performance instead of cancellation, reduction or delivery of a thing or right free from defect (art. 561). Under certain circumstances also the seller has a right to replace the delivered defective thing with another free of defects (art. 560). (iii) The claims under (i) and (ii) are time-barred for immovables in two years, and for movables in six months after delivery (art. 554 ff).

3. The risk of accidental destruction or deterioration passes to the purchaser on delivery. With regard to real property, such risk passes to the purchaser at the time of recordation, if it takes place before delivery (art. 522). If, at the request of the purchaser, the seller dispatches the thing sold to a place other than the place of performance, the risk passes to the purchaser as soon as the seller has delivered it for dispatch (art. 524).

4. *Retention of Title*. If the seller carried out the contract and fixed a time for payment of the purchase price, he may not rescind the contract on the ground of delay in the payment of the price (art. 531). If, however, in the sale contract itself the seller has, by a special clause, retained title until payment of the purchase price, it is to be presumed, in case of doubt, that the transfer of title to the purchaser takes place subject to the condition precedent of payment in full of the purchase price, and that the seller is entitled, if the purchaser is in default with the payment, either to demand payment or to rescind the contract thus retaining his property rights. In case of such retention of title, the purchaser

bears the risk of destruction or deterioration of the thing from the time of delivery (art. 532).

5. The Civil Code provides for the following particular types of sale: (a) sale on approval (arts. 563–564). (b) sale reserving a right of repurchase in favor of the seller (arts. 565–572).

### *B. Lease*

A contract of lease is a two-sided contract whereby the lessor is bound to give to the lessee the use of the leased thing during the term of the lease, and the lessee is bound to pay to the lessor the rent agreed upon (μίσθωση πράγματος, misthosi pragmatos; art. 574). Object of the contract of lease is the use of a thing, not of a right; and only the use of such thing, not the enjoyment of its fruits. Lease contracts are valid regardless of form. A lease does not pass any property rights.

1. (*a*) The lessor is bound to hand over the leased thing to the lessee in a condition appropriate for the use stipulated and to keep it in such condition during the term of the lease (art. 575). (i) If the leased thing has a defect which destroys or diminishes its fitness for the stipulated use, or if a warranted quality is absent, the lessor is liable to the lessee. The lessee is entitled to demand removal of the defect; further, he is entitled to a reduction or non-payment of the rent (art. 576). (ii) If at the time of entering into the contract a warranted quality is absent, or if, at such time, the lessor knew of the defect, the lessee may, instead of reduction or non-payment of the rent, demand compensation for non-performance (arts. 577, 578 I, 578 II 1). If the lessor is in default, the lessee may himself remove the defect and demand compensation for the outlays (art. 578 II 2).

(*b*) The lessor is responsible in a similar way if, through the right of a third party, the stipulated use of the leased thing is wholly or in part taken away from the lessee. But the lessee is not entitled to remove himself the defect in title at the expense of the lessor (art. 583).

(*c*) The lessor shall bear the charges and taxes imposed upon the leased thing (art. 590) and is obligated to compensate the lessee for any necessary expenses incurred for the thing (art. 591 I).

2. (*a*) The rent is payable at the end of the term of lease, or if the rent is measured by periods of time, at the end of each such period, unless there is a different agreement or usage (art. 595). A lessee is not released from payment of the rent by the fact that he is hindered in the exercise of his right of use by a cause personal to himself (art. 596).

(*b*) The lessee is not entitled to use the thing leased in a way which violates the contract (art. 594).

(*c*) The lessee is bound to return the thing after the termination of the lease. He is bound to restitute it in the condition in which he had taken possession thereof (art. 599). However, he is not responsible for wear and tear brought about by stipulated use (art. 592).

3. The lessor of a piece of land has by way of security of arrears of rent a security interest over the things brought upon the premises by the lessee or his wife and children, if they live with him, unless such things are not subject to attachment. Such interest may not be enforced in respect of any rent due for an earlier time than the last two years before attachment (art. 604), and does not prejudice the rights of third parties in the things even if the lessor in good faith believed that they belonged to the lessee (art. 605).

4. A lease terminates on the expiration of the agreed time (art. 608). If the term of the lease is not fixed, either party may give notice of its termination. If a lease is entered into for a period longer than thirty years, or for the lifetime of one of the parties, either party may after thirty years give notice of termination of the lease (art. 610). If the lessee dies, his heir is entitled to give notice of termination of the lease, the term of such notice being at least three months (art. 612). Article 611 provides for an extension of the lease for an indeterminate term if the use of the thing is continued by the lessee, without opposition by the lessor, after the expiration of its term.

5. In the absence of an agreement to the contrary, the lessee is entitled to transfer to a third party the use of the leased thing, particularly to sublet the thing, in which case he is liable towards the lessor for the third party's fault (art. 593).

6. In case of alienation of the thing leased, the principle followed by the Civil Code is that "the sale does not break the lease"; the acquirer is in principle bound by the lease. With reference to leases of land the law makes, however, the following distinctions: (a) If the lease is evidenced by a document bearing a recorded date and no intention to the contrary is expressed therein, the acquirer is subrogated to the rights and obligations flowing from the lease; otherwise, the acquirer is entitled to terminate the lease by giving notice of one or two months according to whether the lease is for up to one year or more (arts. 614–615). (b) A lease entered into for a longer term than nine years is effective against the acquirer only if it has been executed in notarial form and recorded (art. 618). Agreements entered into between the lessee and the lessor in respect of any claim of rent are effective against the acquirer to the extent that they do not relate to the rent for a time later than three months after the acquirer has notified the lessee of the transfer of ownership (arts. 616–617).

7. (*a*) Lease of living accommodations is a particular kind of lease applicable only to civil immovables in which a household is maintained. It is regulated by special laws of which Laws 1598/1986 and 1703/1987 are fundamental, and the provisions of the Civil Code apply in complementary manner. Characteristics of the regulation are the following: (i) Leases of living accommodations must be in writing. (ii) The term may not be for less than two years; if it is not fixed or is fixed for a shorter period, it is deemed to extend to the minimum statutory period. (iii) A system of rent control prevails, whereby the legal levels of rent are calculated on the basis of the market value of the immovable; several factors are, as statutorily fixed coefficients, taken into consideration in order to determine such value. (iv) In the case of a lease of living accommodations in which the lessee has maintained, with his spouse, a

joint or family household (see art. 612A), on the death of the lessee the spouse enters into the lease. The spouse has also a right of termination of the lease.

(*b*) Lease of professional accommodations is another particular kind of lease or of usufructuary lease. The lessee uses the property leased for the purpose of exercising his professional activities in the premises. Fundamental is Law 813/1978, as amended. Characteristics of the regulation are the following: (i) Leases of professional accommodations must be in writing. (ii) The term may not be for less than six, or three years. (iii) Every two years the parties are entitled to demand changes in the rent to adapt it to market rates; such adaptation is effected either by consensus between the parties or by court decision. (iv) The lessee is not entitled either to sublet or to transfer the use of the premises leased. (v) The law provides for the termination of the lease by either of the parties for a number of reasons specially defined.

8. A lease differs from a gratuitous loan for use (χρησιδάνειο, chrisidaneio) in that, by the latter, the lender of a thing is bound to permit the borrower to use the thing gratuitously. The borrower is bound to return the thing lent on the expiration of the contract (art. 810). The lender is responsible only for wilful conduct and gross negligence (art. 811). The lender may demand the thing back before the expiration of the contract if he needs it due to unforeseen circumstances.

### C. *Contract for Services*

1. In articles 648–680, both the contract for independent services and the contract for dependent employment are regulated in detail. The regulation of dependent employment contains, for example, protective provisions about inventions made by the employees (art. 658), the limited availability of set-off against salary or wages (arts. 664–665), overtime pay (art. 659), and paid vacations (arts. 666–667); special reference is also made to collective agreements (art. 680). Besides the Civil Code provisions, many special statutes on the law of employment have imposed a modern system of labor law (see below, Ch. 13).

2. The contract for independent services is a two-sided contract, whereby the employee is bound to furnish, during a fixed or an undetermined period of time, his services to the employer and the latter is bound to pay the remuneration agreed upon.

(*a*) Object of the contract for services are the services as such of the employee and not the result of the work; this is the basic difference between a contract for services and a contract for work (art. 681; see below, under D).

(*b*) If there is no indication of a different intention, the employee shall perform his obligation in person and the claim for services is not transferable (art. 651). The employee is bound to perform his services diligently. The standard of care and diligence for which the employee is liable is established according to the contract, giving consideration to the education or the special, in view of the services to be performed, knowledge and skills of the employee of which the employer had or ought to have had knowledge (art. 652).

(*c*) Remuneration is essential for the contract for services. If services are performed without remuneration, the contract is a mandate (art. 713; see below, under E). The usual remuneration is deemed to have been tacitly agreed upon if, under the circumstances, the performance of the services is to be expected only against remuneration (arts. 649, 653).

(*d*) An employment relationship ends at the expiration of its term. (i) If the duration of the employment can not be inferred from the contract, either party has the right to terminate the relationship by timely notice given to the other party (arts. 669–670). (ii) However, either party may terminate the contract for serious cause immediately. Such right may not be excluded by agreement (art. 672). If the termination is occasioned by the conduct of the other party in breach of the contract, the other party is bound to pay reparations (art. 673). If, on the other hand, the employer terminates due to a change that occurred in his personal or financial situation, the court may at its discretion award reasonable compensation to the employee (art. 674). (iii) The contract for employment ends at the death of the employee. The death of the employer ends the contract only if the parties concluded it mainly with regard to his person (art. 675). (iv) A contract for independent services in which the employee, without being on a permanent basis with a fixed remuneration, has to perform a service entrusted to him because of a special confidence, may be terminated immediately by the employer even if no serious cause can be invoked by him. The employee has an equal right to immediate termination, but if he gives untimely notice, he must compensate the employer for any damage arising therefrom (art. 676).

### *D. Contract for Work*

By a contract for work, the contractor is bound to produce the work promised, and the customer is bound to pay the remuneration agreed upon (μίσθωση έργου, misthosi ergou; art. 681). If the contractor binds himself to produce the work from material provided by him, the provisions applicable to a sale apply, in case of doubt, to such a contract; if the material is to be provided, in the whole or mainly, by the customer, the provisions applicable to contract for work shall apply exclusively (art. 683).

1. If the work performed has minor defects, the customer is entitled to demand either their removal within a reasonable time, in so far as such removal does not entail disproportionate expense or, instead, a proportional reduction of the remuneration (art. 688). If the work performed is effected with substantial defects which destroy its fitness for its ordinary or stipulated use, or if it has not the qualities agreed upon, the customer is entitled, instead of removal of the defect or reduction of the remuneration, to demand cancellation of the contract (art. 689). If the defect in the work is caused by a circumstance for which the contractor is responsible, the customer may demand compensation for non-performance, instead of cancellation or reduction (art. 690). After acceptance of the work by the customer, the contractor is released from any liability by reason of defects in the work unless such defects could not be detected by way of

normal inspection or were intentionally concealed by the contractor (art. 692). The claims of the customer arising out of defective performance are barred by prescription, in the case of work on immovables, in ten years; in all other cases, in six months from acceptance (art. 693).

2. The remuneration is payable at the time of acceptance of the work (art. 694). As security for his claims arising from the contract, the contractor has a right of pledge over the movables of the customer, produced or repaired by him, which he has in his possession (art. 695).

3. If the contract is based upon an estimate of cost and it proves that the work is not practicable without exceeding significantly the estimate, the customer may, instead of bearing the additional cost, terminate the contract for this reason, unless the contractor had expressly guaranteed the correctness of the estimate, in which case the latter bears the risk of any increase in cost and may not demand an increase of the remuneration. In case of such termination, the contractor has a claim for remuneration proportionate to the work performed (arts. 696–697).

4. The contractor bears the risk up to the delivery of the work. This means that, in case of accidental destruction of the work, the customer is released from his obligation to pay the remuneration. But if the customer is in default of acceptance, the risk passes to him, so that he is bound to pay the remuneration even in case of accidental destruction of the work (art. 698). It is a different question whether the contractor is required to produce a new work in order to replace the one lost. The answer to this question is to be found pursuant to the rules related to impossibility of performance in the broader sense explained above, Section I E 2(*c*).

5. The customer may, at any time up to the completion of the work, give notice to terminate the contract in which case the contractor is entitled to claim the remuneration agreed upon (art. 700).

6. Persons employed by the contractor for the construction of a building or other work related to immovables shall have, in respect of their wages and salaries, a direct claim against the customer up to the amount the latter owes to the contractor (art. 702).

## *E. Mandate*

1. By a contract of mandate (εντολή, entoli), the mandatory (e.g., an agent) undertakes to conduct without remuneration the affair entrusted to him by the mandator (e.g., the principal) (art. 713).

(*a*) (i) The mandatory is responsible for any fault (art. 714). (*ii*) In principle, he cannot transfer the execution of the mandate to a third party (art. 715). If the transfer is permitted, the mandatory is responsible only for fault imputable to him in making such transfer and in giving instructions to the third party. If such transfer is not permitted, he is responsible for the fault of the third party as if it were his own fault (art. 716 I and II). In both cases of transfer, either permitted or not, the mandator may in his own name bring directly against the third party the actions which the mandatory has against the third party (art. 716 III). Other possible effects of a contract of mandate on third parties, if any, are covered by the institutes of agency and of power of attorney (arts. 211 ff and 216 ff). (iii) The mandatory is bound to give the mandator information about the affair entrusted to him, and to render an account after the end of the mandate (art. 718), handing over to him all that he had received for the performance of the mandate and all that he obtained therefrom (art. 719). If the mandatory has spent, for his own benefit, money belonging to the mandator, he is bound to pay interest upon it from the time of expenditure (art. 720).

(*b*) The mandator has the burden of paying in advance the expenses necessary for the performance of the mandate and is bound to reimburse the mandatory for all expenses and to pay compensation for any loss the mandatory has incurred in the performance of his duties (arts. 721–723).

(*c*) (i) The mandator may revoke the mandate at any time. An agreement to the contrary shall be null unless the mandate involves also the benefit of the mandatory or of a third party (art. 724). (ii) The mandatory may renounce the mandate at any time, but he may do so with impunity only if he gives timely notice for the mandator to get the task performed conveniently otherwise unless a serious cause exists for a premature renunciation (art. 725).

(*d*) In case there is no indication of intention to the contrary, the mandate is extinguished by the death, or dissolution for legal entities, the bankruptcy, or the placing under interdiction of either the mandator or the mandatory (art. 727).

2. If a person has given advice or made a recommendation to another, he shall not be liable for any loss resulting therefrom, unless he had assumed responsibility by contract or acted fraudulently (art. 729).

3. *Negotiorum gestio* or management without mandate (διοίκηση αλλοτρίων, dioikisi allotrion) is a relationship in which all the features of mandate are present except the instructions of the principal, but the results are quite similar (arts. 713–729).

### *F. Loan*

By a contract of loan, the lender transfers to the borrower the ownership of money or other fungibles and the latter is bound to repay what he receives in things of the same quantity and quality (δάνειο, daneio; art. 806).

1. If the time of repayment of the loan is not fixed nor can it be deduced from the circumstances, the loan shall be repaid upon one month's notice. If interest is not stipulated, the debtor is entitled to make repayment even without notice (art. 807; cf. art. 324, above, Section I B 6).

2. In case of a money loan, if the debtor is in default in repayment he is liable only for legal or contractual interest. An agreement to the contrary is null (art. 808; cf. art. 345, above, Section I B 2(c)(ii)).

3. A person who has promised to make a loan may refuse to make it, if the other party becomes insolvent subsequently. If the insolvency existed at the time

of making the promise, the promisor may refuse to make the loan only if he, without his fault, had no knowledge (art. 809).

### *G. Guaranty*

By a contract of guaranty, the guarantor assumes in regard to the creditor of a third party to be responsible for the fulfillment of the third party's obligation (εγγύηση, engyisi; art. 847). A guaranty may also be given for a future or conditional obligation (art. 848).

1. A guaranty shall be null if it has not been reduced to writing. This nullity is cured by performance (art. 849).

2. The guarantor's obligation being collateral: (a) a valid principal obligation is necessary. However, a guaranty given in respect of a debt contracted by a person lacking legal capacity shall be valid if the guarantor had knowledge (art. 850). (b) The guarantor is responsible at any time for the full extent of the principal obligation at that time, in particular for the legal consequences of any default of the principal debtor (art. 851). (c) The guarantor may raise as against the creditor all defenses available to the principal debtor, even if the latter has, after the guaranty had been concluded, waived any one of them (art. 853). (d) The principal debt having been barred by prescription, the guarantor is freed (art. 864).

3. The guarantor's promise to answer for another's debt being subsidiary to the principal obligation, he may refuse to satisfy the creditor until the latter attempted enforcement by execution against the principal debtor without success (arts. 855, 856). Such defense is barred (a) if the guarantor has waived it, in particular if he has assumed the guaranty in such a manner that he is himself a principal debtor, and (b) in cases where bringing an action against the principal debtor makes no practical sense (art. 857).

4. To the extent that a guarantor has satisfied the creditor and has, on the basis of the underlying relationship with the principal debtor, a cause of action against the latter, he is subrogated to the rights of the creditor (art. 858), unless he omitted to raise justified defenses that belonged to the principal debtor and of which the guarantor had or ought to have had knowledge (art. 859).

5. Plurality of guarantors. If there are several guarantors for the same obligation, they are liable to the creditor jointly and severally, even where they have not assumed the guaranty jointly (art. 854). Co-guarantors are liable to each other and to the co-guarantor who satisfied the creditor only under article 487 (art. 860); see above, Section I L 2(b).

6. The guarantor shall be liberated from his obligation where (a) for reason imputable to the creditor, the satisfaction of the creditor by the principal debtor has become impossible (art. 862), and (b) the creditor has, to the detriment of the guarantor, waived securities concerning exclusively the particular claim for which the guaranty had been issued (art. 863). It is incumbent upon the creditor to proceed without delay to the collection of the claim; otherwise the guarantor is released from his obligation (arts. 866–868).

7. A mandate providing that the mandatory, in his own name and for his own account, shall give credit to a third party is, if given in writing, valid as a guaranty of the third party's obligation arising from the giving of the credit (art. 870).

### *H. Abstract Promise or Acknowledgment of Debt*

#### 1. Concept and Validity

The Civil Code leaves it to be inferred from articles 873–875 that promissory transactions are in principle causal (αιτιώδεις, aitiodeis); that is to say, any promise, however seriously intended, is not binding unless supported by a legitimate cause (*causa*). Article 873 represents an exception to this principle. It provides that a contract whereby an act of performance is promised or a debt is acknowledged in such manner that an obligation is to be created irrespective of the cause of the debt, shall be valid if the promise or the declaration of acknowledgment is made in writing. A written statement of the promise making no mention of the cause of the debt will, in case of doubt, be deemed to have been made for the purpose of creating an obligation. Such unilateral or one-sided contracts are said to be abstract (αφηρημένες, aphirimenes). They create a valid obligation in the sense that the promisee may bring an action against the promisor based upon the agreement without any reference to the *causa*, i.e. to the cause which explains the debt and justifies it in the eyes of the law.

#### 2. Effect on the Burden of Proof

A promise or recognition of existence of a debt, if made under an abstract contract, constitutes thus in effect an act of performance resulting in the enrichment of the promisee to the detriment of the promisor. Would it not be unjust for the promisee to keep the enrichment if there was no legal cause or if the cause has failed? The provisions relating to unjust enrichment stipulate that the enrichment must be returned (arts. 904 ff; see below, Section III). But it is then the promisor who has the legal burden of alleging and proving that there was no legal cause (*causa*), or that it has failed. Abstract contract is thus a sort of legal technique which results in casting the burden of allegation and proof on the defendant. This is an exception to the general principle that, in an action based on contract, the legal burden of allegation and proof of the cause rests on the plaintiff.

#### 3. Formal Requirements

A condition of validity of the said contracts is that the promise or the recognition of debt must be in writing (art. 873). This form is not necessary if the promise or acknowledgment refers to the balance of a stated current account (art. 874). If on the other hand the promise or acknowledgment refers to a cause for which the law prescribes a particular form (e.g., donation, art. 498), the contract shall not be valid unless such form is observed (art. 875).

## III. Unjust Enrichment

*A.* The Civil Code devotes a special chapter to rights arising from unjust enrichment (αδικαιολόγητος πλουτισμός, adikaiologitos ploutismos), and starts out with a comprehensive general clause. Article 904 states that a person who is, without legal ground, enriched from property of, or at the expense of another is bound to return the benefit. This obligation arises in particular if a person has received a payment for a debt which was not owed, or if a transfer or a performance has been made on a ground which did not come about or subsequently ceased to exist or was illegal or immoral. The rule of article 904 applies also where absolute rights other than ownership have been infringed, e.g., infringement – even innocent – of a copyright vested in another.

*B.* A person can not reclaim a benefit he has conferred if he knew that he was not bound to confer it. The burden of proof lies with the defendant (art. 905). A claim of restitution is also excluded if the transfer took place in order to satisfy a moral obligation or for the sake of common decency (art. 906). A benefit conferred on an immoral ground can not be reclaimed if the immoral ground attaches also to the transferor (art. 907).

*C.* Greek courts and the majority of legal writers require 'directness of transfer', in the sense that the loss of the plaintiff and the benefit to the defendant must result from one and the same transaction. This rule derives from the belief that the transferor should only be able to sue the transferee with whom he had a contract and should not acquire an additional debtor just because the object transferred happens to have ended up among the assets of a third party. If, however, the recipient transfers gratuitously the benefit acquired to a third party, the transferor is entitled to claim from such third party the restitution of the benefit so conferred to it (art. 913).

*D.* Extent of liability in restitution. The recipient is bound to restitute the thing received, or whatever he eventually received in exchange for such thing. He is bound also to restitute the fruits collected as well as everything he derived from the thing (art. 908). The obligation to make restitution is released to the extent that the recipient has ceased to be enriched at the time of the suit for restitution of the enrichment (art. 909). As from that moment, the recipient's liability is increased (art. 910).

## IV. Unlawful Acts (Torts, Delicts)

*A.* The Greek equivalent to the concept of tort or delict is the 'unlawful act' (αδικοπραξία, adikopraxia). With a view of mastering, in an accident age, problems of indemnification of the victim and of loss distribution, the Civil Code is supplemented by several auxiliary statutes enacted to deal with particular allocations of risk and liability.[4] They follow, as a rule, the principle of strict liability which is, generally, limited in amount, and they are not integrated in the Civil Code.

*B.* The Civil Code deals with delictual liability in two general clauses, supplemented by a number of special provisions. According to the general clauses, whoever 'unlawfully and culpably' (art. 914), or 'intentionally in a manner which violates the commands of morality' (art. 919) causes damage to another is bound to make reparation to the other for any damage thus caused. The Civil Code thus follows the traditional view of delict. It presupposes an unlawful or contravening *bonos mores* act or omission which has been wilfully or negligently committed by a person and which has caused damage to another. The injured party must establish the elements of liability: damage (ζημία, zimia), unlawfulness of the act or omission (παρανομία, paranomia), culpability of the author of the damage (υπαιτιότητα, ypaitiotita), and an adequate, that is to say legally relevant, connection (αιτιώδης συνάφεια, aitiodis synapheia) between the fault and the damage. The burden of proving these rests on the injured party.

*C.* Financial injury caused to a person as a result of untrue defamatory rumors communicated by another renders the latter liable to compensate the former, if their untruth was known or was culpably unknown to the party who made the communication (art. 920).

*D.* Greek law draws a distinction between unlawfulness and culpability. The requirement of unlawfulness, according to most writers, is satisfied with reference to acts or omissions which are forbidden by law. Thus, according to this view, article 914 of the Civil Code does not itself stipulate which behavior is unlawful. It only imposes sanctions on such behavior, if it has been harmful to a third party.

*E.* Culpability expresses the concept of fault. Fault is the attitude of a person who wilfully or negligently has committed an unlawful act or omission. It presupposes imputability. Imputability is excluded or diminished in cases where the author of the damage is unconscious or he is suffering from a mental disturbance or he is minor or deaf-mute (arts. 915–917). Such persons may, nevertheless, be condemned by the court to make reparations for the damage as is reasonable under the circumstances if, according to the relative position of the parties, equity requires compensation and the damage caused can not be covered from another source (art. 918).

4. E.g., motor vehicle accidents (L. 3950/1911); accidental injury at work (L. 551/1914); accidental injury of persons and accidental loss or damage of goods in carriage by air (L. 596/1937: Warsaw Convention; L.D. 439/1964: Hague Protocol); oil pollution damage (L. 314/1976: Brussels International Convention on Civil Liability for Oil Pollution Damage, 1969).

*F.* The principle of fault is generally the criterion of delictual liability.

1. As an exception, the Civil Code introduces strict liability in two cases: (a) in the case of non-domestic animals (art. 924.1), (b) in the case of liability for employees (art. 922). A person who appoints another to perform a function is bound to make reparations to a third party for the harm caused by an unlawful and culpable act or omission committed by the other in the execution of his task.

2. By means of reversing the burden of proof, liability for fault is in certain cases made to approximate to strict liability. This is true in case of harm inflicted by a person under supervision or by a domestic animal or in case of damage caused by the fall of buildings and structures. The supervisor or, respectively, the keeper or the owner are then presumed to be responsible. The duty to make reparations does not arise only if they satisfy the requirements of the exculpatory proof under article 923, or article 924 II, or article 925 respectively.

*G.* If several persons unlawfully and culpably caused harm, or if several persons are responsible for a certain harm, they are all liable jointly and severally (art. 926). As between themselves, the co-authors of the harm are liable to one another according to the degree of their respective fault, which degree is determined by the court (art. 927).

*H.* In cases of personal injury and death, claims for compensation arise also in favor of persons other than the victim. Those persons may bring action independently. Thus, in the case of death, the person bound to make reparations shall pay the medical expenses and the funeral expenses to the person on whom the obligation of bearing such expenses lies. He is also bound to make reparations, for the loss of maintenance or services, to the person who is entitled by law to claim maintenance or the performance of services by the victim (art. 928). In case of injury to the body or the health of a person, the obligation shall, in addition to medical expenses and the damage already accrued, extend to the detriment which the act occasions to future earnings, and to the additional expenses he will have to bear because of an increase in his needs. There arises also an obligation to compensate the third party who, being entitled by law to claim the performance of services by the victim, is now deprived of the services because of the delict committed against the victim (art. 929). The compensation for future damages under articles 928 and 929 shall be made by payment of an annuity in monthly installments. Instead of the annuity the court may, on request by the claimant, award a lump sum if serious cause exists. The claim for compensation is not barred by the fact that another person is liable to pay compensation or to furnish maintenance to the injured party (art. 930).

*I.* 1. Once an unlawful invasion of a right or of a legal interest has been established, the plaintiff is entitled to have it undone and to demand that it not be repeated. Many legal writers share now the opinion that Greek law grants such a general claim.

2. The main remedy, however, in tort liability is that the plaintiff is entitled to claim reparations. Such reparations may cover not only damages for the pecuniary injury (arts. 914, 919) but also reparation in money for the moral or non-pecuniary harm (ικανοποίηση ηθικής βλάβης, ikanopoiisi ithikis vlavis; arts. 932, 299) which the plaintiff has suffered as a consequence of the unlawful act. Moral reparations may include money for pain and suffering.

(*a*) Indemnity for moral harm is, according to Greek law, compensation; it does not take the character of a civil penalty.

(*b*) In case of fatal injury, the court may adjudicate money for pain to the victim's family.

(*c*) The court has power to evaluate the indemnity to be accorded.

(*d*) The claim for moral reparations is not transferable and does not pass to the heirs, unless it has been acknowledged by contract or an action on it has been commenced (art. 933).

3. The claim for reparations for any damage arising from a delict is barred by prescription in five years from the time the injured party has had knowledge of the injury and of the identity of the person bound to make reparations, and without regard to such knowledge, in twenty years from the commission of the act. Should criminal law prescribe for the act a longer period of prescription, such longer prescription prevails (art. 937).

## Bibliography

*A. Books and Commentaries (in Greek)*

G. Balis, *Law of Obligations. General Part*, 3d ed. (1960).

P. Filios, *Law of Obligations. General Part* (1987); *Special Part*, 2d ed. (1980–1983).

A. Georgiadis and M. Stathopoulos (ed.), *Civil Code. A Commentary on the Articles*, vol. II to vol. IV (1979–1982).

K. Kafkas and D. Kafkas, *Law of Obligations (A Commentary on the Articles). Special Part*, 6th ed., vol. I (1981), vol. II (1982).

A. Ligeropoulos, *Elements of the Law of Obligations*, vol. I, 2d ed. (1968), vol. II (1960).

A. Ligeropoulos (General ed.), *Interpretation of the Civil Code (A Commentary) (ErmAK): Law of Obligations*, vols. II and III (1949–1978).

G. Mantzoufas, *Law of Obligations* (1971) (reprint of the 3d edition of 1959).

M. Stathopoulos, *General Law of Obligations*, vol. I (1979), vol. II (1983).

K. Triantaphyllopoulos, Explanatory Report on the Draft of the Law of Obligations, in: Ministry of Justice (ed.), *Draft of a Civil Code Prepared by the Drafting Committee*, vol. II: *Law of Obligations* (Athens, 1935) 173–254.

P. Zepos, *Law of Obligations*, 2d ed., vol. I: *General Part* (1955), vol. II: *Special Part* (1965).

*B. Articles in Law Reviews and Monographs (in Languages Other than Greek)*

P. Agallopoulos – Zervoyannis, La réparation du *pretium doloris* selon le droit hellénique, *R. Hell. D.I.* 1982–83. 367–377.
A. Bournias, Sur les limites de la liberté contractuelle dans la réglementation des rapports de travail, *R. Hell. D.I.* 1951. 197–200.
P. Kanellopoulos, Products Liability: The Developments of Problems in Foreign Law and Their Treatment Under the Greek Law, *R. Hell. D.I.* 1979. 149–179.
A. Ligeropoulos, Les clauses relatives à la monnaie de paiement et les clauses d' échelle mobile dans les contracts (droit hellénique), *R. Hell. D.I.* 1955. 20–29.
G. Mantzoufas, *Über griechisches Privatrecht* (Athens, 1956).
I. Rokas, Civil Liability and Insurance of Providers of Services Under Greek Law, *R. Hell. D.I.* 1982–83. 271–279.
C. Simantiras, La validité des clauses de non-responsbilité ou limitatives de responsabilité, *R. Hell. D.I.* 1975. 106–126.
P. Zepos, Frustration of Contract in Comparative Law and in the New Greek Civil Code of 1946, *Mod. L. Rev.* 1948. 36–46.
P. Zepos, La théorie de l'imprévision dans les contrats et de la 'Frustration of Contracts', *R. Hell. D.I.* 1950. 27–30.
P. Zepos, Der Schadensersatz nach Ermessen des Richters im griechischen Zivilgesetzbuch, in *Festschrift für Martin Wolff* (1952) 167–173.
P. Zepos, Transfert du risque et de la propriété dans la vente des choses de genre (droit hellénique), *R. Hell. D.I.* 1955. 42–44.
P. Zepos, Le problème du cumul des responsabilités contractuelle et délictuelle en droit hellénique, *R. Hell. D.I.* 1962. 256–262.
P. Zepos, Twenty Years of Civil Code: Achievements and Objectives, *R. Hell. D.I.* 1967. 15–27.
P. Zepos, Equity in Greek Law, in *Equity in the World's Legal Systems* (Newmann, ed., Brussels, 1973) 433–441.

*C. See also:*

G. H. Lawson, *A Common Lawyer Looks at the Civil Law* (Westport, Connecticut, 1977; reprint of the 1953 ed., Ann Arbor).
R. B. Schlesinger, *Comparative Law: Cases, Text, Materials,* 4th ed. (New York, 1980) 692ff, 711ff.
P. Zepos and P. Christodoulou, Professional Liability, in *International Encyclopedia of Comparative Law*, vol. XI: *Torts*, part I (Tübingen – The Hague – Boston – London, 1983) ch. 6.
K. Zweigert and H. Kötz, *An Introduction to Comparative Law.* Translated by T. Weir, vols. I and II [in particular vol. I p. 154–156] (Amsterdam – New York – Oxford, 1977).

# Chapter 6
# Property

*Athanassios N. Yiannopoulos**

## I. Introduction

Book III of the Civil Code, consisting of articles 947 through 1345, contains the basic provisions dealing with property law. The substance of these articles has been derived from the Romanist tradition, indigenous Greek variations developed in the nineteenth century, and from certain modern civil codes. The influence of the French, German, and Swiss civil codes is particularly noticeable.[1]

In Greece, as in most civil law jurisdictions, the number of real rights is limited (*numerus clausus*). The real rights that a person may have are: ownership, personal and predial servitudes, pledge, and mortgage. Possession and detention are *sui generis* rights, neither real nor personal. Real rights other than those enumerated may not be created by juridical act; nor may the features of these rights be altered. Real rights may only be established on things, that is, individual corporeal objects that are susceptible of appropriation. By way of exception, incorporeals are susceptible of usufruct and pledge, and the usufruct of an immovable is susceptible of mortgage.

The creation of a real right is a real transaction, and as such subject to the rule of temporal priority (*prior tempore potior iure*). Real rights may be of limited duration, either by law or by agreement, and may be subject to a term or a condition. When a real right is extinguished with retroactive effect, all real rights granted by the holder of that right are also extinguished in the absence of contrary provision of law.

*W. R. Irby Professor of Law, Tulane University.

1. See P. Zepos, *Greek Law* 104 (1949). The standard works in Greek on the law of property are: G. Balis, *Civil Law Property*, 3d ed. (1955) (Balis); K. Vavouskos, *Civil Law Property*, 6th ed. (1986) (Vavouskos); A. Georgiadis, *Civil Law Property* (1975) (Georgiadis). For article by article interpretation, see A. Papachristou, *Civil Law Property* (1981). For analysis of institutions of Greek property law in the English language, see A. Yiannopoulos, *Civil Law Property*, 2d ed. (1980) (Yiannopoulos, *Property*); id., *Personal Servitudes*, 2d ed. (1978) (Yiannopoulos, *Personal Servitudes*); id., *Predial Servitudes* (1983) (Yiannopoulos, *Predial Servitudes*).

## II. Things

Articles 947 through 973 establish the notion of things as objects of property rights and their division into several broad categories, such as movables and immovables, fungibles and nonfungibles, consumables and nonconsumables, component parts and accessories, fruits and profits, and things 'in commerce' and 'out of commerce.'[2]

### *A. Object and Thing* (αντικείμενο, πράγμα, antikeimeno, pragma)

Following the model of the German Civil Code, the Civil Code distinguishes aptly between *object*[3] and *thing*. The word object applies to anything that may be the subject of a legal relation, with the exception of strictly personal relations. An object may be anything having a pecuniary value, whether corporeal or incorporeal. A thing is a corporeal object that is susceptible of appropriation. Ownership and other real rights may attach, as a rule, on things only and not to incorporeals. Thus, rights having a pecuniary value, though forming part of a person's patrimony, are not governed by the law of property.

Fluid and gaseous substances are corporeal and, as soon as they acquire the mark of individual existence, become things. Natural forces and energies, though incorporeal, are by means of a legal fiction classified as things.[4] Thus, producers of energy enjoy in Greece full proprietary protection. Rights, aggregates of things, and universalities of rights, or of rights and things, such as an entire patrimony or an enterprise, are incorporeal; therefore, they are not things under the Civil Code.

The incidents of human personality are not things susceptible of appropriation. Thus, one's name, likeness, liberty, personal integrity, and honor are not objects of property, but incidents of a comprehensive 'right of personality'[5] that is accorded an almost absolute protection without regard to rules of property law. A living human body and its members or parts are incidents of man's human personality rather than objects of patrimonial rights. Upon death,

2. On the law of things, see G. Balis, *General Principles of Civil Law* 473–544, 8th ed. (1961) (Balis, *Principles*); Yiannopoulos, *Property* §§ 9–27; A. Georgiadis, 1 *Manual of Civil Law Property*, 61–107 (1979) (Georgiadis, Manual); Vavouskos 13–60.
3. Arts. 175, 239, 304 C.C. deal with objects. Cf. BGB § 90; Enneccerus-Nipperdey, 1 *Allgemeiner Teil des Bürgerlichen Rechts* 760, 15th ed. (1959).
4. See art. 947 II. It is otherwise under the German Civil Code; see Kloess, Die Energien in – und ausserhalb des Verkehrs und das Eigenrecht an ihnen, *103 Archiv für die civilistische Praxis* 34, 67 (1908).
5. In accordance with the modern trend, article 57 C.C. establishes an all-inclusive right of personality: 'He who suffers an illegal invasion in his personality is entitled to request the suppression of the invasion and an injunction for the future. If the offense concerns the personality of a deceased, the right belongs to the spouse, descendants, ascendants, brothers and sisters, and testamentary heirs. An additional claim for damages in accordance with the provisions governing delictual responsibility is not excluded.' The Civil Code also recognizes the right to one's own name (art. 58) and the right to the products of one's intellect (art. 60). Cf. Balis, *Principles* 78–83.

however, a human body becomes a thing; and certain parts, such as blood, hair, or internal organs, may become things upon their separation from a living human body.

### *B. Movables and Immovables – Component Parts and Accessories* (κινητά, ακίνητα, συστατικά, παραρτήματα, kinita, akinita, systatica, parartimata)

In Greece, as in other civil law jurisdictions, *things* are divided into movables and immovables. These terms correspond roughly with the division of *property* in common law jurisdictions into personal property (personalty) and real property (realty).

Immovables are the ground and its component parts. Movables are all things that are not classified as immovables. The division of things into movables and immovables applies to corporeal objects only, with one modification: when the law or juridical acts refer to movable property, as distinguished from immovable property, among the movables are included all obligations and among the immovables the usufruct of immovables and predial servitudes.[6] Most provisions of law governing the classification of things as movables or immovables are considered to be rules of public order, from which derogation by agreement is forbidden.

The component parts of an immovable may be either movables or immovables; the component parts of a movable may only be movables. Certain component parts are susceptible of separate real rights but others are not. Things insusceptible of separate real rights are those firmly fixed to the ground, especially buildings, movables incorporated into a structure or building, vegetation and mineral substances, water under the surface, seeds when sown, and plants when planted. The list is considered to be exclusive rather than indicative. The Code provides expressly that things attached to the ground or building for temporary purposes, though firmly fixed, do not become component parts insusceptible of separate real rights. The same rule applies to buildings and other structures erected on the ground of another by a usufructuary or other person having a real right. These things remain movable and are susceptible of real rights separate from those in the land.

The practical consequences of the characterization of a thing as a component part insusceptible of separate real rights are significant. The owner is always free to terminate the status by actual detachment, but as long as it lasts separate ownership and separate real rights are not recognized. Seizure, and any transfer or encumbrance, include all component parts of this kind, even if incorporated subsequently. However, according to special legislation, machinery in industrial plants, in order to be included in a real mortgage, must be mentioned specifically; and standing crops may be seized separately from the land. Real rights affecting movables prior to incorporation are extinguished and do not

6. See arts. 948, 949.

revive upon detachment. Real rights acquired on component parts of a thing by incorporation continue to exist even after the movables are detached. Exception is made as to the rights of a real mortgagee; movables covered by the mortgage may be detached and transferred to third persons free of the mortgage.

Parties may in their private relations establish personal rights with respect to component parts insusceptible of real rights. Thus, the sale of standing crops, standing timber, and mineral substances are valid transactions if made according to the formalities governing movables. But no real rights are created and in case of nonperformance, the purchaser is entitled to damages only.

Component parts are distinguished from accessories. An accessory is a movable which, without being a component part of the principle thing, is destined to serve its economic purpose and has been placed with regard to the principal thing in a space relationship appropriate to its destination.[7] The principal thing may be a corporeal movable or immovable; the accessory must be a corporeal movable.[8] The rules governing classification of a thing as a principal or accessory are suppletive. The significance of the classification is that, in certain instances, the law regards the two as an economic unit and the transfer or encumbrance of the principal thing includes the accessory: *accessorium sequit principali.*[9] However, unlike an inseparable component part one may own the accessory of a thing belonging to another or may have another real right in it.

### *C. Fungibles* (αντικαταστατά, antikatastata)

Fungibles are movables which are ordinarily determined by number, measure or weight. This quality is determined by objective criteria and notions prevailing in trade.[10] The distinction is important in the field of obligations and particularly for the contracts of loan, deposit, and annuity. Responsibility for the loss or deterioration of a fungible is discharged by the delivery of similar things, while with regard to nonfungibles a money judgment is the only permissible substitute.

### *D. Consumables* (αναλωτά, analota)

Consumables are movables the intended use of which consists in their consumption or alienation. Stocks of goods and other aggregations of things the intended use of which is the alienation of the objects singly are likewise considered to be consumables. The quality of consumability depends on objective criteria and prevailing notions in trade rather than physical notions.[11]

7. See art. 956.
8. Accessories are susceptible of separate real rights. See Balis, *Principles* 515.
9. See Yiannopoulos, *Property* 623.
10. See Balis, *Principles* 492.
11. See Balis, *Principles* 493.

The division has practical consequences in that, depending upon the classification, one may be under a duty to return either individual things or things of like quantity and quality.

### E. *Things 'Out of Commerce'* (εκτός συναλλαγής, ektos synallagis)

The Civil Code has retained this special category which includes things common to all, things subject to public use and things dedicated to serve public, municipal, communal, or religious purposes. Things common to all are the air and, perhaps, the open sea. Things subject to public use are, particularly, freely and perpetually running water, roads, public squares, the seashore, harbors and roadsteads, the banks of navigable rivers, large lakes and their shores. The list is illustrative. Things subject to public use may belong to the state, to towns or communities, or to private persons when this is authorized by statute.[12] The owner of a thing subject to public use may exercise all prerogatives of ownership that are compatible with public use.

The last category of things out of commerce encompasses all sorts of things dedicated to a public purpose other than public use including state-owned buildings housing governmental offices and educational and health institutions. Municipal buildings housing municipal offices and institutions belong to the same category. State and municipal enterprises, whether autonomous or not, may serve public purposes. The accepted criterion is whether the main purpose of the enterprise is to produce revenue or to serve the public. The state-owned railroad and telecommunications systems and electric utilities are regarded as serving a public purpose and, therefore, are things out of commerce. Finally, to this category belong religious institutions and cemeteries. Once their special purpose use ceases, things out of commerce lose this quality and become like all other things.

### F. *Fruits* (καρποί, karpoi) and *Profits* (ωφελήματα, ophelimata)

The Civil Code, following the pattern of Roman-Byzantine law, distinguishes fruits into natural and civil. In addition, following the German Civil Code, it distinguishes between fruits of things and fruits of rights and introduces the notion of profits.[13] Fruits of things are organic products, advantages obtained according to the destination of a thing, and any revenue a thing may produce by operation of law or by virtue of a legal relation. According to the prevailing view, organic products are regarded as fruits only if the substance of the principal thing is preserved.[14] The destination of a thing as fruit-producing is

12. See art. 968.
13. See art. 962: 'Profits are not only the fruits of a thing or of a right, but also every advantage which the use of the thing or of the right confers.'
14. See Balis, *Principles* 518.

determined by reference to its nature, prevailing conceptions in society, and the intention of the parties to a transaction. Fruits of rights are royalties and interests deriving from rights other than ownership.

## III. Possession (νομή, nomi)

Possession and possessory actions are dealt with in articles 974 through 998 of the Civil Code. These articles reflect solutions developed by Greek doctrine and jurisprudence in the course of the nineteenth and twentieth centuries. The complicated scheme of the German Civil Code was an example to avoid.[15]

Distinction is made between possession and detention (κατοχή, katochi). *Possession* is the exercise of physical control over a thing with the intent to own it; absent such intent, we have only *detention*. The rules governing possession apply by analogy to quasi-possession, that is, the exercise of a real right with the intent to have it as one's own. Detailed provisions deal with the acquisition, exercise, loss, and protection of possession.

Possession is protected by the privilege of self-help and several actions. Any possessor, however wrongful his possession may be, is entitled to protect his possession by the exercise of reasonable force. The same privilege is accorded to persons possessing on behalf of a master or principal.

A possessor evicted unlawfully and without his consent has an action for the recovery of possession. When possession is exercised through a detentor, such as a lessee, the action may be brought by either the detentor or the possessor. When it is usurped by the detentor, the possessor may bring the possessory action against him. But an evicted detentor has no possessory action against the person from whom he derived his detention, for example, against the lessor.

Defendant is the person who evicted plaintiff, if he is still in possession at the time of the commencement of the action, whether he exercises possession personally or through others. If at the time of the commencement of the action the defendant is out of possession, plaintiff may either sue him for damages under the law of delictual obligations or proceed against any third person whose possession is defective *vis-à-vis* the plaintiff. If, after commencement of the action, the defendant transfers possession to a third person or otherwise loses it, the proceeding continues regularly and the judgment is ordinarily executed against any person who took possession *pendente lite*.[16]

The eviction action may be cumulated with an action for the return of the thing by virtue of a personal right. A disturbance of possession that falls short of eviction is also actionable by a suit seeking judgment suppressing the disturbance and prohibiting future invasions.

The defendant may oppose both possessory actions on the ground of defective possession, i.e., that plaintiff acquired possession wrongfully *vis-à-vis*

15. See Zepos, *Greek Law* 104 (1949). On the law of possession, see Balis 8–85; Georgiadis, 2 *Manual* 127–231 (1980); Vavouskos 61–114; Yiannopoulos, *Property* §§ 206.
16. See arts. 225, 325 C.C. Proc.; Kerameus, *Civil Procedure. General Part* 312 (1986).

the defendant or his ancestors during the year prior to the eviction or disturbance.[17] He cannot assert a right by virtue of which he may be entitled to possession, unless this right has been recognized by final and unappealable decision in litigation between plaintiff and the defendant. Both actions prescribe in a year from the time of the eviction or other disturbance.

Rights to possession may be determined, independently of any possessory action, in a summary proceeding for 'security measures for the provisional regulation of possession or detention'[18] where the court may award possession on the basis of a cursory examination of the merits of the case. The disposition has no *res judicata* effect in a subsequent possessory action. Possession, being a patrimonial right under the Code, is also protected by actions for declaratory judgment, unjust enrichment, and damages under the law of delictual obligations.

## IV. Ownership (κυριότητα, kyriotita)

Articles 999 through 1141 of the Civil Code deal with the institutions of ownership and co-ownership. In these fields, the traditional conceptions have undergone substantial changes. Ownership, though an exclusive right over a thing, no longer enjoys the status of an absolute *dominium*. Clearly defined neighborhood rights are established, expropriation in the interest of the public after due compensation is possible, and acts performed by third persons above or under the soil may not be enjoined if not harmful to the owner's interest. Further, in contrast to the Roman law, horizontal as well as vertical division of immovables and separate ownership of apartments is legally possible.[19]

Compared with the common law doctrine of estates, ownership in civil law jurisdictions is the essence of simplicity. No abstraction such as an estate is interposed between the owner and his property, nor is ownership built on ownership as in the case of a trust. The content of ownership may be limited, as when charges on the land such as servitude are created but these charges are regarded as restrictions on the use of land, rather than as rights of separate or concurrent ownership. Upon the disappearance of an encumbrance, ownership resumes its original plenitude, leaving no room for the concept of a remainder or a reversionary interest.

Trusts are non-existent in Greece. Ordinarily, a person has both the management and the enjoyment of his property, and ownership cannot be fragmented into the components of legal title and beneficial enjoyment. An owner may entrust the management of his property to a mandatory or other representative, and a person may manage the affairs of another without mandate (*negotiorum gestio*). Further, the law allows the separation of management from the enjoyment of property when a person is incompetent to manage

17. See art. 998; Balis 45–48, 55–58.
18. See arts. 733, 734 C.C. Proc.; Vavouskos 91–93.
19. On ownership, see Balis 86–290; Georgiadis, 3 *Manual* 233–434 (1983); Vavouskos 117–327.

his own affairs on account of minority, absence, or unsound mind. In such cases, the management of property is entrusted to a tutor or a curator.

The fragmentation of ownership into a legal estate and an equitable interest is an original common law institution. There is no equivalent institution in civil law jurisdictions, unless one may regard as equivalent a substitution or *fideicommissum*, whereby the instituted heir or legatee is bound to restore the succession to another person. But the analogy fails, because the instituted heir has both management and beneficial enjoyment as long as his right lasts. Nearly everything that a trust can accomplish may be actually achieved within the framework of the civil law, the policies of the law permitting. When something achievable with the trust is not achievable under the civil law, it is usually because the result is forbidden for reasons of social policy.

## *A. Acquisition of Ownership*

Ownership may be acquired in a variety of ways, as by occupancy of things that belong to no one, by transfer from a previous owner or even by a non-owner, by operation of law, by the effect of judgments, and by acts of the public authorities. For systematic purposes, distinction may be made between *original* and *derivative* acquisition of property rights. An original acquisition involves the creation of a new property right; it is independent of any pre-existing rights over the same thing. A derivative acquisition involves a transfer of a pre-existing right from one person to another.

The distinction between the two modes of acquisition is important in the light of the civilian maxim that no one can transfer a greater right than one has. This means that, ordinarily, the transferor must be owner and must transfer the property as it may be burdened with rights of third persons. However, the scope of the maxim has been narrowed by exceptions. Thus, the ownership of movables that are neither lost nor stolen may be transferred by a non-owner to a good faith transferee. Moreover, money and negotiable instruments may be transferred even if they are stolen from, or lost by, their owner. Lands, as a rule, must be transferred by the owner, subject to exceptions established by the system of publicity of transactions.

## *B. Original Acquisition*

There is a variety of original modes of acquisition of ownership, including occupancy, finding, accession, acquisitive prescription, and expropriation.

Occupancy, is the taking of possession of things that belong to no one (*res nullius*). This is limited to certain movables, such as wild animals, birds, fish, and abandoned things. Akin to occupancy is the finding of lost things and the trove of a treasure. Lost things have an owner, but the law attributes ownership to the finder after the lapse of a certain period of time from the completion of certain formalities such as advertisements or reports to the authorities. A treasure trove is divided between the finder and the owner of the property in which the treasure was hidden.

Accession is based on the principle that the ownership of a thing carries with it the right to whatever the thing produces, and to certain other things that are united with it, whether naturally or artificially. The ownership of the soil carries with it the ownership of all that is directly above and under it, unless the contrary is established by provision of law or contract; therefore, buildings and other constructions erected by trespassers on the land of another become the property of the landowner. Moreover, certain fixtures attached to the land of another may become his property even if the annexor acted in good faith and in the framework of a contractual right. Alluvion formations, created by imperceptible additions to the banks of rivers, and islands formed in the beds of non-navigable rivers, belong likewise by accession to the riparian owners. Detailed provisions deal with accession to movables which, apart from the increase of animals, ordinarily takes place in cases of adjunction of materials belonging to different owners, mixture of grains or fluids, and in cases of production of new things by labor bestowed on the materials of another person.

Acquisitive prescription, similar to adverse possession, is predicated on the possession of a thing over a designated period of time with the intent to own it. One who possesses in good faith acquires a movable in three years and an immovable in ten years, whereas one who possesses in bad faith acquires a thing, whether movable or immovable, in twenty years.

Expropriation is essentially a matter of public law (see above, Ch. 3, Section IV D 9). Governing constitutional provisions and other legislative texts provide for notice and the payment of an adequate, fair and just compensation to the owner.

### C. *Derivative Acquisition*

This mode ordinarily involves a transfer from a previous owner. The transfer may be voluntary, such as by agreement, or involuntary, as in the case of a judicial sale. The transfer of ownership by contract is subject to different requirements for movables and immovables. For movables, an informal agreement and delivery of possession of the thing complete the transfer. Exception is, of course, made as to certain movables that may be acquired *a non domino*. For the transfer of the ownership of immovables, the law requires an agreement between the owner and the transferee that the ownership is transferred for a lawful cause, the execution of this agreement in the notarial form, and its recordation in the conveyance records in the district in which the immovable is located.

### D. *Protection of Ownership*

Ownership and other real rights are protected by a variety of personal and real actions. Articles 1094 through 1112 of the Civil Code deal specifically with the revendicatory action, the Publician action and the negatory action.

The revendicatory action (διεκδικητική αγωγή, diekdikitiki agogi) is brought by a dispossessed owner against a possessing nonowner for the recognition of his ownership and return of the thing with its fruits and profits.[20] This action is available for both movables and immovables. Plaintiff is the dispossessed owner or a person to whom such an owner has assigned the revendicatory action. Defendant is a person having possession or detention of the thing at the time of the commencement of the action. The dispossessed owner has against a former possessor an action for damages and against a person out of possession who claims ownership adversely to him an action for declaratory judgment, but may not pursue the revendicatory action.

When the action is brought against the possessor, a judgment against him will be executed against any detentor who has physical control over the thing on behalf of the possessor. When the action is addressed against one exercising quasi-possession, or against a detentor, the defendant is entitled to implead the person for whom he possesses. A judgment rendered against one who exercises quasi-possession or against a detentor has no *res judicata* effect against the possessor unless he has been made a party to the proceeding.[21]

The plaintiff has the burden of proof unless the defendant concedes plaintiff's prior ownership and asserts affirmatively his own right of ownership. In such a case, the burden of proof shifts to the defendant. Proving ownership of immovable property is a hard task that necessitates the tracing of land titles when possession is not in excess of twenty years. The burden of proof is alleviated when one may avail himself of the Publician action. By this action, a prior possessor of immovable property under just title and in good faith may recover it from a possessor in bad faith without having to prove ownership.

Ownership of movable property is proved with the assistance of two presumptions. The present possessor of movables is presumed to be owner, but this may be rebutted on proof of dispossession as a result of loss or theft. In such a case, a presumption arises that the plaintiff was owner during the period of his possession. This presumption is likewise rebuttable.

The Publician action is very similar in its function to the revendicatory action and is governed by the same rules applied by analogy. By its nature, the action may not be brought against the owner or against a person situated in the same position as the plaintiff. The action applies to immovable property only, because under the Civil Code one may acquire the ownership of movables by a transfer from a nonowner and the present possessor of a movable benefits from a presumption of ownership in his favor.

The negatory action (αρνητική αγωγή, arnitiki agogi) is an indirect descendant of the Roman *actio negatoria*, a remedy available to an owner in possession against a person claiming a right of servitude. It is available for the protection of ownership and of other real rights against any interference that falls short of

20. See Yiannopoulos, *Property* § 188.
21. See art. 325 C.C. Proc.; Kerameus, *Civil Procedure. General Part* 274, 276–277 (1986).

eviction. The negatory action applies to both movables and immovables, and its purpose is to secure a judgment ordering the suppression of the interference and an injunction for the future.

## V. Predial and Personal servitudes (πραγματικές και προσωπικές δουλείες, pragmatikes kai prosopikes douleies)

Articles 1118 through 1141 of the Civil Code deal with *predial servitudes*, that is, charges imposed on an immovable in favor of another immovable belonging to another owner.[22] In accordance with the Romanist tradition, predial servitudes may not involve affirmative duties for the owner of the servient immovable. Such duties may be undertaken by virtue of personal obligations only. Detailed provisions in the Civil Code determine the modes of acquisition of predial servitudes by juridical act and by acquisitive prescription, their exercise, their protection by the *confessory* action, and their extinction by nonuse and other causes.

Articles 1142 through 1191 deal with the *personal servitudes* of usufruct and habitation and the various innominate limited personal servitudes.[23] These are charges on property imposed in favor of a person. Usufruct may burden both movables and immovables; habitation and limited personal servitudes may burden immovables only.

Usufruct is a real right of enjoyment of limited duration that is exercised on a nonconsumable belonging to another person under the obligation of preserving the substance of the thing. The usufructuary has the right to draw all the advantages and utility that the thing may produce, as if he were owner, but he must restore the thing at the end of the usufruct. Such a right over consumables is qualified in civilian theory as a quasi-usufruct, under which there is an obligation to return to the owner at the end of the usufruct the value of the things or things of the same quantity and quality.

The usufructuary may protect his right by all sorts of personal and real actions. He is required to deal with the property as a prudent administrator, maintain its destination, and undertake the necessary maintenance and ordinary repairs.

## VI. Recordation (μεταγραφή, metagraphi)

Articles 1192 through 1208 of the Civil Code deal with the requirement, formalities, priority, and effect of recordation of certain acts in the conveyance records. These provisions reflect for the most part the influence of French legislation, doctrine, and court decisions.[24]

22. On the law of predial servitudes, see Balis 291–339; Georgiadis, 4 *Manual* 435–489 (1984); Vavouskos 331–340, 362–364, 366–370. See, also, Yiannopoulos, *Predial Servitudes*.
23. On the law of personal servitudes, see Balis 339–397; Georgiadis, 4 *Manual* 491–550 (1984); Vavouskos 341–361, 364–365, 371–373. See, also, Yiannopoulos, *Personal Servitudes*.
24. On the law of recordation, see Balis 398–427; Vavouskos 236–255.

The acts that are subject to the requirement of recordation are: *inter vivos* juridical acts, including gifts *mortis causa*, by which real rights in immovables are established, transferred, or cancelled; adjudications of real rights in immovables; partitions of immovables; and final non-appealable judicial decisions mandating declarations of will for real juridical acts concerning immovables. In the absence of recordation, there can be neither transfer of ownership nor creation, transfer, or cancellation of another real right in an immovable. The annulment of a recorded act by a final non-appealable decision affects third persons from the time of the recordation of the judicial decision in the margin of the annulled act.

## VII. Real Security Rights (εμπράγματη ασφάλεια, empragmati asphaleia)

The last two chapters of Book III of the Civil Code, consisting of articles 1209 through 1345, deal with real security rights: pledge (ενέχυρο, enechyro) and real mortgage (υποθήκη, ypothiki).

*Pledge* is a real right established on another's movable to secure an obligation by means of preferential satisfaction of the creditor. It is an accessory and indivisible real right that may secure a conditional or even a future obligation. For the creation of a pledge, the law requires an agreement between the owner and the creditor and delivery of the possession. The agreement must be dressed in the notarial form or be made by an act under private signature that has a certain date and adequately describes the debt and the thing.

Negotiable instruments are pledged in the same way as corporeal movables. Incorporeals, that is, rights and claims, may be pledged if they are susceptible of transfer or assignment; they are pledged in the same way as they are transferred or assigned.[25] In the case of a pledge of a claim, notice of the creation of the pledge must be given to the debtor.

The Civil Code provides also for the creation of a *chattel-mortgage*, that is, a pledge that does not involve delivery of possession to the creditor, by virtue of recordation of the agreement in the appropriate public records. This provision, however, remains mostly a dead letter because the contemplated special legislation establishing the appropriate public records has not been enacted.

Mortgage is a real right established on another's immovable to secure an obligation by means of the preferential satisfaction of the creditor. A mortgage is an accessory and indivisible right that may secure a conditional or even a future obligation; it may only be established on an immovable or on the usufruct of an immovable for as long as the usufruct lasts.[26] By virtue of special legislation as well as under the Code of Private Maritime Law, a mortgage may also be established on a ship. For the creation of a mortgage, the law requires

25. On the law of pledge, see Balis 428–497; Vavouskos 374–404.
26. On the law of real mortgages, see Balis 498–615; Vavouskos 405–447.

a *title* granting a mortgage and recordation; the possession of the immovable is not conveyed to the creditor. The requisite title may be the law, a judicial decision, or the will of a private person. Thus, a mortgage may be legal, judicial, or conventional.

The right for the recordation of a conventional mortgage may be granted by the debtor of the principal obligation or by a third person in favor of the debtor of that obligation. Under penalty of nullity, the grantor of the mortgage must be owner of the immovable, and if the mortgage burdens a usufruct, the grantor must be the usufructuary. The mortgage exists from the time of the appropriate recordation in the mortgage records of the district in which the immovable is situated. The date of recordation determines the preference of mortgages; mortgages recorded on the same date enjoy the same ranking.

Detailed provisions in the Civil Code regulate the rights and obligations of the owner of the mortgaged immovable, the rights of the secured creditor, the process for the enforcement of the mortgage, the extinction of the mortgage, and the cancellation of recordation.

# Chapter 7
# Regional and Urban Planning and Zoning

*Anastasia Grammaticaki-Alexiou**

## I. Introduction

Planning in Greece presents a picture of disorder which is due to the gradual formation of the network of settlements in the country, under the pressure of geographical, historic, social and economic phenomena. Few narrow valleys exist in the mountainous land while a considerable part of the country consists of islands. The successive wars have deeply scarred it. The refugees, the immigration and the progressive formation of the Greek state are some of the factors contributing to the disorder. Some other factors are the decrease of rural population due to urbanism as well as the regional inequality with the concentration of productive forces, decision making and cultural activities in the capital and in the major cities. To these one must add the environmental problems created by the large scale degradation of the physical environment all over the country and especially in the big cities.

As a result housing areas are uncontrollably extended, and illegal construction expands in an unplanned and constant manner. The quality of infrastructure is poor. Considerable traffic problems exist, mainly in the city centers, where the density of the population is extremely high.

These problems and deficiencies cannot be attributed to the lack of legal framework. On the contrary, the laws on planning and building are abundant but they are also uncoordinated. The legislator usually faces regional and urban planning problems in a fragmentary manner, with a considerable delay and very often by taking hasty measures of doubtful value. The numerous laws make the concise presentation of the legal frame on planning quite difficult. In the following pages reference will be made to only the most important legal provisions.

## II. The Constitutional Frame of Regional and Urban Planning

The Constitution of 1975 draws the lines within which the legislation and the administration must proceed when taking specific measures concerning regional

*Assistant Professor of Law, University of Thessaloniki.

and urban planning. Article 24 of the Constitution provides for the protection of the natural and cultural environment by the state and subjects regional and urban planning to state control. It also prescribes the means of exercising operational urban planning. Another constitutional provision (art. 17) provides for the protection of property, allowing its taking under eminent domain only for the public benefit and only after full compensation has been paid.

Article 18 IV and VII deals with the redistribution of rural property aiming at the better exploitation of the land.

## III. Forms of Planning Rules

Planning law contains the rules concerning urban programming and planning. These rules may be divided into two categories:

(*a*) Operational planning rules, by which the state creates the necessary legal frame for its intervention to the formation and development of towns and cities.

(*b*) Building regulations, containing the requirements related to the safety, aesthetic and hygiene of buildings, by which the state intervenes and controls the activities of the individuals concerning development.

Besides these forms, regional and urban planning legislation contains a different sort of legal instruments, that is the programs, the plans and the studies, which have a regulatory character. The existing planning laws use these terms without making a clear distinction between them. According to a practice that tends to become a general principle, the regional and urban planning process takes place in two stages. The first stage has a programmatic and directorial character. The second stage is based on the first one and implements its goals. The regional program is made according to the regional plan. The general study for the development of a settlement area precedes the particular urban planning studies. Regional planning stands above the various plans, programs and studies. It must be clarified here that urban planning does not presuppose the existence of completed regional plans and programs.

## IV. The Protection of Regional and Urban Planning

The elaboration of plans, programs and studies is a time consuming process. In the meantime, private development enterprise may create problems if left uncontrolled. Therefore, during the time of elaboration, building activity must be limited or prohibited if it is incompatible with the targets of planning and if it prevents its proper implementation. There must also be certain mechanisms available, which will enable the state to acquire, without resorting to taking by eminent domain, the land it needs for the creation of public areas and the construction of works designed for the public benefit. The measures provided are various, such as the suspension of issuing building permits or the prohibition of building activities or of the division of land properties. Also, the state and the local government authorities have a right of preference under equal terms in purchasing real estate within settlement areas, when these estates are going to be used for planning purposes.

The realization of regional and urban plans, programs and studies requires their observance by both the state and the individuals. This is achieved by the compulsory character of building permits for all building activities, which are thus subjected to the preventive state control.

## V. The Organs of Regional and Urban Planning

The main organs of regional and urban planning are certain ministries and public agencies. Their tasks and extent of competence are often interconnected in such a way that conflicts and confusion may result.

The Ministry of Environment Regional Planning and Public Works is exclusively responsible for the preparation of urban and regional planning studies, environmental programs and housing plans and projects. Evidently it bears the main burden of regional and urban planning. It also supervises all construction activity in the country.

The Ministry of National Economy is responsible for making, completing, modifying or revising national plans and projects. It influences the regional and urban planning policy through the preparation and implementation of national programs of economic and social development. It also supervises the Center of Planning and Economic Research. The Ministry of the Interior intervenes to the administration of the planning system mainly through the departmental Technical Services of municipalities and communes, which undertake plan elaboration on behalf of local government. The Ministry of Agriculture is concerned with agricultural planning, forests and forest roads, landscape and also planning for settlements of up to 4,000 inhabitants in the context of the resettlement of refugees and landless peasants. The Ministry of Industry and Energy is responsible for industrial location policy and planning of industrial estates. The Ministry of Culture and Sciences, the prefects, the municipalities, the Special Fund for the Implementation of Urban Master Plans, the National Tourist Organization, the Autonomous Organization of Workers' Housing, the Autonomous Building Organization of Officers, the Public Corporation for Housing and Urban Planning, the National Mortgage Bank of Greece and the Public Corporation for the Construction of Hospitals are some other organs and agencies influencing planning in Greece.

The approval of all sorts of plans and programs comes from the National Council of Regional Planning and Environment. The national plan and program must be approved by the Parliament as well.

## VI. Planning Legislation

The oldest and basic law on planning is the L.D. of 17.7.1923, concerning the plans of cities, towns and communes of the state. Its provisions were quite advanced for their time and a large number of them are still in force. This statute provides for every settlement to be regulated and developed in accordance with a 'city plan'. Such a plan is subject to constraints regarding plot ratios and dimensions, site coverage, height of buildings, types of housing development etc.

According to this law, the methods of implementation of city plans are (a) the laying out of streets and squares by which properties falling, according to the plan, within areas intended for the public use, are taken away from their owners. This usually occurs when new streets are to be opened or old ones widened; (b) concession, by which the administration confers the ownership of plots to owners of neighbouring sites according to a certain procedure provided by law; (c) the rearrangement of plots through the exchange or the addition and substraction of certain parts of them.

All three methods usually require the procedure of taking by eminent domain. The latter is completed only after the land owner receives full compensation which is assessed by the court. If the compensation is not paid within eighteen months after the date of publication of the relevant court judgment, the taking is cancelled *ipso iure*. The obligation for compensation falls on the land owners who benefit by the new situation and on the local government organizations.

In the 1970s a more modern approach, adapted to contemporary ideas, made its appearance. It widened the city plan and gave to it a dynamic character with emphasis to the large scale planned construction. The state clearly showed its intention to intervene actively in urban and regional matters. The first manifestation of this approach was L.D. 1003/1971, concerning operational urban planning. It was oriented towards an urban planning that takes into consideration physical, economic, social and aesthetic factors, for zones designated for development or improvement.

L.D. 1262/1972 on master plans for urban areas defined the concepts of 'regional plan', 'master plan', 'urban plan' and 'land use'. The regional plan determines the spatial organization of a series of social data in the context of development programs. The master plan refers to the regulation and control of land use and urban networks in the context of wider development programs, or of the national/regional governmental policy. It includes a survey of the conditions which justify the proposal, the forecasts, the targets of development and the proposal for implementation.

Law 947/1979 on planned development areas ('settlement areas') has been intended to replace the 1923 law. It supersedes and extends L.D. 1003/1971 and leaves a very narrow margin of application for L.D. 1262/1972. It analyzes the concept of a planned development area, that is an area where development can take place only as long as it is based on the general principles of urban planning, on an existing regional plan and follows a pattern which is consistent with social or economic goals. The study for a planned development area presupposes a survey of the existing conditions, forecasts of population and of needs for constructed space, an estimation of the consequences of the proposal to the environment, the ways of development or improvement, the stages of implementation and the benefits and costs. General and sometimes specific land uses are defined. According to Law 947/1979, the development or improvement of a planned development area may take place through the exercise of operational urban planning, urban land consolidation or the enactment of normative building regulations. Property owners are required to concede a proportion of their plots to be used for the creation of public open spaces or to make cash contributions for the construction of the basic infrastructure. The compulsory purchase of certain plots may also be necessary.

Of these methods, operational urban planning is the most intense form of state intervention on the land, because it presupposes a series of programmed actions and leads to the reformation of existing urban units or the creation of new ones. In this way the contemporary needs of an organized community and of its working population may be satisfied. Although Law 947/1979 is an important law that brought many innovations, it met strong reactions, mainly related to the contributions of land owners. As a result, it was left to become inactive and the urban development of the country came to a standstill.

In order to satisfy immediate needs of settlement development Law 1337/1983 on the extention of urban plans and on settlement development was promulgated. It allows the extention of urban plans by urban units (called neighbourhoods) and the incorporation of already organized urban units according to a general urban plan (a concept similar to the master plan of Law 1262/1972 but isolated from the national frame) and an urban study. It is not applicable in resort areas. Similarly to the solutions of Law 947/1979, under Law 1337/1983 property owners have the obligation to contribute a proportion of their land analogous to the plot size, as well as to make cash contributions for the construction of basic infrastructure. The cash contributions vary also, according to plot size.

A novelty introduced by Law 1337/1983 is the establishment of zones of special incentives and zones of special aid. The former are parts of urban units where financing and planning incentives are available for the construction or development of buildings that will be used as centers of the urban units (e.g. buildings for cultural activities, recreation, parking etc.). The latter are zones with priority in housing loans and other such aid.

Another category of incentives, aiming at the encouragement of productive investments in the primary and secondary sectors, modern technology, transportation and tourism, is provided by Law 1262/1982. This statute, which must not be confused with L.D. 1262/1972, divides the country into four categories of regions, depending on the degree of development, and offers a variety of incentives, according to the development needs of each region.

In the field of national and regional planning and environmental protection, Law 360/1976 regulates the elaboration and approval procedures of national and regional plans and establishes the competent agencies.

## VII. Building Regulations

Naturally land owners wish to exploit their immovable property. If such a property is a building site, the exploitation usually consists in its development through the construction of buildings for housing or professional use. This development is subject to important restrictions aiming at the rationalization of city and settlement growth and the construction of good and safe buildings. The first target is reached through the rules of regional and urban plans and studies. The second target is achieved through building laws, that is rules which regulate the construction of buildings.

An effective control on the private building activity is exercised by the state through the issuing of building permits, which prevents illegal building. Building sites included in the city plans are subject to different regulations than those outside city plans. The relevant building rules are mainly found in the General Building Code of 1985, which has replaced the General Building Code of 1973. However, the provisions of the Code refer very often to provisions of other previous laws which remain in force. The Code defines basic planning and building concepts and contains provisions on the planning and architectural control of building, exercised by the city plan agencies, on traditional settlements and preservable buildings, on the use of buildings, on the minimum size of plots, on the coefficient of building surface, on the site coverage, on construction ways, on the height of buildings, on open spaces, arcades, fences etc. As the majority of buildings in the towns and cities are multistory buildings, many of the Code provisions deal with relevant problems.

One should not omit here to refer to the special role of the coefficient of building surface in planning and building rules. Every building has its own coefficient and the legislator has decided that, under certain circumstances, the coefficient could be transferred to another plot or another part of the plot. This is done so that architectural and planning needs may be satisfied without depriving the land owners of the benefits they get from the coefficient of building surface of their property. The transfer is possible when it is necessary to save buildings that have been considered preservable or when the state needs space for public use areas.

## VIII. Illegal Building Activity

A major problem in Greece is illegal building activity, mainly due to economic reasons, poor economic conditions of a large part of urban population, high cost of buildings (caused by reasons such as intensive exploitation of land, or safety regulations that require high quality of building materials that will resist to earthquakes), plus the need of the people to possess their own home and avoid paying rent. Illegal building occurs when building takes place without a building permit, in violation of the permit, in the case of an illegal permit or when building regulations are violated.

The legislator has realized that the demolition of buildings constructed illegally would be the solution to the problem and would stand as a threat to future illegal building activities. But political and social pressures have been so strong that most of the legal provisions concerning illegal buildings deal with the conditions under which the latter are exempted from demolition. As an example, Law 1337/1983 contained rules concerning the suspension of demolition of buildings constructed before Jan. 31, 1983 and their eventual legitimation under certain circumstances. The reactions against this law were so strong that Law 1512/1985 attempted to 'correct' the situation by some more lenient provisions. Actually, very few buildings have been demolished and the penal sanctions against the owners, the engineers or building contractors connected with illegal building activities remain inapplicable.

All this shows that the state has been reluctant to attack the phenomenon effectively, while it is evident that the resulting planning and building anarchy is and will be a constant, big problem. It is probably one more weakness of the Greek planning system, along with its ineffectiveness, excessive centralization, lack of real coordination and lack of real participation of non-governmental agencies and individuals.

## Basic Bibliography

(in Greek unless otherwise indicated)

K. Choromidis, *Taking by Eminent Domain* (1975).
D. Christophilopoulos, *The City Plan* (1983).
D. Christophilopoulos, *Regional and Urban Planning* (1984).
P.–M. Efstratiou, Die Raumplanung in Griechenland, *Die Verwaltung* 17 (1984) 355–375.
A.–Ph. Lagopoulos, Greece, in *Planning in Europe*, ed. by R. H. Williams (1984) (in English).
V. Skouris – A. Tachos, *Special Administrative Law*, part 4/I, II: *Regional and Urban Planning Law* (1985).

# Chapter 8
# Family Law

*Anastasia Grammaticaki-Alexiou**

## I. Introduction

Family law is contained in Book IV of the Greek Civil Code. The original provisions of this book were quite conservative even for 1946, when they were adopted, modelled on the idea of a patriarchal family. The majority of family law concepts and institutions of the Code was derived from Byzantine-Roman law, which was applied to family relations of the Greeks at least since Byzantine times. Later, when Greece achieved its independence following Ottoman rule, the same system, as contained in the Hexabiblos of Harmenopoulos, was officially introduced by the Royal Decree of February 23/March 7, 1835 and became the basic legislation in the private law sphere of the country. Byzantine-Roman law along with the Ionian Civil Code, the Civil Code of Samos and the Civil Code of Crete remained in force until the introduction of the Civil Code. Until very recently, the law prescribed different roles for each spouse and considered the husband as the head and main supporter of the family. But gradually traditional ideas changed and the role of the wife became important as well.

The Constitution of 1975, for the first time in the legal history of Greece, establishes explicitly the principle of the equality of the sexes. Article 4 II proclaims that 'Greek men and women have equal rights and obligations'. But under article 116 I, existing inconsistent provisions remained in force until their repeal by law by December 31, 1982. This constitutional mandate made the revision of family law necessary. The process took more than six years and involved a great deal of controversy in the legal press, bar associations, political parties, the Church and women's organizations. The gigantic effort resulted in Law 1250/1982 introducing civil marriage and in Law 1329/1983 on the application of the constitutional principle of equality of men and women as well as on the partial modernization of family law.

No other revision of the Civil Code has been so extensive. The transformation reflects the impact of the changed social context on the law and it is hoped that it will satisfy the anticipated developments of the future. It is worth mentioning

*Assistant Professor of Law, University of Thessaloniki.

that these statutes are drafted in the demotic spoken language and not in the original formalistic language of the Civil Code, thus taking the first step towards the linguistic modernization of all codes. Of the 364 articles in the Book, 264 have been amended or were repealed. Whole institutions, such as dowry, paternal authority (replaced by parental care) and emancipation of minors have been abolished. Most other parts have been reformed.

Greek family law presents, as it is, certain basic characteristics which clearly show its constant progress, balanced between tradition and change. The mandatory character of most rules is an indication of the interest of society, represented by the State, in marriage and family. At the same time family law is liberal, marked by a considerable individualism. Consistent with the contemporary social trends is a tendency of radical renewal. This tendency is hard to reconcile with another characteristic which has always dominated Greek family law, that is the strong influence of the Church, dating back to Byzantine times. Marriage impediments, the compulsory religious form of marriage and certain grounds for divorce are some of the most striking examples of the influence of the Greek Orthodox Church on the law. Today this influence has subsided considerably but it still exists. It produced the main opposition against the establishment of civil marriage as the only form.

## II. Marriage (γάμος, gamos)

### *A. Engagement to Marry* (arts. 1346–1349; μνηστεία, mnisteia)

The term 'engagement to marry' means both the contract between a man and a woman by which they promise to marry each other and the legal relationship existing between the persons engaged. It is remarkable that the provisions of the Civil Code concerning this topic have not undergone any change, notwithstanding that the institution has lost some of its significance in our days. The conditions of an engagement to marry are three: (a) capacity to marry, although minors may become engaged as well, (b) conformity to public policy and morals, and (c) consent of the parties. No formalities are required for an engagement. No legal obligation to marry is created thereby and no legal action may be brought to compel this effect.

The breach of the promise to marry has, however, certain economic consequences for the party who causes it without an important cause: this party owes damages to the other party or to the other party's parents or to any other person who has suffered a material loss as a result of expenditures incurred in expectation of the prospective marriage. As far as the restitution of gifts exchanged between the parties is concerned, each one of them may request their return according to the rules of unjust enrichment. All claims must be made within the two years following the end of the year during which the breach of the engagement took place.

### *B. Essential Requisites of Marriage, Requirements and Impediments* (arts. 1350–1360)

The difference of sex is a basic requirement of a valid marriage which clearly results from the whole concept of marriage. It does not follow, though, that the ability to have sexual intercourse is also an essential requisite. Its lack may only eventually become a reason for divorce.

The minimum age is eighteen years. Thus legal maturity is another requirement. If a minor wants to marry, he/she must apply to the court for an exemption. The exemption will be granted if the marriage, due to extraordinary circumstances, appears to be in the interest of the minor according to the facts presented by the parties and their parents who exercise parental care. Persons of unsound mind or who have been interdicted by the court cannot validly marry. Those under judicial administration may marry only if the administrator gives his consent.

Other impediments to marriage are consanguinity (marriage between persons related to each other in the direct ascending or descending line or between brother and sister is prohibited), collateral relationship up to the fourth degree and adoption.

### *C. The Celebration of Marriage* (arts. 1367–1371)

An investigation as to whether any impediments exist precedes the celebration of marriage. Also a publication of a notice which affords an opportunity of discovering existing impediments is required. If no opposition to the marriage occurs or such opposition has been rejected and the parties have submitted the documents required, the mayor or the chairman of the parish of their domicile issues a marriage licence to each one of them. If the marriage is going to be solemnized in church then the church may issue a marriage licence as well, after checking whether the civil as well as the religious requirements have been met.

The marriage ceremony may be either a church or a civil ceremony, which implies that the couple may choose the kind of solemnization they prefer. If both parties are Greek Orthodox, which is usually the case, and they choose the religious ceremony, then they are entitled to be married by a priest of the parish where at least one of them is registered, according to the rules of the Greek Orthodox Church. If they belong to another denomination, they may be married according to the rules of that denomination. If they belong to a different denomination or faith, then the ceremony has to be performed twice, according to the rules of each denomination or faith each time. Evidently this is a complicated procedure that may create problems; a civil ceremony is the only practical way to avoid them.

The civil wedding is performed by the mayor in the town hall, in the presence of two witnesses, in public ceremony. Marriage by proxy is not allowed. The priest or the mayor who has celebrated the marriage issues a certificate which is recorded in the registry. This recordation serves as proof of the celebration of the marriage.

Statistics show that Greeks still prefer the religious ceremony. This is probably due to the long tradition, the religious influence, or the apparently more formal character of the religious ceremony. Civil weddings are more frequent in the big cities than in the country and rather rare in small towns or villages. A typical example of the preference for the religious ceremony is offered by statistical data for Thessaloniki, the second largest city of Greece. In the year 1984, 2,422 religious weddings were celebrated and only 371 civil ones. Similarly, in 1985 there were 2,628 religious and 365 civil weddings.

### *D. Nullity of Marriage* (arts. 1372–1384)

A marriage contracted while an impediment existed may be annulled pursuant to an action instituted by a spouse, by any other person interested or by the public prosecutor. The same applies if the marriage is celebrated without the free consent of a spouse or if there has been a mistake as to the person, but such marriage may be annulled only upon application of the victim. In the latter two cases, the application for annulment is inadmissible if the victim, after recovering his/her liberty or discovering the mistake, freely and without constraint recognized the marriage.

If one of the parties of a void marriage acted in good faith, he/she has towards the other party who has known the nullity a claim for alimony according to the provisions regulating alimony in divorce. Failure to comply with the provisions on form results in non-existent and not merely void marriages.

### *E. Personal Effects of Marriage* (arts. 1386–1390, 1396)

The principle of equality governs the relations between the spouses. This is more specifically expressed in the principles of mutual assistance, companionship, free allocation of the roles of husband and wife within the family and independence of the spouses in matters that do not affect the marriage directly. For example, marriage does not affect the domicile, the name or the nationality of either spouse.

The husband and wife are required to live together in the matrimonial home under conditions of mutual affection, fidelity, support and assistance. Each spouse has the duty to contribute to the family needs in proportion to his means and condition. The statute of limitations in actions between spouses is suspended so long as the marriage exists. If one of the spouses does not fulfil his/her obligation to live together with the other spouse, the latter may bring an action claiming restitution of cohabitation, so long as such a claim does not appear as an abuse of right.

Decisions concerning family life are taken by mutual consent. A similar approach is adopted by the German, Austrian, French, Scandinavian and other continental legal systems. If such consent is lacking, the disagreement may be resolved by the court. If a natural (absence or illness) or legal (interdiction) reason makes the consent of one of the spouses impossible, the other one decides alone. In an emergency, a decision may be made by only one of the spouses, provided that it is for the benefit of the marriage. Finally, the law also provides that decisions concerning family life must not violate the sphere of the personality of each spouse and they must not obstruct his professional career or activities in general.

As it has already been mentioned, the family name of each spouse does not change. This is quite a liberal solution which finds no exact counterpart in other continental legal systems. However, each spouse may use the name of the other in his social life so long as he/she does not object. For marriages in existence in 1983, when this provision came into force, a transient rule provided that within one year, women who had acquired their husbands' name could have made a declaration to the registry (or to the consular officials, if the spouses lived abroad) to resume their maiden name. However, since many women did not take advantage of that possibility for one reason or another, it is expected that a new rule, which will be soon put into force, will provide that women who have acquired their husbands' family name may resume their maiden name at any time.

### F. *Matrimonial Property* (arts. 1397–1416)

The institution of dowry (προίκα, proika) has deep roots in Greek society. It covered all property, movable or immovable, granted to the wife by her parents or relatives and placed either under the ownership or the administration and usufruct of the husband during marriage. It was connected to the principle that the man bears the burdens of matrimony and has a history of almost three thousand years. It was a practice humiliating women, often creating major economic problems for the woman's family and also degrading to the extent that it allowed women to sue parents who refused to provide a dowry, although they were financially able. The 1983 amendment of the Civil Code abolished this institution as inconsistent with the principle of equality of the sexes. Dowries constituted before that date are returned to the wives. It is, however, doubtful whether the abolition by the law can extinguish the actual practice. Although younger generations appear less inclined to follow the old ways, sociological data show that dowries are rather frequent and it is believed that the practice will cease only when customs and morals change. Still, the attitude of the legislator is a considerable step towards that change.

The matrimonial property regime is governed by the principle of the autonomy of the parties. Thus, the spouses are free to decide about the kind of property relation they prefer. If they do not make use of this freedom, then each one of them owns and manages his/her property separately during the marriage. Naturally, it is possible for them to acquire common property.

Each spouse is responsible to his/her creditors for his/her debts. But as far as movable property is concerned, the law establishes three rebuttable presumptions: (a) for the creditors' benefit, movables being in the possession of either one or both spouses are presumed to belong to the spouse who is the debtor, (b) in disputes arising between the spouses, movables possessed by each spouse or by both of them are presumed to belong to both of them equally, (c) in disputes between spouses and creditors or the spouses only, movables intended for the personal use of each spouse are presumed to belong to the spouse who uses them. There is one more presumption concerning both movable and immovable property, according to which in case of bankruptcy of one of the spouses any property acquired by the other spouse within the two years prior to the cessation of payments belongs to the bankrupt spouse for his creditors' sake.

Very often one of the spouses, usually the husband, manages the property of the other spouse as well. If this happens arbitrarily, he is subject to the general provisions on the management of another's affairs (*negotiorum gestio*, διοίκηση αλλοτρίων, dioikisi allotrion). Otherwise, if the management has been willingly entrusted to the spouse the provisions on mandate (εντολή, entoli) are applicable.

The spouses may modify the legal regime by a matrimonial agreement before or during marriage adopting a community of property. Such agreement is a contract made by notarial act recorded in the public registry. The spouses are free to stipulate which will be common and which will be the separate property of each one of them. If they do not so stipulate, the law provides that community property does not comprise property acquired by each spouse by inheritance or donation to him/her individually, property acquired by each spouse prior to the marriage, property of each spouse intended for his/her strictly personal use or his/her profession, non-transferable claims, rights over his/her intellectual property and acquisitions of each spouse during marriage realized through the sale of his/her private property.

In forming their matrimonial agreement, the parties must take into consideration the mandatory rules concerning matrimonial property. The details of the system of community property are governed by the principle of equality of rights and duties. The spouses may at any time modify the matrimonial agreement by entering into a new one or may terminate it altogether. The form of a notarial act is required in both instances. Community property is also terminated if the marriage is dissolved or annulled, if one of the spouses has disappeared or has gone bankrupt or if the court renders a decision to that effect after a petition of a spouse, because the parties have been living apart for at least one year or because the condition of the private property of the other spouse or the management of the community property is such that the interest of the petitioner is in danger.

In the regime of separation of property, when the marriage is dissolved or annulled, each spouse may claim the distribution of profits and gains deriving from the property of the other spouse to which he/she has contributed. The proof of the size of contributions is usually very difficult. For this reason the law adopts a rebuttable presumption according to which the spouse requesting the distribution is entitled to the 1/3 of the profits and gains. The distribution request belongs to the spouses only and the prescription period is two years after the dissolution or the annullment of the marriage.

### *G. Interruption of Marital Life* (arts. 1391–1395)

This involves a situation where a physical and psychological distance exists between the spouses who wish to share their life no more. In most cases, it is the first step towards divorce and, although it is not the equivalent of the separation from bed and board, it bears many similarities to it. The interruption may be the result of an agreement between the spouses, valid in only a few cases, or of a unilateral action of one of them. It may be either justified or unjustified.

The basic problem related to the interruption of marital life is the support of the economically weaker spouse. The latter is entitled to support if (a) he/she provoked the interruption for good cause or (b) the other spouse provoked the interruption without good cause, or even for good cause when his/her spouse is not at fault. The amount of support depends on the circumstances. As far as the matrimonial home is concerned, each spouse may request that he/she be given the use of the family house, irrespective of rights of ownership, possession or occupancy, if reasons of equity, interest of children or the special circumstances of each party make it necessary. Movables in the house belonging to one of the spouses may be taken away by him/her unless the circumstances show that the use of some of them is absolutely necessary for the other spouse. The right of use of movables belonging to both spouses may be agreed by the parties. If no such agreement is reached then it is for the court to decide.

## III. Divorce (διαζύγιο, diazygio)

### *A. Grounds* (arts. 1438–1440)

A divorce is granted on one of the following grounds:

(*a*) irretrievable breakdown of the bond of matrimony or

(*b*) absence.

Irretrievable breakdown comprises all divorce grounds existing in the law before its amendment in 1983. It does not necessarily imply fault on the part of either spouse. The previous grounds, bigamy, adultery, desertion and attempt on the life of the spouse, have been transformed to rebuttable presumptions that the marriage has suffered an irretrievable breakdown. Another presumption is irrefutable: the separation of the spouses for four consecutive years. The approach adopted by Law 1329/1983 is partly similar to that of French law and partly similar to that of German law. Separation from bed and board is not recognized by Greek family law. Thus the terms 'divorce' and 'dissolution of marriage' have the same meaning.

### *B. Procedure* (arts. 1438, 1441)

Depending on the procedure followed, a divorce petition may be opposed or unopposed. In the latter case, the spouses in reality agree to be divorced. This kind of divorce has often been called divorce 'by consensus'. In legal countenance, however, the consent of the spouses provides only strong proof of the breakdown of the matrimonial bond, which is the 'ground' for such a divorce. The procedural requirements for an unopposed divorce are: (a) duration of marriage for at least one year before presenting the divorce petition and (b) consent in person by the spouses (or their special plenipotentiaries) twice before the court. The second consenting statement must be made at least six months after the first one. The reason for this delay is the need for a reconsideration period, so that overhasty divorces may be avoided. If minor children exist, the spouses must submit to the court and agreement in writing by which they settle the matters of their children's care and of their personal contact with them.

Divorce is granted by court judgment. If the form of the marriage that is dissolved has been a religious one, the divorce is completed by the spiritual dissolution pronounced by the bishop.

### *C. Effects of Divorce* (arts. 1442–1446)

Divorce puts an end to the obligation of spouses for cohabitation and for making common decisions about family life. Dowries which remained valid under the 1983 amendments are returned to the woman. If a comunity property system had been chosen by the parties it is dissolved. If, under the system of separation of property, one spouse had been managing the other spouse's property, he/she is required to make a statement of accounts and to return the income he/she collected from that property. Also each party may claim his/her participation to profits and gains of the other.

As to the children, both parents retain their parental authority in common, but the court regulates its exercise. Thus, parental care may be entrusted to one parent, or to both, if they agree and are able to determine the minor's place of residence. The court may also divide the exercise of parental care between the parents or entrust it to a third person. In formulating its decision, it may take into consideration the ties of the child with each parent, with brothers and sisters and/or existing agreements of the parents on the matter.

The criteria of sex or fault do not play a role anymore in maintenance obligations after the divorce. Both parties have the same rights and obligations and they are expected to support themselves. Nevertheless, if one of the spouses is destitute while the other has sufficient means, the law grants the destitute party a right to alimony as long as there is one of the following reasons: (a) his/her health or age do not allow him/her to acquire proper employment in order to support him/herself, (b) he/she cannot work because he/she has the care of the dependent children, (c) he/she cannot find an appropriate steady employment or needs professional training (in this case the right to alimony cannot last for more than three years after the divorce), (d) alimony is necessary for reasons of forbearance towards the other spouse. This last reason, expressed so generally, is intended to cover cases that do not fall within the other three reasons.

In determining the amount of alimony, the court must take into consideration the needs of the claimant spouse, as they appear after the divorce. Payment is made on a monthly basis, but the spouses may agree otherwise, for example for a lump sum. The court may limit or terminate alimony if the duration of the marriage was very short, if the claimant was at fault as far as the divorce is concerned or if he/she willingly caused his/her destitution. Alimony terminates if the spouse to whom it has been awarded remarries, cohabits with someone else in a form of free union or dies. Nevertheless alimony rights accrued at the time of the beneficiary's death may be inherited.

## IV. Parent and Child

### *A. Establishment of Parentage* (arts. 1463–1472)

Child's maternal descent is established by the fact of birth. The husband of the mother is presumed to be the father of all children born during the marriage. A child born less than three hundred days after the dissolution of the marriage is presumed to have been conceived during the marriage. If a child is born later, then he is presumed to be born out of wedlock. However, he may be retrospectively considered as born in marriage if paternity is proved and established by a court decree. If the mother remarries before three hundred days after the dissolution of her previous marriage have lapsed, the second husband is presumed to be the father of the child unless there is proof that the first husband is the father.

A suit for disavowal of paternity may be filed by the husband in the first place, but also by the mother, the child or, if the husband has died, by his parents. It must be proved that the mother of the child and the presumed father did not have sexual intercourse during the time that the child was conceived or that although there was such intercourse the mother could not have conceived from him. The court may order the production of all relevant evidence, including certain scientific methods of proving (or disproving) paternity. If a party to the action refuses to undergo the appropriate medical test, the court must accept the assertions of the other party.

The exercise of the right of disavowal of a child is subject to certain time limits. The action for disavowal is impossible if the child dies or if the husband has previously acknowledged the child. No formalities are required for such acknowledgment. The husband cannot disavow paternity of a child born as the result of artificial inscmination of the mother to which he consented. Last, the action is impossible if the behavior of the husband has persuaded the child that he is his father and thus a suit for disavowal of paternity would cause an irreparable damage to the child's mental health.

### *B. Children Born Out of Wedlock* (arts. 1473–1484)

Social developments and the international legal order made necessary the amendment of the rules concerning illegitimate children. The Constitution of 1975 also pointed in that direction by containing provisions on the respect and protection of the value of a human being, on equality and on the protection of childhood. The basic characteristic of the new provision of family law is the abolition of any discrimination against illegitimate children and their complete assimilation with children born in marriage. The Civil Code no longer uses the term 'illegitimate' for a child born out of wedlock, although it has not replaced the term with one that would be really different and accurate. Such a child has equal rights with a child born in marriage.

Paternity for children born out of wedlock can be established either by voluntary acknowledgment or by a court decree. The acknowledgment may be made before or after the child's birth by the father or, if he is deceased, by his parents through a last will or a declaration executed before a notary. In all cases the consent of the child's mother is a necessary prerequisite. The acknowledgment may be contested by the mother, the child or his descendants, each one of the mother's parents if she was deceased, declared absent or incapable at the time of acknowledgment, or, under special circumstances, the father or the mother of the child's father. The grounds of the contestation are the existence of vices in the will of the person who made the acknowledgment.

The time limit for the contestation is three months since the contesting party learned of the acknowledgment or, in any case, two years after it. If no acknowledgment has taken place, affiliation proceedings may be initiated by the mother (or her legal representative with the permission of the court), by the child or his representative or by the natural father himself or the parents of the natural father. The basic requirement for the success of the action is the evidence beyond doubt of paternity. The law establishes a rebuttable presumption as well, according to which paternity is presumed if it is proved that the child's mother had sexual intercourse with the man considered as the father during the period that the child was conceived. The prescription for such an action varies.

Still the best way of 'legitimation' of a child born out of wedlock is the subsequent marriage of his parents, accompanied by a voluntary acknowledgment or a court decree to that effect. The acknowledgment may take place before or after the marriage.

## V. Adoption (υιοθεσία, yiothesia)

### *A. The Legal Situation*

The law of adoption was originally contained in certain provisions of the Civil Code (arts. 1568–1588). Social developments led to the amendment of the rules concerning the adoption of minors by L.D. 4532/66 which was later replaced by L.D. 610/1970. In 1967 the member states of the Council of Europe concluded an international convention on the adoption of minors. This convention was ratified in Greece by Law 1049/1980. The basic rules contained in this convention prevail over those of the Civil Code or of L.D. 610/1970. Law 1329/1983 amending family law made very few changes to the rules governing adoption.

### *B. Conditions* (arts. 1568–1578, L.D. 610/1970, L. 1049/1980)

Adoption is permitted only if the prospective adoptive parent or parents have no child of their own at the time the adoption proceedings are initiated. As an exception, the court may allow the adoption of a child to a parent having a child of his own if the latter suffers from an incurable disease or for any other important reason.

Adults may be adopted by persons over fifty years of age. The prospective adoptive parent for a minor must be at least thirty years old. The court may allow the adoption to parents younger than thirty years for important reasons, e.g., if they have no hope of having children of their own or if one spouse wishes to adopt the child of the other spouse. In all cases there must be an age difference of at least eighteen years between the adoptive parent and the child. If a spouse wishes to adopt the child of the other spouse, the court may allow the adoption if the age difference is less than eighteen years but not less than fifteen. Adoption of a child by more than one person is prohibited, unless they are spouses. The natural parent may adopt his minor child born out of wedlock. The adoptive parent and the child must both consent to the adoption. The minor's consent is given through his parents.

The basic consideration for adoption is the welfare of the child. The decision of the court must be preceded by an investigation of all circumstances of the prospective adoption conducted by specialized social workers or governmental organizations.

### *C. Effects* (arts. 1579–1588, L.D. 610/1970, L. 1049/1980)

The adopted person is considered for all purposes as the natural child of the adoptive parent or parents. His former kinship relationships are abolished if he is a minor except where the law provides otherwise concerning hereditary rights, relations towards the natural parent who is a spouse of the adoptive parent or support claims against natural relatives if the adoptive parent does not fulfil his own obligation to this effect.

An adoption is terminated by a court decree for very important reasons or *ipso iure* if the adoptive parent and the child marry each other or if the adoptive father acknowledges the child as his own.

## VI. Legal Effects of Parentage

### A. *Name, Domicile, and Nationality of a Child* (arts. 1505–1506, L. 1438/1984 art. 1,2,8,9 I–III)

Parentage, either natural or created by adoption, entails certain continuous effects, namely those concerning the identity of the person and his rights and obligations towards his family.

The child's family name is determined by a common statement of the future spouses before marriage. It may be the family name of either spouse or a combination of both and it must be the same for all children born in the same marriage. In the absence of such statement the child receives the family name of the father. The adopted child receives the name of the adoptive parent. If he is adopted by both spouses then the rules about the name of children born in marriage apply as well. Children born out of wedlock receive the name of the mother. A child legally acknowledged by his natural father may add his name to that of his own, unless the natural parents of such a child, by a common decision, give to the child the family name of either one of them or a combination of both.

The right to choose the first name of the child is exercised by both parents who decide in common. In case of disagreement the name is decided by the court. If only one parent has the parental care of the child, he/she will decide about his first name. Similar rules apply to the determination of the child's domicile. Greek nationality *iure sanguinis* is acquired from either the father or the mother.

### B. *Obligation for Mutual Assistance and Affection* (arts. 1507–1509)

Parents and children have a mutual obligation for assistance, affection, honour and respect. If a child lives with his parents he is obliged to offer them his services. The parents, also, must offer their children the economic support considered as appropriate.

### C. *Support and Maintenance Obligations* (arts. 1485–1504)

The Civil Code devotes a special chapter to support obligations of ascendants and descendants and of brothers and sisters and to the limited support right of the unmarried mother.

Parents are always responsible for their minor child's support and maintenance as long as his income is not sufficient for this purpose. Adult children are bound to support their father and mother and other ascendants who are in need and the relatives in the direct ascending line are likewise bound to support their needy descendants. The degree of support depends on the needs of the person requiring it and on the circumstances of those who are to provide it since their own subsistence must not be endangered. The amount of support must be sufficient to cover the real needs of the person entitled to it, including those of upbringing and education. If the person entitled to support has gravely offended the person bound to pay it and this reason justifies his disinheritance, the support he receives will cover only the absolutely necessary things for subsistence.

Support is usually furnished on a monthly basis and in advance, unless the person entitled to it is a minor. In the latter case, the parents are free to decide how their obligation can be fulfilled. Support obligations cease when either the person bound or the person entitled to it dies. Their prescription is not allowed by the law.

In special cases, brothers (and sisters) may be responsible for their brother's (or sister's) support. The court may order it for special reasons, such as minority, old age, serious disease or infirmity, which have caused the destitution of such persons. A special kind of support obligation of the natural father of a child born out of wedlock towards the child's mother may also be ordered by the court. More specifically, it may be decided that the mother of a child legally acknowledged by his natural father is entitled to the expenses of childbirth and to support for six months (two months before childbirth and four months afterwards) or, in special circumstances, that is if the mother has health problems due to childbirth, for one year after that event.

## VII. Protection of Minors and of Persons Incapable of Administering their Own Estates

### *A. Parental Care and Custody* (arts. 1510–1541; γονική μέριμνα, goniki merimna)

Parental care is the institution that has replaced paternal authority and is one of the novelties of Law 1329/1983 which entrusts the care, custody and protection of minors and of their property to both parents. Thus, the constitutional principle of equality of sexes is observed. The same attitude is adopted by the Italian and Belgian Civil Codes as well as by all socialist legal systems. Parental care is a duty and at the same time a right of the parents, aiming at the child's welfare. It includes the duty of the parents to provide the child with the appropriate environment and means for the development of his personality as well as the right and the duty of the parents to protect the child and the right of custody, discipline and education. Parental care of a child born out of wedlock belongs to the mother unless the natural father has voluntarily acknowledged the child. In the latter case, parental care is exercised by both parents. If the parents disagree on the exercise of parental care, they may turn to the court which will render a judgment only if it appears necessary for the protection of the child's interest.

The administration of the child's property as part of parental care belongs to the parents. They may use the income to cover expenses of supporting and educating the child and of providing him with professional training or other family needs. The parents are the representatives of their minor child in every legal act or litigation with certain exceptions specified by the law. Parental care may become inactive if the parents are unable to exercise it for reasons of illness, absence or interdiction. It may also become inactive if its exercise is removed from one or both parents by the court for reasons such as violation of their obligations, inability to exercise parental care or at their request. The court order may be revoked or changed if the situation changes.

Parental care terminates if the parent dies, is declared absent or loses the right to exercise parental care because he is convicted of a wrongful act concerning the life, health or morals of the child. Naturally it terminates if the child dies, is declared absent, attains majority, or is adopted or interdicted.

### *B. Guardianship of Minors* (arts. 1589–1667; επιτροπεία ανηλίκων, epitropeia anilikon)

The minor is placed under guardianship if no parental care exists. The guardian may also be appointed by the parent who exercises the parental care. The appointment takes place by will or by declaration before a notary or a justice of the peace. Furthermore the court may appoint a guardian if the parents do not or cannot exercise parental care properly. The guardian's tasks are the care of the ward's person, the administration of his property and his legal representation. In every guardianship there is a deputy guardian who is appointed by the court and whose duty is to supervise the exercise of the guardian's tasks and to replace him whenever the interest of the minor is in opposition to the interest of the guardian.

Greek family law also provides for a body called family council which gives its opinion on the organization and good functioning of guardianship and offers its assistance whenever needed. It consists of the justice of the peace and the six closest relatives of the minor from both sides of the family. If the minor is born out of wedlock the family council is replaced by the justice of the peace. There is no special court to deal with matters of guardianship, as there is no family court in general. The appointment of the guardian and deputy guardian and all other matters concerning guardianship are decided by the district court of the ward's domicile.

Article 21 of Law 1329/1983 abolished the institution of emancipation of minors, according to which a minor over eighteen years of age could have been emancipated and enjoyed a limited civil capacity. Majority now is attained at the age of eighteen and thus emancipation has become meaningless.

### *C. Guardianship of Interdicted Persons* (arts. 1686–1700)

Guardianship of interdicted persons as well as judicial administration are only indirectly connected with family law. Traditionally though they are being included in it.

Persons who are unable to take care of themselves and to administer their property because of a permanent state of insanity or of a physical infirmity, especially blindness, deafness or muteness, may be judicially interdicted. Interdiction is pronounced by the court following a petition of any relative, of the spouse, of the guardian or of the public prosecutor. It brings about the legal incapacity of the interdicted person, who is placed under guardianship. Greek law also recognizes legal interdiction. A person is legally interdicted if he is sentenced for felony as soon as the sentence becomes final and for as long as the penalty lasts.

### *D. Curatorship of Absent Persons* (arts. 1701–1704)

Curatorship of absent persons also is not conceptually a matter of family law. But as the same rules apply to it as to the guardianship of minors, it forms part of family law. Thus, if a person is absent, his residence is unknown and his property is in need of administration, the court appoints a curator to administer it.

### *E. Judicial Supervision* (arts. 1705–1709; δικαστική αντίληψη, dikastiki antilipsi)

Judicial supervision is an institution aimed at the protection of the interests of those persons who are not totally incapable of taking care of themselves and administering their property but whose state (mental illness which does not totally preclude reason, physical infirmity, prodigality or profligacy) requires oversight of their actions. Judicial supervision brings about the partial incapacity of the person who cannot proceed to certain actions concerning his property without the consent of his judicial supervisor.

## Selected Bibliography
(in Greek unless otherwise indicated)

J. Deliyannis, *Family Law*, vol. I (1986), vol. II (1987).
J. Deliyannis – C. Kousoulas, *Family Law. The New Regulation of Parentage and of Protection of Incapable Persons* (1984).
A. Gazis, *The New Family Law. The Problems* (1985).
C. Grammenos, *The Law of Maintenance Obligations* (1986).
G. Koumantos, *Lectures on Family Law*, 4th ed. (1985).
G. Koumantos, Greece: Toward Freedom from Discrimination, 25 *J. Fam. L.* 137–151 (1986).
T. Papademetriou, *Marriage and Marital Property under the New Greek Family Law*, 13 *Int'l J. Legal Info.* 1 (1985).

C. D. Spinellis and C. Shachor-Landau, Reflections on the Law of Adoption in Greece and Israel in the Light of the European Convention, *R. Hell. D.I.* 1972 142–193.

I. Spyridakis, *Family Law* (1983).

G. Statheas, *Religious and Civil Marriage* (1982).

P. Zepos, The Historical and Comparative Background of the Greek Civil Code, 3 *Inter-American L. Rev.* 285 (1961).

# Chapter 9
# The Law of Succession

*Anastasia Grammaticaki-Alexiou**

## I. Introduction

The Greek law of succession has its roots in ancient times and several of its basic concepts, such as testate and intestate succession, legacy or the office of the executor of a will are found in the Attic law of inheritance. Later developments followed mainly the destiny of Roman-Byzantine law in Greece (see above, Ch. 1, Section III).

The Civil Code improved the law of succession and modernised it considerably, introducing new institutions and concepts. Undoubtedly, it is the product of a comparative study of the then existing Greek law and other European laws of inheritance.

The law of succession is covered by articles 1710–2035 of Book V of the Civil Code. It is closely, however, interconnected with other branches of civil law and this is manifested by the fact that certain provisions related to succession are found in other books of the Civil Code or in its Introductory Law. The Code of Civil Procedure as well contains a considerable number of rules regulating matters of succession. Finally, Law 1329/1983, which has widely amended family law, has brought to the law of succession a number of changes which became necessary for the preservation of the systematic unity of the codified civil law.

The task of the legislator in formulating the rules on succession is not easy. The continuation of the economic life must not be upset by someone's death and the family must be protected. This calls for the reconciliation of various and frequently opposed interest: those of the deceased, of his family and other relatives, of the state and of the decedent's creditors. These factors, combined with the pandectist influence, made the Greek law of succession highly technical, formal and detailed. Its structure is often quite obscure. Its language, following Latin or German terms and institutions, is sometimes difficult to translate into English. The problems are further compounded by the many fundamental differences between the continental and the Anglo-American law of property and inheritance. The above characteristics of the law of succession tend to make its concise presentation difficult. For reasons of clarity Latin terms are sometimes also used when the English translation does not appear adequate.

*Assistant Professor of Law, University of Thessaloniki.

## II. Succession in General

### A. *Opening of Succession – Acceptance by Heirs* (arts. 1710–1711, 1846, 1901)

The succession 'opens' at the death of the decedent. In other words, the estate assets and liabilities pass to the intestate or testamentary heirs immediately at death. This process takes place automatically, by operation of law alone, before the heir has taken any step to put himself in possession of the estate or has expressed any intention to accept it. There is no distinction between movable and immovable property. The appointment of an administrator or an executor is neither normal nor necessary.

Although the estate devolves upon the heir from that moment, his right remains in suspense until he decides whether to accept or renounce it. The acceptance is the informal, explicit or implicit, declaration of a person that he wishes to be an heir and that, consequently, he waives the right to renounce the succession. If immovables are part of the estate, the declaration of acceptance must be recorded. If there are several heirs, the estate becomes the common property of them all if they all accept it.

### B. *Acceptance under the Benefit of Inventory* (arts. 1902–1912)

The possession of the decedent's estate passes to the heir with all its advantages and its burdens. Therefore, the heir is personally liable for the charges and debts of the succession. The benefit of inventory is the privilege that the heir obtains, by causing an inventory to be made, of being liable only up to the net value of the estate. To enjoy this privilege, the heir must make a statement of acceptance 'under the benefit of inventory' before the clerk of the court of succession, which is the court of the decedent's domicile.

An heir so accepting the succession is usually in doubt about the solvency of the estate. The benefit allows him to be discharged from the debts of the succession by practically relinquishing the estate to the creditors. The inventory must be made within four months after the declaration. The heir is deprived of the benefit if he does not make the inventory in time, if he intentionally makes an incorrect inventory, if he administers the estate fraudulently or if he sells its immovables or securities without the permission of the court. The acceptance of succession by incapable persons or persons of limited capacity is always made under the benefit of inventory. The benefit is lost if they do not draw up the inventory within a year after they become capable.

### C. *Renunciation of Succession* (arts. 1847–1859; αποποίηση κληρονομίας, apopoiisi klironomias)

A succession may be renounced by a declaration of the heir made before the clerk of the court of succession. The power of renunciation lapses four months after the heir learns of the devolution and its reason. This period is extended to one year if the deceased lived abroad or if the heir learned of the devolution while living abroad.

If renunciation takes place, the devolution of the estate upon the disclaiming heir is considered as never having taken place and the estate passes to the person who would have inherited if the renouncing heir were not alive at the time of death. In the case of several heirs, each one may renounce his succession right. The renunciation (like the acceptance) is irrevocable.

### D. *Unworthiness of Heir* (κληρονομική αναξιότητα, klironomiki anaxiotita)

An heir who is judged unworthy is divested of his succession right by court decision. Persons unworthy of inheriting are those who:

(*a*) intentionally killed or attempted to kill the decedent, his children, his parents or his spouse,

(*b*) were convicted for untruly having accused the decedent of a crime,

(*c*) intentionally and illegaly hindered the decedent from making or revoking a will,

(*d*) fraudulently, illegally or against good morals forced the decedent to make or alter his will, or

(*e*) changed or destroyed the decedent's will.

The relevant suit may be instituted against the heir by any person having an interest thereto. As soon as the judgment becomes final, devolution is considered as never having occurred. Unworthiness may not be invoked if the decedent had pardoned the unworthy heir by his will or by a public document.

### E. *Vacant Succession* (arts. 1865–1870)

A succession is deemed vacant if the heirs are unknown or if it is doubtful whether they have accepted the succession. In such cases the court, on petition of any interested person or on its own initiative, appoints an administrator of the vacant succession, who acts as the legal representative of the heirs. He administers the estate, proceeds to the affixing of seals and the making of an inventory of the succession, collects debts, but cannot sell any asset of the estate nor create any other obligations binding it without the permission of the court. If no heir claims the succession for a long period, the court certifies that the state is the only intestate heir.

### F. *Certificate of Inheritance* (arts. 1956–1966; κληρονομητήριο, klironomitirio)

The court of succession may, at the request of an heir, grant a certificate, stating among whom and for which part is the estate to be distributed. This certificate of inheritance creates a rebuttable presumption that the persons named in it have the rights mentioned there. If it is proved to be incorrect, the court will order its withdrawal or annulment. The true heir or the executor of a will can request the person possessing an incorrect certificate of inheritance to return it to the court.

### G. *Action for the Delivery of Possession of Assets of the Estate* (arts. 1871–1883)

An heir may sue a person unlawfully possessing assets of the estate as heir (possessor of the estate), demanding recognition of his succession right and delivery of the estate or of specified assets. So long as the right to sue has not been prescribed, the possessor may not assert the defense of adverse possession. The extent of the possessor's liability in damages depends on whether he is acting in good or in bad faith.

### H. *Methods by Which Successors, Other than Heirs, Are Established*

#### 1. Legacy (arts. 1967–2010; κληροδότημα, klirodotima)

The testator may devise or bequeath specific property to a person without making him his heir. Usually, he obliges the appointed heir (but also the *fideicommissarius* or a legatee in the case of sublegacy) to give the legatee his legacy. Since he is not an heir, the legatee is not liable for the charges and liabilities of the succession. But the testator may require him to assume them and may, also, impose these obligations on an heir or on a third person.

The legacy is null (ademption) if the legatee dies before the testator. It is also null if the testator devised or bequeathed property belonging to someone else.

#### 2. Fideicommissum (arts. 1923–1941; καταπίστευμα, katapisteuma)

By the institution of *fideicommissum*, the testator may designate not only a present heir but also a future one(s) to receive the estate after the present heir dies. The *fideicommissarius* becomes an heir upon receipt of the succession. He is an heir not of the present heir but of the testator himself.

#### 3. Modus (arts. 2011–2016; τρόπος, tropos)

The testator may impose on an heir or legatee an obligation to do or give something without giving the beneficiary the right to demand performance. For example, the testator may require distribution of an amount of money to the poor, publication of a book or taking care of a favorite pet. However, the enforcement of this testamentary burden may be demanded by an heir, the executor of the will and any other person who would be affected directly. If enforcement is in the public interest, it may be demanded by the competent public authority.

4. Gift Mortis Causa (arts. 2032–2035; δωρεά αιτία θανάτου, dorea aitia thanatou)

A gift *mortis causa* is an act, to take effect after the donor's death, by which he donates the whole or some of his property. What differentiates this type of gift from a gift *inter vivos* is that the donee does not receive the donated goods during the donor's life. A gift *mortis causa* must be made by notarial act and is revocable unless the parties have agreed on irrevocability. In the latter case, revocation may be effected only in the manner prescribed for gift *inter vivos*.

5. Agreements of Inheritance (arts. 368)

Greek law declares null all agreements by which the passing of the succession to a person is required or excluded.

## III. Intestate Succession

### *A. Classes of Intestate Heirs* (arts. 1813–1824)

The criteria of parentage, marriage and nationality are essential for the designation of an intestate heir. In other words, the heirs designated by Greek law are persons related to the decedent by parental or marital ties. There are six classes of intestate heirs. The first four are based on the natural order in which the generations succeed one another. Each class (or parentel) includes all persons who descend from a common ancestor. Acknowledgment of a child born out of wedlock, subsequent marriage of his natural parents or adoption create a bond of filiation as well. The fifth class comprises the surviving spouse and in the sixth class the state is the heir.

The first class includes the descendants of the deceased (children, grandchildren, great-grandchildren) without any distinction of sex or primogeniture. The descendants, who may be born in different marriages, inherit in equal portions by line of succession and *per capita* when they are of the same degree of affinity. The descendant of the nearest degree excludes all other descendants of a more remote degree belonging to the same root. A child born out of wedlock is a relative only of his mother and her relatives and succeeds her in the first class. If he is acknowledged by his natural father, he enjoys the rights of a child born in marriage and inherits as a legitimate child of the father. The surviving spouse is grouped with descendants of the first class and his/her portion is one fourth of the estate. He/she also receives an extra portion, consisting of the furniture, houseware, clothing etc., used by him/her or by both spouses. This extra portion is also given to the spouse when he/she takes with the other three classes of heirs.

The second class of heirs includes the decedent's parents, his brothers and sisters, as well as the children and grandchildren of the brothers and sisters who have passed away before the decedent. Brothers and sisters of half blood concurring with brothers and sisters of full blood receive half the portion of the latter. The third class includes the grandparents of the decedent. For those who do not survive, their children and grandchildren take their portion. The fourth class includes the great-grandparents of the decedent, who inherit *per capita* irrespective of line. The surviving spouse, concurring with relatives of the second, third or fourth class, receives one half of the estate plus the extra portion already mentioned.

If no relatives of the four classes exist, the spouse inherits all the estate in the fifth class. In the sixth class the heir is the state of the decedent's nationality.

### B. *Accretion* (arts. 1807–1808, 1823; προσαύξηση, prosauxisi)

The heir may not be in a position to inherit, because either he died before the opening of the succession, he was disinherited, he renounced the succession, he was declared unworthy to succeed or was not born alive if he had been a *nasciturus*. In the first three classes of intestate heirs, his place and portion passes to his descendants (*successio graduum*).

### C. *Collation* (arts. 1895–1900; συνεισφορά, syneisfora)

Collation takes place only between descendants of the decedent. It is the supposed return to the estate which an heir makes of property that he received from the decedent or of expenditures that the decedent made for the heir's education, if they exceeded the amount appropriate to the economic condition of the decedent. But collation cannot take place if the decedent had expressly excluded it when he gave the property or made the expenditure.

Collation is effected by logistically adding the collated property to the estate. Its value then reduces the share of the heir who had received it in advance. If the property received exceeds the heir's share, he is not obliged to return the excess. The other heirs divide the succession among themselves. In this way the law seeks to maintain equality among children and among other descendants.

## IV. Testamentary Succession

### A. *Capacity to Make a Will* (arts. 1716–1717, 1719, 1720, 1723, 1748)

Every person of sound mind may make a will. Those incapable of making wills in general are the minors, the judicially interdicted persons, the persons under judicial supervision for reason of prodigality and the persons who, at the time the will is executed, are not concious of their actions or do not enjoy the use of reason because of a mental illness.

Incapable of making certain kinds of wills are the persons who cannot read and write and, therefore, cannot make a holographic will and the persons who cannot read and for this reason cannot make mystic wills. Also, mute persons cannot make public wills. If they are unable to write as well, they are incapable of making any kind of will.

Monks are incapable of disposing of their property, which passes to the monastery where they live, with the exception of the share of forced heirs.

### *B. Form of Wills*

Greek law provides for two categories of wills, that is ordinary and extraordinary wills. For ordinary wills, the testator may avail himself of one of the three following forms: holographic, public and mystic (secret). Under extraordinary circumstances a person may make his will in a simpler manner. The law establishes three kinds of extraordinary wills: wills made at sea, military wills and wills made during a blockade.

Except where the law provides otherwise, the formalities to which the wills are subject must be always observed at the price of nullity. The testator must make his will in person; the possibility of willing by the intervention of another person, such as an agent or any other representative, does not exist in Greek law. Likewise, joint or mutual wills are not recognized.

### *C. Ordinary Wills*

#### 1. Holographic Wills (arts. 1721–1722)

A holographic will is handwritten by the testator in its entirety and dated and signed by the hand of the testator. Any additions made in the margins or as a postscript by the testator must be also signed by him. Obliterations, erasures or other such defects are noted by the court which publishes the will and may cause its nullity.

#### 2. Public Wills (arts. 1724–1737)

A public will is made before a notary in the presence of three witnesses or of another notary and one witness. This type of will presents certain advantages: it is a form that may be used by persons who cannot read, write or sign, makes impossible the destruction of the will and limits considerably the possibility of nullity due to vagueness. It also has the increased proving force of a public document and it is an enforceable instrument. But a public will has disadvantages as well: it makes the testator's wishes known to other people, it costs more and, notwithstanding the fact that the wishes of the testator may be stated with absolute clarity and with no faults, the non-observance of one of the many formalities required may lead to the eventual nullity of the will.

The testator states his wishes before the witnesses and the notary, who, after having reduced it to writing, reads it aloud to the testator in the presence of the witnesses, making express mention of the fact that all formalities prescribed by the law have been observed. Deaf testators read the statement themselves. The will of deaf testators who cannot read is made in the presence of five witnesses or another notary and three witnesses. An interpreter is employed where the testator does not know Greek.

### 3. Mystic (Secret) Wills (arts. 1738–1747)

The mystic will is an intermediate form between the holographic and the public. The testator is under no obligation to put down his will in his own handwriting; he must only sign it. The instrument, in a sealed envelope, is then handed to the notary in the presence of three witnesses or another notary and one witness. The testator declares that the instrument is his testament. The notary writes on the envelope the name of the testator and the day of presentation. Then the testator as well as the witnesses sign. If the testator declares that he is unable to sign, a mention of it must be made. The notary then draws an act containing the date and place, the names of the testator, of the notary and of the witnesses and the fact that all formalities prescribed by law have been observed. This act is read aloud to the testator and the witnesses and is also signed by them.

A basic disadvantage of the mystic will is that it may be declared null if a formality is omitted. It may also be drafted in a vague and unclear manner that will raise problems of interpretation. However, its advantages over the other forms of wills are considerable, since the dispositions of the testator remain secret for everybody and are secured by the notary. A will which is not valid as a mystic will may be valid as a holographic will if it satisfies the basic requirements of the latter.

## *D. Extraordinary Wills*

### 1. Testaments Made at Sea (arts. 1749–1752, 1756)

The testament made at sea is a remnant of old times when the duration of voyages by sailboats was very long. A person on a ship flying the Greek flag may, during the voyage, make his will by an oral declaration before the captain or his deputy. Aboard warships the declaration is made before the head of the economic service and, in his absence, before the captain or his deputy. Dispositions in favor of crew members who are not relatives of the testator are null. This latter rule, quite strangely, applies also to holographic wills made during a voyage at sea.

2. Military Testaments (arts. 1753–1755)

A military testament may be made by military personnel during a military expedition, a blockade, a siege or imprisonment or on a warship participating in an expedition. The testament is made orally before an officer in the presence of another officer or two witnesses. The will must be reduced to writing, read to the testator, signed by him and by the receiving person and the witnesses.

3. Testaments During Blockade (arts. 1757–1762)

Similar to the formalities required for a testament at sea are those for a testament made during a blockade before a notary, a justice of the peace, a mayor, a parish chairman, a police officer, or a hospital director.

All types of extraordinary wills become invalid if three months have lapsed since the special circumstances that justified their making ceased to exist and the testator is still alive.

*E. Contents of Testamentary Dispositions* (arts. 1781–1812)

The usual dispositions contained in a will are those by which the testator's heirs or legatees are established. However, quite often complicated or ambiguous ways of expression make it difficult to establish with certainty who are the testamentary heirs and in what shares. To correct this, the law introduces a number of interpretative rules. For example, if the shares left to the heirs do not exhaust the estate, its remaining part is subject to intestate succession. If such shares exceed the disposable estate, they are proportionately reduced.

The testator may leave to an heir part or all of his estate, may set up legacies or *fideicommissa*, attach burdens, conditions and time limits, appoint substitutes, acknowledge his natural child, revoke his previous will, determine the way of distribution of his estate, appoint an executor, etc. Conditions which are impossible, incomprehensible, illegal or immoral are reputed not written.

*F. Validity of Wills* (arts. 138, 1718, 1781–1788, 1796)

It is very important for the testamentary disposition to correspond to the real wishes of the testator. A will made fictitiously, that is with no testamentary intent, is null. A disposition of a will is annulable if the testator was in error concerning the identity of the person he wished to designate or the thing he intended to give. Annulable also is a disposition due to erroneous causes mentioned in the will, without which the testator would not have made such a disposition. A disposition in favor of the spouse, in case of doubt, may be annulable if the marriage is null or was dissolved while the testator was still alive or if he had validly filed a divorce petition.

The whole will is annulable if the testator has omitted a forced heir whose existence was not known to him at the time of his death or who was born or became an heir after the making of the will. Annulment is barred if there is evidence that the testator would have proceeded to the making of his will even if he knew the actual situation. A disposition is annulable if it is the result of threat or fraud. The whole will or a particular disposition is null if it does not conform to the law or public morals.

To summarize, a will is null from the beginning if:

(*a*) the formalities prescribed by the law were not observed,

(*b*) it was made by an incapable person, or

(*c*) there are vices in its contents.

A will becomes wholly or partially invalid if:

(*a*) it was revoked,

(*b*) it was annulable and has been annulled by the court,

(*c*) the establishment of an heir was frustrated, as when he renounces the succession, or

(*d*) three months have lapsed since the special circumstances, justifying the making of an extraordinary will, ceased to exist.

The invalidation may be sought by anyone who directly benefits from it. But if a forced heir has been omitted by the testator it is only he who may request invalidation.

### G. *Substitution of Testamentary Heir* (arts. 1809–1812)

Substitution of an heir takes place if the testator indicated a substitute in case the original heir lost his right of inheritance before or after the estate vests in him. The testator may even indicate a substitute for the substitute. This is called 'common' substitution, distinguished from the different institution of *substitutio fideicommissaria* or specific *fideicommissum*, which applies to legacies and denotes the disposition according to which an asset given to a legatee passes after a certain time or event to another person. The latter disposition is null unless it is for the public benefit or in favor of close relatives of the testator.

### H. *Revocation of Wills* (arts. 1763–1768)

Wills are freely revocable by the testator until his decease. The same capacity for making a will is also necessary for its revocation. Exceptionally, a prodigal under judicial supervision, who is incapable of making a will, may revoke his previous will but may not revoke the revocation.

The revocation must be clothed with the formalities prescribed by the law. There are general forms, appropriate to all wills (by making a subsequent will or by a notarial act), and special ones, appropriate to holographic wills (intentional destruction or crossing out of the instrument) and mystic ones (recovery of instrument from the notary). The revocation of the revocation of a will is always possible in one of the general forms of revocation.

The Civil Code does not contain any provision concerning the destruction or loss of a will due to the action of a third person or an unforeseen event. Both doctrine and the cases agree that such a destruction or loss does not necessarily result to the legal inexistence of the will. The person claiming rights under it may allege and prove that the will had been validly executed, what the content of its dispositions was and that it was destroyed or lost by accident.

### *I. Publication of Wills* (arts. 1769–1780)

The term 'publication' of a will denotes the announcement of its contents by the competent court in a manner similar to probate. The notary in possession of a public or mystic will and any person possessing a holographic will must present it to the court as soon as the decease of the testator becomes known. The will must be accompanied by the death certificate.

For public or mystic wills, the competent court is the one-member district court of the place where the notary performs his duties. A holographic will may be presented to any district court of the country and to any Greek consular authority abroad. Wills made, deposited or published abroad may be published in Greece as well. The person petitioning for the publication of a holographic will may also request the court to declare it authentic. This declaration serves as a rebuttable presumption of its authenticity, as long as it has not been contested within five years following the decision.

### *J. The Executor of the Will* (arts. 2017–2031)

The faithful execution of the dispositions contained in a will may be confided by the testator to one or more testamentary executors who must enjoy full legal capacity. The executor must unconditionally accept his appointment before he can assume his duties. The executor has the right to take actions allowed by the testator or necessary for the execution of the testamentary dispositions. He may also administer the whole or part of the estate and his authority is a limit to the rights of the heirs or legatees or other beneficiaries. However, he may not do certain things such as the sale of immovables or of securities, settlements etc., without permission of the court. The executor's liability for damages caused by his fault is governed by the provisions on mandate. If more than one executors are appointed, they act in common. In case of disagreement, the majority decides. If the administration of the estate is included in the executor's duties, then he may sue and may be sued for claims related to it.

The executor's office terminates if he dies, becomes incapable or resigns. It also terminates if the testamentary heir presents adequate guarantee that he will execute the testamentary dispositions for which the executor was appointed. The court may remove the executor from his office if he violates his duties or is unable to administer the estate.

## V. Forced Heirship (νόμιμη μοίρα, nomimi moira)

### *A. Forced Heirs* (arts. 1825–1826)

The rules on forced heirship protect the family and, more specifically, the closest relatives of the decedent, who is not allowed to leave them out. The forced heirs are always entitled to a certain percentage of the estate and they have all the rights and duties of other heirs. Forced heirs in general are the descendants, the parents and the surviving spouse of the decedent. If there are descendants and/or a surviving spouse the parents are excluded.

### *B. The Legitimate Portion and Its Protection* (arts. 1825–1838)

Forced heirs are entitled to one-half of their intestate share. To determine it, one must include in the estate the shares of disinherited heirs, of those who renounced the succession and of unworthy heirs. Therefore, the legitimate portion does not increase if a coheir has lost his succession right. The forced heir's right may be inherited.

Any testamentary dispositions to the prejudice of the forced heir or any restrictions imposed on his share by the will are null. If other heirs refuse to give the forced heir assets of the estate corresponding to his share, he has the right to institute an action, demanding restitution. Donations of the testator during his lifetime to the detriment of the estate and, consequently, to the legitimate portion, are cancelled if the estate at death does not suffice to cover such share.

## VI. Disinherison (arts. 1839–1849; αποκλήρωση, apoklirosi)

The testator has the general right to exclude from succession any person other than the forced heirs. This is a general form of disinherison which does not require any form or justification. Disinherison in its narrow sense takes place when a forced heir is deprived of his share by the testator for a just cause.

The testator may deprive a descendant of his share if:

(*a*) he attempted to take the life of the testator, his spouse or another descendant of his,

(*b*) he wilfully caused bodily injuries to the testator or his other parent,

(*c*) he was convicted of a crime or a serious intentional misdemeanor against the testator or his spouse,

(*d*) he maliciously neglected his obligation to sustain the testator or

(*e*) he leads an immoral or infamous life against the will of the testator.

The testator may disinherit his parent for one of the (*a*), (*c*) and (*d*) reasons. The disinherison of the spouse is allowed if the testator at the time of death had the right to apply for divorce on a ground due to fault. The reason for disinherison must exist at the time the will is made and must be mentioned in it. In addition to the above-mentioned causes of disinherison, the testator may disinherit a forced heir for his own benefit if he leads a prodigal life or is indebted. This is applicable only in the case of a parent disinheriting his descendant and it is accomplished by bequeathing the forced share to the forced heir's descendants or by designating an executor or by both means. In this case, the testator must also provide for the sustenance of the disinherited heir.

## VII. Relations of the Heir with the Succession Creditors, His Coheirs and Third Persons

### *A. Judicial Liquidation of Succession* (arts. 1913–1922)

The creditors of an estate may request from the court its judicial liquidation. The decision appoints a liquidator who is charged with the administration of the estate. Within one month after the decision is served upon him, he invites the creditors of the decedent to present their claims. He also makes an inventory of the estate, ascertains the claims, collects the debts and sells the movables and immovables of the estate.

When the assets of the estate are sufficient to satisfy all claims, the liquidator pays the creditors. If not, the liquidator requests a court order for the proportionate payment of all creditors who have presented their claims. The creditors of the heir(s) are not entitled to participate in the liquidation and its proceeds.

### *B. Community Among Heirs* (arts. 1884–1894)

Where there are several heirs, the estate constitutes, until partition, their common property and they must deal with it jointly. They are also jointly and severably liable for the debts of the estate in proportion to each portion. An heir may sell his share. But if a particular asset of the estate is to be transferred, all coheirs/co–owners must act in common. However, decisions concerning the administration of the estate are taken by a majority-of-shares rule.

Any heir may demand the partition of the estate at any time. Partition is voluntary, when it is made among all the coheirs by their mutual consent, or judicial, when it is made under the authority of the court. The latter may decide partition in kind if it is feasible. It this is impossible or inconvenient then the court orders the sale of the property in public auction. The testator may prohibit partition for a period not exceeding ten years. He may regulate by his will the mode of partition or leave it to the judgment of a third person. He may also allocate a specific asset to a particular heir.

Partition must be distinguished from the distribution of property to the descendants which the ascendant makes during his life-time. The distribution is effected by a contract and includes property existing at the time the contract is made. The ascendant is not bound by such a distribution when he makes his last will, neither may the distribution prejudice the forced heirs.

*C. Sale of the Estate* (arts. 1942–1955)

The heir may sell the estate including its assets and liabilities or his shares. The buyer does not become an heir but he acquires all that the heir would acquire. The sale is effected by notarial deed. The seller is not liable for any real or legal defects of the estate. The buyer is liable towards the creditors of the estate together with the seller, unless the latter has made use of the benefit of inventory.

## Basic Bibliography
(in Greek unless otherwise indicated)

G. Balis, *Law of Succession*, 5th ed. (1965).
Ph. Drakidis, Incidences de la caducité de la réserve de l'un des conjoints sur la succession testamentaire de l'autre, 19 *R. Hell. D.I.* 60–69 (1966).
P. Filios, *Law of Succession. Special Part* (1988).
P. Ladas, *The Reform of Succession Relations Within the Reform of Family Law* (1984).
A. Ligeropoulos, *Law of Succession*, vol. I, 2d ed. (1957), vol. II (1958).
A. Papachristou, *Law of Succession* (1983).
N. Papantoniou, *Law of Succession*, 4th ed. (1985).
I. Spyridakis, *A Manual on Civil Law. The Law of Succession* (1980).
K. Stefanopoulos, *Elements of the Law of Succession*, vol. I (1976), vol. II (1977).
A. Toussis, *The Law of Succession* (1969).
P. Tsilas, *A Survey of the Greek Law of Inheritance*, Library of Congress Publications, Law Library (1979) (in English).
E. Vouzicas, *The Law of Succession*, vol. I (1972), vol. II (1976), vol. III (1983).

# Chapter 10
# Commercial Law

*Nicholas A. Deloukas**

## I. Introductory Remarks and General Provisions

Upon obtaining its independence from Turkish occupation, the modern Greek State adopted in 1828, by ordinance of its first Governor Ioannis Capodistrias, the Napoleonic Code of Commerce of France of 1807 to regulate commercial relations. Since then such Code underwent many amendments so that actually only a few articles of Book I still remain in force.

In accordance with article 1, 'merchants (έμποροι, emporoi) are those who professionally are engaged in commercial activities'. Such commercial activities are enumerated in a merely indicative way in articles 2 and 3 of a separate enactment, the decree 'On the Jurisdiction of the Commercial Courts' of 1835, which in fact is a reproduction of Book IV of the Napoleonic Code of Commerce. The commercial activities enumerated in article 2 of such decree are the following: purchase for resale or leasing; businesses of manufacture, commissions, transport of goods or persons by land or internal waters; agency, supplies, sales by auction and show businesses; money exchange, banking and broker activities; liabilities assumed on bills of exchange and promissory notes. The commercial activities enumerated in article 3 are: purchase or sale of sea-going vessels; charters; carriage of goods and passengers by sea; marine insurance and generally all operations pertaining to the shipping business. Some other activities such as stock exchange and warehouse operations, as well as liabilities arising from checks, were declared to be commercial activities by subsequent statutes.

Commercial operations are governed in Greece by the special commercial legislation which is distinct from the civil legislation. The main characteristics of the provisions of commercial law, compared with those of civil law, are: a certain degree of informality (except for bills of exchange, promissory notes and checks which are rigidly formal), and proof by witnesses at the discretion of the court without regard to the amount of the claim (see below, Ch. 15, Section VII D in f.). Also, in view of the fact that commercial transactions are considered to be financially risky, the legal capacity to enter into such transactions is restricted. Minors, that is persons who have not completed eighteen years of

*Professor of Law, Emeritus, Athens University.

age, are not allowed to engage in commercial operations (art. 2) and all obligations assumed by a minor in connection with such a commercial operation are null and void.

Since the enactment of the Commercial Code in Greece in 1828, several attempts were made to revise it which, however, remained uncompleted. In 1981, the draft of a new commercial code was submitted to the Minister of Justice. Such draft underwent a new elaboration, especially by being transcribed in the demotic language, but it has not as yet been enacted by Parliament.

## II. Bankruptcy Law (πτώχευση, ptocheusi)

In Greece, as in other countries whose commercial legislation was influenced by the French Commercial Code, bankruptcy law is considered to be part of commercial law. Bankruptcy is governed by the act of 12 December 1878, which replaced Book III of the Commercial Code and was amended by a Law of 22 February 1910 and by N.L. 635/1937. The three-member district court may declare bankrupt those merchants who have stopped their payments or have declared to the clerk that they suspend their payments (art. 525). Bankruptcy may be pronounced also against a deceased merchant within one year from his death if he had stopped his payments when alive. Partnerships may also be declared bankrupt if they were engaged in commercial operations and also limited partnerships and joint-stock companies which have stopped their payments or announced suspension of payments (art. 526). The bankrupt is deprived of the management and administration of his entire estate, but assets acquired by him after he was pronounced bankrupt are exempted from the bankruptcy proceedings and remain his exclusive and free property. One or more administrators (σύνδικοι, syndikoi) are appointed by the court after consulting with the general meeting of the creditors, in order to manage and administer the estate for the purpose of its being liquidated and distributed to the creditors in proportion to the size of their claims. A judge rapporteur is appointed by the court with whom the administrators must consult in all matters pertaining to the bankruptcy. Lawsuits concerning the estate of the bankrupt have to be addressed against the administrator (art. 534). All claims against the bankrupt become due as from the date of the decision pronouncing the bankruptcy (art. 535) and all interest ceases accruing except for the claims secured by a mortgage or a lien (art. 536). However, such secured mortgagees or lienors may not foreclose on the mortgaged real properties before the secured claims mature (art. 655).

The court fixes also the retroactive date, within a year, on which the payments of the bankrupt have stopped, from which date on and within ten days prior to it, all gratuitous transfers of assets are null and void (art. 537). Payments of matured debts as well as any other act for value of the bankrupt which took place within such retroactive period of time may be rescinded if the payees or those who contracted with the bankrupt acted with knowledge of the stoppage of payments (art. 538).

In order for the creditors to participate in the bankruptcy proceedings and to the distribution of the proceeds of liquidation, they must file their claims with the clerk of the court and produce also the documents and the data evidencing their claims within twenty days from an invitation which is published in the daily press and is communicated in writing to them. Such period of time is extended for those residing outside the court's location. The claims so filed are reviewed by the judge rapporteur and the administrators in the presence of the creditors concerned and, eventually, the bankrupt himself and such other creditors whose claims have been reviewed and accepted. All these persons may raise objections. The creditors whose claims are reviewed must also make an oath that their claims are true and honest for the amount accepted. Creditors residing abroad may be absolved from such oath by the judge rapporteur in consultation with the administrators. After the acceptance of their claims, the creditors may participate in the general meetings of creditors (arts. 582–596). Creditors who are secured by a mortgage or a lien are satisfied by preference and participate in the general meetings only for the unsatisfied portion of their claims (art. 648).

Within three days from the expiration of the time fixed for swearing, those who have been duly sworn in are invited to a meeting in order to deliberate on a possible compromise with the bankrupt. The compromise is validly reached if accepted: (a) by a majority of creditors representing three quarters of the aggregate amount of the claims if the sum offered by the bankrupt is at least equal to 60% of the claims, or representing four fifths of the claims if the amount offered by the bankrupt is less than 60% but in excess of 25%, (b) by a majority of two thirds of the amount of the claims if the offered amount is less than 25%, and (c) by a majority of the creditors representing three quarters of the amount of the claims in case of a compromise by means of which the entire estate of the bankrupt is abandoned to the creditors (art. 600). The compromise has to be confirmed by the court (art. 607) and is binding also upon the dissenting creditors (art. 610); it can be rescinded if the bankrupt fails to perform his obligations under it and is *ipso iure* invalidated if the bankrupt is thereafter convicted for fraudulent bankruptcy (arts. 615–616). If no compromise is reached, then the creditors are considered to be *ipso facto* acting jointly (status of junction: ένωση πιστωτών, enosi pistoton) and decide in general meetings convened by the judge rapporteur on all basic matters concerning the bankruptcy (arts. 625–635).

If the bankruptcy proceedings can not continue because of lack of assets, the court may, at the suggestion of the judge rapporteur, after consultation with the administrators, pronounce the bankruptcy proceedings to be terminated. In such a case the creditors resume their rights against the person and the estate of the bankrupt. The bankrupt and any other interested party may request revocation of the pertinent court decision by proving that there exist sufficient assets for continuing the proceedings or by advancing to the administators the necessary sums (arts. 637–638).

All property of the bankrupt is auctioned by the administrator, if it has not been earlier auctioned by the mortgagees and lienors, and the proceeds are distributed among the creditors in proportion to their claims, but mortgagees and lienors are satisfied by preference for the entirety of their claims (arts. 660–667). Negotiable instruments which were sent to the bankrupt for collection and goods which were sent to be sold by him on consignment may be revindicated by the sender under certain conditions (arts. 668–673). Fraudulent bankruptcy constitutes a criminal offense and is prosecuted *ex officio*. The administrators have to deliver to the public prosecutor all documents and data requested (arts. 694–695).

The lifting of the stigma of bankruptcy by the court is effected either: (a) by full satisfaction of all creditors as to principal and interest accrued up to the pronouncement of bankruptcy, (b) by compromise with the creditors, or (c) by the lapse of ten years from the date of pronouncement of the bankruptcy (art. 14 N.L. 635/1937).

A new bankruptcy code is presently under preparation to modernize the existing provisions and to bring them in line with the appropriate harmonization endeavors within the European Economic Community.

## III. Commercial Papers (αξιόγραφα, axiographa)

The various categories of commercial papers are enumerated in articles 68 and 76 of a L.D. of July 17, 1923 'On Special Provisions on Companies Limited by Shares'. Under article 68 of such L.D., the only commercial papers which may be issued to the bearer are shares and debentures of companies limited by shares and their dividend and interest coupons. By virtue of article 5 of Law 5960/1933, checks also may be issued to the bearer.

Under article 76 of the L.D. of July 17, 1923, the commercial papers which may be issued to order are: (a) money orders drawn by a merchant on a merchant, (b) IOU's issued by merchants for money, negotiable instruments and other fungible things, (c) bills of exchange, promissory notes and checks, (d) warehouse receipts, (e) bills of lading, (f) bottomry bonds, and (g) insurance policies. In this part, we will concentrate on: (a) bills of exchange, (b) promissory notes, (c) checks, (d) commercial money orders, (e) commercial IOU's, and (f) warehouse receipts.

### *A. Bills of Exchange and Promissory Notes* (συναλλαγματικές, γραμμάτια εις διαταγή, synallagmatikes, grammatia eis diatagi)

They are governed by Law 5325/1932, by means of which the related Geneva Conventions of June 7, 1930, including the one on choice of law, were ratified.

#### 1. Bills of exchange

A bill of exchange is an assignment in writing by virtue of which the issuer (or drawer) orders another (the drawee or the payor) to pay a sum certain of money at a certain time in a certain place to a certain person (the payee) or to his order.

Such an instrument must contain (art. 1): (a) the denomination 'bill of exchange' in the same language, (b) the simple and unconditional order to pay a sum certain of money, (c) the name of the drawer, (d) the maturity day, (e) the place where the payment is to be effected, (f) the name of the person to whom or to whose order the payment must be effected (this is why the bill may not be issued to the bearer; however, it can be endorsed to the bearer: art. 12 III), (g) the date and place of issuance, and (h) the signature of the drawer. If any of the above indications is lacking, the title is not valid as a bill of exchange. By means of conversion, however, it might be considered valid as a promise, or as an acknowledgment of an obligation to pay. By way of exception to the invalidity: (a) if the indication of maturity is lacking, then the bill is deemed payable on sight, (b) if the indication of the place of payment is lacking, then the bill is deemed payable at the place indicated near the name of the payor and also this is deemed to be the place of residence of the payor, (c) if the place of issuance is lacking, it is deemed to be the place indicated near the name of the drawer (art. 2), (d) if the sum payable is written both in letters and in figures and there is a discrepancy, then the writing in letters prevails, and (e) if the sum was written more than once differently in figures, the bill is valid for the smaller amount; the same applies if the sum is written more than once in letters (art. 6). The bill may be issued to the order of the drawer and it may be drawn also on the drawer himself (art. 3). In case the bill bears signatures of persons incapable to be obligated by it or bears false signatures or those of inexistent persons or which, for any other reason, may not obligate the signatories, then the obligations of the other signatories remain valid (art. 7). Whoever signs a bill as a representative of another without authorization obligates himself (art. 8). The drawer is liable both for the acceptance of the bill and for its payment; he may exonerate himself from liability for the acceptance, but not for payment (art. 9). A bill on which an indication was left incomplete with the express or implied intention of the parties to be completed later, becomes retroactively (as from its issuance) validated as soon as it is completed in conformity with such intention. On the other hand, if the lacking indication was completed in violation of the intention of the parties, then the irregularity of such completion may be opposed to the holder only in case the holder acquired the bill in bad faith or by gross negligence (art. 10).

Every bill, even if it was not issued to order, may be transferred by endorsement; but if the drawer had added the words 'not to order' or any other equivalent indication, then the incorporated claim is transferred subject to all defenses the payor had against the transferor (art. 11). The endorser is liable both for acceptance and payment, but he can exonerate himself from both liabilities. If he prohibits a further endorsement, he is not liable to subsequent endorsees (art. 15). The holder of a bill is deemed to be its lawful bearer (a holder in due course) if he bases his right on an uninterrupted chain of endorsements, even if intermediate endorsements or the last one are in blank. The chain is deemed to be uninterrupted if each endorser appears as the endorsee in the preceding endorsement.

If he bases his right on an uninterrupted chain of endorsements, the holder of a bill may not be deprived of the document, even if it had been lost by the real owner, except if such holder had acquired it in bad faith or by gross negligence (art. 16). Those sued under a bill may not oppose against the holder in due course defenses based on their personal relations with the drawer or with the preceding holders, except if the holder in acquiring the bill had acted knowingly to the detriment of the obligor (art. 17). Where the endorsement includes the words 'value for cover', 'for collection', 'as attorney in fact', or any other indication meaning a mere assignment, the bearer may exercise all rights deriving from it, but any endorsement made by him is considered to be valid merely as an endorsement for collection. In such a case, against the holder can be opposed only such defenses as could have been opposed against his endorser. The assignment included in the endorsement for collection is not repealed in case of death or of subsequent contractual incapacitation of the endorser (art. 18). Where the endorsement includes the words 'value for security' or 'value for pledge' or any other indication of pawning, the holder may exercise all rights deriving from it, but any endorsement made by him is valid again only as an endorsement 'for collection'. Defenses based on the personal relations of the obligated persons to the endorser may not be opposed against the holder, except if the holder upon receiving the bill acted knowingly to the detriment of the obligor (art. 19). An endorsement made after the maturity has the same effects as one preceding it; but if an endorsement was made after protest or after expiration of the term for protest, then it has the effects of a mere cession. An endorsement which is not dated is *prima facie* deemed to have been made before the lapse of the term for protest (art. 20).

In principle, the holder of a bill is free to present it or not to the drawee for acceptance up to its maturity (art. 21). However, the drawer may stipulate in the bill that it may not be presented at all for acceptance (except where the bill is maturing at a fixed term after sight), or that it has mandatorily to be presented for acceptance prior to or after a certain time. Also, any endorser may stipulate that the bill has to be presented for acceptance, by fixing or not a certain time for such presentation, except if the drawer had marked it 'not to be presented for acceptance' (art. 22). The acceptance must be unconditional, but the drawer may restrict the acceptability to a part only of the sum for which the bill was issued. Any other modification of the contents of the bill by the acceptor is assimilated to a refusal of acceptance; provided, however, that the drawee is obligated anyhow in accordance with the terms of his acceptance, even if these modify the terms of the bill (art. 26). The acceptance obligates the drawee to pay the bill at maturity. If payment is not made, the bearer, even if he is the drawer, has against the acceptor a direct action for the amount of the bill increased by costs and interests as of maturity (art. 28).

The payment of a bill may be guaranteed in favor of one or more or of all the signatories, for the entire amount or part thereof, by a third party or by a person who has already signed it; the guaranty must be written on the instrument and be signed by the guarantor; the guarantor's responsibility is the same as that of the persons in favor of whom the guaranty was given (arts. 30–32).

The bill may be issued maturing at sight, at a certain term after sight, at a certain term from the day of issue, or at a certain date. If maturity is fixed in another way, or is fixed in successive partial maturities, then the bill is null and void (arts. 33–37). The holder has to present the bill for payment at the day of maturity or at one of the next two working days on penalty of losing his rights of recourse against all other parties except the drawee (arts. 38 and 53). The drawee, by paying the holder on maturity, is freed except if, in doing so, he was acting in fraud or with gross negligence; he is bound to check the continuity of the endorsements, but not the validity of the signatures of the endorsers (art. 40). If payment is not made at maturity, the holder in due course has recourse against the endorsers, the drawer and the other signatories. He has recourse even before maturity: (a) if the drawee refused acceptance in whole or in part, (b) if the drawee became bankrupt or insolvent, and (c) in case of bankruptcy of the drawer of a bill which was marked 'not to be accepted'.

In order to acquire a right of recourse against all signatories except against the acceptor, the holder has to make a protest before a notary (διαμαρτυρικό, diamartyriko). He is also bound to give a notice of dishonor to his own endorser and to the drawer, but this is not on penalty of losing his rights to recourse. The drawer, the endorsers and the guarantors may, by a clause written on the bill, exempt the holder from making a protest. Such exemption clause, if written by the drawer, has effect against all signatories; if written by an endorser or a guarantor, it has effect only against such endorser or guarantor. The recourse can be exercised by one single lawsuit against all signatories or by separate lawsuits against one or more signatories without obligation to observe a certain priority. Any endorser or guarantor who paid the bill in a recourse against him may exercise a further recourse of his own against the persons (drawer, endorsers, guarantors) who preceded him in signing the bill (arts. 43–54). In case of alteration of the bill, the signatories prior to the alteration are liable in accordance with the initial text; the signatories after the alteration are liable in accordance with the altered text (art. 69).

Claims against the acceptor and his guarantor are barred three years after maturity. Claims against the drawer, the endorsers and their guarantors are barred one year from the date the protest was made and, if there was no obligation to make a protest, one year from maturity. The claims of the endorsers who have paid the bill against the preceding endorsers, their guarantors and the drawer, are barred six months from the time they paid it or they were sued to pay (art. 70). Law 5325/1932 contains also provisions on intervention for payment and for acceptance of a bill (arts. 55–63), as well as on a plurality of originals and copies of a bill (arts. 64–68), but these provisions are obsolete and have no application in the everyday practice.

### 2. Promissory Notes

A promissory note (P/N) differs from a bill in that there is no drawee, so that the main obligor (payor) is the issuer himself; therefore a P/N must contain the same indications as a bill, except for the indication of the payee (art. 75). In accordance with article 77, on promissory notes are applicable the same provisions which apply to the bills, provided they are not inconsistent with the nature of a P/N. Such necessary adaptations include the following: (a) inasmuch as there is no drawee in a P/N, the issuer has the same responsibility as the acceptor of a bill (art. 78 I); (b) in case of a P/N maturing at a certain term after sight, the instrument has to be presented to the issuer to be visaed by him (in lieu of acceptance); (c) inasmuch as there is no acceptor, the provisions on acceptance by intervention (arts. 56–58) and on recourse for refusal of acceptance (art. 43) have no application on promissory notes; (d) if the indication of the place of payment is lacking, the P/N is payable at the place of its issue (art. 76 III); (e) inasmuch as the responsibility of the issuer of a P/N is identical to that of an acceptor of a bill, claims against the issuer are barred three years after maturity.

### *B. Checks* (τραπεζική επιταγή, trapeziki epitagi)

Checks are governed in Greece by Law 5960/1933 which is the Greek version of the Uniform Law on Checks of the Geneva Conventions of the year 1931. The check is, like the bill, an assignment in writing by the drawer and the main differences from a bill are the following: (a) the drawee is always a banker, although a check issued abroad and drawn not on a banker is valid in Greece, (b) while the bill may be drawn always on the drawer himself, the check may be drawn on the drawer only if drawn on a branch office of the same, but in such instance it may not be issued to the bearer, (c) the check can not be accepted by the drawee and any such acceptance is deemed not to have been written (art. 4), (d) the check may be issued to the bearer (art. 5) and (e) the check matures always at sight; any other indication of maturity is deemed not to be written (art. 28 I). The check, if payable in the same country where it was issued, must be presented for payment within eight days from the date of issuance; if payable in another country on the same continent, it has to be presented within twenty days, otherwise within seventy days; checks issued in Europe and payable in a country situated around the Mediterranean, or vice versa, are considered to be payable in the same continent (art. 29).

Revocation of a check is valid only after the lapse of the term for presentation; in lack of a revocation, the payor may pay after the lapse of the time for presentation (art. 32). The check is not invalidated by the death or the incapacitation of the drawer after its issuance (art. 33). Crossed checks can be paid by the payor only to a banker or to a client of the payor; if the crossing is for a specific banker the check can be paid only to that banker or to his client. A banker can acquire a crossed check only by a client of his or by another banker. A check can bear only two special crossings, one of which must be for collection through a clearing house. The banker or other payor not complying with the above provisions is liable to damages up to the amount of the check (art. 39). The drawer, as well as the bearer of a check, may prohibit its payment in cash by writing on the check the indication 'payable in account' (πληρωτέα εις λογαριασμόν, plirotea eis logariasmon) or a similar indication; in such a case the amount of the check has to be credited, deposited in an account, or set off. The recourse claims of the bearer against the endorsers, the issuer and the other liable parties are barred six months after the lapse of the time for presentation of the check for payment. The claims of those who have paid the check after a recourse against them, or against the other signatories who are liable to them, are barred six months from the time they paid it or they were sued (art. 52). All other provisions of the Law 5960/1933 are but a repetition of the corresponding provisions on bills of exchange.

### C. *Commercial Money Orders* (εμπορικές εντολές πληρωμής, emporikes entoles pliromis)

Such money orders may be in the first place *letters of credit* (πιστωτική επιστολή, pistotiki epistoli), which are letters issued by a bank addressed to its 'correspondent' agent (usually also a bank) asking him to pay to the holder or at his order up to a certain amount of money, once or in installments. Letters of credit are normally issued to persons travelling to other countries for business or for pleasure. In Greece, however, this method of financing travellers is not in common practice; it is replaced by traveller's checks or common checks. This is why letters of credit are not regulated by statute in Greece; traveller's checks are, however, regulated in the pending draft of a new commercial code. An overall regulation of commercial money orders is equally lacking in Greek law, except for some very few provisions of articles 77–79 of the L.D. of July 17, 1923. Such provisions are as follows: an instrument issued to order is transferred by endorsement (art. 77); the debtor may oppose to the legitimated holder of the instrument only defenses which regard the validity of his own statement contained in the instrument, which are apparent from the contents of the instrument, or which pertain to him directly against the holder (art. 78). The debtor is bound to satisfy the claim only after he receives delivery of the instrument duly acquitted (art. 79).

Because of lack of sufficient specific provisions on such commercial papers, analogy leads to the application of articles 876–887 of the Civil Code relating to 'delegation' of claims (έκταξη, ektaxi). A 'delegation' consists in a document which is handed by the issuer (the assignor = εκτάσσων, ektasson) to the beneficiary (consignee = λήπτης, liptis), by virtue of which the latter is authorized to collect from an assigned debtor (the drawee: εκτασσόμενος, ektassomenos) an amount of money or other fungible things and the assigned debtor is authorized to effect such payment to the consignee for the account of the assignor (art. 876). If the assigned debtor accepts the delegation by a written acknowledgment on the document itself, he becomes obligated *vis-à-vis* the consignee; the debtor may not oppose defenses arising from his relationship to the consignee or from the relationship between the assignor and the consignee (art. 877). The assigned debtor has to effect payment only upon delivery of the document (art. 878). The claim of the consignee against the assigned debtor who has accepted the assignment is barred three years after acceptance (art. 879). The assigned debtor is not bound to accept the delegation just because he is indebted to the assignor (art. 880). Where a delegation document was drawn for settling a claim of the assigned debtor to the assignor, or of the assignor to the consignee, such settlement, except if otherwise agreed, takes effect only when the assigned debtor has paid the consignee (art. 881). The consignee is bound to advise immediately the assignor if he does not wish to or can not make use of the delegation or if the assigned debtor has refused to accept the delegation or to effect the payment (art. 882). The assignor may revoke the delegation as long as the assigned debtor has not accepted it or has not effected payment. If the assignor has been declared bankrupt, the delegation which has not been accepted is considered to have been revoked (art. 883). The delegation is not repealed by the death or the supervening incapacity of the assignor, the assigned debtor, or the consignee (art. 884). The consignee is allowed to transfer the delegation to another, except if the assignor has excluded such transfer; but such exclusion of transfer is valid towards the assigned debtor only if it is written on the document of delegation, or if it was brought to his knowledge prior to acceptance or payment (art. 884). In any case, the document of the delegation has to be handed over to the transferee (art. 886). If the assigned debtor accepts the delegation *vis-à-vis* the new consignee, he is not allowed to raise against the latter defenses deriving from his relationship with the previous consignee. In all other respects, the provisions relating to the cession are applicable by analogy (art. 887).

### *D. Commercial IOU's* (χρεωστικά ομόλογα εμπόρων, chreostika omologa emporon)

Whilst the commercial money orders are tripartite agreements, involving the assignor, the assigned debtor and the consignee, the commercial IOU's, being promises, involve only two persons: the issuer and the consignee. They are inasmuch distinguished from the promissory notes, as the promise in the commercial IOU's may not only be a promise for money but also a promise to give commercial papers or other fungible things. The main instruments considered to be commercial IOU's are: debenture bonds of corporations (ομολογίες ανωνύμων εταιριών, omologies anonymon etairion), interim convertible bonds (προσωρινοί τίτλοι μετατρέψιμων ομολογιών, prosorinoi titloi metatrepsimon omologion), annuity bonds (τίτλοι ισόβιας προσόδου, titloi isovias prosodou) etc. Debentures are governed by articles 3a–3c of the codified Law 2190/1920 on corporations. Interim convertible bonds are instruments issued on a temporary basis to the holders of convertible bonds of a corporation, pending the issuance of the share certificates to which the debentures were converted. Such bonds, as well as the annuity bonds, are not specifically regulated in Greece, with the exception of life annuities (but not life annuity bonds) (arts. 840–843 C.C.).

### E. Warehouse Receipts

Warehouse receipts are governed by L.D. 3077/1954 "On General Warehouses" (arts. 1, 27–44). They are negotiable and are issued by the warehouseman in connection with goods received for storage; they are delivered to the person who deposits the goods or to whose account they are deposited. They are drawn on model forms in triplicate, cut out of a book; the description of the stored goods and the name of the beneficiary are filled in. The stem stays with the warehouse; the first cut, called 'the deposit certificate' (αποθετήριο, apothetirio), embodies ownership title on the stored goods and serves for proving and transferring such ownership by endorsing the certificate; the second cut, called 'the pawn certificate' (ενεχυρόγραφο, enechyrographo) serves for constituting or transferring a pawn on the stored goods, again by endorsing the instrument. With respect to endorsement, legitimation of the holder, checking of the legitimation, effects of the endorsement and recourse claims, the provisions governing bills of exchange are applicable (art. 80 L.D. of July 17, 1923; see above, Section III A 1).

## IV. Industrial Property (βιομηχανική ιδιοκτησία, viomichaniki idioktisia)

Greece has ratified the Paris International Convention of 1883 on the Protection of Industrial Property, as subsequently revised, so that in regard to nationals of other countries signatories of the Convention, the provisions of such Convention are applicable. Matters covered by the Convention are: the repression of unfair competition, trade names and trade marks, indications of source, patents, utility models and industrial designs.

### A. *Unfair Competition* (αθέμιτος ανταγωνισμός, athemitos antagonismos)

The main statutory provisions on the subject matter are included in Law 146/1914 on unfair competition, as subsequently amended. It consists of a general prohibition in article 1 and of a series of specific prohibitions. In the words of article 1: 'In commercial, industrial and agricultural transactions, any act which is opposed to morality is prohibited. The transgressor may be sued for refraining from such acts and for damages'. Such general provision may concur not only with the specific provisions of the same act but also with provisions of other acts, like the law on trade marks (see below, under B, C) and may also be applicable on matters not covered at all by statutory provisions (see below, under E). The specific prohibitions concern: (a) Any misrepresentation concerning transactions under article 1, made in public communications or in announcements addressed to a larger circle of persons, in particular misstatements concerning the quality, the source of origin, the process of manufacturing, or the pricing of goods or of industrial activities, the manner or the source of procurement, the possession of awards or other honorable distinctions, the cause or the aim of the sale, or the size of the available stock, if such statements are apt to give the impression of a particularly favorable offer. The transgressor may be enjoined from making such misrepresentations and sued for damages (art. 3); if such misrepresentations were made fraudulently, he is subject also to criminal prosecution (art. 4). Depictions or other devices apt to replace such misstatements are equally prohibited (art. 5). (b) Any public announcement of a sale of goods for the purpose of liquidation of a business or a branch thereof. Such clearance sale and the announcement thereof is allowed only by means of a court decision and only in case of actual and final termination of the activities of the entire business or of a branch thereof, and only for the goods of such branch, as well as in case of bankruptcy of such business; provided, however, that seasonal rebates and their announcements are allowed by decisions of the Minister of Commerce; no other announcements for rebates are allowed. Transgressors are subject to an action for refraining from such practice; they are also subject to damages and criminal prosecution (arts. 7–10). (c) Denigration or disparaging of a competitor is prohibited under penalties. The transgressor may be sued for refraining from doing so and is liable for damages (arts. 11–12). (d) Also prohibited is the use of a trade name, a trade mark, an emblem or a distinctive sign of which a third party is the legitimate holder. The transgressor is subject to civil and criminal prosecution and the court may, at the request of the prejudiced party, order the removal and/or the destruction of the injurious sign (arts. 13–15; see below, under B 4). (e) Finally, prohibited under penalties and liability for damages is the disclosure of business secrets by an employee of such business for competition purposes or for prejudicing the business; the same prohibition applies to a third party which obtained knowledge of such secrets through an employee of the business (art. 16) and to any one who discloses to third parties, or makes unauthorized use of, technical data or of particular drawings, patterns, samples or instructions which were entrusted to him in the course of business (arts. 16–18). Claims under this act justify also injunctive relief (art. 19).

## *B. Trade Names and Trade Marks*

### 1. Trade Names

A trade name (εμπορική επωνυμία, emporiki eponymia) is the name which a merchant uses in his commercial activities. Normally, if the merchant is a natural person, his trade name will coincide with his name as a citizen (first name and family name). It is possible, however, for a merchant acquiring by contract or by succession a business in its entirety, to continue using for such business the trade name of his predecessor, provided he adds a distinctive sign.

Thus, if John Ioannides acquires a business formerly owned by George Georgiades he may continue conducting such business under the name George Georgiades by adding, e.g., the words 'successor J. Ioannides'. If the business is conducted under the form of a general partnership (ομόρρυθμη εταιρία, omorrythmi etairia), the trade name has to be formed by the names of the partners (art. 21 Com. C). If the name of only one or of some of the partners is used, then the words 'and Co.' or a similar indication has to be added in order to make clear that there are more partners than those mentioned in the name of the business. In case of a limited partnership only the names of the partners whose responsibility is unlimited may form the trade name (art. 25 Com. C). The trade name of a close corporation (εταιρία περιορισμένης ευθύνης, etairia periorismenis euthynis; *société à responsabilité limitée, GmbH*) can be formed either by the names of the shareholders or by the designation of the kind of the trade engaged in, or by both; in any case, the necessary words must be added. The trade name of a corporation must be formed by indicating its trade; the name of a founder or of another natural person or the name of another commercial association may be added, but in any case the words 'corporation' (ανώνυμη εταιρία, anonymi etairia; *société anonyme; Aktiengesellschaft*) must be added (art. 5 L. 2190/1920).

2. Distinctive title (διακριτικός τίτλος, diakritikos titlos) or emblem (έμβλημα, emblima) is a name or a sign which a merchant or a business uses, in order to distinguish such business for quick reference. Such distinctive title or emblem is affixed on the facade of the shop, printed on the stationery, in advertisings etc. of such business.

3. A merchant or a business may use also distinctive signs of another nature, for example the special shape of the products or of their wrapping (such as the ball-shaped soaps of Pear's, the fancy-shaped bottles of perfumes etc.) or of the shop itself (such as the shape of a cave or of a red windmill etc.).

4. Trade names, distinctive titles and distinctive shapes (διασχηματισμός, diaschimatismos) of goods etc. are protected by virtue of articles 13 and 14 of Law 146/1914 on unfair competition, which read as follows: Article 13. 'Whoever in commercial transactions uses a name, a trade name or a distinctive sign of a shop or of an industrial business or of a printed matter in such a way that it may create confusion with the name, the trade name or the distinctive sign which another lawfully uses, may be compelled by the latter to refrain from such use. He is also held to indemnify the latter for the damage sustained by him, if he knew, or ought to know, that from such use a damage could occur. As distinctive sign is considered also the particular shape of the goods, their packing or wrapper, insofar as these are known to the appropriate market circles as distinctive signs of somebody else's'. By virtue of article 14 I, the intentional use of such a trade name or distinctive sign belonging to another is punished by imprisonment up to six months and/or a fine. In accordance with article 14 II, the provisions of articles 13 and 14 are applicable also in such instances where the use of such other's trade name and/or distinctive sign is done under minor changes, so that by such use confusion might possibly occur.

## 5. Trade Marks (σήματα, simata)

Trade marks are governed by N.L. 1998/1939. In accordance with article 1: '1. Trade mark is any sign which is used to designate the provenance of a product from a certain industrial, agricultural or stock-breeding business, as well as of the trade objects of a certain commercial business. 2. As trade mark is considered also the title of a newspaper or a periodical'. In accordance with article 2 'the right for the exclusive use of a trade mark is acquired only by its registration in accordance with the provisions of this law'. In article 3 are enumerated the signs which may not be accepted for registration: (a) signs commonly used, or which are deprived of any distinctive character, such as signs formed exclusively of lines, words, figures or indications which describe the kind, quality, quantity, weight, destination, value, or provenance of the goods, (b) emblems and symbols of the Greek State as well as of any public or religious authority, (c) those opposed to morality or to public order, (d) those including statements and representations which obviously are untrue and are apt to create confusion, (e) those constituting counterfeits or imitations of duly preregistered and not deleted trade marks which are used for the same or closely resembling products, (f) names and pictures of third persons, even with the latters' consent and (g) those whose registration is opposed to good faith.

A registered trade mark may be deleted by judgment of the administrative courts at the request of a person having a legal interest thereto, in any of the following instances: (a) if the beneficiary fails to market goods bearing such trade mark within three years from its registration; in case of a title of a newspaper or of a periodical within one year, and in case of pharmaceuticals within four years from registration, (b) if the beneficiary has ceased to market products bearing the trade mark for two years and, in case of a newspaper or a periodical, for one year, (c) if the beneficiary business has ceased to operate for at least two years and, in case of a newspaper or a periodical, for one year; in all the above instances (a)–(c) the trade mark will not be deleted if the beneficiary proves that the failure to market products bearing the trade mark, or the discontinuance of the operation of the business, was due to a reasonable cause, (d) if the trade mark became of common use; in such a case the petition for deletion may not be filed prior to the lapse of twenty years from the trade mark's registration, (e) if the registered trade mark constitutes a counterfeit or imitation of a distinctive sign of the same or of a similar product which was already sufficiently known in the Greek market; the petition for deletion in this instance must be filed not later than three years from registration, provided that products bearing the trade mark have in fact been marketed, (f) if the trade mark in accordance with the provisions of article 3 I should not have been accepted for registration; in such a case the petition for deletion must be filed within three years from registration, (g) if the trade mark is a counterfeit or imitation of a foreign trade mark which, although subsequently filed for registration, had priority over the registered one because of its prior registration abroad (in accordance with art. 35 II, foreign trade marks which are filed for registration in Greece within six months from their registration abroad are protected in Greece retroactively from the day of their registration abroad); in such a case the petition for deletion must be filed within six months from registration and (h) if the filing for registration was made in bad faith; in such a case the petition for deletion has to be filed within five years from registration, provided that the products bearing the challenged trade mark have in fact been marketed.

The deletion becomes effective as from the date the judgment of the court pronouncing the deletion becomes final and irrevocable. Both registration and deletion of a trade mark must be pronounced by a judgment. Jurisdiction in this respect is vested now upon the ordinary administrative courts (L. 1406/1983). The decisions pronouncing registration or deletion of a trade mark are published in a special section of the Official Gazette (arts. 7 VI, 13 II, 15 III, 36). The right on a registered trade mark lasts for ten years and can be renewed indefinitely by filing during the last year of protection a petition for renewal; such right is transferable by succession and by contract, but only jointly with the business for the benefit of which it was registered (art. 20). Whoever uses or counterfeits or imitates a trade mark belonging to another may be sued before the district court for refraining from such use and/or for damages; the claim for damages is barred three years from the end of the year in which such violation occurred (art. 24). The claim for refraining from such use may be enforced by interim measures (art. 25). Penalties (imprisonment and/or fine) are inflicted upon those intentionally violating the provisions of this law (art. 26).

### C. *Indications of Source* (*appellations of origin*: ενδείξεις προελεύσεως, endeixeis proeleuseos)

There are some general provisions which are applicable to all indications of origin and specific ones regarding some specific products. General provisions are those of articles 3–5 of Law 146/1914 on unfair competition by virtue of which is prohibited any misrepresentation made in public and addressed to a broad circle of people, especially with regard to the provenance of a product, which may create the impression of a particularly favorable offer. The transgressor may be sued for refraining from such misrepresentations and for damages; he is also criminally liable if he made the misrepresentations with the intention to mislead the consumers. Denominations which in the trade transactions are used to designate species of goods or industrial activities and not the geographic provenance of such goods or services are not subject to the above prohibitions. As a general provision may also be regarded the general clause of article 1 (see above, under A), as well as article 3 I of N.L. 1998/1939 on trade marks, by virtue of which indications of districts of provenance may not be registered as trade marks (see above, under B 5). Specific provisions are included in laws and regulations concerning some specific products like wines (R.D. 423/1970 on recognition of appellations of origin of wines, olive oils and raisins).

### *D. Patents (*διπλώματα ευρεσιτεχνίας, diplomata euresitechnias)

The main statute governing patents is Law 2527/1920 on patents. To new inventions which are susceptible of industrial use are granted rights of exclusive exploitation of limited duration called 'patents' (art. 1). Granting a patent depends on: (a) the novelty and (b) the susceptibility of an industrial use. However, the Patent Office does not examine the actual existence of these requirements in accepting an application for a patent. Greek law follows thus the French system, in contrast to the Anglo-American and German systems where the Patent Office examines the actual existence of the requirements in order to accept an invention for registration. New inventions are not those which, at the time of filing the application for obtaining a patent, are sufficiently known in Greece or have been described in publications or drawings in Greece in such a way as to be susceptible of practical application by an expert (art. 2). Entitled to be granted a patent is whoever first made the declaration of the invention (art. 4). Inventions made by an employee during the performance of his work belong to him, except if they are in the field of the work assigned to him, or if the employer has reserved for himself the right to such inventions; in the latter case the employee is entitled to a reasonable additional remuneration (art. 688 C.C.).

A patent confers to its holder and to his successor in title the right to exclusively produce the object of the invention, to trade and sell it or to use it. If the invention consists of a process, the protection extends also to the products directly produced by such process (art. 5). The rights accruing from a patent may not be invoked against a person who, at the time the declaration was filed, was using the invention in good faith or had made the necessary arrangements for using it; such a person has the right to use the invention for the needs of his own business (art. 6). The term for which patents are granted is fifteen years as from the day of filing the application (art. 7). The holder loses his rights from the patent if (a) he waives his rights, (b) he neglects to pay in time the annual fees or (c) he omits without proper reason to use to a sufficient extent the patent in Greece (art. 9). A patent is declared to be void and of no effect if it is subsequently proven that: (a) the invention was not susceptible of being granted a patent, (b) the holder intentionally omitted to disclose part of his secret or declared it inaccurately, (c) the invention is opposed to public order, to public security, to morality, or to the law or (d) substantial part of the declaration was assembled from descriptions, drawings, models, tools or directions of a third party or from a method applied by a third party without the latter's consent; in such cases the patent may be restricted proportionally. The patent is annulled by judgment of the court (art. 10).

For any modification of his invention, the holder may apply for an additional patent which expires simultaneously with the original patent; it can be converted into a main patent if the appropriate requirements are met; licensees of the main patent may use the modified one (art. 11). For an invention related to the object of another patent, the holder of such related patent may not use the original invention without the authorization of the holder of the original patent, and vice versa (art. 12). The rights accruing from a patent are transferable by contract or succession (art. 14). The holder of a patent may grant to third parties licenses for the use of his patent; such licenses may be transferred by the licensee by means of contract or by succession, but only in conjunction with the business for which the license was granted (art. 15). The holder of a patent which was declared to be of public utility is held to grant licenses against proper indemnification (art. 16). If a patent is annulled all licenses on it are equally annulled (art. 17).

Whoever has applied for a patent out of Greece, and within twelve months applies for a patent in Greece for the same invention, enjoys priority only if he has claimed priority in filing the application in Greece (art. 19). The object of patents accepted for registration together with the registration number, the date, the name, the profession and domicile of the holder and his proxies and authorized agents, is published in a special section of the Official Gazette; so is published also any relevant modification (art. 29). Anyone may get copies of registered patents and of the drawings, specifications and other particulars of the patent (art. 32). Any transfer, license or modification relating to a patent has to be registered within three months from such act, on penalty of their being considered as invalid towards third parties (art. 33). Whoever intentionally or by gross negligence uses an invention in violation of the provisions of the law, is subject to damages (art. 34) and, in case of a fraudulent use, to criminal prosecution (art. 35). Civil actions are barred three years after each violation, taken separately (art. 38). Products illegally produced, as well as tools and equipment used for such purpose may, by court's decision, be destroyed or adjudicated to the prejudiced person (art. 43).

### E. *Utility Models and Industrial Designs* (βιομηχανικά υποδείγματα και σχεδιάσματα, viomichanika ypodeigmata kai schediasmata)

There is no specific legislation in Greece on utility models and industrial designs. Protection of such items may be assured by means of the general provisions on unfair competition (above, under A) and, possibly, by the laws on intellectual property (below, Section V).

## V. Intellectual Property (πνευματική ιδιοκτησία, pneumatiki idioktisia)

Greece is a signatory to the Bern Convention of 1886 on the protection of literary and artistic works, as amended by the Brussels Act of 1948 (ratified by L.D. 3565/1956), which is applicable not only in the instances provided for in the Convention but also to authors and artists of Greek nationality as long as the protection of the Convention is more advantageous than that of Greek law (art. 1 L.D. 4264/1962 on 'Supplementing Some Provisions on Protection of the

Intellectual Property'). The main domestic statute is Law 2387/1920 on intellectual property, as subsequently amended. In accordance with this act, authors, musical composers, painters, designers, sculptors, turners and carvers of originals or adapted and arranged, copied or translated works, enjoy for lifetime the exclusive right of publication or reproduction of their works under any manner and form, of the performance of musical compositions, theatrical plays, fragments and extracts thereof, and of their assignment to third parties (art. 1). The above list of intellectual producers and of literary and artistic works is not exhaustive. The protection of this law extends to all possible creators of intellectual works, such as cinematographic, choreographic and architectural works, radio and television broadcasts and entertainment of any kind.

The rights conferred by this law extend also to the heirs of the beneficiaries for fifty years, calculated from the 31st December of the year in which they died (art. 2) and, in case of joint creators, from the 31st December of the year of death of the last survivor (art. 3). Whoever publishes or makes public a work anonymously or under a pseudonym is equally protected, and such protection continues after he discloses his name (art. 4). The holders of works which were not made public enjoy the rights conferred by the law for fifty years calculated from the 31st of December of the year in which the creator deceased (art. 5). The writers and their assignees and successors enjoy the exclusive right to authorize the translation and, in the case of theatrical works, to authorize the public performance thereof for ten years calculated from the 31st December of the year in which they were published. Thereafter, the right of translation becomes public domain. The same right is enjoyed by the holders of unpublished works of deceased authors. In case of works published in volumes or in incomplete parts, the period of ten years begins from the 31st December of the year in which the last part was published (art. 6).

With regard to reproductions of writings, pictures, drawings etc. in literary collections, anthologies, school manuals, year-calendars or yearbooks etc., the provisions on translations find application; such provisions, however, do not apply to the publication of musical, poetical or dramatic works, either originals or translations, as well as to dramatic or dramatico-musical arrangements of tales, the cinematographic or mimical representation of any literary or artistic work and the performance of musical compositions by phonographic means or through devices of any invention; in such instances the provisions of articles 1–5 apply (art. 7). The purchase of an original writing, or of an original artistic work, does not include the right to its reproduction in any manner (art. 8). The inclusion in a writing of fragments or excerpts from works, pictures and drawings of somebody else's, related to the purposes of the writing, the public recital of literary works and the performance of theatrical, dramatic or musical works and of musical compositions in theaters, cinemas, recreation centers, dancings, restaurants, hotels, cafés and cafés-chantants, are prohibited without the written authorization by the writer, the composer, the assignee of their rights, or their legal representatives. Musical editions may be performed by military or other musicians, without authorization by the appropriate composers and without pay, for educational purposes or for the entertainment of the public in public places without entrance fee, in schools or out of doors. Public performance of music by sonor-films indoors or out of doors or in any public place whatsoever is prohibited without written authorization by the authors, composers and music publishers or their legal representatives (art. 9). This law does not apply to sermons, speeches in the parliament and in conventions and speeches delivered in legal proceedings; publication of shorthand minutes or summaries of such sermons or speeches is free (art. 10).

Whoever publishes against payment and without further agreement a work of his own in a newspaper, periodical, yearbook, year-calendar, anthology etc. is not allowed to republish the same elsewhere prior to the lapse of two years from completion of such publication (art. 11). A work which received an award in a competition and was not published by the prize organizer within three years from the award reverts to the author's ownership. The same applies to a work, the publication of which was assigned by the author against payment and without further agreement; the computation of such three-year term begins from the day the payment was effected to the author (art. 12). Republication by a newspaper or a periodical of originals or translations published in another newspaper or periodical is allowed if there is no written prohibition by the writer or the publisher. However, each such republication has to mention the source from which it was taken and the name of the author or the artist as well (art. 13). Photographic or related works are subject to the provisions of this law, only if on each copy appears the name of the photographer or the publisher, his address and the year of publication. To the same provisions are subject dumb films, and the creators of their particular artistic, literary or musical components and photographic pictures, i.e. the authors, musicians, composers, directors and actors enjoy the same rights with the creators referred to in article 1 (art. 14). The assignees of the rights of a writer or artist are not allowed to cause any alterations to the work without the latter's authorization (art. 15).

Whoever knowingly or fraudulently, in violation of the provisions of Law 2387/1920, publishes or multiplies, by copying or by any other manner and under whatsoever form, writings or artistic works or phonographic records, or publicly performs theatrical works or musical compositions, is punished, at the request of the prejudiced person, with imprisonment and a fine. The works which were marketed in violation of the law are subject to seizure at the request of the prejudiced party, who may dispose of such seized works after the pronouncement of the court's decision. Also, at the request of the appropriate authors, composers or their assignees, the prosecuting authority is bound to prohibit the unauthorized performance of theatrical or musical works and of musical compositions in the places referred to in article 9 (art. 16). Application of this law may be extended also, on condition of reciprocity, to literary or artistic works created abroad, by concluding special conventions with the respective countries (art. 17). With regard, however, to countries belonging to the International Union of Bern or bound by the international convention on the protection of literary or artistic works, this matter is governed by the provisions of such convention.

## VI. Antitrust Law

As a provision of antitrust law can be regarded article 1 of Law 146/1914 on unfair competition (see above, Section IV A), inasmuch as it applies to any agreement aiming at putting competitors out of business by using unethical methods, e.g., by reducing below cost the price of the goods or services offered, with the intention of increasing again such prices after the competitors are put out of business. But, of course, such practice would violate the provision in question even if exercised by a single competitor acting on his own, and not necessarily under an agreement. Specific antitrust legislation was introduced for the first time by Law 703/1977 'On Control of Monopolies and Oligopolies and Protection of Free Competition', as subsequently amended. Such law was enacted in implementation of articles 85 and 86 of the Treaty establishing the European Economic Community and the respective EEC regulations, especially Regulation 17/1962.

By virtue of article 1 of Law 703/1977, '1. Shall be prohibited all agreements between enterprises, all decisions by associations of enterprises and all concerted practices of any kind which have as their object, or which result in, the prevention, restriction or distortion of competition, and in particular those which consist in: (a) the direct or indirect fixing of purchase or selling prices or any other trading conditions, (b) the limitation or the control of production, distribution, markets, technical development, or investment, (c) the sharing of markets or of sources of supply, (d) the application of unequal conditions to equivalent transactions with other trading parties, thereby placing them at a disadvantage in what competition is concerned, in particular by refusing to sell or to buy or to conclude any other transaction without proper justification and (e) the subjecting of the conclusion of contracts to the acceptance by the other party of additional supplies which, either by their nature or according to commercial usage, have no connection with the subject of such contracts. 2. Any agreements or decisions prohibited pursuant to this article shall be null and void except as otherwise provided in this act. 3. Nevertheless, the agreements, decisions and concerted practices, or categories thereof, referred hereinabove may, by decisions of the Minister of Commerce based on recommendations of the Committee for the Protection of Competition, be declared valid wholly or in part, if they meet the following requirements: (a) they contribute to improving the production or distribution of goods or to promoting technical or economic progress, while allowing to consumers a fair share to the benefit deriving therefrom, (b) they do not impose on the enterprises concerned restrictions which are not indispensable for attaining the above objectives, and (c) they do not enable such enterprises to eliminate competition with respect to a substantial part of the market concerned'. Under article 2, 'Shall be prohibited any action by one or more enterprises to take improper advantage of a dominant position of theirs on the whole or on a part of the country's market. Such improper advantage may in particular consist in: (a) directly or indirectly imposing unfair purchase or selling prices or other unfair trading conditions, (b) limiting production, markets or technical development to the prejudice of consumers, (c) applying dissimilar conditions to equivalent transactions with other trading parties, thereby placing them at a competitive disadvantage, especially by refusing without proper justification to sell, to buy, or to conclude any other transaction and (d) subjecting the conclusion of a contract to the acceptance by the other party of additional supplies which, either by their nature or according to commercial usage, have no connection with the subject of such contract'. Article 3: 'Without prejudice to the provisions of art. 1 III, the agreements, decisions and concerted practices of art. 1 I and the abuse of a dominant position referred to in art. 2 shall be prohibited without any prior decision by an authority being necessary to this end'. Article 4: '1. The merger as such of enterprises is not subject to the prohibition of art. 1 I. 2. For purposes of this act, an operation is deemed to be a merger of enterprises in the following cases: (a) when a new enterprise is constituted, (b) when one or more enterprises are absorbed by another, or (c) when one or more enterprises are bought up by another'. Article 5: '1. The provisions of this act apply also to public enterprises or enterprises of public utility; by joint decisions of the Ministers of National Economy and of Commerce may be exempted from the application of this act some of such enterprises or categories thereof which are of importance to the national economy. 2. The provisions of this act apply also to enterprises or associations of enterprises, the object of which consists in the production, elaboration, transformation or marketing of agricultural, livestock, forestry or fishing products, save where certain categories of such enterprises or certain sectors of their activities would be exempt from the application thereof by joint decisions of the Ministers of National Economy, Commerce and Agriculture. 3. The provisions of this act apply also to enterprises and associations of enterprises of transports, save if, by joint decisions of the Ministers of National Economy, Commerce and Communications, in what land and air transports are concerned, or by joint decisions of the Ministers of National Economy, Commerce and Merchant Marine, in what sea transports are concerned, special regulations or exemptions imposed by the national policy as to transports are introduced'. Article 6: 'Without prejudice to the international commitments of the country, the provisions of this act do not apply to agreements, decisions and concerted practices exclusively aiming at securing, promoting or strengthening exports; except if, by joint decisions of the Ministers of National Economy and Commerce, it would be differently ordered as to specific classes of enterprises or products'.

Law 703/1979 provides also the possibility for an enterprise or an association of enterprises to request a 'negative clearance', i.e. a certification by the Minister of Commerce that a certain agreement of theirs does not violate the provisions of articles 1 or 2. Such clearance may be requested also for a future control or a supposed abuse of a dominant position, but granting such negative clearance does not preclude a later adverse decision by the Minister (art. 11). The Minister of Commerce may at any time revoke also his other decisions on the validity of agreements, decisions or concerted practices, if new facts come to his knowledge which provide evidence of a violation (art. 13). Appeal from the decisions of the Minister of Commerce may be filed with the Administrative District Court of Athens within twenty days from notification of such decisions (art. 14).

A special register of cartels is kept in the Ministry of Commerce, including a provisional register of cartels, which is confidential, and the final register, which is accessible to the public. In such final register entries are made of final decisions by the Minister of Commerce, by the administrative district court, by the appellate administrative court, and by the Council of State on matters relating to the provisions of article 1 I, III b (art. 19). Agreements, decisions and concerted practices provided for in article 1 I, as well as mergers provided for in article 4, must be notified by the enterprises and associations of enterprises to the Ministry of Commerce within thirty days from their conclusion (art. 21). Any person or legal entity is *entitled* to report a violation of the provisions of articles 1 and 2, whilst state officials and those working in public enterprises are *required* to do so (art. 24). The Service for the Protection of Competition of the Ministry of Commerce is entitled to collect information necessary for the implementation of Law 703/1979, by conducting investigations and audits, administering oaths etc. (arts. 25 and 26). Penalties are inflicted upon those violating the provisions of that act (art. 29). The scope of application of the act extends to all restrictions on competition having effect within Greece if the respective agreements were concluded abroad; the same applies to abuses of dominant positions which produce effects in Greece (art. 32).

## VII. Banking Law

### *A. The Banking System (provisions relating to the organization and operation of banks)*

The basic enactment is Law 5076/1931 'On Corporations and Banks', as subsequently amended. In accordance with article 10, 'Banks under this act are businesses which notwithstanding any other purpose of theirs, accept as an element forming part of their activity deposits of money or of other values'. Banks within the meaning of said article 10 may be constituted and operate only in the form of a corporation (art. 11). Individual persons, partnerships, limited partnerships, or other types of associations which are engaged in bank operations may not use in their trade name the words 'bank' or 'banker' (art. 12). The equity capital of banks may not be less than a minimum amount fixed from time to time by statute (art. 19). The capital of banks must be deposited fully in cash with the Bank of Greece against receipt, which is submitted to the Ministry of National Economy jointly with the application for the foundation of the bank. Such capital deposited to the Bank of Greece may be withdrawn only after the foundation of the bank (art. 14).

Banks may not engage professionally in a trade or in an industry for their proper sake and may not grant to the same person or entity credits for amounts exceeding a certain ceiling which is determined from time to time; banks may not participate in other businesses for amounts exceeding one fifth of their joint share and reserve capital; they are not allowed to grant credits of any kind whatsoever to members of their board of directors without sufficient real securities, except by virtue of a special decision of the general meeting of the shareholders (art. 16). Banks are subject to the supervision of the Ministry of National Economy and the Bank of Greece; they are bound to submit to the Ministry of Finance and to the Bank of Greece monthly statements on their activities (art. 18b). Values, such as company shares, debenture bonds and other instruments which were deposited in trust or given as a pawn to a bank must not be sold, pawned, or in any other way transferred without the consent of the owner; the transgressor is subject to criminal prosecution even if he had not the intention of appropriating same for himself (art. 26). Governors, members of the board of directors, auditors and employees of a bank are subject to criminal prosecution if: (1) they do not keep orderly the books provided for; (2) they omit to insert a transaction in such books; (3) they submit to the supervising authority or to the Bank of Greece false or inaccurate reports or data; and (4) they hinder in any way whatsoever such supervision and audit (art. 10 of N.L. 1665/1951 on operation and supervision of banks). By virtue of article 1 of L.D. 588/1948 on credit control, 'the granting of credits is henceforth subject to state control and must have the trend of strengthening such economy branches which stress the production activity of the country in accordance with the production policies fixed from time to time by the government'. Such control was originally effected by the Currency Committee, consisting of cabinet ministers, the Governor of the Bank of Greece and some other high-ranking government officials. The Currency Committee was, however, abolished in 1983 and its duties and prerogatives were transferred to the Bank of Greece.

### *B. Private Banking Law*

Statutory provisions with regard to private bank transactions are rather scarce in Greece. Bank transactions are carried on by using printed forms which banks have prepared for each specific kind of transactions. The most important statutory provisions are included in the L.D. of July 17, 1923 'On Special Provisions on Companies Limited by Shares', and in L. 5638/1932 'On Deposits in Joint Account', as amended by L.D. 951/1971.

1. Deposits of cash or securities for the benefit of a third party transfer to the third party immediately ownership title. The purpose of such deposit or acceptance by the beneficiary need not be declared. It may be agreed that the deposited amount shall devolve upon the beneficiary after the death of the depositor; in such a case, if the beneficiary dies before the depositor, the heirs of the beneficiary have no right whatsoever on the deposit. If such deposit violates the lawful rights of another, the latter may claim damages from the beneficiary; however, insofar as no attachment has been imposed on the bank, such claim

does not impede delivery of the deposit to the beneficiary (art. 1 L.D. of July 17, 1923).

2. Inalienable deposits (αναπαλλοτρίωτη κατάθεση, anapallotrioti katathesi) may be made only to the National Bank of Greece (art. 4). They may have as object only: (a) Greek public securities, (b) money or (c) debentures of the National Bank of Greece (art. 6), and may be effected only for the benefit of: (a) an entity not engaged in commercial activities, (b) a minor or a prodigal or a person placed under judicial interdiction or (c) a person in the form of a life annuity, but in such case only by an act *mortis causa* (art. 7). In the case of an inalienable deposit the beneficiary collects the revenue; any alienation of the deposit or its revenue and any attachment thereof is null and void, even if meant to become effective after the inalienability should be repealed (art. 10). The inalienability is repealed: (a) by dissolution of the beneficiary corporation, (b) in case the beneficiary is an incapacitated person, as soon as the incapacitation comes to end, (c) in case of a life annuity, by the death of the beneficiary. Upon making the deposit, the inalienability may be stipulated for a certain period of time or made dependent on a condition, in particular the purchase of a realty (art. 11).

3. Joint Accounts (κοινός λογαριασμός, koinos logariasmos)

In accordance with article 1 I of Law 5638/1932, 'A cash deposit in a current account in the name of two or more persons jointly is a joint account if it includes a condition to the effect that such account may be used in whole or in part by one or more or by all beneficiaries separately without the concurrence of the others'. Such cash deposit may be also stipulated as a savings- or a time-joint account. In such accounts a condition may be added to the effect that in case of death of any of the beneficiaries the deposit and the related account devolves automatically upon the survivors until the last survivor. In such a case the deposit devolves upon such beneficiary or beneficiaries free from any tax or due, but this exemption does not apply to the heirs of the last remaining beneficiary (art. 2). Such deposit may not be disposed of by an act *inter vivos* or *mortis causa*, and the heirs of each beneficiary, except those of the last survivor, have no right whatsoever on such deposit (art. 3). The deposit may be attached but, for that purpose, is deemed to belong to all the beneficiaries in equal shares (art. 4). The interest accruing on such accounts is fixed from time to time by an act of the Minister of National Economy (art. 5). Only some banks and public corporations may accept deposits in the form of a joint account (art. 7).

4. Documentary Credit Contracts (ενέγγυος τραπεζική πίστωση, enengyos trapeziki pistosi)

In accordance with article 25 of the L.D. of July 17, 1923 a confirmed documentary credit contract (*crédit confirmé*) is a contract by virtue of which a bank (the creditor) agrees with another (the debtor) to open a credit in favor of a third party (the beneficiary) by assuming the obligation to pay to the beneficiary, as soon as the latter hands over to the creditor a bill of lading (B/L), the amount of the credit, which amount the creditor will collect from the debtor at the time of receiving delivery of the B/L from the bank. The bank by paying the amount of the credit to the beneficiary acquires a mortgage on the goods covered by the B/L. The B/L is issued or endorsed to the bank or (in case of a bearer B/L) is handed over to the bank; if it was stipulated that the beneficiary shall deliver 'a full set of documents', the bank is bound to require from the beneficiary, in addition to the B/L, also insurance policies and invoices covering the shipped goods. It may be stipulated that the beneficiary will deliver, instead of a B/L, warehouse receipts (art. 26). Payment to the beneficiary may be effected by the bank or by its correspondent either within the country or abroad (art. 27).

Provided there is no agreement to the contrary: (a) if the beneficiary states to the bank that he accepts the credit, it cannot be revoked, unless the bank expressly had designated it as being revocable and (b) if the bank had set in its notification to the beneficiary a term within which the latter is bound to deliver the B/L and the other accompanying documents, the credit, after the lapse of the term, is considered to have been revoked (art. 28). If the debtor gave to the bank money or securities as a guarantee for the opening of the credit, the bank acquires a mortgage on such items *ipso facto*, without the formalities required by the law for constituting a mortgage (art. 29). The bank is not liable for the fortuitous loss of, or damage to, the goods and for possible mistakes of the telegraph service in handling the cables; however, the bank is liable for its proper *dolus* or negligence, including a negligence in appointing its correspondent (art. 30). If the debtor neglects to pay the debt and the bank takes delivery of the goods, the bank is entitled to sell the goods in accordance with the provisions of the law relating to mortgages; such sale can take place only after the lapse of twenty-four hours after notification in case of goods subject to deterioration, and of ten days in case of any other goods (art. 31). If the proceeds from the foreclosure are not enough to cover the claim of the bank the debtor is liable for the outstanding amount (art. 32). If, after expiration of the term, the goods have still not arrived at destination, the bank is entitled, with court's permission, to foreclose on the goods *in transitu* or deposited in a warehouse (art. 33). The above provisions are applicable by analogy if the bank pays to the debtor monies against a B/L handed over by the debtor to it, which monies the bank will collect from a third party by delivering to the latter the B/L (art. 34).

## 5. Chattel Mortgage (τραπεζικό ενέχυρο, trapeziko enechyro)

Articles 35–47 of the L.D. of July 17, 1923 apply where a bank takes as a mortgage movables or a claim, either for a loan (simple or on a current account) or for securing a previous claim of the bank (art. 35). A mortgage is established by an agreement to this effect and by delivery of the mortgaged item to the bank;

the agreement must be in writing and is subject to stamp duties; by a supplementary contract a simple loan may be converted to a current account and vice versa (art. 36). The mortgaged item is handed over either to the bank or to a third party appointed jointly by the contracting parties; the bank is considered to be the holder of the mortgaged goods: (a) if a B/L of a vessel or a railway covering such goods was issued or endorsed to the bank; (b) if the goods are deposited (aa) in a storehouse leased by the bank and the bank holds the keys, or (bb) in a public warehouse and a warehouse receipt was endorsed to the bank; (c) if the goods are stored in a customhouse (art. 37). If the mortgaged thing is a document of title the mortgage takes effect by endorsing the document to the bank; no written contract is required in such a case (art. 38). If the mortgaged item is a personal claim of the debtor against a third party, then the mortgaging entails the assignment of the claim by the debtor to the bank (art. 39).

If the claim becomes in any way due, the bank may foreclose (art. 40). If the mortgage consists in bearer securities which are cited in the bulletin of the Stock Exchange of Athens, they must be sold in the Stock Exchange (art. 42). All other mortgaged items are auctioned by a notary (art. 42). Items subject to deterioration or to severe depreciation may be sold by court permission without an auction (art. 43). Ownership title on bearer securities in case of foreclosure passes upon the highest bidder, even if the mortgagor was not the real owner; the real owner has no claim on the proceeds of the auction up to the amount of the bank's claim, but he may sue the bank if he proves that a collusion took place between the bank and the mortgagor (art. 46). The above provisions apply also to credits under a current account; the bank may close such account at any time (art. 47).

### 6. Bank Hypothecary Mortgages on Realties (τραπεζική υποθήκη, trapeziki hypothiki)

Hypothecary mortgages on realties granted to a bank are governed by articles 48–59 of the L.D. of July 17, 1923. The loan agreement and the hypothecation are effected either by directly giving the loan in accordance with the provisions of the Civil Code or by a promise of loan in accordance with the following provisions (art. 49). The loan contract takes effect by notarial deed which states the terms of the loan and the execution of a mortgage before the money of the loan is paid to the borrower. Such mortgage secures the loan as from its registration, regardless of the time at which the money is paid (art. 50). After registration of the mortgage, the bank may pay the money and the debtor signs a notarial deed acknowledging the receipt of the money; if the bank does not pay the money and does not consent to the redemption of the mortgage, such redemption takes effect by court order (art. 51). If the loan becomes due the bank may proceed to attachment or foreclose on the mortgage or both, in accordance with the general provisions of the Code of Civil Procedure.

## VIII. Private Insurance Law

Statutory provisions with respect to non-marine insurance, which apply also to the mutual insurance (art. 191 Com. C.), are included in articles 196–225 Com. C., while marine insurance is governed by articles 257–288 C. Pr. Mar. L. General terms on the printed forms of the insurance policies are subject to the approval of the Insurance Inspection Authority of the Ministry of Commerce.

### *A. General Provisions*

The insurance contract must be in writing; it has to be dated and must state the name and residence of the insured and the insurer, the insured interest, the sum insured, the premium, the risks undertaken by the insurer and the insurance period (art. 192). If there is no indication in the policy that the insurance is concluded for the sake of a third party or for the sake of whom it may concern, it is considered to be concluded for the sake of the insurance holder (art. 193). The insurer may reinsure his liability under the insurance contract; the insured may insure the premium; the assignment of the claim against the insurer takes effect by transferring the policy with an appropriate statement signed jointly by the assignor and the assignee; in order for the assignment to have effect towards third parties, it must be announced to the insurer or be acknowledged by him in writing (art. 194). Claims arising from a life or a property insurance contract are barred three years after the end of the year within which the claim arose (art. 195).

### *B. Insurance Against Property Loss or Damage*

Any interest on a thing may be insured, such as ownership title, lien, mortgage, liability for keeping a thing (art. 196). The insurance against property losses and damages may be concluded for the entire value of the insured interest, for part thereof, or for a certain sum; expected profits and a crop may also be the object of an insurance (art. 197). If the insurance against property loss or damage is contracted for part only of the value of the insured interest, then the insured must share with the insurer a proportional part of the loss or damage (art. 198). Interests which were insured for their entire value may not be insured anew against the same risks and for the same insurance period; a new insurance is, however, valid in the following cases: (a) if it was concluded under the proviso that the previous insurance was invalid or under the proviso of the full or partial insolvency of the first insurer, (b) if the rights from the first insurance were assigned to the second insurer or were waived *vis-à-vis* the first one (art. 199). If the first insurance does not cover the entire value of the insured interest, then the subsequent insurers are liable for the balance of the value in accordance with the priority of their respective insurance contracts; insurance contracts concluded on the same day are considered to have been simultaneously concluded and concur to covering the loss in proportion to the respective insurance amounts (art. 200). Over-insurance, if effected fraudulently by the insured, has no effects as for him, whilst the insurer, if in good faith, is entitled to the premium; if the insured did not act fraudulently in over-insuring his interest, the insurance is valid up to the real value of the interest and the insured is not bound to pay the premiums corresponding to the excess value; he is, however, liable to damages equal to one-half of the excess premium up to one-half percent of the insurance sum (art. 201).

The insurer is entitled to treat the insurance contract as null and void in case of misrepresentations or of passing over in silence by the insured of facts which, if known to the insurer, would induce him to refuse entering the contract, even if such facts did not have any bearing on the loss or damage; in case of bad faith on the part of the insured, the insurer is entitled to the premium (art. 202). The insurance contract is null and void if the insurer and the insured or the insurance-holder knew that the insurance perils did not exist, or that the loss or damage had already occurred at the time of entering the contract; if only the insurer knew such facts, then the insured is not bound to pay the premium; if the policy-holder knew the loss, he is bound to pay the premium (art. 203). If the interest insured was not exposed to perils the insurance is considered not to have been entered into, but the insurer is entitled to the indemnity referred to in article 201 (art. 204). If the perils change or are aggravated due to circumstances for which the insured is responsible, then the insurer is exempt from his liabilities in case that he would not have entered the contract under such circumstances or would have entered the contract under different conditions; he is, however, not exempt from liability if, after getting knowledge of the changed circumstances, he continued performing the contract (art. 250). If the insured becomes bankrupt before the perils come to an end and before the premium was paid, then the insurer is entitled to demand a guarantee or to rescind the contract; the same right has the insured in case the insurer becomes bankrupt (art. 206).

The insurer is not liable for losses and damage arising exclusively from an inherent defect of the object insured if such defect was not declared; neither is he liable for losses and damages caused by the fault of the insured, his agents, or his assignors; except if otherwise agreed, the insurer is not liable either for war risks or losses arising from civil commotions (art. 207). The indemnity to be paid by the insurer is calculated in accordance with the real value of the insured object at the time of the accident; if the insurance value was fixed in advance and the valuation was acknowledged by the insurer, such valuation may be challenged only for fraud, simulation or bias; in lack of an acknowledged valuation the value may be proven by any means of evidence; contrary to what is the law in the marine insurance, the insured items which were rescued may not be abandoned to the insurer, and the value of such rescued items has to be deducted from the insurance indemnity (art. 208). The insured is bound to give to the insurer notice of the accident within three days from the accident or from his knowledge thereof; he is also bound to do his best for avoiding or reducing the damage; except if they were made inconsiderately, the expenses incurred by the insured for such purpose are at the charge of the insurer, even if the aggregate amount of expenses and damages exceeds the insurance amount and even if the rescue was not reached (art. 209). The insurer who compensated the loss or damage is subrogated to the rights of the insured against third parties, and the insured is liable to the insurer for any prejudice caused by the insured to such rights; if the loss or damage was only partly compensated, the insurer and the insured concur jointly and proportionally to the exercise of such rights (art. 210). In case of transfer of the objects insured, the rights and obligations of the transferor arising from the insurance are not transferred to the transferee, except if otherwise agreed (art. 211). In the marine insurance, however, the transferee is *ex lege* subrogated to the rights and obligations of the transferor (art. 277 C. Pr. Mar. L.).

### C. *Specific Instances of Property Loss and Damage Insurance*

In the case of insolvency insurance, the insurer, before paying the insurance amount, may oppose to the insured the defense of distraint in accordance with article 855 of the Civil Code; after having compensated the insured, the insurer is subrogated to the insured's rights against the debtor (art. 212 Com. C.).

Fire insurance covers all damage effected by fire, except if the fire was caused by personal gross negligence of the insured or by war or riot; also it includes damages caused by inherent defects of the insured building even if such defects were not declared, except if the insured knew such defect at the time he entered into the insurance contract (art. 213). Except as otherwise agreed, the following losses are assimilated to damage caused by fire: (a) damage caused by fire of an adjacent building or by measures taken for extinguishing or confining the fire, (b) loss or a damage occurred during the removal of insured objects for rescuing them from the fire and (c) damage occurred by thunder, explosion or other similar events, even if no fire was caused (art. 214). Except as otherwise agreed, the insurer's risks arising from fire insurance begin at noon of the day following the date of the insurance policy (art. 215). The damage caused by fire is calculated by deducting from the value which the building had before the fire, the value which remained after the fire (art. 216).

In case of crop insurance, the indemnity due by the insurer is calculated in accordance with the value which the crop would have had at the time of its ripeness or at the time of the usual harvest, if the peril had not occurred (art. 218).

Transport insurance may have as its object the value of the transported goods plus expenses until their arrival at destination and the expected profit from the higher value they have in the place of destination; if the expected profit was not separately valued in the policy, it is not included in the insurance value (art. 219). Except if otherwise agreed, the risks for the transport insurer begin at the time the goods are delivered for being transported and continue until the goods are delivered at the place of destination; transient interruption of the transport and deviation from the agreed itinerary or change of the agreed means of transport do not exempt the insurer from his liability if such changes were necessary for effecting the transport (art. 220).

Export credit insurance is governed by L.D. 501/1968 on insurance of export credits and R.D. 229/1971 on extension of the insurance activity of the Credit Insurance Fund. Such fund was created by L.D. 501/1968 as a private corporation to insure any kind of export credits against risks arising from measures of public authorities, Greek or foreign, affecting the exports and from insolvency or rejection by foreign purchasers of goods or services sold to them.

### D. *Life Insurance* (ασφάλιση ζωής, asphalisi zois)

Anyone may insure for an agreed amount of money his own life or of the life of a third person, provided in the latter case that the insured has an interest in such life (art. 221). The insurer is not bound to pay the agreed sum if the death of the insured occurred as a result of a judicial sentence, a duel or a voluntary suicide or had as immediate cause a felony or a misdemeanor committed by the insured, and the insured could have foreseen the consequences; except if otherwise agreed, the insurer in such a case is entitled to the premium (art. 222). Any change of residence, occupation, civil status or life habits of the insured does not affect the insurance contract if such incidents do not aggravate the risk of the insurer, and if the insurer after getting knowledge did not request the contract to be rescinded; in case of such a rescission, the insurer is bound to restitute to the insured one third of the premiums collected (art. 223). The provisions of articles 202 and 203 hereinabove are applicable also to life insurance (art. 224).

### E. *Inspection of the Insurance Business*

Such inspection is governed basically by L.D. 400/1970 on private insurance business, and especially for the marine insurance by L.D. 551/1970 on private insurance business for ships and aircrafts.

1. L.D 400/1970 is divided in nine chapters. The first chapter, entitled 'General Provisions', comprises articles 1–13. In accordance with article 1, all insurance companies operating in Greece, whether Greek or foreign, are subject to supervision by the Ministry of Commerce. The insurance business is carried on in Greece only by corporations engaged exclusively in insurance operations; exceptionally, marine insurance may be carried on through representatives of Lloyd's brokers in Greece (art. 2). In order to operate an insurance business in Greece a license is required, granted by the Minister of Commerce, who is also authorized to recall such license (art. 3); now the respective power is vested upon decentralized authorities, i.e. the prefects. Insurance businesses operating in Greece are bound to issue only in Greece insurance policies to persons residing in Greece. By way of exception the insurance policies for insurance contracts concluded in London by Lloyd's brokers may be issued abroad, but

such policies must be countersigned by the representative of Lloyd's brokers in Greece. Upon official authorization, a life insurance may be transferred abroad if the insured has changed his residence. Insurance policies issued in Greece must be drawn in Greek language, except for such policies covering transport insurance from or to a foreign country, or for ship and aircraft insurances; such policies may be drawn in a foreign language. Insurance indemnities are payable in Greece except in cases of transport insurances where the beneficiary is a consignee residing abroad (art. 4). The share capital and all kinds of reserves of the Greek insurance businesses have to be invested in the way prescribed specifically by articles 6–9. On all insurance investments the insured holds a lien for the insurance indemnities owed to him, which lien ranks over all other general or special liens; such lien is enforceable even in case of dissolution or bankruptcy of the insurance business; attachment of insurance investments is allowed only by an insured or by third parties, beneficiaries of insurance indemnities, and only on the basis of a court order (art. 10).

The second chapter (arts. 14–19) entitled 'on Greek insurance companies' contains provisions: (a) on the documents which a Greek insurance company is bound to submit to the inspecting authority in order to obtain a license (art. 15), (b) on the composition of the board of directors: the majority of the directors must be Greek citizens (art. 16), (c) on the minimum of share capital required for the company's foundation (art. 17), (d) on the amounts to be retained as ordinary reserves: one fifth of the annual profits until the reserves exceed the quadruple of the share capital (art. 18) and (e) on the documents and other information which have to be annually submitted to the supervising authority (art. 19).

Chapter three (arts. 20–24) deals with foreign insurance companies. Under the proviso of reciprocity, a foreign insurance company may establish a branch office in Greece if it meets the standards required by its national law, and its capital is not inferior to that required for a Greek insurance company operating the same insurance branches; such foreign insurance company has to submit to the Greek supervising authority the documents and data enumerated in article 20, as well as a bail in accordance with the branches operated (art. 21). Such foreign company must also have a representative domiciled in Greece (art. 22), and submit annually to the supervising authority certain documents and data (art. 23). Article 24 deals with Lloyd's brokers in London.

The fourth chapter (arts. 25–29) is devoted to the insurance agents, brokers and surveyors, while the fifth chapter (arts. 30–34) contains provisions on tariffs, premiums, dues and commissions. Chapter six (arts. 35–42) provides for mutual insurance associations and funds which are allowed only to insure against risks relating to the profession of their members, and for capital insurance (arts. 39–42). Chapter seven (arts. 43–50) deals with the penalties inflicted for violating the provisions of the act. In the last chapter (final provisions), article 56 is of importance by virtue of which standard general conditions for each insurance branch may be fixed by decrees issued upon proposal of the Minister of Commerce.

2. L.D. 551/1970 was enacted with the manifest aim of securing to the

Greek insurance business conditions apt to resist the competition of foreign underwriters and clubs. In article 1 are defined the risks against which ships and aircraft may be insured. Such risks are: (a) perils to which vessels and aircraft are exposed during their exploitation and while under construction, (b) third parties' liabilities, (c) risks covered by clubs and other mutual insurance associations. As a 'ship' for the purpose of this law is considered any vessel and any other floating structure moving on the sea, on lakes, waterroutes and on an air-cushion over water, by or without proper propulsion. As 'aircraft' is considered any flying device moving by or without proper propulsion. For entering the branch of ships and aircraft insurance, a specific license by the supervising authority is required (art. 2). To such insurance companies certain exemptions are allowed from the general regulations. For example, they may stipulate in their policies foreign currencies, draw same in foreign languages, designate foreign jurisdictions for disputes arising out of them; they enjoy, further, exemption from stamp duties on all their activities as well as from income tax on all profits not distributed to the shareholders (art. 3). They are also exempt from the obligation to effect the technical reserves provided for in articles 7 and 8 of L.D. 400/1970; they may invest their reserves at their free choice (art. 6). In all other matters, the provisions of L.D. 400/1970 find application (art. 8). Articles 4 and 5 provide for the formation of a joint venture by the insurance businesses operating ship and aircraft insurance. Such a joint venture was in fact established by the Greek insurance companies as a private corporation under the name of 'Greek Joint Venture of Ships and Aircraft Insurance'.

## Bibliography

(in Greek unless otherwise indicated)

*Bankruptcy*

T. Liacopoulos, Le redressement des entreprises en difficulté en droit hellénique, *Rev. int'le dr. comp.* 1985. 985–999.

*Warehouse Receipts*

I. Anastassiadis, *Treatise on Warehouse Receipts and Pawn Certificates* (1907).

*Industrial Property*

N. Deloukas, *The Commercial Business. Industrial Property*, 2d ed. (1980).

*Unfair Competition*

E. Alexandridou, *Law of Competition and Consumer Protection*, 3d ed. (1986).

L. Kotsiris, *Law of Competition*, 2d ed. (1986).

A. Liacopoulos, *Economic Freedom as Object of Protection in the Law of Competition* (1981).

N. Rocas, *Unfair Competition* (1975).

N. Rocas – E. Perakis, Greece, in Matthew Bender's *World Law of Competition* (1983) (in English).
G. Simitis, *Unfair Competition* (1929).
C. Voutsis, *Protection of Business* (1982).

*Trade Marks and Source Indications*
N. Deloukas, *The Protection of a Commercial Business*, 2d ed. (1980).
M. Moumouris, *The Cancellation of Trade Marks* (1967).
K. Pampoukis, *The Law of Distinctive Signs* (1965).
N. Rocas, *The Law of Trade Marks* (1978).
N. Rocas, *Indications of Geographic Provenance* (1979).
C. Sokolis, *On Trade and Industrial Marks* (1902).
T. Vosenberg, *The Notion and the Inadmissibility of the Trade Mark* (1969).

*Patents*
A. Argyriadis, *Inventions*, 4th ed. (1984).

*Intellectual Property*
K. Asprogerakas-Grivas, *Questions of Intellectual Property* (1970).
L. Kotsiris, Greek Copyright Law: A Case Study of Copyright Protection in Greece for a Plan of U.S. Division, *16 Int'l Rev. Ind. Prop. and Copyright Law* 734 (1985) (in English).
G. Koumantos, *Intellectual Property*, 4th ed. (1984).
C. Lykiardopoulos – T. Ioannou, *Intellectual Property*, 2d ed. (1962).

*Insurance*
A. Argyriadis, *Elements of Insurance Law*, 4th ed. (1986).
S. Bakas-Tsirimonaki, Les principes généraux du droit hellénique de l'assurance, *Rev. int'le dr. comp.* 1985. 69–106.
N. Deloukas, Grundzüge des griechischen Versicherungsaufsichtsrechts, *Zeitschrift für die gesamte Versicherungswissenschaft* 56 (1967) 137–149.
B. Kiantos, *Insurance Law*, 2d ed. (1985).
J. Passias, *Life Insurance* (1936).
C. Rocas, *Life Insurance* (1936).
C. Rocas, *The Insurance of a Third Party's Life* (1936).
C. Rocas, *Private Insurance Law* (1974).
J. Rocas, *The Private Insurance Law in the Decisions of the Courts* (1979).

# Chapter 11
# Business Associations

*Phaedon John Kozyris**

## I. Introduction

Greece is a civil law country and its laws regulating business associations are in many respects similar to those of the other Continental countries, especially France whose Commercial Code has had a major impact.

Following civil law patterns, the thrust of Greek law is not to enable, as in the U.S., but to regulate. Not only does it contain many mandatory substantive provisions but also subjects business associations to significant governmental controls through an authorization and supervision process.

The statutory scheme for business associations in Greece appears confusing to an outside observer who is lost in the multiplicity and diversity of the relevant texts. In sorting things out, it is important to take cognizance of the generic backdrop provisions of the Civil Code: articles 741–784, which in principle apply to all entities, and articles 61–77 which govern those that have legal personality. For a fuller explication of the regime governing such entities, see above, Ch. 4. Incidentally, most companies constitute legal entities, the exceptions being some civil partnerships and the silent partnership. For commercial companies, one has also to look to the special provisions of the Commercial Code. A project to reform the Commercial Code, including the corporate sections, produced a 1981 draft which was subsequently slightly modified but not as yet adopted by the Parliament. Certain forms such as the corporation and the close corporation are subject to detailed *ad hoc* statutes providing still a third set of governing rules. Special legislation provides comprehensive treatment of 'maritime' corporations formed under it (L. 959/1979). Statutes dealing with certain industries, for example, banking, insurance and transportation sometimes impose additional requirements on companies in those industries. Two recent presidential decrees (409/1986 and 498/1987) harmonized corporate law with the First, Second, Third, Fourth, Sixth and Seventh Directives of the EEC Council. These Directives relate principally to the protection of third parties dealing with the corporation, to corporate consolidation and to the method of presentation of financial information.

The descriptions in this Chapter are necessarily summary, elliptical and

*Professor of Law, The Ohio State University.

oversimplified. The emphasis is on business associations and more particularly on the basic corporate and partnership forms. The peculiarities in Continental law relating to the fundamental distinction between commercial and civil companies are not pursued because they relate principally to the external activities of the companies and not to their structure or governance on which this Chapter is focused.

The most difficult task of the explicator of Greek corporate law in English is selecting the proper terminology. The corporate species in Greece contains creatures that are different and more numerous than those in the Anglo-American world and even under the best of circumstances a translator aims only at an approximation. To illustrate the point from the world of fishes, it is like calling the 'barbouni': red mullet and the 'lavraki': striped bass! *Traduire, c'est trahir, traduttore-traditore*.... My survey of English-language texts dealing with Continental and Greek corporate law discovered a bewildering diversity of terms and all too many inconsistencies and questionable uses. In the absence of an accepted legal esperanto, one has to make his own choices and I use 'company' to encompass the broad generic meaning of the Greek 'εταιρία' and of the French 'société'. Purported synonyms such as association, venture, entity and enterprise are less apt and potentially misleading. For each particular type of company, the closest English term has been selected and, following the Greek name and its customary acronym, if any, the French equivalents are sometimes added in parentheses. The discussion and explication that follows will be centered on those features of the various companies that present significant differences from their Anglo-American counterparts, with the emphasis placed on the second part of the hyphen.

## II. Corporation (ανώνυμη εταιρία, anonymi etairia, A.E., société anonyme)

Relevant sources are articles 29 ff Com. C.; articles 888–900 C.C.; Law 2190/1920, as amended and codified in R.D. 174/1963, P.D. 409/1986 and P.D. 498/1987.

The corporation is the form used by most business enterprises of some substance and dimension and, as a consequence, carries the most prestige. It enjoys all the attributes of corporateness, its governance structure is tripartite and it is taxed as a separate entity.

### *A. Formation*

Instant incorporation by filing a one-page paper signed by an incorporator without the payment of capital, quite common in the U.S., is not possible in Greece. For a corporation to come into existence, certain indispensable steps must all take place:

1. An instrument containing the corporate charter must be executed before a notary by at least two persons (natural or legal) who are the 'founders'

συμβολαιο γράφος

(ιδρυτές, idrytes), and not just ephemeral incorporators. According to the prevailing view, this instrument is in the nature of bilateral or multilateral durational contract.

2. The founders must subscribe to all the shares of the corporation (the minimum required capital is 5 million drs. or about $38,000) at or above par and must pay at least 25% of such subscriptions, but not less than 5 million drs., within two months from formation, except for shares issued for property which must be paid in full. The balance must be paid within no more than ten years. Under a rarely used alternative, for which prior approval of the Capital Markets Committee is required, the capital of the corporation may be opened to public subscription through a bank or financial institution, in which case the minimum capitalization and initial payment must be at least 50 million drs. ($380,000) and an application for listing must be filed with the Stock Exchange within a year.

3. Approval must be obtained by decision of the local prefecture, or the Ministry of Commerce in certain instances, confirming compliance with the legal requirements of formation. Refusal to approve is subject to review by the administrative courts.

4. Publication of the charter and of the decision of approval must be made in a special section of the Official Gazette.

A corporation may be declared null and void for failure to meet the formal requirements on its name and capitalization, if its purpose is unlawful or against the public order, if it has fewer than two founders or if all founders lacked legal capacity at formation. Annulment does not, however, affect past rights and obligations. It is followed by wind up and liquidation.

## *B. Charter* (καταστατικό, katastatiko, statutes)

This document is very extensive and contains most of the bylaws as well. In addition to the usual content of its U.S. counterpart (name, duration, capitalization, seat, first board), the required provisions must deal with the manner of payment of capital, the convocation, composition, operation and authority of the board and of the meetings of shareholders, the statutory auditors, the rights and limitations of shares and shareholders, the balance sheet and method of distributing profits and the dissolution and the liquidation of assets. In addition, the charter's optional clauses may add further restrictions to the minimum legal requirements, for example, by requiring supermajorities for amendment or for board or shareholder action. Duration of the corporation must be for a definite period. General purpose clauses are not valid and the corporate name must have some connection with the purpose.

While the corporate purpose (its object or at least its nature) limits the very capacity of the corporation to act (*ultra vires*), such limitation may not be asserted against third parties who did not and should not have known it. A third party may rely on the authority of the persons who represent the corporation and lack of authority may not be opposed to it unless he knew it. In any event, legal incapacity is deemed to exist for acts expressly prohibited by law, for example, acquisition by the corporation of its own shares. Persons acting for a corporation to be formed are liable jointly and severally but the corporation may, within three months of formation, assume sole responsibility for acts done in its name.

### *C. Capital* (κεφάλαιο, kephalaio)

The features and rights of shares (μετοχές, metoches, actions) are subject to extensive limitations and regulation. The terms of all shares must be defined in the charter. Shares of common stock must have par value; be registered until fully paid when they may be changed to the bearer; have voting rights, equal within each class and, most importantly, proportionate to their ratio to total capitalization so that the number of votes to be cast depends on par value; be subscribed for and issued, there being no such thing as just authorized shares. Preferred stock may also be issued in all sort of variations (cumulative, participating, profit-sharing, interest-bearing etc.) and need not have voting rights. Voting preferred may be convertible into common. The transferability of registered shares may be limited in the charter. The concept of treasury shares is unknown. A corporation may not acquire its own shares except in certain limited circumstances and even then it must either cancel or sell them. Furthermore, a subsidiary (over 50% ownership of capital) may not acquire shares in the parent. Acquisition of all the shares by one person does not affect the corporate existence.

The subscription price of shares may be paid in cash or in property which has monetary value. It is disputed whether intangible property difficult to appraise is acceptable. The valuation of contributions in kind must be made by a special external committee consisting of one or two senior civil servants or certified public accountants and a representative of the Chamber of Commerce. The valuation report is published in the Official Gazette. Future services do not constitute property. Thus, it is virtually impossible to issue watered stock or discount or bonus shares. It should be pointed out, however, that the founders of the corporation may be compensated with special non-voting, no-par value, redeemable shares up to 10% of total capitalization which entitle the owners solely to a share in the net profits over a period of time.

Increases or decreases of capital require a charter amendment adopted by the shareholders at an extraordinary meeting and subject to similar approval and publicity requirements as the initial incorporation. Reduction of capital is subject to certain safeguards to protect the rights of creditors and holders of other classes of securities. An amendment to increase capital may be avoided, however, within the first five years, if the charter so provides. In that case, the board, by a two-third vote of its entire membership, may issue additional stock up to an amount equal to paid-in capital. Similar authorization may be given by the meeting of shareholders for maximum periods of five years at a time. Preemptive rights unavoidably attach to the issuance of all shares of stock other than those issued for property as well as of other securities convertible into shares of stock.

Debt securities (ομολογίες, omologies, obligations) may be issued in registered or bearer form only if and as authorized by the shareholders at an extraordinary meeting and are subject to the approval of the Ministry of Commerce or prefecture. Debt securities may be convertible into common stock but only up to one-half of paid-up equity capital. Debt securities may be open to public subscription through a bank or financial institution but to an amount not less than 50 million drs. ($380,000) and not more than the fully-paid equity capital and only after permission of the Capital Markets Committee. An application for the listing of these securities on the Stock Exchange must be filed within a year. The return on debt securities may include certain profit participation. If shareholders' equity is impaired by more than one-half, the board must call a shareholders meeting to decide whether to restore it, reduce capital or dissolve the corporation.

## D. *Meetings of Shareholders* (γενικές συνελεύσεις μετόχων, genikes syneleuseis metochon)

### 1. Convocation

An annual meeting must be held within six months of the end of the fiscal year. Exclusive authority to call other regular or extraordinary meetings as well is vested in the board who is obligated to do so when the law requires it or at the request of the statutory auditors or of shareholders holding five percent of paid-up capital. A minimum twenty-day notice by publication, including the full agenda, is mandatory unless all shareholders are present. Only matters on the agenda may be acted upon and open-ended clauses such as 'any other business' are not given effect. Within the ten days before the meeting, any shareholder may request a copy of the balance sheet (ισολογισμός, isologismos, *bilan*) and of the reports of the directors and of the statutory auditors. For a shareholder to attend and participate in a meeting it is required that he deposit his shares or proxy documents at least five days in advance with the corporation or with a bank or financial institution in Greece or abroad if so provided. At least forty-eight hours before the meeting, a list of shareholders entitled to vote must be prominently displayed at the corporate offices.

### 2. Quorum, Voting

One-fifth of the paid-up capital constitutes quorum at regular meetings, including the annual and the special meetings. For extraordinary meetings, however, the minimum requirement is two-thirds. Resolutions are adopted by the absolute or two-thirds majority of the quorum respectively. Voting by proxy is permitted. There are no provisions for taking action by consent without a meeting.

3. Authority

The exclusive authority of the meeting of shareholders extends to the following: Charter amendments, election of directors and statutory auditors, approval of balance sheet, dividends, issuance of debt instruments, mergers, extention of life and dissolution and appointment of liquidators. The charter may authorize the board to elect directors to complete itself for the period until the first meeting of shareholders or to fill vacancies.

As part of the government supervision over corporations, its representative may attend meetings at his discretion.

*E. Board of Directors* (διοικητικό συμβούλιο, dioikitiko symvoulio, conseil d'administration) *and Officers*

The board consists of at least three members who need not be shareholders, natural persons or citizens or residents of Greece. The term of a director may not exceed six years and he is removable by the shareholders at any time at will. The charter may provide that no more than one-third of the board is to be appointed and dismissed by certain shareholders who thereby lose their right to vote for the remaining directors. The division of corporate management into an executive and a supervisory branch available in France, Germany and other countries is not known in Greece. The board is required to meet at least once a month. A majority of the directors but not less than three constitutes quorum. Decisions are normally taken by a majority of the quorum. Voting by proxy is allowed but only by a director holding only one proxy.

The board collegially manages and represents the corporation in all respects subject to such limitations as are provided in the charter or adopted by resolution of the meeting of shareholders. In the latter instance, however, they may not prejudice the rights of bona fide third persons.

One of the most remarkable differences between the Anglo-American system and that of some continental countries such as Greece is that in the latter the law does not require or provide for the appointment of officers. This explains why the discussion in the English language literature on the role and powers of the persons who exercise executive functions in continental corporations is usually confused and incomplete. Generally speaking, traditional American law separates the decision-making and the executive functions but allows them to be combined in the same persons whereas Greek law places them in the same persons but allows them to be separated.

The charter may provide that one or more directors or outsiders have the power to represent the corporation in general or on certain matters. Alternatively, the charter may contain a broader provision enabling the board to delegate authority to its members or others relating to matters of representation and business management. Whether functions relating to the structure and governance of the corporation are delegable, for example increasing capital, filling board vacancies or approving the balance sheet, is unclear. It should be noted that delegation is not deemed to be a transfer so that the board always maintains concurrent authority to act and the delegees, unlike corporate officers in the U.S., are not vested, so to speak, with autonomy. A typical pattern is for the board to designate a General Manager (γενικός διευθυντής, genikos dieuthyntis) or to appoint one of its members as General Managing Director (διευθύνων σύμβουλος, dieuthynon symvoulos) making him in effect the Chief Executive Officer of the corporation. The board may also appoint one of its members a Special Managing Director to act jointly with others or on certain matters only (εντεταλμένος σύμβουλος, entetalmenos symvoulos). When the General Manager is not a member of the board the presumption is that he is hierarchically below the managing directors. Many of the executive functions are performed by high-level employees.

Directors are required to perform their duties with the reasonable care that they exercise in their personal affairs. The burden is on them to prove that their subjective standard of care is lower than that of the average reasonable man. The managing director is liable objectively and even for slight negligence. Directors are totally exonerated if their action was based on a lawful resolution of the meeting of shareholders. While the specific concept of 'business judgment' is not used, there is little question that the directors enjoy considerable discretion in choosing alternatives when making management decisions.

Directors and managers are also subject to various duties of loyalty, including confidentiality and non-competition (absent charter authorization or prior approval of the meeting of shareholders). Where unlawful competition has taken place, the profits may be recovered on a theory resembling constructive trust. Loans, credits or loan guarantees by the corporation or a subsidiary to founders, directors, general managers or managers and their spouses and relatives are forbidden, void and subject to criminal penalties. All contracts between the corporation and such persons or corporations managed by such persons not concluded in the ordinary course of business are void if there was no prior approval at a meeting of shareholders by a two-thirds vote. Within two years of corporate formation or of an increase of capital, acquisitions of assets by the corporation from directors or founders or their relatives are void, with certain exceptions, to the extent that they exceed ten-percent of paid-up capital unless approved by the shareholders and by the Ministry of Commerce. Directors generally may not vote on transactions in which they have an interest.

Detailed provisions regulate director compensation. A specific amount may be provided in the charter but usually is not. The annual meeting of shareholders may add other sums and provide for a share in the net profits after deduction of legal reserves and of a 6% allowance for dividends. The court, however, may reduce it if it is found exorbitant and at least 10% of the shareholders voted against it. All these limitations do not apply to payments made to directors for other services rendered under employment contracts.

Directors breaching their duties to the corporation are liable in damages. But the derivative action mechanism is not known in Greece and shareholders have no direct means of redress. The board itself has an obligation to sue if the wrong was intentional or if it is so requested by resolution adopted at a meeting of shareholders or by shareholders holding at least one-third of the paid-up capital acquired not less than three months before. The meeting or the court on petition of the requesting shareholders may appoint special agents to pursue the action.

### F. *Special Protection of Minority Shareholders*

Holders of shares representing 5% or more of paid-up capital may demand: (a) convocation of a special meeting, (b) postponement of action at a meeting, (c) disclosure to a meeting of information on corporate business and more particularly on the amounts paid to directors, managers, employees or parties to corporate contracts within the last two years; such disclosure may be avoided only for good reason, (d) roll-call balloting, and (e) extraordinary audit by judicial order when it appears probable that there were violations of the law, the charter or resolutions of the meeting of shareholders.

Shareholders of at least one-third of paid-up capital not having a representative on the board may also demand: (a) disclosure to them of information on the corporate business and property, which may be refused only for a good and substantial reason and (b) an extraordinary audit by judicial order when it appears that the corporation is not properly managed.

It should be noted here that an extraordinary audit may be requested also by the governmental authorities that supervise the corporate operations.

### G. *Dividends* (μερίσματα, merismata)

Unlike U.S. law, which leaves it to the discretion of the directors to decide if, when and how much is to be paid in dividends, Greek law places this issue within the exclusive authority of the meeting of shareholders, and contains a full set of mandatory rules on the disposition of net profits as follows: (a) at least 5% must be credited to a legal reserve until it equals one-third of the capital, intended to offset future losses; additional reserves may be set up in the charter and (b) after deduction of the legal reserve, at least 35% of the profits equal to at least 6% of paid-up capital must be distributed to the shareholders as a first dividend unless waived as to the 35% element by a 75% and entirely by a 100% vote of the shareholders; to the extent that this dividend exceeds 3% of the paid-up capital, it and other dividends may be paid in stock. Dividends may be paid out of current or retained profits but not out of capital surplus or the legal reserves. Beyond the first dividend, the distribution takes place as provided in the charter. No dividends may be paid if capital is or will become impaired. Stock splits and reverse splits require charter amendment.

### H. *Statutory Auditors* (ελεγκτές, elenktes) *and Financial Statements*

The financial statements to be prepared for every annual meeting of shareholders include the balance sheet and the profit and loss statement. The law requires the appointment at the annual meeting of shareholders of two statutory auditors (or one if he is a Certified Public Accountant) and the fixing of their compensation. These persons follow corporate accounting throughout the year, review and certify the financial statements and report to the next meeting. They are empowered to make recommendations to the board but, beyond that, to blow the whistle to the Ministry of Commerce or prefecture if they detect a violation of the law or of the charter. They may also demand the convocation of a special meeting of the shareholders. Their liability based on fault may not be contractually reduced. These auditors are less dependent on management than their U.S. counterparts and they are supposed to act as watchdogs for the shareholders and the public interest. On the other hand, the control of the government over the CPA organization raises questions of independence in a different sense.

The law prescribes in substantial detail the form of financial statements and the major classifications to be adopted in drawing up the balance sheet. In addition, the law requires their publication before the meeting in the Official Gazette and in two newspapers. Finally, the financial statements require shareholder approval.

Presidential Decree 498/1987 conformed Greek corporate law to the basic requirements of the Seventh Directive of the EEC Council. Extensive and detailed consolidated statements must be prepared for all corporations, close corporations and limited partnerships by shares which are linked together either by parent-subsidiary ties or by other methods of control, for example management contracts. Small enterprises are excluded. Consolidation is required even if some of the enterprises are not subject to Greek law. These provisions have been added as articles 90–109 of Law 2190/1920. It should be also noted that the consolidated statements must be certified by one or more CPAs and are subject to extensive publicity requirements.

### *I. Consolidation, Transformation, Division, Dissolution, Liquidation* (συγχώνευση, μετατροπή, διάσπαση, λύση, εκκαθάριση, synchoneusi, metatropi, diaspasi, lysi, ekkatharisi)

Consolidation may involve only corporations, not a corporation and other companies, and takes the form either of a merger of one into another or of a purchase of the latter's assets or the formation of a new corporation. The agreements require approval of the shareholders of all corporations at extraordinary meetings, as well as of the Ministry of Commerce or prefecture, and substantial notice and publicity requirements must be met. It is also possible to transform a corporation into a close corporation or even into a general or limited partnership in certain circumstances. The law contains extensive regulation of the substantive, financial and procedural aspects of consolidation and of transformation which may not be summarized here effectively.

It should be also mentioned that Greece has recently amended extensively and amplified its corporate law relating to (a) consolidation through long and short form merger (absorption or formation of a new corporation) or acquisition of all the assets of another corporation(s) and (b) division (break-up or spin-off) (P.D. 498/1987). Thus, Greek law now is consistent with the Third and Sixth Directives of the EEC Council which impose disclosure requirements as well as protections of creditors and employees. The new provisions, which are quite comprehensive in their treatment of the entire subject of consolidation and division, appear in articles 68–89 added to Law 2190/1920.

Dissolution of a corporation takes place when (a) its term has expired, (b) it has been declared bankrupt, (c) it is so decided by the shareholders at an extraordinary meeting, or (d) the conditions for dissolution provided in the charter have been fulfilled. In addition, dissolution may be caused by a revocation of the ministerial decision approving formation on the ground that: (a) the required capital has not been paid in at formation, (b) directors or managing persons sentenced to prison terms for actions related to corporate matters have not been removed from office, (c) corporate book net worth falls below one-tenth of paid-up capital, or (d) balance sheets for three or more years approved by the shareholders have not been submitted to the Ministry.

Dissolution, except for bankruptcy, is followed by winding up and liquidation. Liquidators are appointed at a meeting of shareholders. Their task is to inventory and sell the assets, complete pending transactions, make the required publicity and settle all claims and debts, distributing the residue, if any, to the shareholders. Pending liquidation, the board becomes inoperative but the meeting of shareholders retains its powers being the corporate organ to which the liquidators are accountable.

In sum, the legal regime of a Greek corporation is significantly different from that of an American one in the substantial formalities, government approval, publicity, and minimum capitalization required for organization; the combination of charter and bylaws into one instrument and the lack of significant power of the directors over it; the virtually exclusive powers of shareholders over the terms and issuance of securities, the declaration of dividends and the appointment of the staturory auditors; the requirement of proportionality between economic and voting rights; the lack of provisions for executive management through officers and the power given to the directors to set up any desired structure; and the non-availability of the derivative action mechanism.

## III. Close Corporation (εταιρία περιορισμένης ευθύνης, etairia periorismenis euthynis, Ε.ΠΕ., société a responsabilité limitée; L. 3190/1955)

This corporate form, meaning literally, and often called, 'limited liability company', is quite common for smaller businesses and family enterprises.

The principal differences between it and a regular corporation are the following:

### *A. Formation and Charter*

Minimum capital is only 200,000 drs. ($1,500) but (a) it must be subscribed in full and paid in at formation and (b) at least 100,000 drs. must be paid in cash. In drafting the charter, it is important to include all the provisions that depart from the permissive statutory pattern of regulation. The charter needs no ministerial approval but must be registered with the court. Furthermore, special taxes of about 6% of capital are assessed.

### *B. Capital*

Instead of shares, the close corporation issues 'parts' (μερίδια, meridia) which are transferable unless, as is often the case, the charter prohibits or limits inter vivos transfers or provides for preferential purchase at death by the remaining members (εταίροι, etairoi). The transfer, however, may not take place by negotiation but by notarial instrument and is subject again to a substantial tax. In fact, no negotiable instruments of any kind, e.g., debentures, bonds and shares of stock are permissible. Only one kind of part may be issued but the charter may provide for all types of variations in the rights attaching to the part, especially the economic ones, that in a certain sense each part may become a different class of stock. The principle of 'one part one vote', however, must be respected. If all parts come to be held by one person, he becomes prospectively personally liable for corporate obligations as a partner for the duration and the corporation may be dissolved.

### *C. Meetings of Members*

An annual meeting is to be called by the administrator and must be called at the request of any member. Special meetings are called at the request of holders of 5% of the capital. If the administrator fails to call a meeting, the requesters may obtain the permission of the court to convene it themselves. There are no quorum requirements. The partnership aspect of the close corporation emerges in the voting requirements. Ordinary resolutions require approval by the absolute, and extraordinary ones by a three-quarter majority of the members not only per parts but also per capita. Extraordinary resolutions are needed for (a) increases or decreases (but not below 200,000 drs.) of capital, (b) amendment of the charter other than for the appointment or removal of an administrator, (c) the activation of the mandatory contributions to capital to make up capital impairment provided in the charter and (d) dissolution. A unanimous vote is required for any changes in the rights, obligations and responsibilities of members or for releasing the administrator from the non-competition obligation. Actions by the corporation against the administrator or other members for breach of duty require member authorization by an ordinary majority.

Members have full rights of information on corporate business and rights of inspection of the corporate books.

### D. *Management and Interested Transactions*

Theoretically, the close corporation is managed by all the members acting unanimously. In practice, it is almost always run by one or more administrators (διαχειριστές, diacheiristes), who need not be members, natural persons, citizens or residents, appointed in the charter or at a meeting of the members and having such authority as provided therein. The administrator is removable by the meeting of members at will without prejudice to his contract rights, if any, except that administrators who are also members and who have been appointed in the charter may be removed only for an important reason upon permission of the court. All appointments and removals must be published in the Official Gazette.

Loans to members may be made but loans from members may not be secured on corporate assets and are subordinate to other indebtedness. The non-competition obligation may be extended by the charter to the members.

There are no provisions for the appointment of statutory auditors. The financial statements are prepared by the administrator and submitted to the meeting of the members for approval. Close corporations which belong to a corporate group are now required to be included in the consolidated financial statements under the Seventh Directive of the EEC Council implemented by Presidential Decree 498/1987.

### E. *Distribution of Profits*

Beyond the 5% legal reserve requirement for one-third of capital, all the net profits are distributed unless the charter provides otherwise. This is consistent with the treatment of the corporation as a partnership for tax purposes.

### F. *Retirement of Members – Dissolution, Liquidation, Merger, Transformation*

In view of the usual non-transferability of his parts, a member may become locked-in and be oppressed by the majority. The charter may provide for a method of withdrawal but, in addition, any member has the right to retire for an important reason on permission of the court, in which case he must be paid the appraisal value of his parts. Furthermore, the majority may expel and buy out a member again for an important reason, not necessarily fault, as determined by the court.

In addition to the grounds provided for in the law or the charter, including bankruptcy, death and expiration of time, a close corporation may be dissolved by extraordinary resolution of the members or by the court for an important reason on petition of 10% of more of its membership or because of concentration of all the parts in one member. If one half of the capital is lost, the administrator is obligated to call a meeting to decide on dissolution or reduction of capital. Liquidation ordinarily is conducted by the administrator.

A close corporation may merge into another such corporation in a manner quite similar to that for ordinary corporations.

A close corporation may be transformed into a regular corporation upon decision taken by extraordinary majorities of the members and provided that certain formalities, paralleling those of formation of a corporation, be complied with. Dissenting members are automatically relieved of all restrictions on the transferability of their parts. The attractiveness of transformation is its tax-free status which requires, however, that at least 75% of the shares in the new corporation representing old capital be in registered form and non-transferable for five years. In conclusion, the Greek close corporation differs from the typical American one in the requirement for minimum capitalization, the absence of a maximum limit on membership, the detailed provisions for management, the existence of some right of withdrawal of members and the easier availability of dissolution.

## IV. General Partnership (ομόρρυθμη εταιρία, omorrythmi etairia, O.E., société en nom collectif; arts. 20ff Com. C.)

The law governing general commercial partnerships in Greece is similar or identical to Anglo-American law in most major respects, such as unlimited joint and several personal liability of partners; non-transferability of interests without unanimous consent and dissolution on death, retirement, bankruptcy of a partner (*intuitus personae*); control and management by all unless otherwise agreed; authority of partner to bind partnership with third parties regardless of internal limitations; and the like.

A conceptual difference is that the partnership is considered in all respects, not just some, as an entity which means that the 'aggregate' theory is not recognized. This generally simplifies matters in terms of making agreements, acquiring property and suing and being sued. A practical difference of some importance is that a writing is required for its formation as a legal entity which includes data on its name, the partners, the commercial purpose to be pursued (compare the 'business for profit' requirement in American law), the share in profits and losses, the duration which may be indefinite and the management. This writing must be filed with the court within fifteen days of formation and the name must also be registered with the Chamber of Commerce. The Commercial Code project of 1981 would also recognize the informal partnership but without legal personality. The tax on formation is about 4%. As to other taxes, the partnership is not a taxpayer but only a reporter.

Partnership creditors may pursue the partners individually, without joining the others or the partnership, and primarily, without the necessity of first going against the partnership or showing that it is insolvent. What is more, the partners are bound and subject to direct execution, even though they had not been made parties to the related actions, on judgments against the partnership on *res judicata* principles (see below, Ch. 15).

Any partner has the power to dissolve a partnership of indefinite duration at will; however, he may be liable in damages if he acts in an untimely manner and without important reason. If the duration is set, he must affirmatively establish an important reason. In the absence of agreement to the contrary, a partner may not otherwise withdraw from the partnership; and dissolution as above or for the other reasons leads to liquidation and termination, not to the continuation of business among the remaining partners. Absent a different agreement, the management of partnership affairs requires unanimous action. A clause in the agreement that a majority vote suffices in case of doubt is interpreted on a per capita rather than per parts basis. A general or limited partnership may be transformed into a close corporation.

Special mention should be made here of the law governing 'civil partnerships', discussed below, which applies residually to general and limited partnerships as well.

## V. Limited Partnership (ετερόρρυθμη εταιρία, eterorrythmi etairia, E.E., société en commandite; arts. 23 ff, 38 Com. C.)

A limited partnership is in essence a general partnership with the interjection of one or more limited partners who are liable only to the extent of their contribution as also in Anglo-American law. Since the general partner may be a corporation or any legal entity, the limited partnership form may insulate all physical persons from liability.

Failure to comply with the formation requirements which are the same as with the general partnership, in particular with the filing obligations, may produce dire consequences, the limited partner being treated then as general. Contrary to Anglo-American law, a limited partner may participate in management without losing his status but only in the internal dimension, that is with his copartners and not in representing the company in its relations with others. Other significant differences, relating mostly to the equal treatment of general and limited partners, include: the possibility of the limited partner contributing services, not only property; dissolution upon his death or bankruptcy or retirement; requirement of his consent for the admission of any new partners; and non-preference in the distribution of assets at dissolution and liquidation.

Greek law also recognizes a special form of limited partnership (κατά μετοχές, kata metoches, by shares, *par actions*), rarely used in practice, where the parts of the limited partners are transformed into negotiable instruments, even bearer shares.

## VI. Silent Partnership (αφανής εταιρία, aphanis etairia, société en participation; arts. 47–50 Com. C.)

The most important features of this form of partnership are that the silent partner or partners have no representative authority, i.e. no power to act for it with third parties, no property but only contract rights in the partnership property and no direct personal liability to third parties. Unless the agreement provides otherwise, all partners participate in internal management equally and have an equal share in profits and losses. The silent partnership has no name and no legal personality and requires no special formalities or publicity. For the non-silent partner, however, to avoid being taxed individually, the agreement among the parties must be deposited with the tax authorities. It should be pointed out that it differs from a subpartnership, that is a regular partnership whose property consists of partnership interests, and from an informal or unpublished general partnership which is subject to the general partnership rules with some modifications and which is under an obligation to proceed with the formalities and make the required publications. In terms of function, the silent partnership is sometimes used to accomplish objectives achieved in the Anglo-American system through a business trust.

## VII. Civil Partnership (αστική εταιρία, astiki etairia, société civile)

Relevant sources are articles 741–783 C. C.; reference should be also made to articles 27, 62 II, 64, 194 III, 286 Ia, 329, 786, 920 C. C. Proc. which deal with the procedural aspects of corporate matters.

This is the generic form of company and the provisions regulating it apply residually to companies of whatever form except where superseded by or inconsistent with the special legislation governing each particular form.

It is formed by agreement among two or more persons pursuing a common purpose, especially an economic one, through contributions. Unless the agreement provides otherwise certain rules prevail: the members are not required to increase their contributions, have equal management rights and obligations without compensation, decisions being subject to the rule of unanimity, and share in profits and losses equally regardless of amount of contribution; in case of doubt, a majority vote is calculated per capita; management authority extends to external representation; profits are distributed at the end of each year. The death or bankruptcy of a member dissolves the partnership. An agreement totally exempting a member from some share in the profits and/or losses may be invalidated at his request. But an agreement exempting a member from losses is valid if his contribution consisted solely of services. In managing the partnership, members are subject to the diligence practiced in their personal affairs but a managing member is required to satisfy an objective standard of care. Managing members designated as such in the agreement may be dismissed only for an important reason by unanimous vote of the remaining members. Similarly, they may resign only for such reason, otherwise they are liable in damages. In the event of losses, members are liable to third parties in proportion to their shares. Partnership property is owned by them in the same proportion. A member may not transfer his shares and may not demand distribution of property before liquidation. Members have the obligation not to act in their outside affairs in a manner detrimental to the interests of the partnership. A member normally has no right to withdraw but has the power to dissolve the partnership before its expiration date but only for an important reason. A partnership of indefinite duration, however, may be dissolved by any member at any time but then such member may be liable to the other members if he acted in an untimely manner without an important reason. A member may be expelled on court order if he breached his duties to the partnership. On dissolution, following the payment of debts, the contributions are returned and the balance is distributed to the members in proportion to their shares.

While generally the civil partnership has no legal personality, it may acquire such if it pursues an economic purpose and it follows the publicity requirements applicable to general partnerships. This, however, does not affect the personal liabilities of its members. The Commercial Code project of 1981 proposes to abolish the civil partnership with legal personality collapsing it into the general partnership.

## Bibliography

Among the major works on Commercial Law in the Greek language covering also business associations should be included:

I. Anastassiadis-C. Rocas, *Greek Commercial Law*, vol. II, 5th ed. (1949).
K. Karavas, *Commercial Law*, vol. I part 1 (1947), part 2 (1950), vol. II part 1 (1952).
K. Karavas, *Manual of Commercial Law*, vol. I, 2d ed. (1962).
K. Karavas (with K. Pampoukis and A. Kiantou-Pampouki), *Manual of Commercial Law*, vol. II part (a) (1965).
A. Kiantou-Pampouki, *Manual of Commercial Law*, vol. I, 2d ed. (1975).
P. Perdikas, *Manual of Commercial Law* (1952).
T. Petimezas, *Commercial Law*, vol. I (1925).
A. Tsirintainis, *Elements of Commercial Law*, vol. II, 6th ed. (1964).

Works dealing only with business associations law include:

L. Georgakopoulos, *Company Law*, vol. I (1965); vol. II (1972); vol. III (1974) (all business associations but with emphasis on corporations).
L. Georgakopoulos, *Companies* (1985) (student text covering all companies).
E. Levantis, *Law of Corporations*, 7th ed. (1982) (commentary on statute by article).
E. Levantis, *Codification of L.2190 on Corporations Following P.D. 409/1986* (1987) (explanation of changes to conform to some of the EEC directives)
E. Levantis, *Close Corporations*, 2d ed. (1972) (commentary on the statute by article).
K. Pampoukis, *Law of Commercial Companies. General Part* (1979).

I. Passias, *The Law of Corporations*, vols. I and II (1955, 1969).
N. Rokas, *Commercial Companies*, 2d ed. (1984).
A. Toussis, *The Corporation and the Close Corporation* (1971).
A work in French and German is N. Rocas, Company Law, in *Jura Europae, Droit des Sociétés*, vol. III 100: Grèce (1986).

For a discussion of the progress made in the EEC on harmonization, see, e.g., Schneebaum, The Company Law Harmonization Program of the European Community, 14 *L. & Pol. Int'l Bus.* 292–334 (1982), and for a summary of the first nine directives see Nieuwdorp, Status Report on EEC Company Law Harmonization, *Int'l Bus. Law* 425–430 (1984). Since a comparative law perspective would be extremely helpful in understanding the information contained in this chapter, reference should be made here to certain of the excellent chapters in the *International Encyclopedia of Comparative Law* dealing with company law issues: J. Heenen, *Partnership and Other Personal Associations for Profit (1975)*, R. Buxbaum, *The Formation of Marketable Share Companies (1974)*, B. Grossfeld, *Management and Control of Marketable Share Companies (1973)*, and A. Conard, *Fundamental Changes in Marketable Share Companies* (1972).

# Chapter 12
# Admiralty and Private Maritime Law

*Nicholas A. Deloukas**

## I. Introduction

Due to her geographical position, Greece since the most ancient times occupied a predominant place in maritime trade and many of its maritime institutions survived up to the present. The island of Rhodes was famous for its maritime laws. During the Turkish occupation of Greece, which lasted some four centuries until the 1820s, the Greeks developed a very intense maritime trade in the Mediterranean, the Black Sea and the other seas of the world. The French 'Marine Ordinance', enacted in 1681 under the reign of Louis XIV, acquired customary application throughout the Mediterranean, extending also on the maritime trade carried on by the Greeks. The provisions of this ordinance were further elaborated in the second book of the French 'Code de Commerce' of 1807 which Code was eventually adopted by the modern Greek State already in 1828. This book underwent extensive modification in 1911 in order to bring the maritime legislation of Greece in line with some recent international conventions and with the Belgian maritime statute of 1909. In 1958 a new Code of Private Maritime Law was introduced by Law 3816, followed a few months later by L.D. 3899/1958, governing preferred mortgages on ships. A Code of Public Maritime Law was enacted by L.D. 187/1973. As of early 1986, a committee has been appointed to consider amending the Code of Private Maritime Law. Due to space limitations, this chapter will cover only the main provisions of that Code, following its titles and chapters.

## II. The Code of Private Maritime Law

### *A. Ships and Their Ownership* (Title 1)

In article 1, a ship is defined as 'any vessel of not less than ten net registered tons of capacity, destined to navigate at sea by her own means of propulsion'. This is narrower than the definition of a ship in article 3 of the Public Maritime Code comprising 'any vessel destined to move on water for the carriage of persons or

* Professor of Law, Emeritus, Athens University.

goods, towage, salvage, fishing, recreation, scientific research, or for any other purpose'. It is to be noted, however, that the provisions of Titles 3 (master), 4 (crew), 6 (affreightment), 7 (fiduciary transfer of a ship as security), 12 (collision), 13 (maritime assistance and salvage) and 14 (marine insurance) are not limited to ships as defined in article 1, but are expressly extended to all floating structures, such as floating cranes, dredges, caissons etc., which enlarges considerably the application of the Code. Articles 2–4 provide for the compulsory registration of Greek ships in special registers which are kept in all Greek harbors and by the Greek Consular Harbor Masters of some important foreign harbors (London, New York, Hamburg and others). At the owner's discretion, ships under construction may also be registered (art. 4; art. 2 N.L. 136/1967; art. 1 L. D. 375/1974 relating to ratification of the 1967 Brussels Convention on registration of rights on vessels under construction). Unless otherwise agreed, articles 681–702 of the Civil Code relating to construction contracts also apply to shipbuilding contracts except for articles 683 (calling for the application of the law of sales if the construction materials are provided by the builder), 693 (limitation of actions against the builder) and 695 (builder's lien on items repaired by him). Transfer of title to a ship is effected by agreement between transferor and transferee and only after its registration in the ship register (art. 6). The same applies for the transfer of title to a registered ship under construction (art. 7). Rights *in rem* on a ship are governed by the law of her flag (art. 9).

### *B. Co-ownership of Ships* (συμπλοιοκτησία, symploioktisia) (Title 2)

This very old institution, which has become obsolete in most of the current maritime legislations due to the availability of modern financing techniques, is still of some importance in Greece, in particular for small vessels. By virtue of article 10, co-ownership exists on a vessel when her owners operate her jointly. Thus, for a co-ownership on a vessel two factors are needed: (a) joint property of two or more persons (legal or natural), and (b) joint operation by the co-proprietors. There are no formal requirements; it may be established impliedly where all or some of the co-owners begin operating the ship on behalf of all. In Greek maritime practice, the shares of the co-ownership are computed in percentages. Decisions on all matters concerning the co-ownership are taken by the holders of a majority of the shares (art. 11). According to the prevailing opinion in the doctrine, no formalities are required for such decisions; it is enough to inform the other shareholders by any means, even by a mere telephone call. For certain important decisions an increased majority is required: 2/3 for allowing a co-owner to mortgage his share (art. 30 II), as well as for mortgaging the entire vessel with permission by the court (art. 30 I) and for revoking the ship's manager for an important reason (art. 13 II); 4/5 for mortgaging the ship without court's permission, for allowing the sale of shares resulting in the loss of the Greek flag (art. 29) and for the private sale of the entire ship as well (art. 31). On the contrary, a reduced majority of 1/2 of the shares suffices for selling the ship at a public auction with the court's permission (art. 32 I), and 1/4 with the court's permission is enough for deciding the sale of the ship for an important reason (art. 32 II), such as the operation of the ship having become unprofitable because of age, because extensive repairs are needed etc. Finally every co-owner, regardless of the number of shares he owns, may apply to the court for permission to sell the ship at a public auction if she has become unseaworthy (art. 32 III). By a simple majority of the shares the co-owners may appoint a manager and may revoke him by a majority of 2/3 for an important reason, such as incompetent or harmful management (art. 13). In order to be opposable to third parties, the appointment or revocation or resignation of the manager must be entered in the register of ships (art. 14). If more than one managers have been appointed, they must act jointly (art. 17). Co-owners holding the majority of the shares may give directions to the manager (art. 15), but the master must comply with the directions of the manager only (art. 19). The co-owners participate in the profits or losses proportionally to their shares and are bound to contribute at the same proportion to the expenses of the operation (arts. 24 and 26).

### C. *The Master* (πλοίαρχος, ploiarchos) (Title 3)

The master is hired by agreement with the owner or his representative (art. 37). The master may be dismissed at any time without prior notice, any agreement to the contrary being null and void (art. 38). The crew is enlisted by the master, who has to take into consideration the instructions of the owner (art. 39). The master is liable for fault (art. 40). He keeps the ship's log and assures that wireless and engine-logs are properly kept (art. 41). He is bound to keep on board all required documents and books, in particular the certificates of nationality and of seaworthiness, the tonnage measurement certificate, the crew-list, the record of offenders, the cargo documents, the customs documents, and the certificate of mortgages and arrests (art. 42). In entering or in leaving harbors, bays, straights, canals and rivers he must navigate the ship in person (art. 43). In an emergency, when he is not able to communicate with the owner, he may, by permission of the court (when in Greek waters) or of the Greek consul (when abroad), raise monies by selling or pawning the cargo or by borrowing (art. 45). On penalty of fine, he is prohibited from loading cargo for his own account (art. 46). During the voyage, in case of imperative need he is allowed to serve documents in the name of the owner, to take preservative measures and to sue in respect of matters relating to the ship or the cargo; he may also similarly act on behalf of the shippers (art. 47). In case the ship is away from the owner's place of business, judicial or extra-judicial documents may be served upon the master (art. 48). In case of shipwreck, or in the port of destination, or in an intermediary port of necessity, he is bound, within twenty-four hours from entering port, to present the ship's log and the crew-list for inspection (art. 49). In case of extraordinary events affecting the ship or persons on board, the master is equally bound to submit within twenty-four hours from arrival a report to the district court or, as the case may be, to the justice of the peace (abroad to the Greek consular authority) (art. 50).

*D. The Crew* (πλήρωμα, pliroma) (Title 4)

In accordance with article 53, the engagement of a seaman as crew-member is contracted with the master and is finalized with its entry (in Greece by the local harbor master, abroad by a consul) in the crew list. It must contain certain data relating to the identification of the seaman and the ship as well as to the terms and the duration of the contract (art. 54). In case the seaman fails to board the ship without proper cause on the day he was signed on, the master may rescind the contract of engagement (art. 56). In emergency cases, the master may assign to the seaman duties additional to, or different than, the ones for which he was signed on, provided that these are not incompatible with his rank, and provided further, that he gets additional pay (art. 57). The crew-members are not allowed, without the master's permission, to load goods on the ship (art. 58). In case his wages were agreed on a monthly basis, the seaman is entitled to wages for the months and days his engagement lasted, but for engagements lasting less than one month he is entitled to a full month's wages (art. 60). Where the wages were agreed on a per voyage basis, they are increased proportionally if the voyage is extended but they are not decreased if the voyage is shortened (art. 61). The seaman is entitled to an advance on his wages at amounts that depend on the circumstances; such advance may not exceed one month's wages; the balance is to be paid at the end of each voyage, even if the wages were agreed on a monthly basis (art. 64). No wages are due where the seaman withholds his services without proper cause (art. 65). The seaman is entitled to medical treatment. If his engagement is terminated because of illness, he is entitled to treatment on board throughout his illness; if he disembarked for such reason, he is entitled to expenses for treatment and to wages for four months starting from disembarkation or termination, whichever happened last (for such instances, reduced wages may have been agreed in the engagement contract). The same provisions apply in case of illness or injury caused by a violent event, but if the seaman suffered permanent disability or died as a result thereof, the special provisions of Law 551/1920 'Regarding Labor Accidents' are applicable (art. 66). In such instances, no additional compensation by virtue of article 75 is due to the seaman (art. 19 N.L. 373/1968). The above provisions are not applicable if his illness or injury was caused intentionally by the seaman himself (art. 67). The engagement contract is terminated in case of loss of the ship, loss of the Greek flag, or sale at a public auction (art. 68). The master may rescind a seaman's contract in case of unseaworthiness of the ship or unauthorized absence of the seaman (art. 69). An engagement contract stipulated for a fixed term which expires during a voyage of the ship is extended *ex lege* until the arrival of the ship at the port of destination (art. 70). A contract for a certain voyage or voyages is terminated upon the discharge of the cargo at the last port of destination; it comprises the voyage under ballast; on regular line voyages, the contract ends upon discharge of the cargo at the port where the seaman was signed on (art. 71). The master is entitled to terminate the seaman's contract at any time without prior notice (art. 72). The seaman may terminate a contract of engagement of indefinite duration after nine months from its conclusion, but if the port of destination lies outside the Mediterranean, or the Red Sea, or the Persian Gulf, or Europe, he may not cancel the contract before eleven months have lapsed, by giving notice of not less than seven days. The above time limits do not apply if the ship is lying in a Greek port (art. 73, as amended by art. 1 L. 451/1976). A seaman may terminate the contract for serious breach of duty by the master towards him (art. 74). The seaman is entitled to fifteen days' wages as compensation where his contract is terminated by reason of loss of the ship or of the Greek flag, of a public sale of the ship, of unseaworthiness of the ship, or of undue conduct of the master (arts. 75 and 76). After termination of his contract, the seaman is entitled to repatriation (art. 78). Agents in Greece of shipowners or ship-operators not residing in Greece who engage a seaman in Greece are liable jointly and severally with the employer for any liabilities arising out of such contract and are also deemed to be the employer's agents for the service of process. In case of bankruptcy of the employer, the agent's liability is confined only to claims which arose during the six months preceding the bankruptcy; claims against agents are subject to a six-month limitation period except that claims for the seaman's injury in the course of his employment are subject to a thirty-month limitation (art. 1 L. 762/1978). The provisions of title 4 apply also to the engagement contracts of alien seamen. The right to repatriation of an alien seaman consists in his being given the financial means to return to the port of his engagement or to the country of his nationality or to the port the voyage was initiated or to the place his contract was signed (art. 83, as amended by L. 451/1976).

### *E. Shipowner's Liability* (ευθύνη πλοιοκτήτη, euthyni ploioktiti) (Title 5)

This title reproduces basically the system of the Brussels Convention of 1924. The Brussels Convention of 1969 was also later ratified by Law 314/1976. Under article 84, the shipowner is bound by the contractual acts of the master within the scope of his duties; he is also liable for torts committed by the master, the crew and the pilot in the performance of their duties. The owner is released from such liability by abandoning the ship and the gross freight of the respective voyage to the claimants, even if, being also the master, he himself has committed a tort. Except as to claims arising out of accidental harm to persons, the abandonment does not include insurance benefits; amounts deducted from the value of the ship and the freight to satisfy claims for which the owner may not release himself by abandoning the ship and freight, have to be added back by the owner (art. 85). In lieu of abandoning the ship and the freight, the owner may offer in respect of each voyage a sum corresponding to three tenths of the value of the ship at the commencement of the voyage and an additional sum corresponding to a further three tenths for claims arising out of accidents to persons; in case such additional sum is insufficient to satisfy personal injury claims, the unsatisfied claims attach to the first sum and to the freight; the option under this article applies also if the ship was abandoned to the underwriters; however, such option does not apply to claims arising out of maritime assistance or salvage (art. 86). The right of abandonment does not apply to claims arising out of contracts concluded with the specific consent of the owner or ratified by him, or out of his obligations under contracts for the employment of the master or the crew (art. 87). In accordance with article 105, 'operator of the ship' ('disponent owner', εφοπλιστής, efoplistis), as distinguished from the 'shipowner', is he who 'exploits' (operates) a ship belonging to another. A further distinction is made between a 'shipowner' (πλοιοκτήτης, ploioktitis) who operates his own ship, and a 'mere proprietor' (κύριος του πλοίου, kyrios tou ploiou) who owns a ship but has assigned her operation to another (the 'operator'). The act of assigning the ship's operation by the 'owner' to an 'operator' must be declared in writing to the port of registry of the ship in order to be entered in the register and be noted in the ship's nationality document. Absent such declaration and entry, there is a rebuttable presumption that the proprietor operates the ship for his own account; the operator has the right of limiting his liability by abandoning the ship or by paying the sums provided for in this title, as if he were the owner (art. 105). Unless otherwise agreed, the ship's operator is entitled to appoint the master; claims arising out of the operation of the ship may be exercised against the ship; if the operator abandons the ship to the claimants, the proprietor is entitled to substitute to such abandonment the amounts provided for in article 86 (art. 106).

### *F. Affreightment* (ναύλωση, naulosi) (Title 6)

#### 1. General Provisions (Chapter 1)

Title 6 incorporates the major part of the substantive provisions of the Brussels Convention of 1924 on Bills of Lading (the Hague Rules), although Greece is not a party to such Convention. However, instead of limiting the applicability of the regulation only to the common carriage of goods by sea, the Code extends it to cover the affreightment in general, with the exception of the "demise charter", which was left to be regulated by agreement of the parties and the provisions of articles 574–587 of the Civil Code on lease. In accordance with article 107, the contract of affreightment may consist either: (a) of using the whole or part of the capacity of the ship for sea transport, or (b) of the carriage of goods by sea, or (c) of the carriage of passengers by sea. Unless otherwise specifically provided in the law, the provisions relating to affreightment in general apply also to the carriage of goods by sea (art. 107), whilst the carriage of passengers is separately regulated in chapter 7. The contract of affreightment must be evidenced in writing, merely *ad probationem* (not *ad solemnitatem*); in the contracts for the carriage of goods by sea the bill of lading may be replaced by a charter party; in the coastal trade the contract may be evidenced by any means of proof admissible in commercial matters, i.e. by testimony (art. 108).

2. Obligations of the Owner (υποχρεώσεις εκναυλωτή, ypochreoseis eknauloti) (Chapter 2)

In this and the following chapters of title 6, the Code uses the term 'εκναυλωτής' (eknaulotis; the equivalent French term is *fréteur*, the German *Verfrachter*) which we translate as the "owner", although it includes also the "disponent owner" of the ship. Under article 111, the "owner" is bound to make the ship fit for navigation and for the performance of the contract of affreightment (seaworthiness) as well as for the proper stowage and preservation of the cargo (cargoworthiness). He is also bound to bring the ship to the port of loading and to the appropriate loading place within such port and to load and stow the cargo at his own expense and see that it is properly kept during the voyage (art. 112). He is not entitled to effect the transport by another ship than the stipulated one, or to transship the cargo, except in emergency (art. 113). Neither is he entitled to stow the cargo on deck, except in coastal navigation (art. 114). In whole charters, if the charterer does not use the entire available capacity of the ship, the owner is not allowed to load in the unused space, otherwise he is bound to pay to the charterer the corresponding freight. The owner is bound to accept a cargo different than the one stipulated in the contract, provided this does not cause to him an additional burden (art. 115). If the time of loading and unloading is not stipulated in the contract, the local custom is applicable (art. 116). The owner is bound to keep the ship at the place of loading or unloading without additional pay for the entire period required (laytime); if the laytime is not agreed upon in the contract, it is determined equitably in accordance with local custom and the circumstances of the case; holidays or inactive time due to other circumstances causing impossibility for anybody to load or unload are not computed in the laytime (art. 117). For demurrage time, stipulated or customary, which begins after expiring of laytime and after proper notice is given to the charterer, additional equitable compensation is due to the owner; holidays and days of impossibility to load are computed in the demurrage time (arts. 118, 119). In contracts for the carriage of goods, the carrier is not bound to wait for loading beyond the time specified in the contract or made known publicly by press announcements or reasonably allowed by him to the charterer. After the expiry of such time, the carrier is released and the shipper is bound to pay the freight (art. 123). The owner, at the charterer's request, is bound to deliver to him a bill of lading containing: (a) description of the owner (or carrier), the charterer (or shipper), the consignee, the ship and the master, (b) ports of loading and destination, (c) the agreements on the freight, (d) the marks identifying the loaded goods as furnished in writing by the shipper, provided such marks have been attached to the goods or their packing in a way that they may be expected to remain legible until the end of the voyage, (e) the number of packages or pieces or the weight, as such items are furnished in writing by the shipper, (f) the apparent general condition of the goods at the time of loading, and (g) the date of issue. The carrier is not bound to include in the bill identifying marks or statements as to the number or weight of the goods loaded if he has reasonable grounds to believe that they do not correspond to the goods or if he has no reasonable opportunity of checking the accuracy thereof (art.

125). Upon arrival of the ship at the port of discharge and her being ready to discharge, the owner must give notice of readiness to the consignee; in case the consignee is unknown, as well as in the case of a contract for carriage of goods, such notice may be replaced by an announcement in accordance with the local custom (art. 128). Laytime for discharge begins on the day following the notice of readiness; if not stipulated, laytime is determinable equitably in accordance with local custom and the circumstances; the provisions of articles 117–119 regarding loading laytime and demurrage apply by analogy (art. 129). The cargo has to be delivered to the proper consignee, provided the freight and any other amounts have been paid (art. 130). If the consignee does not appear or refuses to accept the cargo, the cargo must be deposited in escrow and the consignee must be notified accordingly (art. 131). The provisions of articles 130–131 are applicable by analogy to contracts for the carriage of goods (art. 132). In case of a subcontract for the carriage of goods, the provisions of articles 128–131 continue to apply to the relationship between the original carrier and the charterer (art. 133).

### 3. Liability of Owner (ευθύνη πλοιοκτήτη, euthyni ploioktiti) (Chapter 3)

Contrary to the principle of absolute liability, which for about two thousand years (since the Roman *receptum nautarum*) governed the carrier's liability in Greece, the Code introduced the 'due diligence principle' of the Hague Rules. In article 134, the owner is liable for any loss of or damage to the goods from their receipt until their delivery, unless such loss or damage were due to events which were unavoidable even by exercising due diligence; he is also liable for any damage because of delay due to his fault in sailing, during the voyage, or during discharge. He is further liable: (a) for any damage caused by unseaworthiness or lack of cargoworthiness, except if he could not detect such deficiency by exercising due diligence (art. 145), (b) for misrepresentations as to tonnage (art. 136), except if the charterer or the shipper knowingly caused the nature, weight, or value of the cargo to be inserted falsely in the charter party or the bill (art. 137). He is liable for the fault of his agents and servants, in particular the master and crew, except if the loss or damage occurred because of an error in the navigation or in handling the ship, or because of fire, which fire was not caused by his own fault (art. 138). The compensation for loss of, or damage to the cargo may not exceed an amount per package or unit fixed from time to time by decree, unless a higher amount was agreed upon, or both the nature and value of the goods were declared by the shipper in writing before loading (art. 141). Any stipulation releasing the owner from his obligations and liabilities under this chapter, or reversing the burden of proof, is null and void (art. 142), except as regards: (a) obligations prior to loading or after discharge of the cargo, (b) matters purporting to general average, (c) cargo carried on deck, (d) carriage of livestock, (e) exceptional and unusual cargo (art. 143), (f) all the "excepted perils", as specified in article 4 II of the 1924 Brussels Convention (art. 144). Claims for partial loss of, or damage to loaded goods are barred one year after their receipt by the consignee (art. 148).

### 4. Charterer's Obligations (υποχρεώσεις ναυλωτή, ypochreoseis nauloti) (Chapter 4)

The main obligation of the charterer is to pay the freight agreed upon, possible demurrage monies, compensation for delay in taking delivery of the goods, expenses and the like; in the absence of an agreement, the freight customary at the port of loading is owed; for goods in excess of the agreed quantity an additional proportionate freight must be paid (art. 149). For time charters, in the absence of an agreement, the freight is computed from the day the loading began until discharge was completed (art. 150). The owner may not detain the cargo for not payment of the freight, but must deposit it in escrow (art. 152). The consignee, in taking delivery of the goods at the port of destination, is liable, jointly and severally with the charterer, to pay the freight and all related additional amounts (art. 153).

### 5. Rescission of Contract – Impossibility of Performance (υπαναχώρηση – αδυναμία παροχής, ypanachorisi – adynamia parochis) (Chapter 5)

Prior to the beginning of loading and during laytime, the charterer may rescind the charter contract by paying one half of the freight; after the beginning of loading or after the expiry of laytime he must pay the entire freight (art. 155). For contracts for carriage of goods by sea, if he rescinds after loading, he must pay half of the freight plus the expenses for loading, discharging and reloading other loaded goods and any other damages for delay (art. 156). If the statement for rescission was made after the sailing, the charterer is bound to pay the entire freight plus all expenses caused by the discharge of the goods; the owner may refuse to discharge the goods if such discharge is especially onerous for him or for the other shippers. If the contract is rescinded for reasons attributable to the owner, he must discharge the goods at his expense and pay for all damages and expenses resulting therefrom (art. 157). The contract of affreightment is cancelled at no cost to the parties if: (a) before sailing, the ship was lost accidentally or became unseaworthy, or the sailing was prevented by order of a public authority, or navigation to the port of destination was prevented in any way (art. 159), (b) before loading, specifically described goods forming the object of the charter contract were accidentally lost, (c) before sailing, the goods loaded or received by the owner for shipment were lost by accident, except if the charterer brought within the laytime other goods for loading and assumed the obligation to compensate the owner for any damage arising therefrom (art. 162), (d) after sailing, the goods were lost by accident (art. 163). In case of cancellation by accident the owner bears the discharge costs and the charterer bears any other expenses (art. 165).

### 6. The Bill of Lading (φορτωτική, fortotiki) (Chapter 6)

The bill of lading is issued by the master to the name of a certain person or to order (but not to the bearer) at the shipper's choice; copy signed by the shipper is delivered to the owner (arts. 168, 169). On an order bill at lading the provisions on bills of exchange (art. 170; see above, Ch. 10, Section III A 1) apply by analogy to the defenses which may be brought against the holder. The carrier is bound to deliver the cargo only upon return to him of the bill of lading and of a written receipt-statement of the consignee, even where the carrier has rescinded the contract (art. 173).

### 7. Carriage of Passengers (σύμβαση μεταφοράς επιβάτη, symvasi metaforas epivati) (Chapter 7)

The contract of carriage of a passenger is evidenced by a ticket, which is not transferable if it bears his name (arts. 174, 175). Unless otherwise agreed, passage-money does not include victualling during the voyage but the passenger is entitled to be properly victualled at a reasonable cost (art. 176). If prior to sailing the passenger rescinds the contract he must pay half of the fare (art. 178). The contract is cancelled at no cost to the parties if the voyage is frustrated due to a fortuitous event regarding the ship (art. 179). If sailing is delayed, the passenger is entitled to stay on board and be victualled at a reasonable cost; if the delay is extended, he may rescind the contract at no cost without prejudice to his right to damages (art. 180). In case the passenger disembarks at an intermediate port he owes the entire fare, but if this is due to his illness or to another fortuitous event affecting his person or the ship, he owes only a proportionate fare (arts. 181, 182). No additional fare is due for baggage, except for overweight (art. 186). On the carrier's liability for baggage, the provisions of carriage of goods apply by analogy (art. 187), but if a passenger retains custody of his baggage the carrier is liable only for a tort by the master or the crew under the provisions of article 142 (art. 188). In the case of a whole or part charter for the carriage of passengers of an unspecified number, the provisions of affreightment apply, unless otherwise either expressly agreed or obvious under the circumstances (art. 189).

### G. *Fiduciary Transfer of Ownership of a Ship as Security* (μεταβίβαση κυριότητας πλοίου για εξασφάλιση απαιτήσεως, metavivasi kyriotitas ploiou gia exasphalisi apaitiseos) (Title 7)

This is a rather obsolete institution actually not used any more in practice. The shipowner transfers ownership title on the vessel to the creditor for securing a claim, but retains management and operation thereof, which he must exercise diligently (art. 190). The creditor may change the master (art. 191). Upon entrance in the ship's register of the creditor's statement that his claim has been satisfied, the ownership reverts automatically to the original owner (art. 192). If upon maturity of the claim the creditor is not paid, he may foreclose by selling the ship at a public auction; agreement to the effect that he may keep title on the ship is null and void; however, an agreement that he may take over management and operation of the vessel is valid (art. 193). Where the ship is lost or suffers damage which reduces substantially her value, the creditor may ask immediately for satisfaction unless the debtor offers adequate security (art. 194).

## *H. Mortgage of Ships* (υποθήκη σε πλοία, ypothiki se ploia) (Title 8)

### 1. Simple Mortgage (απλή υποθήκη, apli ypothiki)

A mortgage may attach even on a ship under construction, provided she is registered (art. 195). A mortgage takes effect by notarial deed and its entry in the register of mortgages of the port where the ship is registered (arts. 197, 198). Any mortgage registered after the arrest of a ship is void in respect of such arrest (art. 199 in conjunction with arts. 715 and 997 C. C. Proc.). After the registration of a mortgage, the port of registration or the name of the ship may not be changed without the consent of the mortgagee (art. 201). Transfer of title on a mortgaged ship causing loss of the Greek nationality is null and void if effected without the consent of the mortgagee (art. 202). In case a ship acquires the Greek nationality, mortgages which were acquired by registration in a public register according to the law of her previous nationality continue to be valid if registered in a Greek register of mortgages within sixty days from the ship's acquisition of the Greek nationality (art. 203). The provisions of the Civil Code on mortgages have analogous application as to other matters (art. 204).

### 2. Preferred Mortgage (προτιμώμενη υποθήκη, protimomeni ypothiki)

The preferred mortgage on a ship was introduced and is regulated by L. D. 3899/1958. The main differences from the simple mortgage consist in that: (a) the preferred mortgage takes effect by two-sided contract drawn in Greece by a notary (abroad also in accordance with the local law) plus registration (art. 2), (b) it may be agreed that the mortgagee shall be entitled to assume the ship's management in order to satisfy his claim from the proceeds of her operation (arts. 1 and 2), (c) it may be agreed in favor of the mortgagee any other right for increasing his security, including that the mortgagee may foreclose on the ship without public auction (art. 5), (d) the preferred mortgage may attach only to the whole of a ship (art. 4), and (e) while a simple mortgage secures interest accruing only one year preceding the arrest, the preferred mortgage secures all accrued interest (art. 12).

## *I. Maritime Privileges (Liens)* (ναυτικά προνόμια, nautika pronomia) (Title 9)

The maritime privileges in Greek law (as well as on the European Continent in general) are *quasi in rem* claims attaching to the ship, but the appropriate proceedings have to be directed against the owner or the disponent owner at the time the proceedings are initiated, and not against the ship as such as in Anglo-American law. Greece is not a signatory of the Brussels Conventions of 1926 and 1967 governing maritime liens and mortgages. In order to facilitate the procuring of financing by means of mortgages, Greek law accepts a very limited number of maritime privileges. Under article 205 only the following four categories of claims give rise to a privilege: (a) legal costs incurred in the common interest of the claimants; public dues and charges on the ship; taxes levied in connection with navigation; costs for the preservation of the ship in the last port, (b) claims of the master and crew in connection with their employment contract and charges in favor of the Seamen's Pension Fund, (c) expenses and claims on account of maritime assistance and salvage, and (d) compensation owed to ships, passengers and cargo by reason of collision. These liens enjoy priority over mortgages (art. 205); claims of each category rank before the following ones, while claims of the same category rank concurrently and proportionally, except for claims for assistance and salvage which rank in inverse order of their coming into existence (art. 206). The *quasi in rem* action of the said privileges exists in that, if title on a ship is transferred by contract, the privilege continues to exist against the new owner, provided it is acknowledged by court order in legal proceedings initiated within three months from the registration of the transfer in the register of ships (art. 207). In addition to the general grounds of extinction, privileges are cut off by the sale of the ship at public auction (art. 208). Privileges may not attach to the insurance benefits (art. 209).

### J. *Arrest and Foreclosure on Ships* (κατάσχεση και αναγκαστική εκτέλεση επί πλοίων, kataschesi kai anangastiki ektelesi epi ploion) (Title 10)

Most of the provisions of this title have been repealed by the Code of Civil Procedure which entered into force in 1968, and those which remained in force are of purely procedural nature. For interstate relations, Greece has ratified and applies the Brussels International Convention of 1952 on the arrest of seagoing ships.

### K. *General Average and Contribution* (κοινή αβαρία και συνεισφορά, koini avaria kai syneisfora) (Title 11)

The provisions of this title have basically as a model the York-Antwerp Rules as elaborated by the Brussels Convention of 1950. In accordance with articles 219 and 220, general average exists where a damage or an extraordinary expense was caused intentionally and reasonably in order to save a ship and her cargo from a common sea peril, if the intended beneficial result was achieved, or where a total sacrifice of the cargo was made in order to save the ship, or of the ship in order to save the cargo. As general average is also accepted an expense incurred in order to avoid another expense having the character of a general average, but only up to the amount of the expense avoided (art. 222). So is it also with wages and victualling of the crew and other expenses incurred by the fact that the ship was impeded during her voyage by public authority or was compelled to stay in a harbor because of war or a similar cause, or for undertaking repairs necessary for the continuation of her voyage, provided that such repairs consist in a general average (art. 223). Jettison is decided and performed by equitable judgment, in particular by taking into consideration weight, value and position on board of the jettisoned items (art. 224). Sacrifices in general average are apportioned in the way of contribution between the saved and the sacrificed cargo on one hand and ship and freight on the other (general average adjustment) (art. 225). In the absence of a different express agreement of the parties, the apportioning is effected in accordance with the provisions of articles 226–234, which correspond in substance to the York-Antwerp Rules of 1950.

### *L. Collision of Ships* (σύγκρουση πλοίων, synkrousi ploion) (Title 12)

This title is mainly based on the provisions of the Brussels International Convention of 1910 relating to collision between vessels. Adopting the principle of doubtful fault as laid down in article 2 of this Convention, article 235 provides that in a collision between ships, if it was caused by accident or *force majeure* or if its cause is doubtful, the damage is borne by those who suffered it. In case the collision was due to the fault of one of the ships, liable for damages is such ship; if two or more ships are at fault, they are liable in proportion to the degree of their fault; if the proportion can not be ascertained or the faults are equal, they are all equally liable (art. 236). For death or personal injuries, all ships at fault are liable jointly and severally (art. 237). Liability under the above provisions attaches also where the collision was due to the fault of the pilot, even a compulsory one (art. 238). Such liability of the ships does not affect the personal liability of the persons at fault towards the damaged persons and the shipowners (art. 239). After collision, the master of each ship is bound to provide assistance to the other ship, her crew and passengers, if this can be done without serious danger to his own ship, crew and passengers; he has also to possibly make known to the other ship the port and number of registration of his ship and the ports of her sailing and destination; violation of these obligations does not impose a liability upon the shipowner (art. 240). The above provisions are applicable also in case of wrongful maneuvers causing damage to other ships, and/or persons or property on board of such ships, even if no collision was caused (art. 241). Greek courts have jurisdiction in collision cases if: (a) the defendant has his domicile or residence in Greece, (b) the ship flies the Greek flag, (c) the collision took place in Greek waters, or (d) the sequestration of the ship was effected in Greece, even if it was lifted before the suit was filed (art. 242). The findings of administrative inquiry commissions as to the cause, the fault and the extent of damage in case of collisions have the force of presumed evidence and are not binding upon the courts, which may consider other evidence too (art. 243). The master or owner of a ship may act on behalf of the crew, the persons interested in the cargo, and the passengers of his ship for damage suffered by them by reason of a collision; they have to notify accordingly such persons before the hearing (art. 244). The provisions of this title are applicable also on collisions of anchored ships (art. 245).

### *M. Maritime Assistance and Salvage* (επιθαλάσσια αρωγή και διάσωση, epithalassia arogi kai diasosi) (Title 13)

The major part of this title was modelled on the related Brussels International Convention of 23 September 1910 and applies to assistance and salvage of ships in distress, property on board, freight, cargo, passengers, and services of a like nature rendered by one vessel to another (art. 246). Any act of assistance to or salvage of a ship which had a beneficial result confers the right to a reasonable remuneration, even where it was rendered between ships of the same owner (art. 247). The remuneration may not exceed the value of the property saved (art. 248). The master and crew of the assisted or salvaged ship, as well as any persons who rendered assistance against the express and reasonable refusal of the master of the ship in distress, are not entitled to salvage-monies; the latters not even to costs (art. 249). A tug is not entitled to salvage-money for assistance rendered to the tow and the cargo, except for exceptional services beyond the scope of the towage contract (art. 250). One half of the salvage-money is earned by the owner, one quarter by the master and the remaining quarter by the crew of the ship having rendered the assistance, any agreement to the contrary being null and void (art. 251). The law of the flag of the ship that rendered the assistance or salvage applies to the distribution of the salvage-money (art. 252). A contract for assistance or salvage entered into during and under the impact of the danger may be rescinded or reduced by the court if the remuneration agreed upon is excessive or disproportionate to the service rendered (art. 253). In case no agreement is reached, the salvage-money is fixed by the court; the court may reduce the salvage-money or not allow it at all if the savors by their fault caused the need of assistance (art. 252). In the court proceedings, the master represents also the crew members if they are not otherwise represented (art. 255). No remuneration is owed for saving human lives, but the savors are entitled to a reasonable share of the salvage-money due for assistance to, or salvage of ships and property (art. 256).

### *N. Limitation of Actions* (παραγραφή αξιώσεων, paragraphi axioseon) (Title 15)

The following claims are subject to a one-year limitation: (a) of the master and crew for their wages, (b) of the owner against the master and the crew for torts in the performance of their duties, (c) for supply of materials and victuals, services rendered in connection with the construction, repair, armament or equipment of a ship, as well as claims arising out of acts of the master done pursuant to articles 45 and 46, (d) arising out of a contract of affreightment or of carriage of goods or passengers, (e) arising out of general average for paying the contribution, and (f) from collision of ships (art. 289). A two-year statute bars claims: (a) of co-owners against each other or the manager, (b) arising out of marine insurance, (c) for salvage-money and recover of costs in case of assistance and/or salvage, and (d) against a shipbuilder for deficiencies in the constructed ship (art. 290). In all these instances, the limitation time begins to run at the end of the year in which the claim accrued. The institution of proceedings for abandonment of the ship against the underwriter interrupts the running of the limitation period against him for damages (art. 291). Whoever possesses a ship for three years in good faith by virtue of a duly registered title acquires ownership of the ship; and whoever possesses a ship for ten years acquires ownership without the above prerequisites (art. 292).

## Basic Bibliography

(in Greek unless otherwise indicated)

N. Deloukas, *Maritime Law*, 2d ed. (1979).
D. Kamvyssis, *Private Maritime Law* (1982).
Ph. Potamianos, *Elements of Maritime Law*, 2 vols. (1963–1966).
C. Rocas, *Maritime Law* (1968).
K. Kerameus, Admiralty Jurisdiction in Continental Countries, *The Maritime Lawyer* 329–343 (1983) (in English).
N. Lolis, Notes on International Maritime Law as Applied By the Law of Greece, *R. Hell. D.I.* 1965. 126–137.
An English translation of the Greek Code of Private Maritime Law, including brief comments, by T. Karatzas and N. Ready was published in 1982 by Martinus Nijhoff.

# Chapter 13
# Labor Law

*Alexandros G. Karakatsanis**

## I. Introduction

Modern Greek labor law can be traced back to the end of the first decade of our century. Many of the laws of that early period were so important, dominated by a clearly protective character for the employee and his job security, that they remained in force for many decades; some of them are still in force. Since then legislation has given to Greek labor law step by step its current features.

Systematically, Greek labor law is divided into two parts, employment law and collective labor law.

Its sources are:

(*a*) The Constitution of 1975. Some of its articles are of direct interest. Specifically: article 22 I 1, which proclaims the right to employment as a programmatic principle: the state is bound to protect it and to follow policies aiming at full employment and the improvement of the condition of workers; article 4 I–II, which provides equality before the law and equal rights and obligations for men and women; article 22 I 2, which postulates equal pay for work of equal value, irrespective of sex or any other distinction; article 12, in which the right to establish trade unions and employers' associations as well as their protection are founded; article 22 II, which offers a constitutional base to collective bargaining and to the right to conclude collective agreements; article 23 I, which commits the state to proceed to the proper measures for securing the freedom of association and the respective rights of the trade unions; article 23 II, which recognizes the right to strike except for judges and the security forces (this right is, however, limited for civil servants and the personnel of public enterprises and of public utilities).

(*b*) International conventions ratified by Greece, such as ILO Conventions 87 (freedom of association), 98 (organization and collective bargaining), 100 (equal pay for both sexes), the European Social Charter of 1961, the UNO Convention of 1966, the EEC legislation and others. Ratified international conventions become part of domestic Greek law and they prevail over any contrary provision of the law (art. 28 I Const.)

* Professor of Law, Athens University.

(*c*) Numerous statutes. Several attempts to codify labor law brought to success. A labor code is still missing.

(*d*) Collective agreements as well as arbitration decisions on trade disputes.

(*e*) The majority of the internal regulations of firms.

## II. Employment Law

### *A. The Contract of Employment* (σύμβαση εργασίας, symvasi ergasias)

The employment contract normally requires the employee to perform services of a certain kind for pay at a place, time, manner and other conditions fixed by the employer. The rights of the parties are subject to judicial control under article 281 of the Civil Code which prohibits the abuse of rights. The terms of employment are generally a matter of private agreement between the parties under the condition of equal treatment of men and women (L. 1414/1984 art. 9). The contract may be for a definite or an indefinite term. In the public sector, however, to which several large enterprises also belong, the employees have to retire when they complete thirty-five years and reach the age of fifty-six.

#### 1. Working Hours (ώρες εργασίας, ores ergasias)

Working hours have been fixed by a law dating from 1932 providing for a maximum of eight hours per day and forty-eight hours per week. A gradual reduction of working time began in 1975 through collective agreements and arbitration decisions. The current regulation, deriving from the National General Collective Agreement of 1984, provides for forty working hours per week. Recently, again by collective agreements and arbitration decisions, the voluntary or, as far as industry is concerned, compulsory five-day week has been introduced. Extended working hours are permitted in exceptional cases, under certain conditions, and they are paid at higher rates. The overtime rates (an increase of 25–100% of the respective hourly wage) depend on the number of the extended hours, which in any event cannot exceed the limit set each year by the law (as a rule, 120 hours).

#### 2. Welfare, Health and Safety, Injury at Work (πρόνοια, υγεία, ασφάλεια, εργατικό ατύχημα, pronoia, ygeia, asphaleia, ergatiko atychima)

The employer (εργοδότης, ergodotis) is required to take all the necessary measures for the welfare, health and safety of the employees (εργαζόμενοι, ergazomenoi) at the places of work. Workmen's compensation without fault is payable by the employer to employees injured at work or in connection with it. The sum payable depends on the seriousness and the degree of the injury as well as on the duration of any disability, and it may reach the wages of six years in case of a total and permanent disability (L. 551/1914, as amended). This obligation of the employer is extinguished if the injured is insured, as is the rule, at IKA, the largest institution of social insurance (see below, Chapter 14). In this case, IKA comes up with the payment of the related benefits. However, the employer remains responsible for intentional injury.

3. Leaves (άδειες, adeies)

Employees with a minimum continuous employment of twelve months by the same firm are entitled to paid annual leave. Recently (L. 1346/1983 art. 1 I) the duration of such leave has been fixed between 24–26 days (or 20–22 days for employees with a five-day week). During the leave, the employee receives regular wages plus an extra half-month. On termination of employment, earned leave is compensated at two-day wages for every month at work; if twelve months of work were completed, full leave remuneration is payable. There are also special leaves for students and teachers for their examinations (L. 1346/1983), for parents having to take care of family (L. 1483/1984) and for trade union officials in order to fulfill their duties (L. 1264/1982).

4. Wages (μισθοί, misthoi)

In practice, collective agreements have become the regular instrument for fixing the minimum wage either generally or for each branch, district or firm. Arbitration decisions and, in exceptional cases (when a collective agreement, which could cover the 3/5ths of the concerned employees, can not be concluded because an employers' association does not exist), ministerial decisions are also of importance and effect. Employment contracts may fix the wage only above these minimum levels. A recent statute (L. 1363/1983 art. 6) opens the way for collective agreements as well as arbitration or ministerial decisions to establish the automatic adjustment of wages every four months according to the price index, that is the cost of living. The rate of this adjustment is, however, fixed by ministerial decisions.

Collective agreements, arbitration or ministerial decisions, firm regulations and employers must provide equal pay for work of equal value (art. 22 I 2 Const.; EEC Directive 75/177; L. 1414/1984). This principle is not applicable to civil servants. Another point to be mentioned is the wage ceiling (L. 1256/1982). The net wage of employees in the public sector, to which a great number of enterprises belong (banks, enterprises of public character or interest, insurance companies etc.) may not exceed the gross wage of the President of the Supreme Court. The same limit applies equally in case of cumulation of wages or of wages and pensions.

*B. Termination of Employment – Job Security* (λήξη της συμβάσεως – ασφάλεια θέσεως, lixi tis symvaseos – asphalia theseos)

The distinction between a contract of definite duration and a contract of indefinite term is very important.

1. Contract of Definite Duration (σύμβαση ορισμένου χρόνου, symvasi orismenou chronou)

Under the law, the premature termination by either party is permitted only for important reasons. If the reason is the breach by the other party, full compensation may be claimed. On the other hand, if the employer terminates the contract because his personal or economic condition has changed, the court may impose upon him the payment of a reasonable severance pay (arts. 673–674 C.C.).

2. Contract of Indefinite Term (σύμβαση αορίστου χρόνου, symvasi aoristou chronou)

Theoretically, such a contract may be terminated by either party at any time and without reason. But the law imposes certain requirements and provides for severance pay. The dismissal (απόλυση, apolysi) must be in writing, and the employer must provide severance pay even if the dismissal is due to the employee's fault (breach of duty, disobedience, repeated absences), with the exception of committing a work-related crime. The amount depends on the kind of the dismissal, prenoticed or summary. In a prenoticed dismissal, the compensation is half of the compensation owed for a summary dismissal. In the latter instance, the amount is in direct relation to the length of the employment. Clerical employees are entitled from one up to twenty-four months of wages and workers are paid the wages of five to fifty-two days.

As for the judicial control of the right to dismiss, case law has established two categories of reasons accepted as not involving an abuse of right: (a) reasons relating to the employee (inadequacy, breach of his duties) and (b) reasons referring to the needs and interests of the firm (economic difficulties, diminishing activity, introduction of new working methods or new technology, changes in organization).

A dismissal is valid, when these three conditions (written notice, offer of the compensation and fair use of the right) have been met.

## III. Collective Labor Law (συλλογικό εργατικό δίκαιο, syllogiko ergatiko dikaio)

### *A. Trade Unions*

Freedom of association (συνδικαλιστική ελευθερία, syndikalistiki eleutheria) is constitutionally guaranteed. Trade unionism is a reality at all organization levels, which are three. The first level covers unions of a certain profession and, as a rule, of a certain enterprise or of local character. The majority of them – actually the most important ones – are registered as associations with legal personality and have, because of this registration, the right to conclude collective agreements in their own name. Employees have the right to be members of only one professional and one enterprise union. At least two unions of the first level are needed to form a trade union of the second level, that is a federation or a labor centre. A federation is an association of unions representing employees of the same profession or service sector in different regions, practically all over Greece. It has the authority to conclude collective agreements and to declare a national strike for the employees of a certain profession. Labor centres comprise unions of a particular place regardless of the profession and enterprise of the employees represented. Labor centres represent and assist their members in various ways. Every union of the first level has the right to be member of one federation and of one labor centre. The next and highest organization level is that of the confederations which consist of at least two federations and/or labor centres. The most important among them is the General Confederation of Workers of Greece.

### B. *Collective Bargaining and Collective Agreements* (συλλογική διαπραγμάτευση, συλλογική σύμβαση, syllogiki diapragmateusi, syllogiki symvasi; L. 3239/1966, as amended)

Collective agreements can be concluded only between parties having the requisite legal capacity. These are the trade unions with legal personality, and among them only the two more representative per bargaining unit, and the employers' associations. Employers or firms individually do not possess this capacity, with the exception of corporations of public utility, banks as well as the state and other institutions of the public sector (for employees under a private law contract).

Collective agreements according to their scope of application are either of a national-general level (for the employees of the whole country, qualified participants are the confederations), or of a national-professional level (for the employees of a certain profession, qualified participants are the federations), or of a local professional level (qualified participants are the local trade unions representing employees of the profession in question), or of the enterprise level (qualified participants are the firm or local unions or, in the case of more than one enterprise, the respective federations).

A consequence of this peculiarity is that the labor relationship of an employee often falls at the same time within the coverage of more than one collective agreements. An inconsistency among collective agreements results, and the problem of selecting the one to be applied is often quite difficult although the law ranks collective agreements of different levels in a clear priority sequence. At the top there is the national general collective agreement; the national professional collective agreement is second, followed by the local professional one and/or the collective agreement on the enterprise level. The rule is that a collective agreement of a higher level prevails over collective agreements of lower level grades. Exceptionally, special circumstances may justify prevalence of the supplementary or different treatment of certain questions by the narrower bargaining unit of a lower level collective agreement, but only on the condition that this different treatment proves to be more favorable for the employee.

Collective agreements apply only to employees and employers belonging respectively to the trade unions and to the employers' associations which have concluded the agreement. Membership is necessary on both sides. An extension of application can take place either by a ministerial decision or by originally signing the agreement in the presence of the Minister of Labor or his representative. In both cases the result is the same: this agreement applies to all employers and employees of the field covered, no matter whether they are members or not of the respective unions and associations. Typically, minimum wages are governed by the collective agreement. Other usual provisions refer to working conditions, working hours and leaves, and they apply only if they are more favorable to the employee than rules deriving from other sources. Further, a collective agreement may regulate the relationship of the concluding parties themselves (negotiations, cooperation, obligation to keep peace; the latter is, anyway, inherent to the collective agreement).

Collective agreements are not just 'binding in honor'; they have legal effect. They control the individual labor relations in an automatic and compulsory way; they are self-executing and enforceable through judicial proceedings between employee and employer. The employee can claim directly the wage provided for his group by a collective agreement which means that a collective agreement, in effect, has the force of law.

### C. *Arbitration* (διαιτησία, diaitisia)

In case of failure of the collective bargaining process, a procedure of arbitration is provided for the settlement of collective industrial disputes (Const. art. 22 II and L. 3239/1955). A preliminary attempt at conciliation and mediation is undertaken by an officer of the Ministry of Labor or its local branches. In important cases, the minister intervenes personally. If this effort fails, the dispute is taken to the arbitration tribunals. These tribunals (arranged at two levels) are administrative bodies, not tribunals in the real sense of the word. They are composed of one (on the appellate level two) representative of the trade union and of the employers' association respectively, one officer of the Ministry of Labor and one professional judge, who is the president. While these proceedings are pending, striking is forbidden. The decisions of the arbitration tribunals have the same legal effect as the collective agreements; they also prevail, in their scope of application, over employment contracts. This arbitration has been criticized as incompatible with the freedom of association and the right to strike, and consequently as inconsistent with the Constitution.

### D. *Strikes* (απεργία, apergia)

The right to strike is secured by the Constitution in article 23 II. On the other hand, the lock-out (ανταπεργία, antapergia) is prohibited (L. 1264/1982 art. 22

II) Only trade unions have the right to declare a strike to support the protection and promotion of economic and labor interests or interests relating to the right of association or to the social insurance of the employees. Wild strikes are illegal; so are also the clearly political strikes. On the other hand, strikes with a political character are tolerated, if they are related to labor problems and interests, provided that they are of short duration. Further, a strike is illegal if the union does not give the other side the 24-hour-notice required by the law (L. 1264/1982 art. 19 I) or does not provide the necessary personnel for the security of the employer's installations. The right to strike must not be abused of (art. 25 Const.; art. 281 C.C.). Abuse makes a strike illegal. A lawful strike does not cause a breach of the labor contract; neither the contract is dissolved nor the employer has the right to dismiss the strikers. During a lawful strike the performance of the labor contract is merely suspended and, therefore, wages are not payable during this interval. On the contrary, an illegal strike is considered a breach of the labor contract with heavy consequences. The employer may claim damages and also may dismiss the strikers, provided however that is done in a manner not constituting an abuse of right.

## Basic Bibliography

A. Karakatsanis, *Labor Law*, vol. I, revised ed. (Athens, 1987), vol. II/1, II/2 (Athens, 1977, 1980) (in Greek).

T. Koniaris, Greece (1982, p. 1–181) in *International Encyclopaedia For Labour Law and Industrial Relations* (R. Blanpain, ed. in chief), vol. V (Deventer).

I. Koukiadis, *Labor Law, Employment Law and Social Policy* (Thessaloniki, 1984) (in Greek).

I. Koukiadis, *Collective Labor Law* (Thessaloniki, 1981) (in Greek).

# Chapter 14
# Social Insurance Law

*Konstantinos D. Kremalis**

## I. Introduction

With the onset of industrial reform in Greece in mid-19th century, we observe the first legislative moves towards the establishment of independent social insurance institutions such as the Naval Veterans Fund (1836), the Miners' Insurance Fund (1882) and others. A large number of institutions were subsequently created for the protection of special professional groups of employees, independent professionals and public servants. The idea to build a national insurance system for the protection of individuals was first conceived in 1929.[1] This idea has not materialized to this date, however it has not been abandoned.

A composite social protection system is presently in existence. We call it social insurance system (σύστημα κοινωνικής ασφαλίσεως) because it is mainly what the term denotes. Characteristic trends of contemporary social policy are the personal and territorial expansion of protection, the concentration of social insurance on certain basic institutions and the establishment of a minimum level of social protection.

The law of social insurance draws basically its rules from the Constitution, international conventions, European Community law, special legislation, various regulations, and certain principles of law. More specifically under article 22 IV of the Constitution (1975), social insurance for working people has become the object of public concern (κοινωνική μέριμνα, koinoniki merimna). This means that the state is bound to establish and ensure better conditions for the fulfillment of the social insurance system. Thus, a social right directed to social insurance is recognized for the working people,[2] the content of which is defined by the legislator within the framework of social insurance institutions. Financing of social insurance is provided for according to one opinion by these compound legal relationships, and according to another opinion by two independent legal bonds.[3] The first opinion favors, of course, the reciprocity

*Associate Professor of Law, Athens University.

1. Chr. Agallopoulos, *Social Insurance* (1955) 18–27.
2. The S.S.C. 16/1983, EDKA 1984. 320 held, however, in close adhesion to the constitutional wording, that only the social right of those who offer dependent work is secured.
3. K. Kremalis, *Social Insurance Law* (1985) 58–64.

(interdependence) between contributions and benefits, while the second disregards the insurance techniques in favor of a general protection on a tolerable level.

## II. Organization and Administration of Social Insurance

### *A. Multiplicity of Social Insurance Systems*

The services of social insurance are provided by independent institutions of public and of private law and aim at protecting the individuals of a certain community (profession, enterprise, region etc.) against any risk. The diffusion of social protection into various insurance regimes may, as stated above, be historically justified; nevertheless it is characterized by strong social inequalities and by a high degree of uncertainty, as far as the existence and extent of social insurance rights are concerned.[4]

As a rule, social insurance institutions (ασφαλιστικοί φορείς, asphalistikoi phoreis) have their own legal personality and exercise public authority in the form of legal entities of public law. There are, nevertheless, certain institutions of social insurance that have been created by private initiative or have been qualified by the legislator as belonging to the 'private sphere of law'. According to the social budget estimate of 1986, there are today 330 general and special institutions of social insurance.

### *B. Self-Governance of Social Insurance Institutions*

The social insurance institutions hardly ever had their own self-governance. The basic reason for this is the lack of representativeness of their organs and their budgetary dependence on state resources.

Since the early days, the governing boards of the insurance institutions have been established by decisions of the competent minister (art. 2 L. 1022/1946) and are composed of representatives of the state as well as of the insured, the pensioners and the employers, who have been recommended by the respective organizations. Recently, however, according to article 20 of Law 1539/1985 in every new board 'the majority of its members shall consist of representatives of the insured and pensioners'. The minister here is bound to appoint the representatives elected by professional organizations representing the total of the insured or the pensioners.[5]

With regard to the budgetary dependence of the insurance institutions, it should be noted that the ministry's approval is required for any qualitative or

4. A. Petroglou, *Social Insurance Law*, vol. I (1974) 61–63; P. Kyriakoulakos, *Social Policy. General Notions-Social Insurance* (1970) 96.
5. G. Psilos, Representation of Insured in the Social Insurance Institutions, *Syndicalistic Review 2* (Athens, 1985) 23–30.

quantitative improvement of insurance benefits. On the other hand, insurance institutions are not allowed to make free use of the reserve funds (αποθεματικά, apothematika) which are blocked at the Bank of Greece at relatively low interest rates (arts. 1, 2 L. 1611/1950).

## III. Financing of Social Insurance

### A. *Insurance Contributions*

The insured are required to make contributions (ασφαλιστικές εισφορές, asphalistikes eisphores) to the respective social insurance institutions. The contributions paid by farmers and public servants are rather insignificant. Theoretically as well as practically interesting is the determination of the parties that are bound to contribute in the social insurance of the employees. The correlation between persons bound to contribute in the social insurance of the employees and those that must pay the salaries is almost self-evident. Article 8 V 1 of Law 1846/1951, however, defines 'employer' (εργοδότης) in the law of social insurance on the basis of extra-legal considerations, that is profit resulting from work. In fact, an emphasis on the criterion of economic interest strengthens even more the financing of the institution, especially in the so-called tripartite employment relationship (τριμερής σχέση εργασίας), established between three contracting parties. There is a controversy, however, as to what extent the law of social insurance borrows the terms of labor relations unaltered, i.e. employer, employee, remuneration etc., or whether these terms are to be interpreted in the context of the specific needs of the relevant branch of law.[6] I find the second version more appropriate.

The legal nature of contributions has given rise to scholarly debates. The view of a charge similar to tax is based on the provisions that disconnect the obligation of contributions from (a) the payment of remuneration (art. 29a P.D. 278/1982) and (b) the immediate expectation of benefits (art. 4 VII L. 1302/1982). The courts, however, adhere accurately to the view that contributions constitute literally a part of remuneration temporarily removed to be used for future needs.[7]

When the insured or other persons bound to make contributions, like the employers for instance, deny or delay such payments, compulsory measures may be taken against them.

The public institutions of social insurance are authorized by the law to immediately order the payment of contributions without having recourse to ordinary legal remedies. Within this authority (administrative constraint), the individual administrative acts are regarded as enforceable instruments, which

6. G. Papachatzis, *System of Greek Administrative Law*, 5th ed. (1976) 148; K. Kremalis, *Social Insurance of Workmen* (1982) 57–76. SE 1104/1963, EDKA 1963. 516; 2253/1980, EDKA 1980. 594; 626/1981, EDKA 1981. 331.
7. SE 900/1983, EDKA 1984. 10; D. P. Athens 7301/1983, EDKA 1984. 35.

determine the extent of payment to be made and call the debtor to effect payment within a fixed period of time.[8] There are also other administrative and economic sanctions, like the prohibition of obtaining loans from credit institutions (art. 2 L. 1239/1982) and the surcharge of additional penalties (art. 19 L. 1469/1984). A limited penal responsibility forms equally part of these measures (art. 1 I L. 86/1967).

According to a general principle expressed in article 26 VII of Law 1846/1951, any violation in the payment of these contributions does not jeopardize the payment of social insurance benefits to salaried employees. It does, however, cancel the insurance protection provided to independent professionals,[9] owing to the strong element of reciprocity in the insurance legal bonds.

### *B. Social Sources and State Economic Support*

The legislator often places part of the burdens of a certain insurance community to the society at large by establishing the so-called social sources (κοινωνικοί πόροι, koinonikoi poroi). In assessing the value of goods or services rendered in some transactions, a certain percentage is earmarked for the insurance institutions. For instance, in order to obtain a driver's license a person must pay a sum in favor of the Automobile Owners Pension Fund. Despite their variety, the social sources are nothing else but indirect taxes in favor of third parties. Greek courts correctly hold that the extraordinary support of an institution through social sources is inconsistent with the principle of proportionality between contributions and benefits and justifies the imposition of a ceiling on insurance benefits contrary to proper insurance doctrine.[10]

Each time that the insurance protection of a substantial group of people is actuarily underrated, the machinery of wider social solidarity, that is of general taxation, is put in motion. This explains for instance the exceptional state economic support to the Professional and Handcraftsmen Fund of Greece afforded by article 1 II of Law 1275/1982, in an effort to increase the lowest limits of pensions provided by that Fund.

The state contributions for the creation of socio-insurance capital consists of fixed sums where the state itself emerges as an institution of social insurance for public servants, or when it has committed itself to make regular, often yearly, contributions as in the case of the insurance regime of the Social Insurance Organization (Ίδρυμα Κοινωνικών Ασφαλίσεων: IKA; art 24 VIII L. 1846/1951). The last mentioned provision, however, was in my opinion erroneously construed as a guarantee of the state only in cases of economic insufficiency of this insurance institution.[11] This resulted in a far-reaching

8. F. Chatzidimitriou – G. Psilos, *Insurance Legislation* (1984) 391–406.
9. AP 840/1976, EDKA 1976. 559; 986/1979, Epitheorisis IKA (Athens, 1980) 782.
10. S.S.C. 9/1980, EDKA 1981. 46; SE 3215/1976, EDKA 1977. 72; D. P. Athens 8515/1982, EDKA 1982. 749.
11. Chr. Agallopoulos (above, n. 1) 155; K. Kremalis (above, n. 3) 185–187.

inapplicability of this provision as well as in economic deficits which cannot be remedied without sacrifices by the insured.

## IV. Social Insurance Benefits

### *A. Important Characteristics*

The basic substance of insurance benefits (ασφαλιστικές παροχές, asphalistikes paroches) corresponds to the immediate targets of social insurance plans. Accordingly, they are divided into measures taken for the restitution of the labor capacity of the insured and measures taken in order to balance out the lost income due to social risk. Benefits are distinguished specifically in (a) compulsory and permissive, (b) periodical and lump sum, and (c) monetary and in kind.

There is a strong controversy with regard to the legal nature of insurance benefits. The legislative command which orders the insurance institution to issue an administrative act in favor of the insured, that is to grant him a pension, actually means the recognition of the party's right to such benefit; such right is of public character. On the contrary, payment of insurance benefits by a private institution of social insurance does not go beyond the fulfillment of a debtor's contractual obligations towards his creditor (insured).

### *B. Prerequisites of Insurance Benefits*

The requirements for the establishment and the implementation of insurance rights present a great variety. This is due to the deep differentiation of Greek social insurance plans based on professional categories. In systematizing, to some extent, the requirements for social benefits as they stand today, we can classify them into two main groups, the substantive and the formal. Substantive are the requirements needed to determine to which person and for what purpose the benefits will be granted. The formal requirements refer to the procedural steps which have to be taken before insurance benefits are granted.

The substantive requirements cover: (a) the circle of protected persons, (b) the presence of an insured risk (ασφαλιστικός κίνδυνος, asphalistikos kindynos), and (c) a certain duration of insurance (ασφαλιστική περίοδος, asphalistiki periodos).

The circle of protected persons, i.e. the working individuals, spouse, children, parents, brothers and sisters, grandchildren, is expanded or restricted by the legislator, depending on the insurance institution and the kind of insurance benefit provided thereunder. Regular insurance risks are: sickness, maternity, disability, industrial injury or disease, old age, death of a family protector, lack of housing, and the destruction of agricultural production.

In laying out time prerequisites, the legislator is often satisfied with the mere running of insurance time (art. 28 I L. 1846/1951); in other instances, however, he imposes a specific time of actual insurance in relation to a specified period or to the occurrence of a protected risk, such as illness (art. 35 I 2 L. 1846/1951). The insurance period runs, as a rule, together with the work period. The facility, however, to include, for purposes of estimation, periods during which no work was performed is often provided for (fictional[12] or permissive insurance[13]). This, along with the problems of formal[14] and consecutive[15] insurance, give rise to some interesting questions of interpretation that occupy Greek courts daily.

The formal requirements include: (a) filing of an application and (b) initiative taken by the insurance institution.

## C. *Types of Insurance Benefits*

The most important monetary benefits are the pensions (συντάξεις, syntaxeis). Old age pension is granted after a certain age limit has been reached (55–56 years), that varies according to each insurance regime, and after a certain period of work has been completed (25–35 years). The pensioners are often permitted to retain a parallel limited professional activity. Disability pension is granted after assessment of the influence of the injury that caused loss of income to the individual. The medical diagnosis does not have, as a rule, binding force with regard to the percentage of disability. A percentage of disability between 50% and 67% provides only reduced pension, while full pension is granted to those that are disabled beyond 67%. Death benefits are given to the widow(er) and to other dependent members of the family. All pensions, except those granted to farmers, purport to replace the loss of income from the related activity. They are therefore estimated at a percentage of 70–80% of the earnings or income recently received. There are lowest and highest limits of pensions which are readjusted usually automatically according to the increases of the consumer price index determined by the state.

The monetary benefits also include certain benefits which have a periodical character such as allowances (επιδόματα, epidomata) for sickness, maternity, industrial injury or disease, unemployment, family charges and mobilization and other lump sum payments (εφάπαξ παροχές, ephapax paroches) like marriage and birth allowances, funeral expenses, housing loans and indemnification for destruction of agricultural production.

The most important benefits in kind (παροχές σε είδος, paroches se eidos) are the medical, hospital and pharmaceutical relief. After the establishment of the national health system (Εθνικό Σύστημα Υγείας, Ethniko Systima Ygeias) (art. 1 L. 1397/1983), which is gradually taking shape, these benefits will result in social services independent of any special social insurance institution. In this respect, Greece is now at a period of transition.

12. A. Petroglou, Case-Law Achievements Regarding Recognition and Redemption of Fictional Periods of Insurance, *EDKA* 1965. 129.
13. F. Chatzidimitriou – G. Psilos (above, n. 8) 271–287.
14. V. Rotis, *Formal Insurance and Formal Non-Insurance* (1977).
15. A. Metallinos, *Evolution of the Institution of Consecutive Insurance* (1982).

The benefits in kind also include labor exchange and professional orientation, as well as training services carried out by the competent social policy organization OAED (Οργανισμός Απασχόλησης Εργατικού Δυναμικού). There are various programs now under way (especially arts. 15 I L. 1346/1983, 29 I L. 1262/1982), often sponsored by EEC. The basic rules however governing the legal relations and the relevant rights have not yet been systematically dealt with.

# Chapter 15
# Judicial Organization and Civil Procedure

*Konstantinos D. Kerameus**

## I. Introduction

Judicial organization and civil procedure have grown in recent years to relatively high stature in Greece. This is true both at the level of scholarly production as well as in the field of the practice of law. The reasons for such a comparatively privileged treatment of procedural matters within the whole Greek legal system may be traced in two directions: the first one pertains to the statutory regulation of procedural issues, the second to the conditions of law enforcement in the Greek courts.

In Greece, judicial organization and procedure have always possessed clear and numerous constitutional underpinnings. The new Constitution of June 9, 1975, has stressed still more the immediate relevance of constitutional commands. First of all, a whole section of the Constitution (Section V of Part Three, arts. 87–100) deals with the 'Judicial Power' in two chapters: chapter one (arts. 87–92) bears the title 'Judicial Officers and Staff'; chapter two (arts. 93–100) is devoted to the 'Organization and Jurisdiction of Courts'. Secondly, a large number of other constitutional provisions have a direct or indirect procedural impact[1]. Thirdly, the right of access to the courts has been raised to constitutional preeminence: according to article 20 I of the Constitution, 'everyone is entitled to legal protection by the courts and may plead before them his position on his rights or interests, as specified by law' (see also above, Ch. 3, Section V C 1). It is not surprising that these normative arrangements of the third branch of government have come to be regarded in Greece, as in some other countries, as a kind of 'applied constitutional law'.

Parliamentary activity has equally contributed to expanding the relevance of procedure, as compared to other legal disciplines. Between 1835 and 1968, Greece operated under the old Code of Civil Procedure, which had come into force shortly after the establishment of the modern Greek State and was the

* Professor of Law, Athens University.

1. Cf. arts. 1 II, III; 2 I; 4 I, II, IV; 5 II–IV; 6; 7 II–IV; 8; 9 I 3; 10 II; 12 II, IV 1; 13 V; 14 III 2, IV, VI 2, VII; 16 VI 4; 17 II, IV 1, 2, 4; 18 V 4; 19.2; 22 II; 23 II 2; 25 I, III; 26 III; 28 I 1; 29 III; 47 I, II; 48 I 1; 49 III, IV; 51 III 2; 52; 56 I, III 1; 58; 61; 62; 65 VI 2; 76 VI; 77; 86; 102 V 2; 103 IV 2, 3; 104 III; 105 V 2; 106 IV; 109 II; 111 III b, V; 115 I–V; 118 I, II; 119 I.

work of the Bavarian jurist Georg Ludwig von Maurer. The current code, elaborated over some thirty years (1933–1964), was mainly influenced by mid-European models, especially German and Austrian law. This major work of codification, in force since September 16, 1968, as well as its subsequent frequent amendments, has been feeding a lively discussion on procedural issues among the members of the legal community. Procedure has thus become a matter of actual and permanent preoccupation for all lawyers – practitioners, judges and scholars alike.

The conditions of law enforcement in the Greek courts have been exceptionally favorable to such a procedural orientation, or disorientation, of legal thinking and legal action. Leading scholars of the law of procedure in the nineteenth century were either high judges themselves, or extremely influential upon judges. In more recent times, the large number of practicing attorneys and the intensely competitive climate that exists among them opens the door of opportunity creating incentives for the use, or abuse, of procedural tactics. Some aggressive features of the Greek national character come out as well when people become litigants. Many judges regard procedure as their own professional ambit *par excellence* and cherish, in their opinions, a preference for procedural over substantive issues. Against such a background, one can well understand the exclamation contained in an important Greek novel of the 30's: 'Procedure, my friend, procedure. As long as you keep procedure under control, you have the upper hand' [2].

## II. Judicial Organization

The law governing judicial organization is not contained in a single enactment. Relevant provisions are to be found either in the Constitution or in many special laws, some of them quite extensive. In December 1987 a comprehensive code on judicial organization and the status of judicial officers (comprising 113 articles) was compiled and forwarded to Parliament for adoption.

### *A. Principles*

Out of these scattered sources some general principles emerge:

1. Justice is administered by three hierarchies of courts: administrative, civil and criminal (διοικητικά, πολιτικά, ποινικά δικαστήρια, dioikitika, politika, poinika dikastiria; Const. 93 I). In terms of judges, however, this distinction is reduced to a twofold scheme, since the same persons regularly alternate between civil and criminal courts.

2. Judicial officers are divided into ordinary judges (τακτικοί δικαστές, taktikoi dikastes) and public prosecutors (εισαγγελείς, eisangeleis; cf. Const. 87 III). The latter mainly participate in criminal proceedings; in civil matters, only

2. G. Theotocas, *Argo*, 8th ed., vol. II (Athens, 1980) 39.

the Supreme Court prosecutor or his substitutes are required to submit their views on all pending cases.

3. Judicial officers are career lawyers, entering early and remaining for life. They are appointed after passing an entrance examination administered by Supreme Court judges and law professors. There is no jury nor other lay element in civil and administrative cases. Only in criminal proceedings do jurors take part in mixed courts competent to try some serious felonies (see below, Ch. 18, Section III A 1).

4. There is some preference for judicial panels rather than single judges. Recent amendments, however, have markedly expanded the subject matter competence[3] of one-member tribunals. What remains true is that at least all appellate courts consist of more than one judges.

### *B. Ordinary Civil Courts*

The Code of Civil Procedure provides for three types of district courts in civil matters: justices of the peace (ειρηνοδικεία, eirinodikeia), one-member (μονομελή πρωτοδικεία, monomeli protodikeia), and three-member district courts (πολυμελή πρωτοδικεία, polymeli protodikeia). The justices of the peace, divided into approximately 300 districts throughout the country, handle mostly cases of low monetary value or involving agricultural disputes. The one- or three-member district courts, sixty-three in each category, sit in jurisdictional areas which coincide roughly with the boundaries of the respective prefectures (νομοί, nomoi).

The three-member district courts have general original jurisdiction and also hear appeals from the justices of the peace (C. C. Proc. 18 no. 2). Appeals from the other district courts, however, go to the twelve courts of appeal (εφετεία, efeteia) which sit in the largest cities of the country in panels of three judges and review the judgments below both on the law and on the facts. The Supreme Court (Άρειος Πάγος, Areios Pagos) sitting in Athens and normally hearing cases in panels (τμήματα, tmimata) of five justices, or in full bench (Ολομέλεια, Olomeleia) with all justices (about fifty-five) entitled to participate, a quorum being eleven, is not considered a regular appellate court but only a court of cassation which confines its extraordinary review to questions of law, not having authority to reverse findings of fact (see below, Section VIII E).

### *C. Ordinary Administrative Courts*

A similar structure has been extended in recent years to the administrative courts as well. Law 1406/1983 (cf. also Const. 94 I–II) granted them jurisdiction

3. The appropriate American term here would have been, of course, subject matter jurisdiction. However, Greek law as well as the continental legal systems in general adopts a clear distinction between jurisdiction and competence. See the text, Section III A.

over all substantive administrative disputes. There are twenty-eight (one- and three-member) administrative district courts and seven (three- and five-member) administrative courts of appeal. Supreme court in the administrative jurisdiction is the Council of State (see above, Ch. 3, Sections II B 6 and V C 1).

### D. *Judicial Independence*

Both the Constitution (art. 87 I) and legal doctrine distinguish the personal from the functional aspect of judicial independence. Under the former, all judicial officers, after a probationary period of at least one year, acquire life tenure. Compulsory retirement is now fixed at sixty-five or sixty-seven years according to rank. During tenure, they may be dismissed only upon conviction for a serious offense, or upon adjudication of grave breach of discipline, illness, disability or professional incompetence, but not merely because their court or post is abolished. Even beyond that, the status of judicial officers (promotions, assignments, transfers, detachments) is within the authority of the Supreme Judicial Council (Ανώτατο Δικαστικό Συμβούλιο, Anotato Dikastiko Symvoulio), composed exclusively of members of the Supreme Court, with no participation of governmental or parliamentary representatives; only the promotion to the presidium of the Supreme Court (president, prosecutor, vice-presidents) is decided by the Cabinet. The concept of judicial self-governance is rounded out by entrusting supervision of judges only to superior judges and also by conferring disciplinary authority over them to councils consisting of these higher judges.

The functional aspect encompasses the independence of the judiciary as a separate branch of the government. Legislation and administrative acts are subject to incidental judicial review. Functional judicial independence exists within the judiciary itself as well; as in other civil law countries, the binding force of judicial precedents is not formally recognized. In practice, however, courts tend to follow prior cases; see below, Section VIII E.

### E. *Judicial Staff*

A high degree of personal independence is also granted to the secretarial staff (γραμματείς, grammateis) of all courts and prosecutor's offices (Const. 92 I–III). Notaries (συμβολαιογράφοι, symvolaiografoi), for whom full legal education is required, record some important legal transactions in authentic documents; they also hold public auctions. Marshals (δικαστικοί επιμελητές, dikastikoi epimelites) officially serve judicial and extrajudicial documents, and discharge numerous functions during enforcement proceedings (see below, Section XIII).

For all legal professions, graduation from one of the three law schools of the country (Athens, Thessaloniki, Komotini) is required. Students enter law school at the age of eighteen, immediately after high school. Law study takes four years. Following graduation and a period of apprenticeship (eighteen months), mostly in a law firm, the candidates take a bar examination conducted by the courts of appeal. All practicing attorneys (δικηγόροι, dikigoroi) must be members of one of the Greek bar associations (δικηγορικοί σύλλογοι, dikigorikoi syllogoi), which are public entities. The promotion of lawyers to the appellate courts is generally a formality, depending mainly on time. Otherwise, there is no formal distinction among practicing attorneys with regard to the functions undertaken by them. Their number is high and their degree of specialization rather low.

## III. Jurisdiction and Competence

### *A. Definitions*

In modern Greek law, there has always been a sharp distinction between jurisdiction (δικαιοδοσία, dikaiodosia) and competence (αρμοδιότητα, armodiotita). Jurisdiction refers either to the state's judicial power as a whole (cf. the 'international jurisdiction' of the Greek State; see below, Ch. 16, Section III), or to the divisions of judicial authority according to the nature of the matter to be adjudicated; with respect to the latter, one speaks of civil, criminal, and administrative jurisdiction, exercised by the corresponding kinds of courts as prescribed in article 93 I of the Constitution. The distinction between civil and criminal matters does not cause any significant problems; as far as administrative, in contrast to civil, disputes are concerned, they always originate from some administrative action undertaken in the exercise of public power.

Competence, on the other hand, pertains to the allocation of judicial power within each jurisdictional division. It describes a court's power to adjudicate specified matters. These matters, if identified by class, are assigned to one of the three types of district courts (see above, Section II B), constituting their subject matter competence (αρμοδιότητα καθ'ύλη, armodiotita kath'yli). Additional links are, however, required to bring a dispute to a particular court and, thus, make up its territorial competence (αρμοδιότητα κατά τόπο, armodiotita kata topo), which is similar to the American notion of venue. Besides subject matter and territorial competence, there also exists the so-called functional competence (λειτουργική αρμοδιότητα, leitourgiki armodiotita), which denotes the respective adjudicative powers of various judicial authorities with regard to the same litigation, for example through the consecutive appellate levels.

### *B. Subject Matter Competence*

As a rule, subject matter competence depends on the amount in controversy. The current lines of demarcation (art. 14 C. C. Proc.) run at 300,000 drs., or about $2,300, as between justices of the peace and one-member district courts; and at 1,000,000 drs., or about $7,650, as between the latter and the three-member district courts. The amount in controversy stands as defined in the complaint, without taking into account interest or other accessory claims (art. 9). Along with this value-conditioned competence, the Code of Civil Procedure adopts a parallel method of allocating civil disputes among these three courts, regardless of the amount in controversy, by expanding the competence of the justices of the peace and the one-member courts, according to the nature of particular species of disputes. Thus, to the former are allotted many cases involving farming, restrictions on property, transportation or performance of some other services, and the internal working of associations and cooperatives (art. 15); to the latter, leases, employment, insurance and car accident disputes, claims of lawyers and of some other professionals, as well as some family litigation with financial impact, especially maintenance applications (art. 16).

### C. *Territorial Competence*

Territorial competence usually depends on the defendant's domicile (art. 22), i.e. a person's main and permanent establishment consisting of *corpus* and *animus* (art. 51 C. C.).[4] Business 'domicile' is an additional ground for related claims (art. 23 II C. C. Proc.). If domicile is lacking, its place is taken by residence. Legal entities are deemed to be domiciled at their real seat.[5]

### D. *Exclusive Jurisdictions*

Special jurisdictions (ειδικές δωσιδικίες, eidikes dosidikies) are divided into exclusive and concurrent. There are six kinds of exclusive or 'local' jurisdiction where the action may not be brought anywhere else but there, even to the exclusion of a defendant's domicile: (1) *Forum rei sitae*: actions relating to property interests in immovables, including leases but not purchase and sale contracts, are allocated to the courts of the situs (art. 29); (2) *Forum hereditatis*: descent and distribution claims among heirs and legatees as well as in favor of third parties go to the probate courts which are those of the decedent's domicile or residence at death (art. 30); (3) *Forum connexitatis*: auxiliary claims, such as for interest on loans or for guaranties, are tried before the courts having jurisdiction over the main claim (art. 31); (4) *Forum societatis*: 'internal affairs' corporate claims are adjudicated at the real seat (art. 27); (5) *Forum gestae administrationis ex decreto iudicis*: where a court has appointed an administrator of the affairs or property of a person, all related claims are to be tried

4. The defendant's domicile covers even causes of action unrelated to the forum, thus providing the basis of 'general jurisdiction'. Cf. *Helicopteros Nacionales de Colombia v. Hall*, 466 U.S. 408, at 414, 415, 418 n. 12, 421 with n. 1, 423, 424, especially 414 n. 9 (1984); *Burger King v. Rudzewicz*, 105 S. Ct. 2174, at 2182 n. 15 (1985).
5. The 'real seat' is located not necessarily in the place of incorporation, nor in the principal place of business, but where the decision-making authority over the affairs of the legal entity originates.

there (art. 28); and (6) *Forum reconventionis*: counterclaims, which generally are only permissive and need not be related to the cause of action, belong, if asserted as such, to the exclusive jurisdiction of the court of the claim, provided they do not exceed its subject matter competence (art. 34).

### *E. Concurrent Jurisdictions*

Concurrent jurisdictions, available at plaintiff's option, include another six categories, resembling the U.S. long-arm system: (1) *Forum negotii*: suits on contracts and other juridical acts may be brought either at the place of making or of performance (art. 33); (2) *Forum delicti*: actions on tort constituting simultaneously a criminal act may be brought at the place of either conduct or its effects (art. 35); (3) *Forum gestae administrationis ex causis variis*: disputes relating to various agency and administration relationships are adjudicated where the related conduct took place (art. 36); (4) *Forum continentiae causarum*: suits against joint obligors may be brought at the domicile or a concurrent jurisdictional basis of any one of them; likewise, actions among the same persons involving multiple immovables may be brought at the situs of any one of the immovables (art. 37); (5) *Forum matrimonii*: personal marital and divorce matters go to the courts of the common residence, with certain exceptions where the spouses are aliens (arts. 39, 611, 612); and (6) *Fora bonorum*: suits on monetary claims may be brought also either at the (a) residence of the defendant if it is of a certain duration or (b) situs of any property of the non-domiciliary defendant even for unrelated claims (arts. 38, 40), which is akin to *in rem* and *quasi-in-rem* jurisdiction except that, because the judgment is not limited as to amount, it can be classified as potentially 'exorbitant'.

### *F. Prorogation*

It should also be mentioned that the parties may choose a specified district court by express written agreement in advance as to a particular matter, or by tacit informal acceptance expressed through failure to object in court at the first opportunity (prorogation = παρέκταση, parektasi; arts. 42–44). This confers jurisdiction except for non-pecuniary claims and claims relating to out-of-state immovables. No similar freedom of choice exists for the parties with regard to subject matter competence, which is mandatorily fixed by law.

### *G. Review of Jurisdictional Issues*

Any court having competence is required to take the case: the *forum-non-conveniens* doctrine is unknown in Greek law. If the court lacks competence, it may not dismiss the case, but must transfer it to the competent court within the same jurisdictional division (art. 46). Such transfers are not allowed among different jurisdictional divisions, be they civil, criminal or administrative. A judgment can be attacked for lack of competence; null and void, however, is only a judgment which transgresses the lines demarcating the three jurisdictional divisions (cf. art. 313 I lit. b).

## IV. Parties and Types of Actions

### *A. Capacity and Standing to Sue*

According to article 68 of the Code of Civil Procedure, 'he who has a direct legal interest may request judicial protection' (plaintiff = ενάγων, enagon). This provision grants standing to sue (νομιμοποίηση, nomimopoiisi) only to persons whose substantive rights constitute the object of the relief sought in the action. In conformity with traditional continental patterns, Greek law does not allow third persons having only an indirect or remote interest, or fighting merely *pro bono publico*, to institute civil proceedings. Therefore, neither the *actio popularis* nor modern American developments in the field of class actions have found their way into Greek civil procedure. A similar position is taken with regard to the proper party defendant (εναγόμενος, enagomenos): only a person who is liable under substantive law may be made defendant (cf. art. 216 I lit. a).

Joinder of parties (ομοδικία, omodikia) relies equally on substantive law considerations. Permissive joinder of plaintiffs or defendants is available to all those sharing in the right or duty in dispute, or in cases in which joint parties prosecute or face claims based on similar causes of action (art. 74). The code (art. 76) also acknowledges, however, the concept of necessary and indispensable parties: if several persons are required in order to bring or to defend a particular action (e.g., for partition of a thing in common), or if no inconsistent judgments should be rendered as among them, then parties must be joined. An expansion of the subjective confines of litigation is further provided for through the use of the intervention (παρέμβαση, paremvasi; arts. 79–85) and the impleader (προσεπίκληση, prosepiklisi; arts. 86–90).

As far as capacity is concerned, every natural person and every legal entity, since they are capable of holding rights (see above, Ch. 4, Sections II A–B, III B 2), may be made a party. However, capacity to be a party (ικανότητα διαδίκου, ikanotita diadikou) is to be clearly distinguished from the capacity to conduct litigation in one's own name (ικανότητα δικαστικής παραστάσεως, ikanotita dikastikis parastaseos). The latter is granted only to persons enjoying the capacity to enter into juridical acts (see above, Ch. 4, Sections II A and V B), i.e. to all persons above the age of eighteen and not being interdicted or mentally ill. Therefore, a party not capable of conducting litigation in his own name as well as all legal entities have to act through their legal representatives.

A further and more general requirement is for a party to be represented by an attorney in any court other than a justice of the peace. The choice of attorney is free but must be made from among the members of the local bar. A power of attorney may be granted either by a document prepared by a notary or through personal appearance in court (art. 96); it is revocable at any time (arts. 100–103).

The requirements discussed in this section are called 'procedural prerequisites' (διαδικαστικές προϋποθέσεις, diadikastikes proypotheseis) and have to be scrutinized by the court on its own motion (art. 73). If any one of them is lacking, the court will not proceed to the merits of the case, but will dismiss the action as 'inadmissible' (απαράδεκτη, aparadekti)[6]. Such a dismissal does not prevent, however, the defeated plaintiff from remedying the defect and coming back with a new action.

## *B. Types of Actions*

Several criteria are used in order to classify the various types of actions. The classical categories of complaints were developed in Roman law and rely heavily upon substantive law concepts (e.g., *actio in rem*, *actio in personam*, *actio mixta*; further examples on similar lines of thinking would be the hereditary action or the family law action). More important, however, is the procedural classification based on the type of relief requested by the plaintiff. In this respect, a tripartite division emerges: actions for performance, actions for declaratory judgment, actions for judicial modification of legal relationships.

The action for performance (καταψηφιστική αγωγή, katapsiphistiki agogi) is the most ancient and remains today the most usual type of action. It aims at a judgment ordering the defendant to perform as obligated; the performance may be a specific one, or consist in the payment of money. Article 69 of the Code of Civil Procedure rather broadly allows even an action for future performance, thus turning an originally repressive remedy into a preventive one. The practical relevance of an action for performance lies in the field of enforcement: it is the only type of action which, if successful, opens the way for enforcement by execution. By contrast, declaratory judgments are not, strictly speaking, enforceable. They make a binding determination of a legal relationship capable of becoming *res judicata*. Therefore, an action for declaratory judgment (αναγνωριστική αγωγή, anagnoristiki agogi; art. 70) (1) must concern a specific legal relationship, and (2) requires a legal interest on plaintiff's part especially worthy of protection. There is increasing recourse to such actions in Greece, since their litigation is exempted from the fee levied by the state on the trial of an action for performance. Finally, an action for judicial modification of legal relationships (διαπλαστική αγωγή, diaplastiki agogi; art. 71) is available only in cases provided for by law, for example to obtain a divorce or to set aside a contract on account of fraud, threat or mistake. Greek law does not permit the courts to alter existing legal relationships between the parties without an express statutory authorization which is granted only in exceptional cases.

6. In continental civil procedure, 'inadmissibility' of the action, or of the appeal, is a technical term. The term means that the court may not examine the merits of the case, and covers situations like lack of capacity or standing, prematurity, *res judicata*, or untimely filing of an appeal.

## V. Procedural Principles

The Code of Civil Procedure devotes a central chapter of its Book I to the so-called 'fundamental procedural principles' (arts. 116–126). In so doing, it conforms to the continental tradition of procedural codifications, with the new French Code of Civil Procedure (1975) being the latest and most spectacular example (arts. 1–24: *les principes directeurs du procès*). Such principles mainly deal with the allocation of power and initiative as between the court and the parties, and with the guidelines for conducting litigation. They are formulated in the code in highly abstract wording. Yet they are not mere precepts for general inspiration but rules of positive law, requiring and enjoying immediate application.

### *A. The Dominant Position of the Parties*

*Domini litis* are the parties. They determine whether, on what subject matter, to what extent, and upon what allegations of fact there will be civil proceedings. The judge remains a neutral, more or less passive and more or less silent, observer of the procedural scene, introducing on his own motion mainly the rules of law applicable to the dispute. Compared to his Anglo-American counterpart, the Greek judge displays less visible power in controlling the courtroom but, as far as evidentiary matters are concerned, he seems to have greater leeway for initiative.

The dominant position of the parties with regard to the subject matter and the conduct of civil litigation becomes apparent in three respects:

1. A court may not award the plaintiff relief not requested nor go beyond the request submitted (art. 106). Conversely, the plaintiff may withdraw the complaint and the defendant may acknowledge the claim, meaning that, as a rule, the proceedings are terminated to the detriment of the party taking such initiative, without any further inquiry by the court (arts. 294, 296, 298).

2. The court has no authority to rely on facts not submitted nor proven by a party (art. 106). The court may, of course, order the taking of evidence (art. 107), but it is then for the parties to collect and to present to the court the various means of proof. By contrast, the field of the applicable rules of law constitutes the court's own domain: with regard to domestic law, there is neither need nor possibility of 'proving' its contents. Foreign law is also covered by judicial notice (art. 337), even on appeal, including the final appeal to the Supreme Court (arts. 559 no. 1.1, 560 no. 1.1). If, however, the court does not know the relevant foreign law, it may order the taking of evidence or rely on any, even unofficial, methods of cognizance (art. 337).

3. All consecutive procedural steps are to be taken, as a rule, by the parties, not by the court (art. 108). For instance, all hearings of the case are fixed upon a party's motion; judicial documents, including judgments, are served on a party's initiative and not on the motion of the court (art. 123); even moving the appellate proceedings forward after an appeal has been filed depends always on any party's diligence (art. 498).

### B. Concentration on the First Hearing

In its endeavor to expedite proceedings, Greek law requires all factual allegations of the parties to be submitted to the court at the first hearing of the case; only in exceptional instances are parties permitted to plead additional facts at a later stage (art. 269: σύστημα συγκεντρώσεως, systima syngentroseos). This rule and its exceptions apply equally to appellate proceedings (art. 527).

### C. Oral and Written Proceedings

The drafters of the code strongly favored oral proceedings. Nevertheless, both practice and subsequent amendments relied heavily on the exchange of written pleadings, making thus a full oral hearing an optional and rather rare phenomenon in civil litigation. By contrast, Law 1478/1984, in force since March 1, 1985, has now made oral proceedings mandatory before the justices of the peace and in the one-member district courts (arts. 115, 270 C. C. Proc.).

### D. Good Faith and Morals

In an optimistic spirit of innovation, article 116 introduces a general duty to tell the truth in civil proceedings, and requires the parties, their legal representatives and their attorneys to conduct litigation according to good faith and morality. Little has changed, however, as an immediate result of this provision, since the sanctions are restricted to moderate fines (cf. arts. 205 no. 2, 185 no. 1) seldom imposed and thus regarded as a negligible threat.

## VI. Ordinary Proceedings in First Instance

### A. Commencement of the Action

Regardless of the type of action, ordinary proceedings in the courts of first instance follow the same pattern. A civil action (αγωγή, agogi) is commenced by filing a complaint with the clerk who appoints a day and time for the first hearing of the case; he then enters the action in the docket (πινάκιο, pinakio; arts. 215, 226). The defendant will then, on plaintiff's initiative, be served at his home or at his place of business with a copy of the complaint containing also the day and time fixed. Service must be made at least thirty days before the first hearing (art. 228). After service is completed, the action is considered as having been brought (art. 215 I 1) and the litigation as pending. This has both procedural and substantive effects: on the former level, no future extension or modification of plaintiff's claim is permitted (arts. 223, 224), and the resulting *lis pendens* (εκκρεμοδικία, ekkremodikia) prevents any court from hearing the same claim (art. 222); on the latter, as from the service on the defendant, among other things, the running of the statute of limitations is interrupted – which is considered, according to continental tradition, a substantive effect – and interest accrues on all monetary claims (art. 221 C. C. Proc.; arts. 261, 346 C. C.).

### *B. Contents of the Complaint*

The complaint is drawn up and signed by plaintiff's counsel. It mentions the court in which the action is being brought, states plaintiff's and defendant's names and domiciles, and contains the grounds establishing the cause of the action as well as an unambiguous specification of the relief requested (art. 216 I C. C. Proc.). Failure to allege sufficient facts to support the claim will lead to the dismissal of the complaint even on the court's own motion. By contrast, the legal aspects need not be articulated at this initial stage of the litigation or even later (*ius novit curia*; see above, Section V A 2) – the only exception being, of course, the proceedings in the Supreme Court, which are restricted to legal issues. However, since both the complaint and the subsequent pleadings are prepared by lawyers, they, not surprisingly, often include extensive legal arguments.

Joinder of separate claims between the same parties is allowed even if they arise out of entirely unrelated facts, provided they (1) do not contradict each other, and (2) fall within the competence of the court (art. 218). Subsidiary claims may likewise be included in the same or in another complaint should the main claim be dismissed (art. 219). There exists, however, neither a compulsory joinder nor any general prohibition against splitting a single claim or cause of action.

### *C. Pleadings*

Formal preparation for litigation is not necessary for either plaintiff or defendant. The plaintiff may bring an action without any previous notice to the prospective defendant. The defendant is not required to answer the complaint immediately but may wait until the first hearing of the case when both parties develop in their pleadings their factual and legal positions. Written pleadings are never required to be served or even sent to the other party; they are to be filed with the court's clerk before the hearing, in one-member district courts at least three days before the hearing (cf. arts. 237–242, as repeatedly amended).

The first hearing of the case is indeed the most important phase of the entire proceedings. Both parties articulate their statements of fact which also limit the evidence to be produced. For proceedings before justices of the peace or one-member district courts, which are oral, the first hearing is for all practical purposes the only one (art. 270 C. C. Proc., as amended by art. 11 L. 1478/1984): the parties have to produce all their means of proof at that hearing, after which the judgment is handed down; only in exceptional cases may the court order further evidence to be taken.

### *D. Defenses and Counterclaim*

In formulating his pleadings, the defendant is also not subject to strict pleading rules. He may raise two types of objections:

1. Exceptions (ενστάσεις, enstaseis) which either prevent the court from reaching a decision on the merits, for example a plea of lack of jurisdiction or of lack of standing, or plead subsequent facts, for example a plea by way of confession and avoidance or of set-off. The former type of exception must also be considered by the judge *ex officio*.
2. Defenses related strictly to the grounds of the action, which means to deny the facts as alleged by plaintiff, or to put them in another context (art. 261 C. C. Proc.; άρνηση της βάσεως της αγωγής, arnisi tis vaseos tis agogis).

The defendant may interpose a counterclaim at the first hearing (arts. 34, 268; ανταγωγή, antagogi; see above, Section III D (6)). Counterclaims follow their own procedural course, regardless of the outcome of the action. It is thus possible for the action to be dismissed, yet an affirmative judgment may be rendered on the counterclaim.

### *E. Default*

A judgment may also be obtained by default, either on plaintiff's or on defendant's side (ερημοδικία, erimodikia). Default may result when a party is not adequately represented at a hearing; adequate representation requires a duly appointed lawyer and the timely filing of pleadings. Any party's default requires the court to ascertain whether proper service of summons was made on the defaulting party; if not, the case cannot proceed and a new service becomes necessary (arts. 271 I, II; 272 II, III). If service was proper, then plaintiff's default leads to dismissal of the action (art. 272 I). Default by the defendant is tantamount to admitting the grounds for the action, resulting in the rendition of judgment for plaintiff, provided all procedural prerequisites have been met (see above, Section IV A in f.) and the complaint states a cause of action (art. 271 III). These rules refer to default at the first hearing of the case. Default at a later hearing compels the court to examine the merits of the case, with the defaulting party regarded as a fictional or silent presence (art. 279).

### *F. Attempt at Conciliation*

At any stage of the case, the court is expected to attempt a settlement of the dispute (art. 233 II; συμβιβασμός, symvivasmos). Furthermore, articles 209–214 provide for a permissive conciliation by the justice of the peace before a complaint is filed with the clerk of any civil court. Such an attempt at conciliation becomes mandatory in cases falling within the subject matter competence of the justice of the peace (art. 208) and in labor cases (art. 667). Nevertheless, the practical relevance of conciliation is minimal. Skipping a mandatory attempt at conciliation does not trigger any sanctions. With regard to optional conciliation, the parties are usually unwilling to expose themselves by undertaking a settlement which may not succeed. The intensely belligerent image of Greek advocacy also contributes to a rather unfavorable attitude towards conciliation.

### *G. Court Costs and Legal Aid*

Another factor accounting for the same result is the comparatively low level of court costs and attorney's fees. Court costs (δικαστική δαπάνη, dikastiki dapani) are borne in advance by each party with respect to his own expenses. *Ex post*, they are allocated by the judgment according to the so-called 'defeat principle' (art. 176): after the suit is terminated, the loser pays the other party's expenses, including attorney's fees. This principle is, however, mitigated by an important exception: the court may and actually often does depart from the all-or-nothing cost charge and allow no recovery of expenses whatsoever, if it deems that the loser had 'justified doubts as to the outcome of the case' (art. 179). This consequence may also follow in cases of partial victory and partial defeat by both parties (art. 178).

Legal aid (ευεργέτημα πενίας, evergetima penias) is provided for by articles 194–204 of the Code of Civil Procedure. Its availability depends, however, on proven need. Such a strict limitation has so far prevented an extensive recourse to legal aid.

## VII. Evidence

### *A. Ordering Evidence*

Matters of evidence (απόδειξη, apodeixi) occupy a central place in Greek civil proceedings. At the first hearing of the case, if the court deems that the relief requested by plaintiff is provided for by the law and, further, that the facts alleged in the complaint are sufficient to constitute a cause of action, but the defendant denies their truth, then the court's preeminent task is to establish the controversial facts. It does so by first ordering, and then by evaluating the appropriate means of proof. The taking of evidence was formerly ordered by an extensive and fully reasoned opinion of the court. Recently, Law 1478/1984, amending article 341 of the Code of Civil Procedure, replaced this full statement of the reasons in a formal decision with a simple and short judicial act, containing only the subject matter of evidence, the allocation of burden and the allowed means of proof, as well as the place and time of evidence-taking. In addition, before one-member courts, parties are required to produce their means of proof at the first hearing, since the court is expected to render judgment, as a rule, at once without further taking of evidence (art. 270, as amended by art. 11 L. 1478/1984; see above, Section VI C in f.). In any event, discovery and other pretrial devices are not known to Greek law, since evidence is confined solely within the time limits of a formal lawsuit except in cases of imminent danger, for example destruction of a means of proof (arts. 348–351: συντηρητική απόδειξη, syntiritiki apodeixi).

### *B. Subject Matter of Proof*

Only those facts contested by one party and relevant to the outcome of litigation make up the subject matter of proof (art. 335). The court takes judicial notice (art. 336) of the general teachings of human experience (e.g., notions of psychology, geography, history, even generally accessible concepts of modern technology) as well as of facts practically known to everyone (e.g., the nuclear accident at Chernobyl). The court is further allowed to infer from proven facts conclusions as to other facts.

### *C. Burden of Proof*

Matters of proof are extensively regulated in the Code of Civil Procedure in some 130 articles (335–465). Nevertheless, only one of them establishes a general statutory rule allocating the burden of proof (art. 338). According to this rule, each party has to prove the facts which are necessarily required to support his claim or counterclaim. Further elaboration of this abstract principle is left to the substantive rules dealing with the specific legal relationships and contained mainly in the Civil Code. Thus, in a contract case, plaintiff bears the burden of proving both the existence of the contract and its breach. However, lack of capacity, fraud or the plea of the statute of limitations are affirmative defenses which must be proven by the defendant (cf. arts. 277–278 C. C.).

These rules refer to the burden of proof as the duty to produce evidence. However, to the party bearing this 'subjective' burden of proof is also allocated the burden of proof in an 'objective' sense, that is the risk of nonpersuasion[7], which will in most cases ultimately mean losing the suit. Persuasion implies the full conviction of the court, i.e. requires clear and convincing proof; only in cases specifically provided in the law, the 'objective' burden of proof is satisfied by a showing of probability (art. 347 C. C. Proc.).

### *D. Means of Proof*

Although the Code of Civil Procedure does not contain exclusionary rules of evidence in the American sense, it deals in some detail with the admissibility of the various means of proof. There are eight such means under the code (art.

7. On this distinction, see, e.g., F. James and G. Hazard, *Civil Procedure*, 3d ed. 313–321 (Boston, Toronto, 1985).

339): confession (ομολογία, omologia), direct proof, especially viewing the premises (αυτοψία, autopsia), expert reports (πραγματογνωμοσύνη, pragmatognomosyni), testimony (μάρτυρες, martyres), examination of parties (εξέταση των διαδίκων, exetasi ton diadikon), party-oath (όρκος, orkos), documentary evidence (έγγραφα, engrapha), and presumptions (τεκμήρια, tekmiria). Party-oath is a relic of medieval procedure, conferring binding force to a party's sworn affirmation. It is imposed by the court only if there is no other sufficient evidence (art. 421 III); in actuality, it is used infrequently. It has been replaced in part by the testimony of parties, sworn or unsworn, which is also a subsidiary means of proof (art. 415 I).

In recent years, the use of expert reports has risen greatly in importance and frequency, particularly in connection with blood tests, the explanation of air-photographs, the authenticity of tape recordings, or the account of other technological events. Courts are encouraged to take judicial notice of technical elements relevant to the litigation, for example of the value of an estate or the proper functioning of a machine. Only if the required level of knowledge is qualified as 'highly specialized' and expertise is requested by a party, must the court order it (art. 368 II). In practice, however, expert evidence is often ordered even where the court was not bound to resort to it. In all cases of expert evidence, the parties are entitled to appoint their own 'technical counsels' (arts. 391–392; τεχνικοί σύμβουλοι, technikoi symvouloi) in order to highlight their viewpoints on the technical aspects and to assist the court-appointed experts. The latter may be public officers or private individuals; no formal consequences are derived from this distinction.

Testimony and documentary evidence remain the most common methods of proof. Still under French influence, Greek law is suspicious of the credibility of witnesses. It requires a contract or other juridical act to be in writing and admits testimony only as an exception which is, however, rather broad. The exception encompasses all cases in which production of written proof is literally or practically impossible. Also within the exception are most commercial transactions as well as all juridical acts, even of non-commercial nature, the value of which does not exceed the sum of 120,000 drs., or about $920 (arts. 393, 394).

### *E. Documentary Evidence*

Documentary evidence consists of notarial and other authentic instruments or of instruments drawn privately. The former bring about conclusive proof: the court must deem established as against the world the facts recorded in an authentic instrument witnessed by a notary or other public official, provided that he has acted within the scope of his authority (arts. 438, 440–441). The latter have a more limited probative effect in two respects. First, the facts recounted are considered as established, but only as against the person(s) who signed the private instrument; however, any form of counterproof can overcome this effect (arts. 446–448). Furthermore, the authenticity of a private instrument, if contested, has to be proven by the party producing the instrument (art. 445). All documents may be challenged for falsification (arts. 460–465; πλαστογραφία, plastographia).

### *F. Administration of Evidence*

As a rule, evidentiary proceedings take place before the court (arts. 270, 341 III 1). However, in courts consisting of more than one member, judges are usually reluctant to allow these proceedings to transpire in front of the whole panel. Instead, one judge among them or an out-of-town judge is charged with the task of administering this matter (art. 341 III 2–4, V–X). In proceedings before a one-member court, witnesses may also be examined by a notary provided that the adverse party has been notified two working days in advance (art. 270 II 2). In any case, it lies within the province of the court to order the reintroduction of such evidence before the full court, especially a witness's deposition which may seem exceptionally important (arts. 344, 411; cf. also arts. 245, 414). Documentary evidence and expert reports are kept in the record of the case and may be examined by the whole panel.

### *G. Evaluation of Evidence*

In principle, there are no mechanical rules of proof, prescribing in a general way the probative weight to be accorded to the various types of evidence. Such legal weight irrespective of the particular circumstances is provided for by the law only in exceptional cases, as with regard to notarial or other authentic instruments (see above, under E), confessions (art. 352), or party-oath (art. 430). Otherwise, the judges must decide controversies on the basis of their inner conviction and are free to ponder the opposed means of proof in any way they deem proper (art. 340. 1). This rule applies even to highly technological explanations contained in some expert reports (art. 387). In any event, the judges have to state in their opinion the reasons which led them to make up their minds (art. 340. 2).

## VIII. Appeals

### *A. Function and Distinctions of the Methods of Appeal*

Greek law, like most continental legal systems, does not conceive of appeals as left to the discretion of the judge, either the judge below who rendered the judgment to be attacked or the superior judge called upon to review it. All methods of appeal (ένδικα μέσα, endika mesa) are as of right: they are provided specifically by the law and there is no other way of reviewing a judgment. On the other hand, appeals are not necessarily addressed to a higher court: although not often used, two kinds of attack are directed to the same court which rendered the decision under challenge.

Following again French patterns, Greek civil procedure distinguishes between ordinary and extraordinary methods of attack. Reopening a default decision, as well as the regular appeal leading to a review on the law and on the facts, make up the former group. To the latter group belong the two remaining methods of attack: (1) the reopening of contested judgments, and (2) cassation, the request to the Supreme Court for a review on the law only. The functional consequences of such distinctions lie with the effect of *res judicata* and the enforceability of judgments. Generally, both come into play after the ordinary methods of attack have been exhausted (arts. 321, 904 II lit. a), that is either rejected or left unused within the time limitation provided. By contrast, extraordinary methods of attack neither suspend the *res judicata* effect nor stay execution of the judgment under challenge. Whereas, however, *res judicata* cannot be precipitated or deferred by order of the court in its discretion, the procedural maturity of the judgment for enforcement purposes may vary in both directions: the court may, or sometimes must, allow the provisional enforcement of a judgment (προσωρινή εκτέλεση, prosorini ektelesi), with the one or the other ordinary method of attack still pending (arts. 907–914); it may also suspend the enforcement of a judgment already having *res judicata* effect until the exhaustion of the extraordinary methods of review (arts. 546 II, 565 II).

From a technical point of view, all methods of attack are initiated by filing a written complaint with the clerk of the court which rendered the judgment (arts. 495–497; for the next steps see above, Section V A 3 in f.). From a general point of view, appeals are not considered to be protected either through the constitutional guaranty of the right to sue (art. 20 I Const.) or through article 6 of the European Convention on Human Rights. Therefore, Parliament is in principle free to reduce the availability of appeal in some matters; it has done so, for example, with regard to small claims (up to 60,000 drs., or about $460; arts. 466, 512 C. C. Proc.).

### *B. Reopening of Default*

The reopening of default (ανακοπή ερημοδικίας, anakopi erimodikias) is a twofold method of attack. It means, first, that a party who has not been duly summoned to a hearing of the case may demand reopening of the decision (cf. art. 501 II). In this sense, reopening is premised on the right to be heard in court (art. 20 I Const.) and does not produce a suspensive effect (art. 506 III C. C. Proc.). However it is rarely successful, since it is unlikely that the court, when issuing the default decision, did not consider the question of proper service on the defaulting party (cf. above, Section VI E).

The second meaning of the reopening of default is more technical and peculiar to Greek civil procedure. It covers the cases in which the default judgment was handed down in the first hearing of the case, in first or second instance (intermediate appellate level). In such circumstances, the defaulting party may demand, and the court must reopen the default regardless of whether the party had been duly served (art. 501 I: 'unjustified' reopening of default). This latter attack is provided with suspensive effect and often serves only defendant's dilatory tactics.

Under any form, a reopening may be asked for within fifteen days from the date of service of the default judgment, or sixty days if the defaulting party resides abroad (art. 503).

### *C. Regular Appeal*

The most important and frequent attack on judgments is provided through appeal (έφεση, ephesi). The term has a technical meaning, denoting the attack on first instance judgments, addressed to an (intermediate) court of appeal authorized to review the judgment on the law and on the facts. In this sense, appeals may generally be taken from judgments rendered by any trial court (arts. 511, 13). As a rule, only final judgments are appealable; non-final decisions, for example interlocutory orders, can only be attacked jointly with the final judgment following them and terminating the entire case before the trial court (art. 513 II). Time for appeal is thirty days from the date of service of the judgment attacked, or sixty days if appellant resides abroad (art. 518). Grounds for appeal may refer to pure questions of fact, including the evaluation of evidence, to questions of (substantive or procedural) law, or to alleged procedural mistakes of the court below. Consequently, an intermediate appellate court has potentially the same powers as the trial court which issued the judgment appealed from. It cannot, however, grant relief beyond the issues to which appellant has restricted his appeal (art. 522); new claims may not be presented on appeal (art. 525). Yet, a cross-appeal is allowed to the party who has not appealed, but only within the challenged portions of the decision below or those necessarily related to them (art. 523). The court of appeal conducts a trial *de novo* on all matters before it: a regular appeal on the record alone is unknown to Greek civil procedure.

Upon reversal, the court of appeal usually retains the case and reexamines its merits. If the court below did not have the opportunity to pass on the merits, for example if it dismissed the claim because it thought that the action was barred by *res judicata* or by lack of standing to sue or of jurisdiction, and the court of appeal reverses precisely on this ground, at its discretion the appellate court may either decide the case on the merits or remand (art. 535).

### *D. Reopening of Contested Judgments*

Reopening of contested judgments (αναψηλάφηση, anapsilaphisi) has been modelled in Greece on the French *requête civile* and the German *Wiederaufnah-*

*me des Verfahrens.* This avenue is open to a party aggrieved by a judgment having *res judicata* effects, regardless of the availability of a cassation to the Supreme Court, yet on very narrow grounds. The grounds may be either purely procedural or have simultaneously some substantive connection (see art. 544). To the former category belong the existence of falsified or of inconsistent judgments, a knowingly improper method of service of process, as well as a party's improper representation or the absence of a power of attorney. Along with these procedural improprieties, contested judgments may also be reopened in cases of fraud or misconduct, provided that a criminal sanction has been already inflicted thereon through an unappealable decision; also if existing, yet concealed, documentary evidence has been discovered afterwards; finally in cases in which a judicial decision supporting the judgment under attack has been vacated. Under all these quasi-substantive grounds, the defect subsequently disclosed must have materially affected the outcome of the concluded proceedings.

### *E. Cassation*

Compared to regular appeal (see above, under C), proceedings on cassation (αναίρεση, anairesi) in the Supreme Court take on a much narrower scope. Here, the grounds for review are quite limited, and may involve violation of either a rule of substantive law, or of some specified rule of procedure (arts. 559–560). Cassation thus proceeds on the record and is not allowed in principle to touch upon findings of fact (art. 561 I). It may nevertheless be founded on a distortion of clear and precise documentary evidence or on a lack of legal basis (*manque de base légale*), i.e. whenever the findings of fact contained in the decision below are so inconsistent or insufficient that the Supreme Court cannot determine whether the law has been correctly applied.

Apart from these marginal grounds for cassation, a violation of rules of substantive law may result from either erroneous interpretation or mistaken application of the legal norm concerned. In the latter alternative, the Supreme Court reviews also the characterization attached to facts, for instance whether or not they constitute negligence or whether they comply with abstract legal notions, such as good faith or important ground, incorporated in the applicable rules. Here, however, emerge mixed questions of law and fact which cause difficulties in delineating the exact scope of review and spawn a somewhat inconsistent case law. Upon reversal the case may be either remanded to a lower court or referred to another panel of the same Supreme Court for reexamination of the merits (cf. art. 580, as amended through L. 1738/1987 art. 5 XV).

Even though precedents are not a formal source of law (see above, Section II D in f., and Ch. 2, Section III), opinions of the Supreme Court have a considerable impact upon the decisions of all other courts in the country and they are, as a rule, followed by the Supreme Court itself in subsequent cases.

## IX. Effects of Judgments

### *A. Drafting and Contents of Judgments*

In order to prepare the judgment (απόφαση, apophasi) in any judicial panel, one of its members is appointed by the president or the presiding judge, immediately after the hearing, to be the drafter of the opinion (*juge rapporteur* = εισηγητής, eisigitis). Only in the cassation panels of the Supreme Court is the drafter already appointed at the time of fixing a date for the hearing. He must file his draft opinion at least eight days before the hearing (art. 571), and will read it in public at the hearing (art. 574.1). In all other judicial panels, the drafter will prepare and develop orally the terms of the judgment only in a closed conference to be held among the members of the panel. The judges speak and vote in the reverse order of seniority (art. 301), except the drafter who presents his point of view first. Dissenting opinions are allowed in all Greek courts according to article 93 III 2–3 of the Constitution (see also L. 184/1975 arts. 35–38); they appear, however, not very often and are, as a rule, anonymous. Judgments are pronounced at a public audience (art. 93 III 1 Const.; art. 304 II C. C. Proc.) and are thereafter reported, with varying degrees of frequency and comprehensiveness, in the current legal periodicals.

The text of a judicial decision opens by mentioning the composition of the court, including the name of the judge who drafted the opinion; identifies the parties and their representatives; indicates the subject matter of the dispute and the course followed in the proceedings; and then goes on stating the reasons adopted in the case by the court. The operative part of the judgment (διατακτικό, diataktiko) comes at the end (cf. art. 305). Greek opinions, compared to English, American or German ones, are rather short, tending more to French style, especially in the Supreme Court. With the exception of the latter, they usually contain some references to scholarly works, and even more to case law.

### *B. Binding Effects of Judgments*

A civil judgment is not automatically binding. In the first place, it may be null and void if it was beyond the jurisdiction of the civil courts, or against a non-existing party, or not publicly pronounced (art. 313). Apart from these truly rare cases, a non-final judgment may always be modified or revoked by the court which rendered it, at a later hearing of the same case (art. 309). However, the scope of application of this rule has been reduced since all one-member civil courts are expected to hand down their final judgment after the first hearing of the case, which practically leaves no room for non-final judgments in these courts (see above, Section VI C). But even a final judgment, binding though it is upon the court which rendered it, is not yet genuinely binding upon the parties. *Res judicata* (δεδικασμένο, dedikasmeno) accrues to a final judgment only after it is no longer subject to an ordinary method of attack, i.e. reopening of default or regular appeal (see above, Section VIII A). According to traditional Greek doctrine, the *res judicata* effect operates within limits which are objective (preclusion between the same parties; below under C), subjective (preclusion with respect to non-parties; below under D), or depending on time (mutability of *res judicata* because of changed circumstances; below under E).

### *C. Claim and Issue Preclusion*

The *res judicata* effect between the same parties produces in Greek law both a merger or bar with respect to the claim involved and a preclusion of issues determined in the first suit. Both preclusions require a judgment on the merits. By contrast, a judgment dismissing the action on procedural prerequisites becomes *res judicata* only with regard to the procedural question decided on direct estoppel grounds (art. 322 I). Claim preclusion is restricted to the same cause of action, both in factual and legal terms (art. 324). Therefore, according to prevailing case law, if plaintiff, after having lost the first suit on the merits, comes back with a new complaint based on other allegations of fact or on a legal theory pertaining to different substantive rules, no plea of *res judicata* can be entertained. While Greek law does not know rigid forms of action, still the legal foundation of a claim helps in delineating and identifying it.

Issue preclusion on collateral estoppel principles is specifically provided for in article 331 of the Code of Civil Procedure and distinguishes Greek law from most other continental systems. Under this rule, issues determined in the first suit are covered by *res judicata* insofar as (1) they fell within the subject matter competence of the court, and (2) their determination was necessary for the outcome of the litigation. The latter requirement particularly causes recurrent problems and induces the second court to define the scope of *res judicata* in a sometimes unpredictable, case-by-case approach.

### *D. Preclusion with Respect to Non-Parties*

As far as the subjective limits of *res judicata* are concerned, Greek law adheres to the principle that only parties and their heirs or other successors are bound thereby (art. 325). To a certain extent, however, substantive relationships lead to a broader conclusive effect. Thus, judgments concerning property are equally binding to non-parties holding the thing in dispute in their possession or detention (art. 325 no. 3). Judgments in matters of succession, where the administrator of a vacant succession, the liquidator of an estate, or the executor of a will is a party, are conclusive also upon the heirs (art. 327; cf. art. 326). Judgments for or against a legal person become *res judicata* also with respect to its members (art. 329). The mutuality rule is prevailing, with a slight statutory exception concerning the relationship between the principal debtor and the guarantor (art. 328).

### E. *Time Limits of Res Judicata*

Judgments are often based upon judicial forecast of future developments, for example with regard to lost profits; if reality turns out to be different from predictions, *res judicata* remains nevertheless undisturbed. Not so, however, in cases of periodic performances, for instance future maintenance claims. Here a substantial change of circumstances, including a substantial increase of the price index, allows the court to modify the previous judgment for the future (art. 334).

## X. Special Proceedings and Provisional Remedies

### A. *Function of Special Proceedings*

Along with ordinary civil proceedings, there have always been in modern Greece special proceedings (ειδικές διαδικασίες, eidikes diadikasies) statutorily provided for. The latter are distinguished from the former essentially through a simpler and speedier procedure, accompanied by wider powers of the court. They have grown step by step mainly in the first half of the twentieth century, and they have been integrated into the system of Greek civil procedure in order to counterbalance the exaggerated formalities and considerable delays under the old Code of Civil Procedure of 1834. The new code tried to reduce both the necessity and scope of special proceedings by concentrating on ordinary proceedings and improving their efficiency. However, in the less than twenty years that the new code has been in force, the reform of ordinary proceedings has lost a good part of its impact. Accordingly, the legislature expanded the sphere of application of special proceedings by increasingly assigning to them additional kinds of disputes.

Law 1478/1984 attempted to revitalize ordinary proceedings. It simplified them, as far as one-member courts are concerned, by essentially imposing the pattern of the most typical of special proceedings: the procedure in labor cases. In this fashion, traditional ordinary proceedings are now observed only before the three-member district courts, or on appeal from their judgments, while in all other cases proceedings may still be technically 'ordinary', yet they are actually modelled on typical patterns of special proceedings.

### B. *Groups of Special Proceedings*

Special proceedings are now provided for with respect to the following groups of cases: matrimonial matters, such as divorce or annulment of marriage (arts. 592–613); relationships between parents and children (arts. 614–622); orders to pay debts on the basis of documentary evidence (arts. 623–634); disputes concerning negotiable instruments (arts. 635–646); disputes between landlords and tenants (arts. 647–662); labor cases (arts. 663–676); disputes related to the performance of independent services (arts. 677–681); car accidents (art. 681 A); and maintenance and custody cases (art. 681 B).

Along with these specified special proceedings, particular rules (ειδικές διατάξεις, eidikes diataxeis) apply to the collection of small claims (arts. 466–472; see above, Section VIII A in f.), to the action seeking an accounting (arts. 473–477), and to the action for partition (arts. 478–494, as amended through L. 1562/1985 arts. 10–21). Here, both the low degree of deviation from ordinary proceedings and the technical rather than substantive delimitation of the disputes in question prevented the legislator from elevating the particular rules to the level of actual special proceedings.

## *C. Common Procedural Features*

It is difficult to identify common procedural features connecting all special proceedings. With regard to matrimonial cases and parent-child disputes, one could stress the non-availability of the party-oath and the statutory demotion of confession to the position of a non-conclusive method of proof (art. 600); the public procecutor's potential participation as a party (art. 607); a wider demarcation of international jurisdiction (see below, Ch. 16, Section III), depending as well on a party's Greek nationality (arts. 612, 622; cf. also art. 611); and a broader *res judicata* effect operating as against the world (arts. 613, 618).

As far as the other types of special proceedings are concerned, one has to keep in mind that labor disputes should be regarded as their prototype as well as their most important specimen in reality. In this respect, the following features emerge: parties are not necessarily represented by lawyers and they may also assume their defense themselves (art. 665). Defaulting parties are by statutory fiction considered as silently present, so that the court must examine the merits of the case, oblivious to the default (art. 672); accordingly, no reopening of defaults is allowed without cause (art. 673 I). Standing to sue is granted not only to immediately interested parties, but also to trade unions, professional chambers, or other associations (art. 669). Finally, admissibility of evidence in a substantially broader sense is acknowledged, including as well 'means of proof not complying with the terms of law' (art. 671 I). Thus, even unsigned private instruments or depositions of biased witnesses are taken into account.

## *D. Provisional Remedies*

In terms of practical significance, provisional remedies (arts. 682–738; ασφαλιστικά μέτρα, asphalistika metra) are still more important than special proceedings. As a rule, they are administered by the one-member district court (art. 683 I), with a decision usually being rendered within a couple of weeks after the hearing. Their scope is extremely broad. They provide for the possibility of provisional relief on each and every claim under the condition of an urgent need or in order to evade an imminent danger (art. 682 I). They may be used, indeed, for all sorts of substantive rights or property matters as well as contract or tort cases. Thus, rather promptly, the victim of a traffic accident may obtain an order against the tortfeasor for part of the damage (art. 728 I lit. e), or, to secure the future enforcement of an eventually affirmative judgment, an attachment of the debtor's property may be authorized (arts. 707–724). Real property litigation between neighbors may equally support a grant of relief consisting in the provisional preservation of the situation (arts. 731, 733, 734). Provisional remedies may even be granted on an application *ex parte* (art. 687 I) and allow the court to issue immediately a provisional order upon the filing of the request (art. 691 II). They are generally available as soon as two requirements are met: (1) an urgent case, and (2) the existence of an underlying substantive right seeking provisional protection. Both requirements need only be shown as probable.

The aforementioned remedies are termed provisional under two meanings of the term. First, their granting may be combined with an order specifying a time limit within which plaintiff must bring the principal action; in case of non-compliance, the provisional remedy expires as of right (art. 693). Second, the court before which the main litigation is pending always has the power to modify or to revoke provisional remedies (art. 697). Revocation becomes mandatory whenever the judgment on the principal action ripens into *res judicata* (art. 698 I lit. a).

In Greece, provisional relief has been enjoying increasingly practical importance. The rather slow progression of ordinary proceedings makes recourse to provisional remedies highly desirable. An identifiable tendency among the courts which subsequently examine the merits, not to depart light-heartedly from the terms of an earlier provisional relief, although they are statutorily authorized to do so (art. 695), adds to their attraction. Taking into account these developments, the legislature time and again assigns to these efficient proceedings for provisional remedies disputes which in themselves do not present an urgent character.

## XI. Non-Contentious Proceedings

### *A. Doctrinal Foundation*

According to both article 93 III of the Constitution and article 1 lit. a of the Code of Civil Procedure, the jurisdiction of the ordinary civil courts includes not only the adjudication of disputes but also the regulation of the so-called 'affairs of voluntary jurisdiction' (υποθέσεις εκουσίας δικαιοδοσίας, ypotheseis ekousias dikaiodosias) which are assigned to them by statute. A distinction is thus drawn between contentious or adversary (*iurisdictio contentiosa*) and non-contentious or voluntary or *ex parte* jurisdiction (*iurisdictio voluntaria*). The criterion is to be found in the nature of the subject matter of jurisdiction as well as in the function of the judicial decision on it. Disputes involve the violation of a substantive right as between at least two persons; they seek a decision evaluating the behavior of persons in the past, inferring therefrom the consequences provided for in the law. By contrast, non-contentious affairs do not refer to relationships between persons, but contemplate one person as an individual and his legal situation; they aspire to protect it through judicial measures taken not as a sanction for past deficiencies but in anticipation of future needs. Functionally, therefore, voluntary jurisdiction looks more similar to public administration than to proper civil justice. This tenuous relationship between non-contentious affairs and civil procedure explains why the former require a specific statute for them to be assigned to the jurisdiction of ordinary civil courts.

### *B. Examples of Non-Contentious Matters*

According to the Code of Civil Procedure, the list of non-contentious affairs to be dealt with by the ordinary civil courts is quite long (arts. 782–866) and includes topics dispersed over the entire realm of private law. For instance: declaring a person whose death is strongly probable, as an absentee, or revoking such a declaration (arts. 40, 46 C. C., arts 783–785 C. C. Proc.; see above, Ch. 4, Section II C); declaring a lost negotiable instrument as void (art. 895 C. C.; arts. 850–860 C. C. Proc.); authorizing the alienation of a thing pledged (art. 1237 C. C.; art. 792 C. C. Proc.); pronouncing the interdiction and guardianship or judicial supervision of persons, as well as revoking such status (arts. 1688, 1699, 1706 C. C.; arts. 801–806 C. C. Proc.; see above, Ch. 8, Section VII C, E); granting, retracting, annulling, revoking, or amending a certificate of inheritance (arts. 1956–1966 C. C.; arts. 819–824 C. C. Proc.; see above, Ch. 9, Section II F) are all examples of non-contentious matters.

### *C. Procedural Features*

The procedural characteristics of non-contentious proceedings are highlighted in articles 740–781 of the Code of Civil Procedure. Subject matter competence belongs to the one-member district courts; in exceptional cases (e.g., bankruptcy proceedings) to the three-member district courts (art. 740 C. C. Proc.; art. 44 Introductory Law to the Code of Civil Procedure). There exist no actual parties, but only the person introducing the request. A copy of the request is in many cases served on the public prosecutor or on such third persons as the judge may order (art. 748 C. C. Proc.). The court exercises quasi-inquisitional powers in establishing the relevant facts (art. 744). Even final judgments are subject to revocation or modification upon a showing of new facts (art. 758). Appeals may be taken even by persons who, although having participated in the proceedings below, were not aggrieved by the decision under attack (arts. 761, 769). Regular appeal (arts. 763–766), reopening of contested proceedings (arts. 767, 768), and cassation (arts. 770–772), as well as third-party opposition (*tierce opposition*; arts. 773–775; cf. arts. 586–590 within contentious jurisdiction) are available here also. It must be noted that the benefits of a suspensive effect do not follow as of right any of these methods of attack (cf. art. 763; see above, Section VIII A).

## XII. Arbitration

### *A. Legislative Status*

In addition to being a party to the New York Convention on the Recognition and Enforcement of Foreign Arbitral Awards (ratified through L. D. 4220/1961), Greece modernized her domestic law of arbitration (διαιτησία, diaitisia) in Book VII of the Code of Civil Procedure (arts. 867–903). The code treats arbitration as a method of settling private law disputes, which method is quasi-equal to litigation in the ordinary courts. Particularly in both international and domestic commercial relations, arbitration has expanded in frequency and importance. It has even obtained constitutional status with respect to the protection of foreign investments through the reference made in article 107 II of the Constitution to Law Decree 2687/1953 which provides for arbitration as the exclusive way of resolving all related disputes. Recent critics arguing against arbitration as an unconstitutional and inadvisable deprivation of the powers of the judge assigned to everyone by law (art. 8 I Const.) are truly isolated.

### *B. Arbitration Agreement*

Nearly all private law disputes are arbitrable under the sole condition that the parties may dispose of the relationship in question by agreement (art. 867 C. C. Proc.); accordingly, arbitration is not allowed in divorce and other matrimonial cases of personal nature. A further exception pertains to labor cases which are not arbitrable either. Both existing controversies and eventual disputes, provided that the latter will result from a present legal relationship, may be likewise submitted to arbitration (art. 868). In both instances a document in writing, not necessarily a notarial one, is the only formal requirement (art. 869). An arbitration agreement (συμφωνία περί διαιτησίας, symphonia peri diaitisias) is most often a part of a civil or commercial contract. The scope of the agreement depends entirely on the parties' will. If, as is often the case, it extends to all disputes arising out of the contract then any claim related to the contract and its performance, including a tort claim, is excluded from the jurisdiction of ordinary courts and has to be submitted to arbitration.

### *C. Arbitral Procedure*

There are detailed statutory rules concerning the nomination of arbitrators (arts. 871–880, 883); in case of disagreement, arbitrators are appointed by the one-member district court (art. 878). The parties may determine in the arbitration agreement the procedure to be followed, otherwise this task falls on the arbitrators themselves (art. 886 I). Institutional arbitration (art. 902; μόνιμη διαιτησία, monimi diaitisia) generally utilizes permanent rules enacted by presidential decree. However, no arbitral procedure can infringe upon the equality of the parties and their right to an adequate hearing (arts. 886 II, 897 no. 5, 902 II 2 lit. c). Case law has further tightened these limits to arbitral activity. It has been held for example that an arbitrator's private knowledge of relevant facts may not be used because this knowledge would prevent the parties from verifying the sources of information, thus turning a supposedly neutral arbitrator into an involved witness[8].

### D. *Authority of Arbitrators*

The authority of arbitrators depends on the will of the parties combined with some principles of public policy. Unless the parties have provided otherwise, the arbitrators are entitled to inquire into the validity and scope of the arbitration agreement (art. 887 II). Even if the main contract, of which the arbitration agreement is a part, is invalid, the authority of the arbitrators to judge this invalidity and its consequences usually remains unimpaired. Subject to an agreement to the contrary, arbitrators abide by existing rules of substantive law. They may, nevertheless, be authorized to issue an award *ex aequo et bono*, but provisions of public policy must be complied with (art. 890). For similar reasons arbitrators are not allowed to grant, to modify or to revoke provisional remedies (art. 889).

### E. *Control by the Ordinary Courts*

Unless the parties have agreed to the contrary, no methods of review are allowed with respect to awards (art. 895). A certain control is, of course, exercised by the ordinary courts, both in the beginning and at the end of arbitral proceedings. In the beginning, it can happen that a party to an arbitration agreement brings suit in the ordinary courts; the court then, assuming that the defendant pleads the arbitration agreement, will refer the dispute to arbitration after ascertaining that the agreement is valid and that the dispute falls thereunder (arts. 264, 870 I). At the end, a party aggrieved by the award may bring an action in the three-member district court where it was rendered to set it aside (arts. 897–900; αγωγή ακυρώσεως διαιτητικής αποφάσεως, agogi akyroseos diaititikis apophaseos). However, the grounds for this remedy are rather narrow. They include (art. 897): invalidity of the arbitration agreement; exceeding its terms or the scope of the authority of the arbitrators; infringement of the right to equal treatment or to an adequate hearing; violation of public

8. AP 1509/1982, NoB 31 (1983) 1355–1356.

policy; or any ground for the reopening of contested judgments (cf. above, Section VIII D).

The courts have given expansive construction to the grounds for setting aside an award, and a significant percentage of awards are subsequently annulled. This remedy can go all the way to the Supreme Court. However, it has no suspensive effect. The award (διαιτητική απόφαση, diaititiki apophasi), unless set aside, becomes *res judicata* (art. 896) and can be enforced upon its filing with the clerk of the one-member district court (arts. 893 II, 904 II lit. b, 918 II lit. d).

## XIII. Enforcement Proceedings

### *A. Enforceable Instruments*

The Greek law of execution allows the creditor to resort to public authority to enforce his claim. Instruments which are enforceable by execution (εκτελεστοί τίτλοι, ektelestoi titloi) essentially include three groups (art. 904 II):

(1) All final affirmative judgments, i.e. those which order specific performance or payment of money *and* are no longer subject to ordinary methods of attack or, pending such an attack, are given provisional enforcement (see above, Section VIII A).

(2) Arbitral awards.

(3) Notarial documents enforceable by reason of their form.

Foreign judgments and arbitral awards are likewise enforceable after being granted an *exequatur* under articles 905, 906, 323 and 903 of the Code of Civil Procedure, as is explained below, Ch. 16, Section IV.

### *B. Creditor's Initiative and Control by the Court*

Regardless of the kind of enforceable instrument, the intervention of judicial authorities during enforcement proceedings (αναγκαστική εκτέλεση, anangastiki ektelesi) is not a preventive, but rather a controlling one. Execution is considered to be a continuation of adjudication in cases of non-voluntary compliance. Therefore, in accordance with the dispositive principle of adjudication (see above, Section V A 1), it is subject to party initiative, especially that of the creditor holding the enforceable instrument.

Enforcement proceedings start with a formal notice by the creditor to the debtor, inviting the latter to voluntary performance, otherwise threatening execution. This notice (επιταγή, epitagi) is placed at the bottom of a certified copy of the enforceable instrument (απόγραφο, apographo; art. 924). If the debtor remains silent, the creditor proceeds with enforcement by giving an order (εντολή προς εκτέλεση, entoli pros ektelesi; art. 927) to a marshal who is the agent authorized to levy execution and to perform various other related functions (arts. 927–931, 954, 960 I, 993, 999 I, 1049 II). Should the debtor deem that the enforceable instrument is invalid, that the enforcement rules have not been complied with, or even that the creditor's claim has been paid or set off, it is up to him to make the respective motion (ανακοπή, anakopi) before the one-member district court (arts. 933–937). Only then are the courts called upon to judge on the prior steps of enforcement proceedings. On appeal, the motion can go all the way to the Supreme Court; however, it does not stay execution unless otherwise ordered by the court (arts. 938–939).

### C. *Execution with Respect to Specific Performance*

With respect to methods of execution, distinctions are drawn between direct specific performance and enforcement to satisfy a money claim which usually results in a levy on property. Specific performance applies to duties to transfer title to movable (arts. 941–942) and immovable property (art. 943, cf. also art. 944 for ships and aircraft), as well as to obligations to perform (arts. 945–946) or not to perform or not to oppose a specific act (art. 947). If, however, the debtor fails to meet the obligation to perform a certain act, enforcement becomes necessarily indirect: the creditor is authorized to have the act performed at the debtor's expense (art. 945). Where the specific act cannot be performed by a third person or the debtor does not omit or opposes an act, the latter will be subjected to a fine of up to 100,000 drs., or about $760, and to imprisonment for debt for a period up to one year (art. 946).

### D. *Execution to Satisfy a Money Claim*

Of greater practical significance is enforcement on property to satisfy a money claim. There are four types of attachment (κατάσχεση, kataschesi) for the purpose of bringing property under judicial control ultimately leading to a public auction and, in the meantime, suspending the debtor's power of disposal:

(1) Enforcement on chattels (arts. 953–981).

(2) Enforcement on land, ships and aircraft (arts. 992–1016).

(3) Garnishment, which also includes reaching chattels of a debtor that are not in his possession (arts. 982–991).

(4) Enforcement on debtor's special assets, like copyrights, patents and film exploitation rights (arts. 1022–1033).

Detailed rules provide for the orderly distribution of funds realized in a public auction (arts. 974–978, 1007, 988 I 3, 1030 III 3–4), with special treatment granted to secured creditors (arts. 976 no. 2, 977 I 2, 1007 I 2, 1008). In essence, creditors other than the petitioning one are entitled to assert their claims (art. 972; αναγγελία, anangelia). Distribution will follow on an equal footing among all announced creditors, allotting to each the same percentage on his claim. Greek law thus rejects the Germanic system which accords preference to the petitioning creditor, and follows the Romanic system of proportional distribution. Proportionality is, however, disturbed in two respects: First, to the benefit of creditors enjoying a real security right, i.e. pledge or mortgage (see above, Ch. 6, Section VII); and second, to the benefit of creditors enjoying specific priorities (art. 975; προνόμια, pronomia). Creditors with specific priorities rank before creditors with real security rights; this precedence is, however, limited only to one third of the sale proceeds, so that the remaining two thirds are reserved for the satisfaction of secured creditors (arts. 977, 1007).

There are two additional methods of execution to satisfy, directly or indirectly, a money claim; the first was enacted in recent years through Law 2810/1954 and integrated then in the Code of Civil Procedure (arts. 1034–1046); the second is very old but still in existence, and occasionally effective. The former is a form of receivership called 'compulsory administration' (αναγκαστική διαχείριση, anangastiki diacheirisi) of a debtor's immovables or business which are henceforth managed by an administrator appointed by the court. The creditors receive quarterly distributions on their claims out of the profits of the new management (art. 1043). The latter method consists in the debtor's imprisonment for a period up to one year (arts. 1047–1054; προσωπική κράτηση, prosopiki kratisi). This measure is imposed by specific judicial decision only on merchants for commercial debts; it is also generally allowed for the satisfaction of tort claims. Imprisonment is not often utilized and is subject to serious constitutional doubt, but may still function as an effective threat.

## Bibliographical Note

1. Under the old Code of Civil Procedure (in force between 1835 and 1968), the two leading treatises, which are still of use today, were V. Oikonomidis, M. Livadas and L. Gidopoulos, *Manual of Civil Procedure*, 7th ed., vols. I–III (1924–1926) and S. Eukleidis and K. Papadopoulos, *Interpretation of Civil Procedure*, 3d ed., vols. I–II (1932). The most complete digest of judicial opinions was A. Kitsikopoulos, *Civil Procedure. A Commentary by Article*, vols. I–X plus annex A (1934–1955).
2. The materials and other preparatory works for the new Code of Civil Procedure in force since September 16, 1968 are to be found in the *Draft of Civil Procedure*, elaborated by the Drafting Committee and published by the Ministry of Justice in Athens, vols. I–IX (1940–1974), as well as in the *Minutes of the Meetings of the Revision Committee for a Draft Code of Civil Procedure and its Introductory Law* (Athens, Ministry of Justice, 1967). There is only one complete translation of the Code of Civil Procedure in a foreign language (German): G. Baumgärtel and G. Rammos, *Das griechische Zivilprozessgesetzbuch mit Einführungsgesetz* (Cologne, Carl Heymanns Verlag, 1969); but even this translation refers only to the initial text of the code, without taking into consideration subsequent important amendments.
3. There exist numerous treatises and commentaries (in Greek) on the Code of Civil Procedure of 1967. They are mentioned in alphabetical order:

*A. Treatises*

K. Kerameus, *Civil Procedure*, vol. I, 2d ed. (1983).
K. Kerameus, *Civil Procedure. General Part* (1986).
G. Mitsopoulos, *Civil Procedure*, vol. I (1972).
T. Oikonomopoulos, *Manual of Civil Procedure under the Code*, vols. I–IV (1969).
G. Rammos, *Manual of Civil Procedure*, vols. I–IV (1978–1985).
A. Vernardos, *Civil Procedure*, 2d ed. (1972).
A short presentation in English is A. Iatrou, *Civil and Criminal Proceedings in Greece* (Athens, 1981).

Narrower areas are dealt with in:

K. Beis, *Introduction to Procedural Thinking*, 3d ed. (1981).
I. Brinias, *Enforcement Proceedings*, 2d ed., vols. I–V (1978–1982).
Ch. Fragistas and P. Yessiou-Faltsi, *Enforcement Proceedings*, 2d ed., vols. I–II (1978–1983).
L. Dassios, *Labor Procedural Law*, vols. I–IV (1980–1984), the 1st vol. in second edition (1986).
L. Sinaniotis, *Special Proceedings*, 2d ed. (1984).
P. Tzifras, *Provisional Remedies*, 4th ed. (1985).
P. Yessiou-Faltsi, *Evidence*, 3d ed. (1985).

*B. Commentaries by Article*

K. Beis, *Civil Procedure* (incomplete), fasc. 1–14 (1973–1983).
S. Delikostopoulos and L. Sinaniotis, *Interpretation of the Code of Civil Procedure* (incomplete), vols. I–III (1968–1974).
S. Stavropoulos, *Interpretation of the Code of Civil Procedure*, 2d ed., vols. I–II (1979).
P. Theodoropoulos, *Code of Civil Procedure*, 3d ed. (1986).

4. The most complete digest of judicial opinions under the new Code of Civil Procedure is P. Kostakos – G. Nikolopoulos, *Code of Civil Procedure. Collection of Cases* 1968–1984, vols. I–III (1984–1986). For cases decided by the Supreme Court and otherwise remaining partly unreported, see *Basic Cases of Civil, Commercial, Labor and Procedural Law of the Years 1967–1982*, published by the Bar Association of Athens, vols. I–VI plus Indexes (1983–1984), especially vols. I–II which are devoted to civil procedure. For a continuation of this collection covering the years 1983–1986, and partly 1987, see *Supplement to Basic Cases*, vols. I–II (1987), particularly vol. I p. 1–417, vol. II p. 1617–1646.
5. Many Greek proceduralists have published separate volumes with their essays, articles and other contributions to questions of civil procedure: K. Beis I–II (1980), Ch. Fragistas (1980), and two more volumes in 1987, K. Kerameus I (1980), G. Mitsopoulos (1983), G. Rammos I–VI (1948–1968),

P. Zissis I–IV (1963–1972), P. Yessiou-Faltsi I (1981). One should mention also four collections of essays in honor of Ch. Fragistas I–VI (1966–1971), E. Michelakis (1973), G. Oikonomopoulos (1981) and G. Rammos I–II (1979), consisting mainly of procedural studies. Two volumes in honor of G. Mitsopoulos are in preparation for 1988.

6. Quite a number of articles on special questions of Greek civil procedure and judicial organization have been written by Greek authors in foreign languages, often in German. Most of them are published in *Revue Hellénique de Droit International* (Athens) (recent articles in English include Kerameus, The Use of Conciliation for Dispute Settlement, *R. Hell. D.I.* 1979. 41; Kerameus, The Function of Conciliation as a Means of Avoiding Litigation and Settling a Dispute, *R. Hell. D.I.* 1982–83. 227; Kerameus, Judicial Independence in Modern Legal Developments, *R. Hell. D.I.* 1982–83. 335; Yession-Faltsi, Judicial Responsibility in Greece, *R. Hell. D.I.* 1982–83. 281; Yessiou-Faltsi, The Production of Evidence in the Case According to the Greek Code of Civil Procedure, *R. Hell. D.I.* 1979. 88.); *Zeitschrift für Zivilprozess* (Cologne, Berlin, Bonn, Munich), especially vols. 74 (1961), 78 (1965), 79 (1966), 81 (1968), 91 (1978), 92 (1979), 96 (1983), 99 (1986); *Revue critique de droit international privé* (Paris), as well as in volumes of essays dedicated to eminent lawyers (*Festschriften* or *Gedächtnisschriften*). There are also doctoral dissertations submitted by Greek jurists to German, French and English Universities and published in the respective languages.
7. For arbitration, see Union Internationale des Avocats, *International Commercial Arbitration*, vol. I (1956) as well as the journals *Revue de l'arbitrage* (Paris, since 1955) and *Yearbook of Commercial Arbitration* (Deventer/The Netherlands, since 1976).

# Chapter 16
# Conflict of Laws, Nationality, International Jurisdiction and Recognition and Enforcement of Judgments and Awards

*Phaedon John Kozyris**

## I. Conflict of Laws

### *A. Introduction*

The Greek system, in the civil law tradition, consists of statutory rules which, quite commendably, are generally bilateral, select a single applicable law and use terms which are broader than those of the corresponding domestic substantive law. The principal repository of these rules is Book I, chapter two of the Civil Code comprising articles 4–33.

### *B. Obligations*

#### 1. Contracts

The autonomy of the parties occupies center stage in article 25 as it also did under prior law. Failing submission by the parties to the law of their choice, however, article 25 abandons the *lex loci* approach of prior law and, under English and German influence, opts for the 'proper' law of contract which is to be selected on the basis of 'all special circumstances.' These two rules of article 25, which incidentally are considered 'successful' by the writers, are quite open-ended.

First, is this autonomy without limit as suggested by the unqualified language in the text? The answer appears to be in the negative. Autonomy comes into play only for multistate contracts, not for purely domestic ones, and even then the law chosen must have a 'significant' (major? substantial? reasonable?) connection with the contract. The choice by the parties may be expressed or

* Professor of Law, The Ohio State University.

implied and may take place even at a later time up to and during the adjudication of a particular dispute. Subject to the vested rights of third parties, article 25 does not treat separately the preliminary question of what law governs the validity of the choice itself which question article 30 of the Maridakis project of the Civil Code subjected to the law of the place of the making. Thus, we do not know whether 'bootstrapping' is legitimate.

Second, as should have been obvious to the drafters, the invitation to the courts to apply the 'proper' law of contract was not likely to solve the conflicts problem by some kind of magic. The liberation was matched, if not exceeded, by the aggravation and uncertainty that accompanied the attempt to define 'propriety' and make it work. In decisions that can be counted in the hundreds, if not thousands, many of them involving maritime law, the courts struggled to make sensible choices based mostly on some combination of the usual connecting factors including the presumed intention and nationality of the parties and generally excluding the *lex fori* as such. The *lex solutionis* which usually prevailed under prior law is just one possible choice, especially since no clear-cut distinction is drawn now between matters of execution and matters of performance. This does not mean that place of making and place of performance are not relevant, even perhaps important, connecting factors but only that their propriety must be explicated or at least specifically invoked each time. Once the choice is made, the applicable law governs all issues arising under the contract and *depeçage* is in principle rejected. It is too early to distill a manageable set of conflicts rules or at least some system from these cases which operate in a manner resembling the 'most significant relationship' standards of the Second Restatement in the U.S.

In accordance with the Civil Code systematics, article 25 is subject to the general conflicts provisions governing the capacity of the parties and the form of all juridical acts including contracts. Thus, it does not apply to (a) capacity to contract, which is generally governed as to each party by the law of his nationality under article 7 (but most contracts made in Greece by an alien natural person consistently with the Greek rules on capacity are validated even where the alien had no such capacity under his own national law; art. 9) and (b). form of contract, including issues under the statute of frauds, which is subject to the alternative reference rule in article 11 validating a contract as to form if it complies with either the law of the place of making or the national law of the parties or the law governing its substance (*lex causae*).

As a party to the Geneva Conventions on negotiable instruments, Greece has enacted special legislation (arts. 90 ff. of L. 5325/1932 and 70 ff. of L. 5960/1933) governing choice of law questions in those fields. In general, the capacity of each party is governed either by his national law, including its conflicts provisions, or by the law of the country of signature whichever would validate the obligation. With respect to form, compliance with the law of the country of signature or of payment suffices for checks, whereas for promissory notes and bills of exchange only the law of the country of signature applies. The law of the country of signature governs also the obligations of all parties other than those of the primary debtor of a note or of a bill which are subject to the law of the country of payment. The law of the country of payment also extends to issues of loss, theft and destruction of the document as well as of consent, negotiability, and defenses.

Although article 25 refers only to 'contractual' obligations, the prevailing view appears to be that it applies by analogy to obligations based on quasi-contract and perhaps also on *negotiorum gestio*.

Powers of attorney are characterized as contractual and, therefore, subject to articles 7, 11 and 25. Even when the applicable law is that of Greece and a notarial instrument is required for some judicial act such as a conveyance or a will, the Greek authorities generally have been accepting U.S. notarization as sufficient under the liberal rules governing questions of form despite the significant differences in the role and function of the notary and in the notarial form in the two countries.

As a member of the European Economic Community, Greece signed but not yet ratified the EEC Convention on the Law Applicable to Contractual Obligations of 1980 which supersedes article 25 *pro tanto*. The Convention validates party autonomy except when all the relevant elements are connected with one country in which case the mandatory rules of such country must be respected. The existence and validity of the choice of the parties are governed by the law applicable without reference to the choice. In the absence of choice, the applicable law is that of the country with which the contract is most closely connected. The most important difference between the Convention and article 25 is the presumption that the country most closely connected is that where the obligor of the characteristic performance has his habitual residence, principal place of business or central administration. Also, for matters of performance reference is made to the *lex solutionis*. *Depeçage* is permitted. The mandatory rules of the forum always apply. Special rules apply to consumer and employment contracts. The Convention does not extend to certain contracts and issues such as: negotiable instruments, family agreements, internal corporate matters, insurance and capacity of natural persons. The Convention applies in a global manner, that is irrespective of whether the law to be chosen is that of an EEC member state.

## 2. Torts

The *lex loci delicti commissi* is enshrined in a single-sentence provision of article 26. This represents a major departure from article 6.2 of the Civil Law of 1856 which, under Savigny's and Wächter's influence, contained a unilateral rule applying always the *lex fori*. Conflicts writers neglect tort issues and the only doctrinal dispute worth mentioning is whether a tort is 'committed' at the place of the conduct or of its effects. Even here the discussion is inconclusive, with some tendency to favor conduct over effects or to give plaintiff the choice. For traffic accidents, the *lex loci delicti* reigns supreme, Greece not having become party to the Hague Convention on the Law Applicable to Traffic Accidents of 1971. Whether the victim has a direct action against the insurer is characterized as a matter of contract rather than tort and subject to the law governing the insurance policy. The same law appears also applicable to the subrogation rights of an insurer against a tortfeasor.

The courts have been developing special rules for certain maritime torts on the high seas. Thus, the *lex fori* applies to collisions of ships registered under different flags. Torts on board a ship are subjected to the law of the flag. In this latter case, if the ship is in the territorial waters of a state the views are divided on whether the law of the flag or the *lex loci delicti* is applicable.

### *C. Property*

Property rights, including possessory rights, in movable and immovable things are governed by the *lex rei sitae* (art. 27). The same law applies to the form of 'property' contracts and other juridical acts having *in rem* effect, i.e. those which create, convey, modify or reduce property rights (art. 12). Where a movable is transferred to another country before a certain property right has been fully affected, it is the new *lex rei sitae* that applies to the entire right. Documents of title are treated as things. According to the prevailing view, however, other intangibles are not 'things'. If they are part of a personality right, they are governed by the national law of the person. Under Law 2386/1920, intellectual property rights are governed by Greek law if the first publication took place in Greece. It has been suggested that the 'first publication' connection should be expanded to a general conflicts rule. Ships are subject to special laws to be discussed below. Finally, an Anglo-American trust, at least so much of it as has *in rem* effects, appears to fall within the realm of a 'property' contract or juridical act and, therefore, should be subject to the *lex rei sitae*. The use of trust terminology is not necessarily determinative, however, of the characterization question. A 'trust' may in substance be a contract or an agency depending on its contents.

### *D. Domestic Relations*

The most comprehensive conflicts provisions of the Civil Code deal with family matters where nationality is the prevailing connecting factor. It is also in this field that the recent reforms to implement the constitutional equality of the sexes (L. 1250/1982 and L. 1329/1983) have taken place.

The substantive requirements for adoption, including judicial or other approval, are governed as to each party by his national law (art. 23). It appears that these laws are to be applied cumulatively but certain provisions of substantive Greek law are interpreted not to extend to aliens, e.g., the prohibitions against adoption by a person who (a) has children of his own, (b) is not at least fifty years old, (c) is the parent of the adoptee out of wedlock or (d) has already other adopted children. Other prohibitions, however, are not so limited, such as the ones against adoption by a second parent while the first is still living, by or of a spouse without the consent of the other spouse and between persons having an age difference of less than eighteen years. The relationship between adoptive parent and child is governed by the law of their last common nationality or, in its absence, of the nationality of the parent at adoption. The guardianship of children and others is subject to their national law (art. 24). Whether a child is born in wedlock is determined by the law applicable to the personal relations of the mother and her husband at birth or at the prior time of dissolution of their marriage (art. 17). The relationship between a parent and a child born out of wedlock is governed, in order of priority, by the law of their common nationality, common habitual residence, or nationality of the parent (art. 19–20). In this situation, the relationship between the parents themselves is subject to the law of their last, during pregnancy, common nationality, habitual residence or residence in that order (art. 21). The legitimization of a child (a) by subsequent marriage, is governed by the law applicable to the personal relations of the spouses at marriage and (b) by public act, is subject to the then national law of the father (art. 22).

A marriage is valid as to substantive requirements under the national law of either of the parties. It is valid as to form if it meets the requirements either of the law of either party or of the law of the place of celebration. A Greek abroad now may also be married at a Greek consulate (art. 13). A retroactive provision of major practical significance was adopted in article 7 of Law 1250/1982 to the effect that prior marriages abroad involving at least one Greek spouse are considered valid as to form *ab initio* if they complied with the requirements of the *lex celebrationis* except where (a) at least one of the spouses validly remarried subsequently, (b) they have lived apart for at least three years, (c) there exist other special circumstances or (d) a divorce has been already granted or an irrevocable declaratory judgment of nullity has been obtained in a Greek court. Despite the exceptions, the children are considered born in wedlock. This validates many marriages of Greeks abroad previously considered non-existent for failure to comply with the required religious formalities.

The personal relationship of the spouses is subject, in order of priority, to the law (a) of their last common nationality if one of them still has it, (b) of their last common marital habitual residence and (c) to which they are most closely connected (art. 14). As to property relations, the same rules apply and are fixed at the time of celebration of the marriage (art. 15). Divorce and judicial separation are also subject to these rules but as of the time of the commencement of the proceedings (art. 16).

Finally, reference should be made to the fact that Greece has signed but not as yet ratified the Hague Convention on the Law Applicable to Child Support Obligations of 1956 and the Hague Convention on the Recognition and Execution of Judgments Relating to Child Support Obligations of 1958.

## *E. Descent and Distribution*

According to article 28, descent and distribution as to all property, movables and immovables, is governed by the law of the decedent's nationality at death.

The reach of this law is quite comprehensive but certain issues escape it either because they are subject to the general choice rules applicable to all juridical acts or because they are characterized as belonging to another branch of the law. Thus, capacity to make a will or to accept or reject an inheritance is subject to the national law of the testator or the actor respectively. The form of a will is subject to the law of the testator's nationality at execution or death or of the place of execution, whichever will uphold it (art. 11). In addition, under article 1 of the Hague Convention on the Conflicts of Laws Relating to the Form of Testamentary Dispositions of 1961, to which Greece is a party, five other connectors toward validation are added: the domicile or habitual residence of the testator at either execution or death and the location of immovables. The probate proceedings are subject to the *lex fori*. The method of acquisition of property rights in the estate assets is governed by the *lex rei sitae* as is the issue, according to one view, of to whom property escheats in the absence of heirs. Gifts *causa mortis* are treated as contracts and are allocated to the *lex contractus*. The special Greek institution, modelled after German law, of a 'certificate of inheritance' (κληρονομητήριο) which certifies that a certain person is an heir or legatee of an estate is generally treated as having only probative value and, therefore, its acceptability is subject to the *lex fori*.

### *F. Legal Entities, Corporations*

A single provision in article 10 calls for the application of the law of the 'seat' of a legal entity to questions of its 'legal capacity.' This is interpreted to make such law the 'personal law' of the entity which governs not only matters of formation, capacity, consolidation, dissolution and the like but also the entire gamut of its internal affairs. Seat means the situs of management and, according to the majority view, it must be real and it will not suffice for it to be merely stated in the charter.

An important consequence of the neutrality and bilaterality of the seat rule is that foreign corporations formed and operating under the law of their seat are automatically recognized in Greece. Article 16 in the Maridakis project of the Civil Code would have imposed a recognition requirement by presidential decree. Many bilateral treaties also equalize the recognition of foreign and domestic entities. It should be pointed out, however, that recognition is not enough for purposes of establishment and that special legislation subjects the establishment of certain foreign entities to additional requirements. Foreign corporations must follow a procedure with the Ministry of Commerce similar to qualification to do business. Foreign close corporations are subject to an even more complex qualification process and, in addition, must show that the country of their seat grants the same rights to Greek corporations (reciprocity). Special 'doing business' requirements apply to banking, insurance and certain other legal entities. Entities formed in a EEC country and having their registered seat, central administration or principal place of business in an EEC country are entitled to national treatment with respect to establishment under article 58 of the Treaty of Rome as implemented.

Limited deviations from the 'real seat' connecting factor appear in certain treaties and statutes. For example, under article 24 III 2 of the U.S.-Greece Treaty of Friendship, Commerce and Navigation of 1951, companies formed under the law of a party are treated as its nationals and their legal personality is to be recognized in the territory of the other party regardless of their seat. Similar provisions are found in the treaties with the United Kingdom, Spain and Argentina. Furthermore, article 1 I of Law 791/1978 provides that the existence and legal capacity of maritime companies formed abroad which own Greek-flag ships or are established in Greece are subject to the law of their registered seat regardless of the actual situs of management.

Whether one is a 'merchant' for purposes of the applicability of the special provisions of commercial law is determined by the law of his principal place of business.

### *G. Maritime Law*

The Code of Private Maritime Law of 1958 contains a couple of interesting conflicts provisions. The law of the flag applies to property rights on a ship (art. 9). This includes conveyances and mortgages. The law of the flag of the helping ship governs questions relating to compensation for salvage (art. 252). The bulk of the labor law provisions regulating employment contracts of Greek nationals on Greek-flag ships are governed by Greek law. This is substantially extended also to aliens on condition of reciprocity (art. 83). The other aspects of such contracts are subject to the general conflicts rules for contracts. As regards employment of Greek nationals on foreign-flag ships, the courts tend to favor Greek law as the proper law especially when the flag is of convenience and the owners have major Greek connections.

Article 2 of L.D. 3899/1958 provides that a preferred mortgage on a Greek-flag ship may be executed either in Greece in notarial form or abroad according to the form either of Greek law or of the law of the place of execution.

### *H. General Matters*

#### 1. Renvoi

Article 32 contains a general rejection of *renvoi*. By way of exception, however, under the Geneva Conventions discussed above (Section B 2) the capacity of a person to be bound by a promissory note, check or bill of exchange is governed by his whole national law including its choice-of-law component.

#### 2. Public Policy

Foreign law is not applied if it contravenes morals or, generally, public policy (art. 33). While it is agreed that this exception, which in practice is invoked rarely, may operate both negatively and positively, whether and to what extent the rest of the foreign law still continues to govern or is replaced by the *lex fori* is unclear.

## 3. Statutes of Limitation

It is well settled that they are considered substantive rather than procedural and, therefore, are subject to the *lex causae*.

## 4. Nationality, Habitual Residence, Residence

The acquisition and loss of nationality by natural persons, which is one of the major connecting factors in Greek conflicts law, is in principle determined by the law of each country whose nationality is at issue (art. 29). Where a person has more than one nationality, the one selected for Greek choice of law purposes is (a) the Greek one or, in its absence, (b) the one with which the person is more closely connected (art. 31). In the event that a person has no nationality, article 30 provides that its place is taken first, by habitual residence and second, by simple residence. It is noteworthy that this language was amended in 1983 to replace 'domicile' with 'habitual residence' to bring it into line with the prevailing view that 'domicile' in the international sense means habitual residence and to conform it to the modern trend as demonstrated especially in the Hague Conventions.

## 5. Proof of Foreign Law

Greek courts are more receptive to the application of foreign law than their U.S. counterparts and quite adept at handling it. Article 337 of the new Code of Civil Procedure of 1968 abandoned the old and much criticized treatment of foreign law as 'fact' by providing that the court must take it into account *ex officio* and without proof. This does not preclude an order for or offer of proof in aid of discovering its content. In addition, article 559 treats an error about foreign law the same way as one about domestic law for purposes of reviewability on final appeal to the Supreme Court. Under the prevailing conflicts theories, the court is required to apply foreign law when called for by a choice of law rule *proprio motu* and regardless of whether any of the litigants so requests. Whether the new system will eliminate the practice of presuming explicitly or implicitly that, in the absence of proof or knowledge to the contrary, foreign law is identical to domestic law is not yet clear. A valuable source of information on the content of foreign law is the Hellenic Institute of International and Foreign Law which is extensively used by the courts. It is this same Institute that Greece has designated as the organ for the receipt and processing of requests for information on Greek law under the European Convention on Information on Foreign Law of 1968 implemented by Law 593/1977.

6. Status of Aliens

An alien is entitled to the same rights as a national under the law applicable pursuant to the Greek choice of law rules (Art. 4). Many bilateral treaties of Greece also call for national or most-favored-nation treatment of aliens. Furthermore, since the accession of Greece to the European Economic Community, all discrimination against Community persons based on nationality is being eliminated. The Office of the Legal Counsel of the government, by majority vote, has upheld the right of Community legal entities to establish private schools in Greece on conditions of equality against challenges deriving from their non-commercial character and from the exercise of public authority in education.

The most publicized unfavorable treatment of aliens under Greek civil law relates to their disability to acquire title and certain other property rights on land situated in the border regions broadly defined which cannot be avoided by forming a Greek corporation if the controlling interests are in foreign hands. The disability may be waived by the government in certain circumstances and does not apply generally to descent and distribution. For restrictions of this type to be legitimate under the Treaty of Rome and under bilateral treaties having national treatment clauses without limitation, they must be tailored to meet the specifications of the national security exception. A draft bill submitted to Parliament in late 1987 requires a government waiver for both Greeks and Community persons. In addition, a more limited definition of "border areas" is under consideration.

Special percentage limitations apply to co-ownership of interests in Greek-flag ships by aliens. The Code of Mines, which regulates alien ownership of mining enterprises, has been challenged as discriminatory by the Commission before the Court of Justice of the European Communities also because it uses criteria of 'control,' such as ownership of capital, and not formal or general ones, such as place of formation, registered seat, central administration or principal place of business, in determining the nationality of companies; the same provisions have been denied application by the Greek Council of Stare (2152/1986) because of discrimination against Community companies. The concept of 'control' has been used also in other contexts such as sequestration of enemy assets, oil exploration and air transportation.

## II. Greek Nationality

### *A. Acquisition*

There are at least six methods of acquisition of Greek nationality:

1. At birth, (a) *iure sanguinis*: birth to a Greek father or mother, (b) *iure soli*: but only where the person does not at the same time acquire another nationality.

2. By legitimization before age 18, through marriage of a Greek father to the mother and otherwise or by recognition as legitimate by a Greek father.

3. By adoption before age 18, by a Greek parent.

4. By naturalization: (a) ethnic Greeks living abroad and having no other nationality may request the authorities that they be recognized as Greek nationals *ex nunc*; their unmarried children less than eighteen years old automatically acquire Greek nationality at the same time; (b) regular naturalization requires (i) age of eighteen years, (ii) a declaration before the municipal authorities, (iii) for persons who are not ethnic Greeks and were not born in Greece and have their domicile out of Greece, domicile of 3 years after such declaration or 8 out of the last 10 years before the application, not interrupted by long absences, (iv) application to the Ministry of Interior, (v) approval of the application at the discretion of the Ministry, and (vi) oath of allegiance. The naturalization of the father or mother automatically extends to the unmarried children below the age of eighteen but they may, if they are not ethnic Greeks and maintain their nationality, reject Greek nationality within the year between their 18th and 19th birthdays.

5. By joining the Greek Army, for ethnic Greeks.

6. Through special laws, applicable to certain narrow categories of ethnic Greeks.

### *B. Loss*

A Greek having or acquiring another nationality voluntarily or through public office with the permission of the Ministry of the Interior loses his Greek nationality. Greeks who were naturalized abroad before 1914 even without permission also lost their nationality. A Greek who is legitimized or recognized as legitimate by an alien before age 18 loses his nationality if he acquires that of the father. A non-ethnic Greek who leaves Greece permanently or who is abroad and has no intention of living in Greece may be deemed to have abandoned his nationality by decision of the Ministry of Interior. Finally, in certain extraordinary circumstances a person may be deprived of his Greek nationality by ministerial decision.

### *C. Reacquisition*

The reacquisition of Greek nationality is possible in certain contexts.

## III. International Jurisdiction of the Greek Courts

Primarily under French influence, the nationality of either the defendent or the plaintiff was the principal general jurisdictional basis for suits in Greek courts before World War II. The Introductory Law to the Civil Code of 1946 in articles 7 I and 126 went the other way by establishing instead the principle of equal jurisdictional treatment of litigants regardless of nationality. This is also consistent with the 'national treatment' obligation in some treaties. The courts, however, continued to subject Greek citizens as such to their general jurisdiction. Article 3 I of the Code of Civil Procedure of 1968 repeated the equality language even more emphatically and it is now accepted that the Greek nationality of the defendant standing alone and regardless of domicile or any other special jurisdictional basis does not generally suffice. In any event, in certain limited matters involving the family relationship, the nationality of either party constitutes an independent jurisdictional basis. Putting nationality aside, the jurisdiction of Greek courts consists of the sum total of the amenabilities to suit or jurisdictions in various other contexts. For these amenabilities, see above, Ch. 15, Section III A–F. An express or tacit prorogation can expand the international jurisdiction of the Greek courts. Conversely, the Greek courts will usually recognize foreign forum choice clauses except in matters of immovables situated in Greece.

The fundamental differences between the Anglo-American and Continental concepts of personal jurisdiction also affect the Greek courts especially in that neither service of process nor doing business within the state are sufficient or even relevant general bases of their international jurisdiction. However, see above, Ch. 15, Section III E (1) on the *forum negotii.*

For admiralty, the Code of Private Maritime Law contains certain specific jurisdictional provisions. Disputes relating to co-ownership of Greek-flag ships are to be brought before the court of the port where the ship is registered (*forum domicilii navis*). Claims arising from collisions may be pursued before the Greek courts if (a) the defendant is domiciled or resides in Greece, (b) the ship carries the Greek flag, (c) the collision took place in Greek territorial waters or (d) the ship was sequestered in Greece (*forum arresti*).

Foreign sovereign and diplomatic immunity is recognized in accordance to the Vienna Conventions on Diplomatic Relations of 1961 and on Consular Relations of 1963 to which Greece is a party. Foreign states are immune to suit for sovereign acts (*iure imperii*) but not for commercial, contractual or tortious acts (*iure gestionis*). Immunity is also extended to heads of state and diplomats and their families. Consular immunities are more limited in that they cover only acts performed in the course of duty and do not extend to families. In general, there is no immunity with respect to claims to immovables (with certain exceptions for embassy and diplomatic residence grounds), descent and distribution matters and the exercise of an occupation or a trade in Greece. Furthermore, when a foreign state brings an action it is deemed to waive its immunity for related counterclaims.

The Greek courts may address to or receive from foreign authorities letters rogatory and render international judicial assistance where this is not contrary to public policy or a treaty obligation. They may also seek the aid of the Greek consular authorities abroad. Greece is also a party to the Hague Convention on the Service Abroad of Judicial and Extrajudicial Documents in Civil or Commercial Matters of 1965.

Finally, the Greek membership in the European Economic Community brought with it the obligation to become party to the Brussels Convention on

Jurisdiction and the Enforcement of Judgments in Civil and Commercial Matters of 1968 as amended. Greece signed and is expected to ratify it soon. The Convention limits the availability of certain jurisdictional bases, especially the exorbitant ones, for actions against domiciliaries of the EEC but for non-domiciliaries each member is free to use its own jurisdictional rules. Other members must recognize and enforce judgments rendered according to the Convention or to national jurisdictional rules when applicable.

## IV. Recognition and Enforcement of Foreign Judgments and Awards

Foreign judgments and awards may be either only 'recognized,' that is given *res judicata* effect in domestic proceedings, or also rendered directly enforceable by being invested with a local *exequatur*. The Code of Civil Procedure contains detailed provisions on both these matters which, contrary to prior law, treat nationals and aliens and domiciliaries and non-domiciliaries equally and non-discriminatorily. Furthermore, no reciprocity is required; and recognition and enforcement take place without reexamination of the merits.

Article 323 of the Code of Civil Procedure enunciates five requirements for the recognition of the judgments of a foreign civil court rendered in contentious, that is adversary, proceedings. First, the court must have had international jurisdiction according to Greek law, which is tested under the rules regulating the jurisdiction of the Greek courts themselves discussed earlier in this chapter. It suffices for such jurisdiction to have been concurrent. That the court complied with its own rules of international and domestic jurisdiction under certain circumstances may be testable not in itself but within the confines of the second and third requirements. Second, the judgment must have the claimed *res judicata* effect under the law of the country of origin. For example, whether mutuality of estoppel is required is first determined by the law of such country. Since, however, the scope of *res judicata* recognition is generally determined by the country of enforcement, this means that the judgment will be given the lesser of the origin or the recognition effects. Third, the losing party must have been given an opportunity to defend not less favorable than that available to nationals of the country of origin. Fourth, the judgment must not be inconsistent with a Greek judgment on the same matter binding the same parties. Apparently this extends not only to subsequent but also to prior Greek judgments in violation of the usual rule that the judgment later in time prevails. Fifth, the judgment should not be contrary to morality and generally to Greek public policy. In this context, public policy is less demanding than in choice of law and it is possible for a court, especially where foreign parties and events are involved, to recognize a judgment applying a rule of law that it would have refused to apply in the first place on public policy grounds. Most of the cases where the public policy exception was raised involved divorce or other family related decrees.

The authority of judgments rendered *ex parte* (voluntary or non-contentious jurisdiction), is recognized more easily: it is sufficient that the foreign court had jurisdiction under the applicable substantive law and that the decision is not contrary to good morals and Greek public policy. However, the court also must have chosen the applicable law consistently with the Greek conflicts rules (art. 780).

Greece should be commended because, unlike some other European countries, does not require, except for judgments rendered in non-contentious proceedings, that is *ex parte*, that the court of origin applied the law called for by the Greek conflicts rules.

While the recognition itself takes place automatically and without the institution of any proceedings, in practice a claimant may encounter difficulties in persuading particular authorities, especially within the executive branch, that the judgment satisfies the criteria of the law and should support the requested action. To remove this uncertainty, a claimant presumably may institute a declaratory judgment proceeding seeking verification of the recognition.

While recognition is often sufficient for declaratory or constitutive foreign judgments, when the judgment orders the payment of money or the doing of an act its enforceability must also be obtained.

Article 905, which deals with enforceable instruments, provides for a special *exequatur* proceeding before the one-member district court of the defendant's domicile or residence or, in their absence, of Athens. The defendant need not be summoned or notified but he usually is in order to be precluded from challenging the *exequatur* later through any available remedies. If the defendant appears, he may challenge only matters related to the *exequatur* but he may not raise substantive issues, such as set-off, payment etc. The latter can be asserted against the execution of the judgment itself.

For an *exequatur* to be obtained it must be shown that the foreign document is judicially enforceable (not necessarily final or non-appealable) under the law of the country of origin and not contrary to good morals or generally to Greek public policy. In addition, when it comes to judgments, the recognition requirements of article 323 must be met. Furthermore, an ambiguous paragraph 4 added later to article 905 provides that the *exequatur* procedure also applies to the recognition of the *res judicata* effect of foreign judgments relating to personal status. It is not as yet settled whether this investiture with an *exequatur* is mandatory or merely permissive and at the choice of the claimant. What accompanies the *exequatur* application is the document itself and evidence of its enforceability at the country of origin and of the notification of or participation by the defendant. The court may not alter, interpret or correct the document but only order its enforcement in whole or in part.

An arbitral award that is foreign, that is rendered abroad or under foreign law, is recognized as having *res judicata* effect if (a) the arbitration agreement was valid under the applicable law, (b) the subject matter was arbitrable under Greek law, (c) the award is not subject to review (but need not be enforceable) in the country of origin, (d) the loser was not deprived of the right to defend, (e) the award is not inconsistent with a judgment of a Greek court on the same matter among the same parties having *res judicata* effect and (f) the award is not contrary to morality and generally to Greek public policy (art. 903). In addition, such awards may be enforced through the *exequatur* proceedings (art. 906).

Greece is a party to eight bilateral Conventions dealing with matters of recognition and enforcement of judgments (Cyprus, Czechoslovakia, Federal Republic of Germany, Hungary, Poland, Rumania, Syria, Yugoslavia). These Conventions prevail over the Code of Civil Procedure but the matter is not important in practice since there are no significant differences. A conflict may, for instance, arise under some of the Conventions in situations where a Greek court rejects a judgment because of inconsistency with a prior Greek judgment.

Greece is also party to two Geneva (1923, 1927) and the New York (1958) Conventions dealing with arbitral awards as well as to the ICSID Convention of 1965 on the settlement of investment disputes.

A major change in the recognition and enforcement of judgments in Greece rendered in the countries of the European Economic Communities will occur when Greece ratifies the Brussels Convention on Jurisdiction and Enforcement of Judgments in Civil and Commercial Matters of 1968.

Finally, a Greek court will normally stay a case if the same issue between the same parties is in the process of being adjudicated abroad.

## Bibliography

There is no comprehensive treatise on Greek conflicts law. The two best relatively recent works in Greek are: D. Evrigenis, *Private International Law* (1973) and G. Maridakis, *Private International Law*, 2d ed., vol. I (1967), vol. II (1968). See, also, S. Kalogeropoulos-Stratis, *Private International Law*, 2d ed. (1962) and E. Krispis, *Private International Law*, vol. I (1967–68), vol. II (1970).

Among the many Greek-language monographs and articles in the field, special mention should be made to:

### *1. Choice of Law*

#### *(a) Contracts*

D. Evrigenis, *Problems of the Applicable Law in Contracts* (1970).
A. Grammaticaki-Alexiou, *The Law Applicable to Employment Contracts Under the EEC Convention of Private International Law of 1980* (1984).
Z. Papassiopi-Passia, *New Trends in Private International Law in the Area of Contractual Obligations* (1986).

#### *(b) Torts*

E. Kounougeri-Manoledaki, *Tort Liability in Automobile Accidents in View of the Modern Trends in Private International Law* (1974).
A. Tenekidou-Frangopoulou, *The Delict in Private International Law* (1956).

*(c) Legal Entities*

E. Krispis, *Legal Persons, Especially Corporations, in Private International Law* (1950).
S. Menglidou, *The Establishment of Foreign Companies in Greece* (1971).
D. Papasteriou, *The Seat of Legal Persons in Private Law* (1979).
See, also,
D. Evrigenis, *Elements of the Law of International Transactions and International Economic Organizations* §§ 22–25, vol. I (1976).

*(d) Family Law*

E. Bendermacher-Geroussis, *Divorce and Separation in Greek Private International Law* (1960).
J. Deliyannis, Choice of Law in Spousal Relations, *Greek Review of European Law* 227–261 (1986).
A. Grammaticaki-Alexiou, *Private International Law. Questions of Family Law* (1983).

*(e) Maritime Law*

K. Kardoulis, *The Flag of a Ship as Connecting Factor in Private International Law* (1970).
D. Kokkini-Iatridou, *The Charter in Private International Law* (1962).
P. Vallindas, *Private International Law in the Greek Code of Private Maritime Law* (1959).

*(f) Other*

A. Grammaticaki-Alexiou, *The Domicile of Natural Persons in Private International Law* (1980).
K. Ioannou, Freedom of Establishment, Public Security and Border Regions, 3 *E. Eur. Koin.* 160 (1982).
E. Krispis, *The Monetary Obligation in Private International Law* (1964).
E. Krispis, *The Form of Juridical Acts in Private International Law* (1960).
S. Metallinos, *The Cession of Claims in Private International Law* (1971).
V. Papadimas, *The Preliminary Question in Private International Law* (1981).
Z. Papassiopi-Passia, *Problems of Applicable Law in Legal Cessions. The Case of Insurer Subrogation* (1981).
S. Vrellis, *Fraud in the Law in Private International Law* (1979).
S. Vrellis, *Trademarks in Private International Law* (1972).
S. Vrellis, *The Guaranty in Private International Law* (1983).

*2. Nationality*

E. Bendermacher-Geroussis, *The Greek Law of Nationality*, 3d ed. (1975).
E. Krispi-Nicoletopoulou, *Nationality* (1965).
Z. Papassiopi-Passia, *Nationality Law* (1986).
P. Vallindas, *Nationality Law* (1957).

*3. International Jurisdiction and Foreign Judgments*

A. Georgiadis, Execution and Recognition of Foreign Judgments, *Harm.* 599–612 (1974).
G. Maridakis, *The Execution of Foreign Judgments*, 3d ed. (1970).
*Eranion* (Festschrift) for G. Maridakis 4 vols. (1963–1964, 1972, various authors).
Metallinos, The Recognition of Foreign Ex Parte Judgments, *Diki* 176–203, 344–360 (1978).

Reference should also be made to the general treatises on Civil Procedure by Professors K. Beis, K. Kerameus, G. Mitsopoulos and G. Rammos and to the older writings of Professor C. Fragistas.

In English, a useful work, although a bit out of date, is A. Ehrenzweig – C. Fragistas-A. Yiannopoulos, *American-Greek Private International Law* (Bilateral Studies, Parker School 1957). See, also, Evrigenis-Kerameus, Report on the Accession of the Hellenic Republic to the Community Convention on jurisdiction and the enforcement of judgments in civil and commercial matters, *Offical Journal of the European Communities* C298/24.11.1986, p. 1–27; Markianos – Guggenheim, *International Cooperation in Litigation: Greece*, Smit ed. (1965);

P. Massouridis, The Enforcement of Foreign Judgments in Greece, *Rev. Hell. D.I.* 186–224 (1970); G. Nicoletopoulos, Private International Law in the New Greek Civil Code, 23 *Tul. L. Rev.* 452–477 (1949). In French, see D. Kokkini-Iatridou, *Introduction au Droit Hellénique* 15–43 (1969). In German, see K. Kerameus, Rechtsmittelfestigkeit und Vollstreckung von ausländischen Entscheidungen, in *Multitudo legum ius unum: Essays in Honor of W. Wengler*, 383–395, vol. II (1973).

Finally, attention should be called to the Revue Hellénique de Droit International, now in its thirty-seventh year, which often publishes summaries of conflicts cases.

# Chapter 17
# Tax Law and Investment Incentives

*John C. Dryllerakis**

## I. Introduction

The Greek Constitution provides for certain restraints and limitations on the direct or indirect authority of the Government to impose taxes. Under its article 78: (a) A tax may be imposed only by law passed in Parliament, (b) the Parliament may not delegate its legislative power to the Government or other authority concerning the object and the rate of taxation as well as the tax exemptions and (c) a tax or other economic burden may not be imposed by retroactive legislation extending beyond the previous economic year. Also under article 4 V, all Greek citizens are required to contribute to public expenditures without distinctions and in relation to their financial ability.

We define tax (φόρος, foros) as the monetary payment imposed, without specific consideration, by the State to raise revenue and pursue its various objectives. Taxes are distinguishable from fees (τέλη, teli), which are payable for specific services offered to the taxpayer by the authorities (e.g., cleaning fees) and from contributions (εισφορές, eisphores), which constitute mandatory payments by a group of people benefited from a certain program or action of the authorities (e.g., development of the area where they live). The Greek tax system relies heavily upon indirect taxation, due both to its lack of effectiveness to catch directly the real income of natural persons and legal entities and to the structure of the economy (extent of black economy). In the 1986 Budget, the direct taxation represented approximately only 35% of the total revenue (481 billion drs.), while indirect taxes contributed the remaining 65% (890 billion drs.).

## II. Income Taxation (φόρος εισοδήματος, foros eisodimatos)

### *A. General Principles*

1. Natural persons domiciled in Greece and Greek legal persons are subject to income tax for their worldwide annual income. Domicile is acquired by physical

*Attorney at Law, Athens.

presence in a place and intent of the natural person to have this place as the center of his social, economic or professional activity (see above, Ch. 4, Section II D).

2. Natural persons not domiciled in Greece and foreign legal persons are taxed only on their income deriving from a source in Greece (e.g., rentals of premises in Greece). Foreign legal persons are also taxed on their income from their 'permanent establishment' in Greece, which may be physical (office, branch, or other place of operation) or deemed (e.g., participation in a close corporation). However treaties for the avoidance of double taxation (see below, Section D) between Greece and other countries adopt certain variations to the definition of permanent establishment and to the taxation of foreign domiciliaries. Another deviation has been introduced by Law 89/1967, which exempts from taxation branches or offices of foreign companies established in Greece after a special approval of the Ministry of National Economy exclusively to coordinate their offshore activities; these foreign companies are not allowed to carry any business in Greece. Despite their 'permanent establishment' they are not subject to income taxation in Greece in exchange for their obligation to import foreign currency (minimum $50,000 per year) to finance all their local expenses. Certain other facilities are also available to these companies (for shipping enterprises see below, Section III C).

3. For the reasons explained below under 4 and 5, the law classifies the sources of income into seven categories and distinguishes income from: (a) buildings, (b) land leasing, (c) securities, loans etc., (d) commercial enterprises, that is business activities – regardless of legal form – in commerce and industry or any other operation for profit, excluding professional activities, (e) agricultural enterprises, (f) employment and (g) professions and all other sources. Nevertheless income tax is computed on the aggregate income from all sources and loss from one source is offset against profit from another.

4. In general, gross income is reduced by (actual or presumed) expenses to arrive at the net income. This way, the annual gross income of enterprises and professionals (income of sources (d), (e) and (g)) is reduced by the depreciation of fixed assets and by the expenses incurred related to their activity ('productive expenses'). Branches of foreign companies may deduct part of their head office expenses too, as related to their local operation. A tax audit may not disallow an expense as unnecessary or unreasonable, but only as unrelated to the enterprise or the profession or as not actually incurred. In general, reserves for contingencies are not deductible and the same is true for certain categories of legitimate expenses; for example royalties and fees payable for technical and other assistance to foreign enterprises are deductible in the year that they are actually remitted or paid to the beneficiary and not in the year in which they were invoiced and the assistance was received.

Booking and documentation of expenses must be in full compliance with the 'Tax Data Code', a highly technical and bureaucratic piece of legislation, which in many instances enables the tax audit to disallow expenses as inappropriately booked or supported or even to disregard the books of an enterprise and to recalculate the profits arbitrarily.

Small and medium scale enterprises are subject to lesser bookkeeping obligations. Their net income is computed as a predetermined percentage on their purchases or sales, as the case may be. Also net income of constructing enterprises is computed as a percentage of their gross income, and the same applies to other technical enterprises.

For the other categories of income, the law defines specifically the actual or presumed expenses, which are deductible; for example in sources (a) and (b) the law allows mainly a deemed depreciation and maintenance ranging between 5–25% as well as interest payable on mortgages.

5. The law also discriminates among the various categories of income, burdening certain income with surtaxes (for example sources (a) and (c)) or favoring others (e.g., 50% or 340,000 drs. – whichever is lower – of salaries was tax exempt, while for 1987 salaries and pensions were taxed at a lower scale; agricultural gross income up to 1.65 million drs. is also tax exempt; journalists, authors and artists enjoy a special tax exemption).

6. The law taxes presumed income as follows: (a) a house or building owned and used by the taxpayer is presumed to generate income calculated by reference to rental value after allowing a deduction of 210,000 drs. increased by 45,000 drs. for each dependent child, and (b) ownership of a passenger car is presumed to generate income calculated by reference to its horsepower; this presumption however does not apply to cars owned by non-Greek-domiciled foreign personnel of the above mentioned companies under Law 89/1967. Presumed income is also imputed, based on a formula, in case of ownership of a private yacht or airplane. However, in these cases (under b), the imputed income is additive only to the extent that declared income or capital spending is lower. Exceptionally, income may also be assessed, based on a taxpayer's general spending (rentals, housemaids, travels, tuition fees etc.), while a recent law established, for enterprises and professionals, the principle of 'presumed minimum income' which ranges between 550,000 and 700,000 drs. (viability presumption).

7. An extensive system of tax withholding aims at catching the tax at source. Withholding and reporting obligations are imposed on enterprises and professionals which pay salaries, fees and other types of income to taxpayers. In addition, part of next year's tax – to the extent it is not withheld – is advanced, calculated on prior year's tax. Especially for payments of royalties, fees or remuneration of any kind and rentals of equipment to foreign companies not having a permanent establishment in Greece, a tax withholding of 10, 20 and 25%, as the case may be, is provided for.

Full scale withholding is made from the income of foreign residents, even if a treaty provides for a reduced tax rate or a total exemption. The beneficiary may apply afterwards for a refund, having lost the use of the funds in the meantime and bearing the risk of drachma devaluation *vis-à-vis* the invoicing currency and the cost of the procedure. Exceptionally, interest on loans and royalties is subject to tax withholding only on the basis of the provisions of the tax treaties.

8. As a general rule, Greek law allows full tax credit for taxes paid in foreign

countries for income from sources within those countries. Such tax credit may not exceed, however, the amount of the Greek tax.

### *B. Taxation of Natural Persons*

Natural persons are taxed on the basis of a progressive tax scale on their aggregate net income from all sources. A tax reform has been officially announced and will apply retroactively effective Jan. 1, 1988. The number of brackets has been drastically cut (from 18 to 9) and the highest income tax rate has been reduced to 50% (from 63%), applying to income over 4.7 million drs., while the average tax rate up to that level has been brought down to 36.7% (from 48.3%). In addition, a different system of floating tax credits has been introduced.

Up to the end of 1987, there were small fixed tax credits for the taxpayer and dependent family members, while certain allowances or types of expenses were reducing the taxable net income. According to the new system, the net income is not reduced any more by allowances or special expenses. Instead, allowances and expenses are summed up to create a 'negative income'. The tax corresponding to this negative income on the basis of the above scale, calculated separately, constitutes the amount of tax credit corresponding to the individual taxpayer. The separate calculation favors the lower incomes.

This 'negative income' is the aggregate of: (a) personal allowances for the taxpayer and his dependents (currently 600,000 drs. for a family with two children), (b) certain allowances depending on the kind of income (e.g., up to 400,000 drs. for income from employment or from agriculture), and (c) certain other expenses incurred by the taxpayer. These latter expenses are classified in two categories. The first has no maximum ceiling and includes (i) medical expenses, (ii) social insurance contributions, (iii) donations to the state, state agencies etc., and (iv) interest on loans for acquisition of new assets. The second has a ceiling varying on the basis of family status of the taxpayer (currently 500,000 drs. for a family with two children) and includes expenses such as for the purchase of electrical appliances, house maintenance, clothing, car repairs, insurance premiums etc., provided that they are formally established. The purpose of this radical reform is double. First, to reduce the tax burden, which in an inflationary environment had become unbearable, and second, to catch taxable income by inducing the taxpayers to collect receipts from enterprises and professionals.

### *C. Taxation of Legal Persons*

1. Greek corporations are subject to a flat income tax rate of 49%. For manufacturing, mining and quarrying enterprises the tax rate is 44% or 39%, depending on whether their stock is quoted on the Greek Stock Exchange or not. Such rate applies to net profit, after deduction of carried forward losses (of the last three years for commercial and agricultural enterprises or five years for

industrial enterprises), dividends, directors' fees, profit sharing and tax-free reserves (see below, Section VII F). The rate of 49% applies to all kinds of foreign corporations or branches of foreign corporations operating in Greece and, in general, of all foreign legal persons for profit. However, as branches do not constitute separate legal persons, they do not declare dividends but have undistributed profits which may be transferred to the head office.

2. Dividends are taxed separately in the name of the shareholders at a flat rate of 42% or 47% for registered shares and 45% or 53% for bearer shares respectively, depending on whether such shares are quoted on the Greek Stock Exchange. The tax is withheld by the corporation and this exhausts the tax liability of the shareholder. Shareholders have the option of adding this income to their total income and receiving the corresponding credit or refund for the amount withheld.

Treaties for the avoidance of double taxation, which always prevail over the general legislation (see below, under D), provide for a lower maximum rate of taxation of dividends (for example 35% Dutch Treaty, 25% German Treaty).

3. Cooperatives (συνεταιρισμοί, synetairismoi) are taxed at the rate of 28% or 33% while Greek or foreign entities not for profit are subject to taxation at the flat rate of 23% only on their income of sources (a), (b), (c) (rentals, interests, dividends etc.) but not on the revenue they earn in pursuing their purposes.

4. Unlike corporations, general partnerships and close corporations are not taxed as separate legal entities. The tax liability rests on the members who have to include their attributed share of the entity's profit in their own tax return.

5. It has been announced that, effective Jan. 1, 1988, the taxation of legal entities will be reduced. The general tax rate will be cut down to 46% (from 49%). The tax rate of the manufacturing, mining and quarrying enterprises will become 40 or 35% (instead of 44% or 39%), while the dividend withholding tax for bearer shares will be 50% from 53% (the other rates remaining unchanged).

### *D. Bilateral Treaties for Avoidance of Double Taxation*

Greece has entered into such treaties with the following fourteen countries: (1) Austria (2) Belgium (3) Cyprus (4) England (5) Finland (6) France (7) Federal Republic of Germany (8) Hungary (9) India (10) Italy (11) Netherlands (12) Sweden (13) Switzerland (14) U.S. The treaties with Germany, England and U.S. are older. The other treaties mainly follow the OECD model. These treaties in general define certain important terms, such as permanent establishment or place of taxation, and provide for certain local tax exemptions in favor of nationals of the other country or for special treatment of certain types of income.

The Constitution provides in article 28 I that ratified international treaties constitute an integral part of the Greek legal system and that they prevail over any contrary provision of the internal law. Thus, the above tax treaties are superior to the general tax legislation.

## III. Other Direct Taxes

### A. *Gift, Succession and Lottery Gains Taxation*

A succession tax is imposed on the assets of an estate situated in Greece or, regardless of their situs, which belong to Greek decedents (domiciled in Greece or abroad) or to foreign decedents domiciled in Greece at the time of their death. Debts of the estate are deducted from its gross market value. The net value thus derived is subject to taxation on the basis of a progressive scale ranging between 6 and 72%, depending on the degree of relationship between the decedent and the heir or legatee. The latter are classified in five categories: spouse and children; descendants – other than children – and ascendants; brothers and sisters; other relatives of third degree (nephews/nieces and uncles/aunts); and finally all the rest.

The span of tax rates for these categories is from 6 to 27%, 7 to 29%, 12 to 50%, 16 to 61% and 19 to 72%. A tax credit of 80, 60, 40, 30 and 20,000 drachmas respectively is allowed for each of the above categories. The maximum of the above rates applies to the part of the net value of the estate exceeding 10 million drs.

Greece has entered into a few bilateral treaties which mainly define the situs of the assets of the estate. The most important treaty is with the U.S.

The same tax is imposed on gifts. Successive gifts to the same person by the same donor are calculated cumulatively for purposes of computing the tax. Gifts to certain close relatives (children), in greater use after the institution of dowry was abolished (see above, Ch. 8, Section II F), are subject to half of the regular tax. The law taxes all gains from lotteries at the flat rate of 10%.

### B. *Property Tax*

Real estate located in Greece is taxed annually for market values in excess of 25 million drs. for natural persons or 30 million drs. for legal persons. The rate for legal persons is fixed at 1.5%, while for individuals it is slightly progressive (0.5% to 2% over 55 million drs.).

### C. *Taxation of Ships and Shipping Enterprises*

Ships under Greek flag are classified in two categories (L. 27/1975). Income from ships of category A is taxed at a flat dollar rate ($0.772–1.383 per ton depending on the age of the ship). The tax rate is further increased or decreased (factors ranging from 1.2 to 0.8) depending on the gross tonnage of the ship between 100 to 80,000 tons and over, to favor big ships. Ships of category B are taxed in drs. (100 to 2,300 drs. per MT) based on their gross tonnage. There are several exemptions; for instance ships built in Greece and registered under the Greek flag are exempted from tax until they reach the age of six years.

Branches or offices of foreign companies dealing exclusively with administration, exploitation, chartering, insurance, average adjustments, brokerage of sale, shipbuilding, chartering or of insurance of ships under Greek or foreign flag may be exempted from income taxation, although they have a permanent establishment in Greece, in exchange for their obligation to import foreign currency to finance their local operation (minimum $50,000 per year) according to Law 89/1967 and Law 378/1968 (see also above, Section II A 2).

### *D. Capital Gain Tax*

There is no capital gain tax in Greece. Only in the context of the income taxation of source d (enterprises) there are provisions which treat as income certain specific gains such as the realized appreciation of fixed assets of an enterprise, while the assignment of goodwill or intangible rights is taxed at a flat rate of 30%. Capital gain from shares of stock, real property and ships is tax exempt.

## IV. INDIRECT TAXATION

### *A. Transaction Taxes*

#### 1. Value-Added Tax (φόρος προστιθέμενης αξίας, foros prostithemenis axias)

Effective January 1, 1987 the Greek indirect taxation has undergone a major change. The value-added tax (V.A.T.) system was introduced by Law 1642/1986 under the EEC Treaty to replace totally or partially many other indirect taxes and, more particularly, the turnover tax and stamp taxes.

V.A.T. is payable when any person engaged in independent economic activity supplies goods or services in Greece or imports goods into Greece. Certain categories of transactions are exempted from V.A.T. (such as lawyers', notaries' and medical services, post office services, building leases, delivery of newspapers etc.) while special treatment is provided for small enterprises, farmers, travel agents and petroleum products.

In principle, V.A.T. is a neutral tax, paid ultimately by the consumer, but collected gradually in all stages of production by the persons liable. They collect V.A.T. on their outputs and pay it to the State after deducting the V.A.T. paid on their inputs. If the balance is positive, they get credit and, occasionally, a refund. Export of goods is exempted from V.A.T. Still, however, the exporter is entitled to a full credit of V.A.T. on his inputs.

Transactions of the State or state agencies are not subject to V.A.T. with the exception of selected list of services and deliveries of goods (like telecommunications, distribution of energy, transportation, storage). All other transactions are divided in three categories attracting low, normal and high rates respectively (currently 6%, 16% and 36%). Agricultural goods and services are subject to special treatment.

### 2. Stamp Tax (χαρτόσημο, chartosimo)

With the exception of those subject to V.A.T., all other transactions, including reports and applications to the Government, certified copies of documents, lawsuits and other legal documents, drafts and promissory notes as well as all contracts which take place within the jurisdiction of the Greek tax authorities are subject to stamp tax, calculated either as a percentage of the value of the transaction or as a fixed, usually low, amount. The fixed amounts are collected normally by sticking special stamps to the various documents.

Rates are set out in the 'Stamp Tax Code', the general rule being that business contracts are subject to a rate of 2.4% on their value, while non-business contracts to 3.6%. There are many exemptions and variances. The most common stamp tax was 3.6% on the value of all sales invoices and on imports which currently is replaced by V.A.T.

### 3. Turnover Tax (φόρος κύκλου εργασιών, foros kyklou ergasion)

In a manner resembling the V.A.T., this tax (t.o.t.) was imposed on the gross revenue of industrial or handicraft enterprises from the sale of their products, on the gross revenue of banking institutions and insurance companies, on the value of imported goods and finally on the gross revenue from certain categories of services. The general rate was 8 to 10%, but reduced or increased rates ranging from 4–15% applied in certain cases. Gross revenue was calculated by deducting from sales the value of raw materials which actually had been subjected to t.o.t. (as a product of another industry or at importation) or which were exempted from t.o.t.

The main differences of t.o.t. from V.A.T. are that: (a) V.A.T. applies to all and any deliveries of goods (including self-consumption) and services as well as to the import of goods, while t.o.t. has a more selective application, (b) V.A.T. applies to retail sales as well, (c) technically any V.A.T. already paid at previous stages will be credited to the payable one (while in t.o.t. the sales revenue subject to t.o.t. is reduced only by the supplies subjected to t.o.t.), and (d) V.A.T. is refunded upon export of goods.

Following the introduction of V.A.T., t.o.t. has been limited only to insurance companies.

### 4. Banking Tax and Capital Concentration Tax

Law 1676/1986 imposed a special tax of 3% on bank loans and of 8% on the revenues of banks in Greece. Both taxes are passed over to the banks' clients. The same law introduced a special tax of 1% on capital concentration, i.e.

establishment, conversion or merger of a company, capital increase or capital contribution. Some of the above taxes replaced existing stamp tax burdens.

### *B. Sales Taxes*

Special sales taxes (consumption tax = φόρος καταναλώσεως, foros katanaloseos, and luxury tax = φόρος πολυτελείας, foros polyteleias) ranging from 10 to 40% apply to sales in Greece of several goods such as televisions, cameras, etc. and on TV commercials. The tax is on their sale price. Consumption taxes also are levied on petroleum products as well as on certain other categories of goods.

### *C. Transfer Tax* (φόρος μεταβιβάσεως, foros metavivaseos)

New buildings transferred for value by contractors (developers) are subject to V.A.T. effective January 1, 1989. In all other cases where rights in real property located in Greece are transferred for value, a transfer tax is due. The rate is 9% on the market value of the real property (which is not necessarily the transfer price) up to 4 million drs. and 11 % on any excess. A surtax of 2% is levied if the real property transferred is located in an area served by a fire station. Reduced rates apply in certain cases such as mergers, distributions and when Greek emigrants import foreign currency to cover the market value of the acquired property. In the (greater) Athens and Thessaloniki areas as well as in other urban areas, the market value is imputed pursuant to official tables prepared on the basis of different parameters (location, place, floor, age, joint ownership etc.). Expansion of the same system to more areas is planned.

### *D. Import Duties and Taxes* (δασμοί-φόροι εισαγωγής, dasmoi – foroi eisagogis)

Greece entered into the EEC on January 1, 1981 and after the expiration of a five-year transitory period it has become a full member effective January 1, 1986. Goods imported from other EEC countries are basically duty and tax free subject to minor exceptions. Imported goods from outside the EEC are subject to the Common Customs Tariff (CCT) and classified as per the Brussels Standard International Trade Classification of Commodities. The value of imported commodities for calculation of duties and taxes is determined based on CIF market price increased by taxes and expenses. The preferential treatment provided for countries or groups of countries by EEC treaties (LOME, GSP, EFTA countries, Israel etc.) is also applicable.

Import of products duty-free for manufacturing and reexport is allowed. Storage of products in transit in free zones in Piraeus and Thessaloniki is also provided, while petroleum products may also be imported and stored in transit in 'Free Customs Zones' until they are reexported or, in certain cases, sold locally. Finally, refineries operating in Greece are subject to a special custom supervision.

Greece introduced in 1984 with the approval of the EEC a 'regulatory tax' to assist the Greek economy to adapt to the Community system. The tax is gradually reduced and is expected to be abolished in 1989.

### *E. Other Taxes*

It would be wrong if the impression was created that the above exhausts the list of indirect taxes. On the contrary, there is a great number of different taxes, some well known – such as the taxes on car sales or imports and the circulation taxes on vehicles – and others less visible – like the tax on alcohol and beer. They are, however, gradually reduced. The law which introduced the V.A.T. has recently abolished some of them.

## V. Municipal Taxes and Taxes in Favor of Third Parties

### *A. Municipal Taxes* (δημοτικοί φόροι, dimotikoi foroi)

The revenue of the municipalities is very meager as they have no independent power to impose taxation and the taxes voted in Parliament in their favor are occasional, do not secure equal opportunities or a continuous flow of income and are insufficient to cover the needs.

The main sources of revenue for municipalities, apart from state subsidies, are the following taxes and fees: (a) cleaning and lighting fees (τέλη καθαριότητος καί φωτισμού, teli kathariotitos kai photismou), payable by the owners or users of buildings for the collection of garbage and waste and for the lighting of the streets; the amount is calculated based on the size of the building, (b) fees for use of streets, squares and pavements, (c) a general tax, payable by the owners or users of buildings or spaces. The tax ranges between 6 and 16 drs. per sq. m. and it is within the discretion of each municipality whether to activate it or not, (d) tax on hotel and restaurant bills, (e) tax on building licenses and for the expansion or amendment of zoning, (f) annual tax on undeveloped real property, (g) tax on advertisements, and (h) tax on sales of beer.

### *B. Taxes in Favor of Third Parties* (φόροι υπέρ τρίτων)

Certain provisions impose numerous taxes in favor of third parties, such as the Lawyers Pension Fund, the Universities, other Funds and non-profit organizations. The constitutionality and the fairness of these taxes have been repeatedly questioned as they enforce contributions to organizations which are not connected to the taxpayer. The trend is to eliminate this type of taxes, not an easy task. It is true, though, that the number of taxes of this kind is continuously reduced.

## VI. Enforcement of Tax Laws – Penalties – Litigation

The operation of the tax system relies upon the reporting obligation of the taxpayer. The tax payable is computed on the basis of the tax return submitted. The tax audit, which may follow, assesses additional taxes, if any, and penalties. The latter vary from 25 to 300% on the additional tax, depending upon the kind of tax involved. Fines are also provided for delayed submission of tax returns, while criminal sanctions for tax evasion became lately extremely severe, covering even technical failures.

In the past, all enterprises had to undergo a regular audit. The inability of the tax authorities to meet the tremendous load of work led to repeated tax amnesty laws allowing finalization of unaudited (and sometimes audited) tax returns upon payment of predetermined amount of taxes. Effective 1986, regular audits are made at random.

The findings of the audit are incorporated in the 'audit report' which is the basis of the 'tax assessment' (φύλλο ελέγχου, phyllo elenchou) issued by the tax commissioner or any other competent authority (municipalities). The assessment may be appealed, within 20 days from its service, before the administrative district courts. Normally, the appeal (προσφυγή) suspends payment of 80% of the total amount assessed (taxes and penalties). The court decision may be appealed (both by the taxpayer and the tax authorities) before the administrative courts of appeal, but it is immediately enforceable. Ultimately, any legal issues may be brought to the Council of State, the Greek administrative Supreme Court. Litigation can be avoided if settlement is reached with the tax office. The drastic reduction of penalties at that stage compared with the alternative of immediate payment of 20% of the total amount, the long time required for finalization of litigation and the ever-present ambiguity of the outcome of litigation constitute major incentives for an out-of-court settlement, which of course has little to do with law and justice and does not promote the tax consciousness of the taxpayers. Still, though, it is a current reality.

## VII. Investment Incentives

### *A. General*

The population of Greece is approximately ten million living in an area of 133,000 sq. km of which nearly 25,000 sq. km consists of about 2,000 islands – small, medium and large – scattered in the Ionian, Aegian and Cretan seas. Four-fifths of the country is mountainous, while more than three million inhabitants live in the greater Athens area and another million in Thessaloniki and four other large cities.

To encourage dispersion of industry throughout the countryside, a system of incentives has been established. The law (L. 1262/1982) currently provides for (a) capital aids in the form of cash grant and/or government's participation in the share capital of a company, (b) subsidies of bank loans interest, (c) reduced income tax rate for corporations, and (d) tax-free reserves as well as accelerated and free depreciations.

### *B. Development Regions and Qualifying Investments*

1. For the purposes of differentiating the available regional development aids, Greece is divided into four regions. Region A includes the developed districts of Attica and Thessaloniki and B the semi-developed districts running along the major part of the national road from Patras (in northwest Peloponnese) to Thessaloniki (in Macedonia) on which axis most of the industries (outside of Athens and Thessaloniki) have been concentrated. The remaining districts constitute region C with the exception of the north and east border areas and the islands along the Turkish coast which are classified as region D. For investments in the tourist industry, the four regions do not completely coincide. The major difference is that region B consists of selected, highly developed areas (like Corfu, Rhodes, and parts of Crete) and not the above axis of the national road.

In general, investments in region A are not subsidized. There are few exceptions to the above rule, when investments serve general economic and social goals (environmental protection, energy conservation and projects of exceptionally advanced technology or of applied research).

2. Only 'productive new investments' made in certain defined 'activities' are eligible for the incentives of the law. 'Productive investments' include buildings, machinery and equipment, computers and automation systems, installations and miscellaneous expenditures. Land, passenger cars up to six seats and office furniture and equipment are excluded. The 'activities' qualifying for aids include: (a) general manufacturing, (b) mining, (c) certain enterprises in the primary sector (agricultural, cattle-breeding and fishing enterprises of advanced technology etc.), (d) shipyards and similar activities, (e) coast liners, (f) tourist business (hotels, campings, spas, winter tourism centers), and (g) miscellaneous activities, such as enterprises exploiting agricultural or industrial effluents or wastes. Purely trading activities (supermarkets) and services in general do not qualify as productive activities.

### *C. Capital Aid and Loan Subsidy* (επιχορήγηση, επιδότηση επιτοκίου, epichorigisi, epidotisi epitokiou)

1. The capital aids range between 10–50% of the value of the subsidized investment, depending on the region as well as on the type of activity and its contribution to the national economy (export activity, substitute of imports, added value, foreign currency capital expenditure etc.). Enterprises owned by municipalities and cooperatives or repatriated Greek emigrants are further subsidized by an additional 15%.

2. The total capital aid is divided into a cash grant and a state participation in the share capital of a corporation or of a close corporation. While the cash

grant is a free payment to the enterprise (reducing the cost of investment and increasing the return on capital invested), the capital participation component constitutes equity financing of the investment by the State as a shareholder. Although the cash grant was known in prior legislation, the participation in the share capital has been introduced for the first time by the above Law 1262/1982. Allocation of given subsidy between these two forms is as follows: (a) investment up to 1.2 million drs. is eligible to cash grants, (b) the portion of the investment between 1.2 million and 1.5 billion drs. receives 50% of the aid in cash grant and the remaining 50% in share capital contribution, and (c) capital aid is entirely in the form of share capital participation for the part of the investment exceeding 1.5 billion drs. Investors can choose to limit the capital aid to the first portion of 1.2 million drs., foregoing state participation in the share capital.

3. The subsidy of bank loan interest is proportionally equal to the capital aid which the enterprise is entitled to receive; for example should the capital aid be determined at 20% of the value of the investment, 20% of the interest expenditure from investment bank loans is covered.

### *D. Requirements for Capital Aids*

The aids are granted by a decision of the Minister of National Economy published in the Official Gazette and are not automatically available to eligible enterprises. The decision defines the amount of aid and particular terms and conditions which apply to the investment. Two basic requirements are that the investor must provide share capital to finance part of the investment ranging between 10–30% (depending on the region and the type of investment). Reduced participation is provided for investments by cooperatives, municipal enterprises and repatriated Greek emigrants. Dissolution of the enterprise or transfer of shares or assets of subsidized investments is not allowed before ten years from the completion of the investment without prior ministerial approval.

### *E. Reduced Tax Rates*

The income of corporations coming within the protection of Law 1262/1982 is subject to a lower tax rate, 39% or 44% (depending on the type of business), as compared to 44% or 46% which applies generally (see above, Section II C 1, 5). Such rate applies only to the profits from the new investment.

### *F. Tax-Free Reserves – Accelerated and Free Depreciation* (αφορολόγητα αποθεματικά, αυξημένες αποσβέσεις, aforologita apothematika, auximenes aposveseis)

1. An enterprise making a 'productive investment' in any of the special 'activities' identified in the law (see above, under B) qualifies for a 'tax-free

reserve', which is a deduction from its taxable profits of an amount equal to a certain percentage of the expenditure of part of the 'productive investment' up to 400 million drs. in the protected activities (see above, under B). This amount is kept as a special nontaxable reserve and its taxation is suspended until its distribution on the sale of the corresponding assets.

The size of the annual reserve varies depending on three factors: the cost of the investment, the region in which it is made (regions B, C & D) and the size of the enterprise's profits. The allowance (and the corresponding reserve) may not exceed a percentage of the investment (40, 55 and 70% respectively for investments in regions B, C and D) and a certain percentage of annual profits (60, 75 and 90% respectively). Any balance of the allowance not covered by the above percentages may be carried forward to future years.

2. Under corporate and tax law, fixed assets are carried in the accounts of an enterprise at their acquisition value (and not at replacement cost or current value) less depreciation. Unlike commercial law which does not define depreciation rates, considering them as a matter of judgment in each case, tax law details compulsory annual depreciation percentages for each kind of fixed assets.

The incentives legislation allows eligible enterprises to accelerate depreciation. The allowable increment on the statutory schedules depends on the region in which the industry operates and the intensity of use of the equipment (double or triple shifts). The increased percentages are optional and can be used for investments made between June 1982 and December 31, 1992.

3. For purposes of social policy, the law provides for free depreciation (total write-off in the year of the expenditure) of certain fixed assets such as buildings and facilities for recreation or dining as well as works of art of Greek artists (sculpture, mosaics, frescoes etc.) up to 3% of the value of the building in which they are to be placed.

4. Unlike the capital aids and the reduced income tax rate which require prior approval by the Minister of National Economy, tax-free reserves and accelerated depreciations can be utilized by all eligible enterprises for their qualified investments without any prior approval by any governmental authority (automatic application). Aids, however, are incompatible and may not be cumulative with tax-free reserves while depreciations (single, accelerated or free) are calculated on the value of the assets, reduced by the aid granted for their acquisition.

### *G. Other Investment Incentives*

L.D. 2687/1953 authorizes the Government to grant certain privileges to investments made with imported foreign capital. Repatriation of loan or share capital (up to 10% annually), cumulative remittance of profits (up to 12%, net of tax, on the imported and non-repatriated capital), remittance of interest (up to 10%) are the main advantages of this law which is endowed with constitutional power (i.e. neither this law nor the ministerial approval can be amended even by legislation). All major investments made in Greece have been protected under this law. Despite the liberalization of capital movements in accordance with the Treaty of Rome (P.D. 207/1987), these privileges will still have limited significance for investors from EEC countries (escape clauses to be claimed by Greece will not affect L.D. 2687/1953 approvals). Recently, investors from third countries have been also vested with the right to remit the profits from their future direct investments, following approval by the currency authorities (Bank of Greece). Still, though, the provisions of L.D. 2687/1953 will maintain their importance in the above cases in view of the increased security and secondary additional benefits they offer to the investor.

## Bibliography

There are few general works in the Greek language about taxation, while there are many works pertaining to special parts of tax law (stamp tax, transfer tax, tax data code etc.) with practical orientation. There are also many loose-leaf publications following up legislation and cases. The 'Bulletin of Tax Legislation' (Δελτίο Φορολογικής Νομοθεσίας) is a fortnightly review of tax legislation and judicial decisions as well as of administrative practice. A selection of books follows.

J. Anastopoulos, *Tax Law* (1983).
J. Anastopoulos, *Public Subsidies of the Economy* (1982).
J. Dryllerakis, *Incentives for Industrial Investments* (1979).
J. Dryllerakis, *Investment and Protection of Foreign Capital* (1975).
C. Finokaliotis, *Constitutional Guarantees of Legality and Certainty of Taxes and of Prohibition of the Retroactivity of Tax Laws* (1984).
M. Kypraios, *Elements of Tax Law* (1980).
E. Papadopoulos, *Tax Data Code*, vols. I–III (1980).
J. Photopoulos, *Tax on Real Estate and Ship Transfers*, vols. I–III (1979–1983).
L. Theocharopoulos, *Tax Law. General Part* (1981).
N. and C. Totsis, *Income Taxation*, vols. I–III (1984).
N. Vilos, *Tax Data Code* (1966).

Works in English and other languages on special subjects can be found in the 'Cahiers de Droit Fiscal International' of the International Fiscal Association. There is a BNA Tax Management Portfolio on Greece which is kept reasonably current. Reference should also be made to the various '*Doing Business in Greece*' guides published and updated by the major accounting firms.

# Chapter 18
# Criminal Law and Procedure

*Dionysios D. Spinellis**

## I. Historical Development and Sources

During the Greek War of Independence (1821–1829), a first effort was made to draw up a codified law governing criminal matters (1823). However, this resulted in a rather unsystematic and incomplete enactment, which was applied only for a short period. It was replaced by the Penal Law of 1833 and the Criminal Procedure Act of 1834. After being applied for more than a century and amended several times, these two Codes were in their turn replaced by the Penal Code and the Code of Criminal Procedure of 1950 which entered into force on January 1, 1951.

Apart from these two codifications, however, a great number of special statutes containing penal provisions exist. Among them is the Code of Traffic Regulations, the Code of Market Regulations, the Military Penal Code, several laws governing labor matters, the laws on drugs, firearms, antiquities, etc. According to the statistics (1985), out of the total number of recent convictions for crimes and misdemeanors, a substantial majority (83.6%) concerned offenses criminalized in such special statutes.

The Greek Penal Code, following the continental European tradition, is divided into a General Part and a Special Part. While the former includes the provisions applicable to all offenses or to abstract categories of them, the latter comprises the definitions of the various offenses and the penal sanctions provided for each of them. It should be noted that the provisions of the General Part are applicable also to the offenses provided in the special penal statutes, unless otherwise provided in them (art. 12 P.C.).

## II. Substantive Criminal Law

### *A. General Principles*

#### 1. The Two Functions of Criminal Law

Greek criminal law, as well as the similar laws of other countries, is meant to

* Professor of Law, Panteios School of Political Science.

have two functions. Its primary function is to protect the legal interests of the individual and of the community from certain harmful forms of behavior. It is considered that penal provisions can achieve this goal first by influencing the public at large so that it will abstain from such forms of behavior (general prevention: deterrence, moral and social education); then by deterring the individual perpetrator of a criminal offense in various ways (special prevention: individual intimidation, reform, rehabilitation, incapacitation) so that he will not commit any more offenses in the future.

It is obvious that this function of the penal law corresponds to relative and utilitarian theories of punishment. However, retribution, although not considered as the purpose of punishment, is recognized as useful upper limit to it: penalty for an offense shall not exceed the proportions of what is deemed a just retribution for it. This limit must be taken into consideration both by the legislator when introducing penal provisions and by the courts when imposing penal sanctions.

The second function of the penal law is a derivative one: while criminal punishment is considered as having the greatest coercive leverage, it is also the most painful means of coercion. Therefore, Greek penal law includes a series of guaranties to protect the individual from abuses connected with the exercise of its primary function. The most important such guaranty is the principle 'nullum crimen, nulla poena sine lege'.

## 2. The 'Nullum Crimen, Nulla Poena Sine Lege' Principle

This principle is consecrated in article 7 I of the Greek Constitution of 1975, and it is also included in article 1 of the Penal Code. The constitutional provision reads as follows: 'There shall be no crime nor shall punishment be inflicted unless provided by law in force prior to the perpetration of the act, defining the constitutive elements of the act. In no case shall punishment more severe than that provided at the time of the perpetration of the act be inflicted.' From this provision, the following more specific principles are deduced:

(*a*) A penal law must be a written (statutory) law. No penalty may be based on customary law or on judge-made law. This is no obstacle, however, to the free interpretation of statutes by the courts.

(*b*) No penalty may be imposed in application by analogy of a penal law not directly applicable to the particular case.

(*c*) No penalty may be imposed on the basis of a penal law not describing specifically the criminal behavior and not providing the applicable penal sanctions within upper and lower limits.

(*d*) Penal laws have no retroactive effect.

It should be noted that while criminal liability cannot be founded or made more severe where the above principles do not permit, it may be excluded or mitigated even if the conditions under (*a*)–(*d*) are not fulfilled: grounds for exclusion or mitigation of criminal liability may be based on custom, on inference by analogy, and on retroactive recent laws. It is expressly provided (art. 2) that if between the perpetration of a criminal act and the final judgment on it more than one legal rule was in effect, the most lenient one shall be applied.

## *B. The Structure of the Criminal Offense*

### 1. The Definition and Elements of an Offense

Article 14 I of the Penal Code defines a criminal offense in the following way: an offense is (a) an act, (b) illegal, (c) imputable to the offender, and (d) punishable under the law. We are going to discuss these elements below.

### 2. An Act or Omission

As act is considered any external and voluntary human conduct. Therefore, bad thoughts alone cannot constitute a crime. Since the conduct must be human, an offense cannot be committed by or attributed to a legal entity such as a corporation. The law specifies that the term 'act' includes also omissions (art. 14 II). Some statutory crimes are specifically defined as omissions to act, e.g., failure to save someone's life (art. 307). In other cases, the statute requires a certain result, for example the death of a person; then the criminal conduct may not be an active one which caused the result but also a failure to prevent it whenever the offender had a special legal duty to act (art. 15). For instance, failure to save a child's life may constitute a murder if the defendant had such a duty based upon statute, contract, voluntary assumption of care, or the creation of a peril.

### 3. An Outline of the Method of Analysis

Greek criminal law theory, like that in some other countries, is characterized by a tripartite analysis. Whether an act or omission may be a criminal offense must be examined from three different viewpoints in three consecutive steps:

First, does it fall within the definition of a statutory offense and thus constitute *prima facie* an offense? If it does, in the second step it is examined whether a justification exists in which case the analysis stops here. A prosecutor would not prosecute the person concerned, a court would acquit him. If no justification exists, then the act or omission is considered illegal. An illegal act is not necessarily a punishable one, as we will see, but the illegality may have other legal consequences; for instance it may be countered with self-defense; or the offender, although he is not criminally responsible by reason of insanity, may be committed to a mental institution; or it is a condition for accomplice liability. In the third step, the analysis is focused on the person of the offender in order to find whether any grounds exist which exclude his imputability or his guilt.

To the above basic three steps a fourth one may be added in which it is examined whether any grounds exist which prevent punishment even for a complete criminal offense, such as statute of limitations, immunity or amnesty.

## 4. Justification

The Penal Code includes several grounds of justification, some of which are provided in the General Part and others in the Special Part. The most important ones are:

(*a*) Exercise of right or of legal duty (art. 20): An act is justified if it consists in the exercise of a right (e.g., the right of the possessor, provided by the law, to recover a stolen object) or of a legal duty (e.g., the duty of a police officer to use reasonable force to make a lawful arrest).

(*b*) Self-defense or defense of another: Under article 22, an act constituting *prima facie* an offense is justified if it was necessary to defend the person or the property of the perpetrator or of another person against an unjustified and present aggression. The amount of force permitted to be used against the aggressor depends on the value of the threatened harm, the degree of danger and other circumstances. If the perpetrator exceeded the above limits of defense, he is punished. In the event that the excess was intentional, the punishment is that for the offense committed, mitigated according to article 83. If it was due to negligence, then the offense is punished to the extent that such an offense is punishable when committed by negligence (art. 23). But if the perpetrator intentionally provoked the aggression in order to commit the offense under the pretext of self-defense, he is subjected to the normal penalty for this offense.

(*c*) Necessity justifying the act (art. 25): An act is justified if committed in order to prevent a harm threatening, through no fault of the perpetrator, his person or his property or those of some other persons. The harm prevented must be substantially greater than the one produced by his act. If the perpetrator exceeded the limits of harm permitted, the provision pertaining to excess of defense (see above, under (*b*)) applies also here.

(*d*) An order of a superior justifies the act of an inferior civil servant or soldier, if and to the extent that the law does not permit him to examine the legality of the order. In such a case, only the superior is punished (art. 21).

(*e*) The consent of the victim in some cases negates an element of the offense, and then not even a *prima facie* offense exists: for example illegal imprisonment, rape or theft. In other cases, the consent of the victim has no influence at all on the legal situation, for example in a murder or a serious bodily injury. But there are some offenses where the consent of the victim justifies the *prima facie* offense. The Penal Code provides this rule expressly only with respect to the simple bodily injury (art. 308 II); it is also applied by analogy to other offenses where the victim can dispose of the legal interest protected, for example defamation, verbal injury or intentional damage to property.

## 5. Imputability and Guilt

According to the Greek doctrine, imputability (καταλογισμός, katalogismos) is a judgment by which a person is blamed for something and therefore he is disapproved and becomes personally responsible for his act. Guilt (ενοχή, enochi) is called whatever circumstance, concerning the person of the offender, justifies such a disapproval.

In Greek criminal law, the 'principle of imputability' or 'principle of guilt' is of great importance. It is based on article 2 I of the Constitution which obligates the state to respect and protect human dignity. By this principle, no penalty may be imposed for a criminal offense unless the offender can be blamed for such offense. Therefore Greek criminal law does not recognize any cases of strict or absolute liability.

## 6. The Elements of Imputability

The prevailing classification in the Greek criminal law doctrine includes three elements within the realm of imputability:

(*a*) Capacity to appreciate and conform.
(*b*) Mental culpability (subjective fault).
(*c*) Possibility to behave differently, or lack of reasons of excuse.

### (*a*) *Capacity to Appreciate and Conform*

Two tests are included here: first the defendant's capacity to appreciate the illegality of his act, and second his capacity to conform his conduct to the requirements of the laws in case he appreciated them.

(*i*) Minors: The law takes for granted that children of up to twelve years of age have not the above capacities, therefore they are not criminally responsible. However, children of seven to twelve years may be subjected to educative or therapeutic measures (art. 126; see below, under D 2). Adolescents of twelve to seventeen years of age are also presumed not to have the above capacities and, as a rule, only educative and therapeutic measures may be imposed to them. But the court may judge that they are criminally responsible; in that case it imposes to them a special penalty: confinement in a correctional institution (art. 127).

(*ii*) Adults: With respect to adults, the opposite presumption applies. They are deemed criminally responsible, except in the cases provided in the law. These cases may concern also minors, but the minority as we have seen is in itself a ground against criminal responsibility. The exceptional cases are:

- mental insanity (psychosis, neurosis, organic brain disorder, congenital intellectual deficiency),

- disturbance of conscience (unconsciousness, semiconsciousness, intoxication), or
- deaf-muteness,

provided that, due to one of these conditions, the offender was deprived of the capacity to appreciate the illegality of his act or to conform his conduct to the requirements of the law where he appreciated such illegality (arts. 33, 34).

### (*b*) *Mental Culpability*

Culpability is the state of mind of the offender toward his offense, due to which he is considered as its mental cause. Greek criminal law provides two basic forms of culpability: intention and negligence.

(*i*) Intention

The intention comprises the offender's knowledge of the material elements of a criminal offense (physical conduct, result, circumstances) and his will or acceptance that his act causes the consequences included in these elements (art. 27). Physical elements of the crime and state of mind must concur at the same time. If the knowledge at this time does not include certain elements, then a mistake of fact exists (see below, under (*iii*)).

The will to produce the consequences may show the following variations:

- Intent or purpose: The offender aims at causing the consequences (e.g., A shoots B in order to kill him).
- Acceptance by the offender of a consequence as necessary by-product of his intended act (e.g., A places a time bomb in an airplane in order to kill B, accepting also to kill all the other passengers).
- Acceptance of consequence as possible by-product of his intended conduct (art. 27 II: e.g., A burns his own building with intent to defraud an insurance company; he accepts the possibility that an invalid living there may perish).

As a rule, in all offenses which by definition must be committed with intention any of the three variations is sufficient. In some offenses, however, the law requires only the first, or the first and the second variations.

(*ii*) Negligence

According to article 28 of the Penal Code, negligence consists in lack of care or circumspection, because of which the offender

- either did not foresee at all the consequence of his conduct (negligence without realization of risk);
- or he foresaw this consequence as possible but he trusted that it would not occur (negligence with realization of risk).

When negligence as a state of mind exists, it is accompanied by a violation of a standard of conduct.

The law sets two criteria for care and circumspection. First, the due care and circumspection according to the circumstances. Thereby, the rules and standards of the average diligent person in the relevant branch of social activity are taken into account. If the offender has shown such amount of care and circumspection, no negligence exists. Any harm caused in spite of his care is considered as fortuitous.

If, however, the offender has fallen below such standards, then it must be examined whether he could have complied with them in view of his personal circumstances and capabilities. If he could not, then he is not responsible (e.g., a surgeon during an operation is required to use all antiseptic means; but if he makes an urgent operation at the site of an accident where no such measures are available, he cannot be considered as negligent).

(*iii*) Ignorance or Mistake of Fact

As we have mentioned, if the offender did not have knowledge of certain facts or circumstances which constitute material elements of the offense committed by him, he has no intention; therefore his offense cannot be imputed to him as an intentional offense (art. 30). If he knew the elements of the basic form of an offense but not the additional elements which make it an aggravated form of it, only the basic form is imputed to him; e.g., A knows that he is entering a building without being entitled to and steals. He ignores, however, that this building is a church or a museum. Therefore he is responsible for simple theft (art. 372), and not for aggravated theft (art. 374).

If the ignorance of the elements of an offense may be attributed to the negligence of the perpetrator, then he is responsible for an offense by negligence, if such an offense is provided in the law; for example, A shoots B who is working in a garden, thinking that he is game. He is not liable for intentional homicide but he may be liable for criminal negligence manslaughter.

### (*c*) *Human Possibility to Comply with the Law*

The impossibility of an offender (i) to appreciate the illegality of his act and (ii) to conform his conduct to the requirements of the law may be due to the particular circumstances of each case.

(*i*) Appreciation of the Illegality – Ignorance or Mistake of Law

According to article 31 I of the Penal Code, the fact that the perpetrator just did not know that his act is punishable under the law does not exclude the imputability and therefore is not a defense. The imputability is excluded only when the offender due to ignorance or mistake believed that it was permitted to him to commit the offense. The law provides, however, that this ignorance or mistake must be excusable (art. 30 II). Whether this is the case is usually judged according to the circumstances.

(*ii*) Possibility to Conform: Grounds of Excuse

A perpetrator who is generally capable to appreciate the illegality of his act and to conform his conduct to the requirements of the law, may commit a criminal act because exceptionally he was operating under certain circumstances which created in him such a mental or emotional condition that he could not be expected to behave differently. The Penal Code does not include a general rule governing such conditions but only provides for certain typical situations which usually create such a mental or emotional condition. In these situations, it is 'presumed' that the perpetrator could not behave differently. The most important of such cases are the following:

(*aa*) *Necessity as an Excuse (art. 32)*
A perpetrator is excused and the act is not imputed to him if it was committed in order to prevent a harm threatening, through no fault of such perpetrator, the person or the property of himself or of a close relative. The harm prevented must be in this case not disproportionate to the one caused. As we see, the necessity as an excuse differs from the necessity as a justification (see above, under 4 (*c*)) as to the circle of the persons threatened by harm and as to the proportion between harm caused and harm prevented.

(*bb*) *Excusable Excess of the Limits of Defense*
Under article 23 II, if the excess of the limits of defense (see above, under 4 (*b*)) was the result of fear or confusion caused to the perpetrator by the attack, such excess is not imputed to him and he is not punished.

### 7. Grounds for Non-Punishment

An act which is punishable under the law, illegal and imputable to the offender is a criminal offense. The person who committed it may be prosecuted and punished. However, the law provides several grounds under which this is not done. A general reason for abstaining from punishment in the relevant cases is that such punishment would not be socially necessary, or that it may be contrary to other social expediencies. Some of these grounds are:

(*a*) Grounds relevant to the important office of the offender, e.g., certain immunities of the President of the Republic or of members of Parliament.

(*b*) Grounds extinguishing the right of the state to punish. These are: (i) the statute of limitations, (ii) the voluntary desisting from an attempt, (iii) practical repentance after the crime (e.g., return of stolen property), (iv) amnesty, and (v) waiver of complaint. It should be noted that, although the prosecution of offenses is in Greece mandatory, in some cases a complaint of the victim is a necessary condition of the prosecution. If it is not submitted within three months, the right to punish is extinguished.

## *C. Special Forms of Crime*

Greek criminal law doctrine considers (1) the attempt (uncompleted crime) and (2) the accomplice liability (more parties to a crime) as special forms in which a crime may appear. As a third such form is considered the accumulation of offenses which leads to concurrent sentences, and is discussed below, under D 3.

### 1. Attempt

Article 42 of the Penal Code provides that the attempt (απόπειρα, apopeira) of any felony or misdemeanor (see below, under D 1) is punishable by a reduced penalty (art. 83). The attempt presupposes an intent to commit an offense and an act which may be considered as (only) the commencement of such offense. Therefore, an attempt is not conceivable in the offenses by negligence. Under article 43 of the Penal Code, in case of factual impossibility (e.g., shooting with intent to kill while the victim was already dead) the penalty is further reduced; but if the impossibility was due to the stupidity of the perpetrator (e.g., attempting to kill by using magic words) the attempt is not punished.

With respect to the abandonment of an attempted offense the law provides that the offender is not punished if he has started an act toward the commission of the offense but he abandoned it on his own free will (moral motives are not necessary) and not due to external obstacles. If, however, the offender has finished his act but later he prevented the harmful consequence which was part of the offense, he is punished by the penalty of the attempt once more reduced; but the court may even decide not to punish (art. 45).

### 2. Accomplices

Greek criminal law follows the system of the distinction between principals and accessories. The parties to a crime provided in the law are the following:

(*a*) The principal or actor (αυτουργόος, autourgos), who committed in whole or in part the act or omission constituting the offense as defined in the law. There can be more than one principals (art. 45).

(*b*) The instigator of a principal (ηθικός αυτουργός, ithikos autourgos), who has intentionally brought about the decision of the principal to commit the crime (art. 46), for example the person who paid a professional killer to commit a murder.

(*c*) The direct accessory (άμεσος συνεργός, amesos synergos), who intentionally assisted the actor directly in and during the commission of the crime.

(*d*) The simple accessory (απλός συνεργός, aplos synergos), who intentionally aided another in any way before or during the commission of the offense.

The accomplice liability of the persons (*b*)–(*d*) depends on the commission by the principal of an illegal act, punishable under the law but not necessarily imputable to the offender. Therefore accomplices are liable even if the offender is not punished due to mental insanity, mistake of law, or a ground of excuse (cf. art. 48). The persons (*a*)–(*c*) are punishable with the same penalty, i.e. the one provided in the law for the principal. The simple accessory is punished by a lesser penalty.

## *D. Penal Sanctions*

The Greek Penal Code follows a bifurcated system of sanctions, which includes penalties and security measures. Penalties are imposed only to criminally responsible offenders for offenses imputable to them. Measures of security are imposed first, as substitutes of penalties, to persons who are not criminally responsible, and second, to persons criminally responsible in addition to penalties (supplementary measures). The reason for imposing measures of security is the danger emanating from certain persons or objects.

## 1. Penalties (ποινές, poines)

The following main penalties are recognized:

(*a*) The death penalty (arts. 50 and 86). It is provided for few very serious offenses and – with one exception – alternatively with term for life. The death penalty may be imposed only if the circumstances of the offense show it to be especially hideous, or if the offender is dangerous to public safety. It should be noted that since 1972 no capital punishment has been executed in Greece. It is also imposed very rarely. Article 116 of the Correctional Code provides that a death penalty not executed within three years after the judgment becomes unchallengeable is automatically converted into a term for life. The presently governing party has declared its intention to abolish the death penalty also formally, but this has not materialized so far (December 1987).

(*b*) Custodial penalties. These are: (i) term for life; (ii) temporary term (5–20 years); (iii) imprisonment (ten days to five years); and (iv) jailing (one day to one month). The law provides also certain special custodial penalties for habitual criminals, for dangerous criminals with reduced criminal responsibility, and for adolescents.

(*c*) Pecuniary penalties. There are two kinds: (i) the pecuniary penalty (2,000–1,000,000 drs.) and (ii) the fine (350–10,000 drs.)

(*d*) Supplementary penalties. They presuppose always a main penalty. They are the following: (i) the deprivation of civil rights (permanent or temporary); (ii) the prohibition to exercise a profession; (iii) the publication of the conviction; (iv) the confiscation of the instruments or products of crime. Special penal laws provide also for certain offenses special penalties, for example the deprivation of the driving license.

On the basis of the penalties threatened against them, offenses are classified into three categories: (i) an offense punishable by death or a term is called felony (κακούργημα, kakourgima); (ii) an offense punishable by imprisonment or pecuniary penalty is called misdemeanor (πλημμέλημα, plimmelima); (iii) an offense punishable by jailing or fine is called petty violation (πταίσμα, ptaisma) (art. 18).

## 2. Measures of Security (μέτρα ασφαλείας, metra asphaleias)

(*a*) Measures of security in substitution for penalties are: (i) the custody of non-criminally responsible but dangerous offenders in psychiatric institutions, (ii) the educative and therapeutic measures applied to minors.

(*b*) Supplementary measures of security are: (i) The reference of alcoholics and drug addicts to a therapeutic institution, (ii) the reference of persons who have an aversion to work and a tendency to an irregular life to a workhouse, (iii) the prohibition of residence in certain areas, (iv) the expulsion of alien criminals after their release from prison, and (v) the confiscation of dangerous objects (e.g., explosives, false money, drugs), irrespective of who is their owner.

### 3. Sentencing

The Penal Code includes several articles providing how a court shall fix the sentence within the limits set forth in the provisions of the Special Part and the special penal laws. The most important of them is article 79 which provides that the court in sentencing must consider: (a) how serious is the offense committed and (b) the personality of the offender. Under each of these two concepts the law states what circumstances must be considered in particular. It is also provided that the court must set forth in its sentence the reasons justifying its decision as to the imposed punishment (art. 79 IV). In practice, however, the Supreme Court has held that a general mention of the terms used by the law is sufficient without any specific reference to particular circumstances.

According to article 82 of the Penal Code, all custodial penalties not exceeding six months as a rule must be converted into pecuniary penalties. The court may do the same with respect to penalties of up to eighteen months, if it judges that the defendant's incarceration is not necessary. The courts apply these possibilities in most cases, so that out of the custodial sentences only approximately 3% are executed in prisons.

Articles 99–104 of the Penal Code provide for the suspension of sentences of first-offenders which do no exceed eighteen months. Such suspension is granted in approximately 12% of cases. Articles 88 and 93 define a recidivist as a person who, after being convicted for a felony or misdemeanor to a certain punishment, commits a new such offense within a certain period of time provided in the law. To recidivists are imposed more severe punishments according to certain scales.

In case of accumulated offenses (more than one distinct offenses, committed either by a single act or by several acts) for which the court must pass concurrent sentences, article 94 of the Penal Code provides the following procedure: After determining the sentence for each one of them, the court proceeds to fix a compound sentence, which is composed of the severest of the concurrent sentences (or one of them in case they are equal), increased in consideration of the others according to a certain scale in the case of several acts; while in the case of more offenses by a single act the court increases according to its discretion the severest sentence up to the maximum limit of the relevant kind of penalty (e.g., the total imprisonment may be increased up to five years).

*E. Special Part*

In this section, some characteristics of certain important offenses provided in the Special Part are discussed.

1. Homicide (ανθρωποκσονία, anthropoktonia)

Article 299 of the Penal Code provides for two forms of intentional homicide:
(*a*) Murder and
(*b*) Heat-of-passion homicide.

The murder is characterized only by the lack of heat of passion. Other criteria, such as premeditation or immoral motives, do not exist under Greek law. We should keep in mind, however, the 'hideous act' circumstances provided in article 86 as a condition for imposing the death penalty.

The law provides further for the following mitigated forms of homicide:

(*c*) Homicide with consent of the victim (art. 300). This provision is applied only if the offender acted after a serious and persistent demand of the victim, who was incurably suffering, and out of compassion for such victim.

(*d*) Accomplice to a suicide (art. 301). The offender is punished if he persuaded or assisted another to commit or attempt suicide.

(*e*) Infanticide (art. 303). The offender must be a mother who intentionally kills her child during the childbirth, or after it but during the period of disturbance of her organism due to such childbirth.

(*f*) Homicide by negligence (art. 302). On the concept of negligence see above, Section II B 6 (*b*) (*ii*). According to a recent amendment (1984), it is provided that if the victim was a close relative of the defendant, the court may not impose a punishment if it judges that due to pain and suffering from this loss no such punishment is necessary (art. 302 II).

2. Abortion (άμβλωση, amvlosi)

Abortion may be committed (a) by a pregnant woman herself or by another person acting (b) with or (c) without her consent. The most serious punishment is provided in the last case, and the most lenient one in the first case (art. 304 I–III).

The abortion is justified, provided that it is performed in a hospital by competent medical doctors, in the following cases (art. 304 IV):

(*a*) without any indication, if it takes place before twelve weeks of pregnancy are completed,

(*b*) when indications of serious anomalies of the embryo exist, which may result in the birth of a pathological infant, and the pregnancy has not lasted for more than twenty-four weeks,

(*c*) in the case of medical indications, i.e. when an abortion is performed in order to avert an otherwise unavoidable danger to the life of the pregnant woman or a serious danger to her bodily or mental health; the necessity of the abortion must be certified by a specialist medical doctor,

(*d*) in the cases of criminological indications, i.e. if the pregnancy is a result of a criminal act, such as rape, incest, seduction of a minor under fifteen years, and the pregnancy has not completed nineteen weeks.

It should be noted that, while cases (*c*) and (*d*) were already included in the original text of the Penal Code, case (*b*) has been first provided by Law 821/1978 and case (*a*) was introduced only recently by Law 1609/1986.

### 3. Bodily Injury (σωματική βλάβη, somatiki vlavi)

Bodily injury is defined in the law as bodily harm or detriment to health (art. 308).

The law distinguishes the following forms: (a) simple bodily injury, which may be justified by the consent of the victim, provided that it is not against good morals (art. 308), (b) unprovoked and (c) dangerous bodily injury, in which forms the circumstances of commission are taken into account (arts. 308A and 309); (d) severe bodily injury (e.g., serious sickness, amputation); as a rule, it is not required that this result was intended by the offender; it is sufficient that he intended simple injury but was negligent as to the further result; if, however, the result was intended, then the offense is punishable as a felony (term of five to ten years), (e) deadly bodily injury; intended injury plus negligence as to its fatal result is the characteristic of this form and its difference from intentional homicide, (f) bodily injury by negligence; it should be noted that also here (cf. above under 1 (*f*)) the court may refrain from punishment (art. 314).

### 4. Torture (βασανιστήρια, vasanistiria)

In conformity with article 7 II of the Constitution and with article 4 of the U.N. 1984 Convention Against Torture and Other Cruel, Inhuman or Degrading Treatment or Punishment, Law 1500/1984 has introduced in the Penal Code articles 137A–137D by which torture as such is criminalized. An act of torture is defined as any systematic infliction of acute physical pain, or of physical exhaustion endangering the health of a person, or of mental suffering leading to severe physical injury, as well as any illegal use of chemicals, drugs, or other natural or artificial means capable of bending the victim's will (art. 137A II). The offender must be a public official or anybody who has usurped public duties (art. 137A I).

As aggravated forms of torture are provided the cases in which certain methods of torture are used, or the acts of torture resulted in the death or serious bodily harm of the victim, or the offender has committed such acts habitually, or he gave orders to others to commit them in his capacity as their superior (art. 137B). It is further provided that the state of emergency or a superior's order do not justify any acts of torture (art. 137D I and II).

### 5. Theft (κλοπή, klopi)

Under article 372 of the Penal Code, theft commits he who takes from another's possession movable property (including any forms of energy) belonging to another, with intent unlawfully to appropriate such property. An aggravated form of theft exists if the stolen property is of especially high value. More aggravated forms amounting to felonies are thefts of certain objects (e.g., used for religious worship from churches, works of art from museums) or by certain persons (e.g., habitual or professional criminals).

### 6. Embezzlement (υπεξαίρεση, ypexairesi)

Embezzlement is the unlawful appropriation of movable property belonging to another person, which had come to the possession of the offender in any (lawful) way (art. 375). The law further provides that object of embezzlement can also be the substitute of an object or money which were entrusted to the offender by the victim with instructions to sell, purchase or exchange them.

### 7. Fraud (απάτη, apati)

Fraud commits he who persuades another person to act or to omit or to tolerate an act by representing false facts as true or by illegally concealing or suppressing true facts, and this causes damage to the property of another with intent to enrich himself or a third person unlawfully (art. 386 I). The person persuaded and the person damaged need not be the same. The fraud, which is normally a misdemeanor, becomes a felony if committed as a profession or habitually or under circumstances proving that the offender is especially dangerous (art. 386 III).

## III. Criminal Procedure

The Greek criminal justice system is based on the continental tradition. The structure of authority may be considered as 'hierarchical', and criminal procedure is often characterized as following a 'mixed' model. It would be more accurate to say that, although basically investigatory, it has also strong adversarial elements, perhaps stronger than in other Continental countries. We are going to discuss first the institutions and the persons involved in criminal proceedings and then to give an outline of the procedure.

## *A. Institutions*

### 1. The Criminal Courts

Greek criminal courts are classified according to two principles. First, according to their competence with respect to categories of offenses. Crimes are divided into felonies, misdemeanors and petty violations (see above, Section II D 1). Therefore:

(*a*) The following courts are competent to adjudicate felonies:

(*i*) The mixed court (composed of judges and jurors) which tries the most usual felonies such as murder, severe bodily injury, rape, etc.

(*ii*) The (three-member and, at second instance, also five-member) court of appeal. Although initially it was only an appellate court, now it is also competent to try several felonies which present complex legal problems, such as aggravated theft, fraud, forgery and drug offenses.

(*b*) Misdemeanors are tried before the two misdemeanor courts (one-member and three-member), sharing this competence according to the gravity of the offenses.

(*c*) For petty violations is competent the petty violations court.

(*d*) All offenses committed by children and adolescents are tried before the juvenile courts.

The second principle according to which authority is allocated is based on the distinction between first instance and second instance courts. Most criminal offenses may be tried *de novo* twice, once at each level. Some criminal courts judge only as first or only as second instance courts, but most of them alternate both functions. The Supreme Court (Ἄρειος Πάγος, Areios Pagos) is competent to judge on appeals for error of law from most of the lower criminal courts (see below, under C 4 (*c*) (*ii*)).

### 2. The Public Prosecutor's Office

The public prosecutor (εισαγγελέας, eisangeleas) is competent to press charges for criminal offenses and to represent the state throughout all stages of the proceedings. Before any decision of a criminal court, the public prosecutor must be heard. He may submit applications, make motions, he pleads at the end of the trial, and he may lodge appeals. Since he has the same rights as the parties to the proceedings, he may be considered as a party in the formal sense of the term. However, he is not a party in the substantive sense since he does not represent interests contrary to those of the other parties. He is considered as an objective authority, concerned only with finding the truth and with the proper application of the law. Therefore, he may summon also witnesses for the defense (art. 327 I C. Crim. Proc.), he may plead in favor of the defendant, make a motion for his acquittal, and lodge appeals in his favor.

The public prosecutor's office is characterized by the following principles:

(*a*) Indivisibility: The office is represented each time by one of its members, but it functions as an indivisible entity. Therefore, any act performed by one incumbent is considered as act 'of the office'.

(*b*) The second principle, 'hierarchical subordination', correlates logically with the other. The office is organized in three levels corresponding to the organization of the courts. Each prosecutor has a deputy who is bound to follow his instructions, and each prosecutor likewise the instructions of those at higher levels. To a certain extent, the office is bound to follow the instructions of the Minister of Justice. However, this subordination is limited in two respects: (i) By the principle of legality, which does not allow an inferior prosecutor to carry out an order which he deems illegal; (ii) as to the expression of personal conviction: while a subordinate is bound to act according to the instructions of his superior (e.g., to press charges or to lodge an appeal), when he submits a motion or pleads he is free to express his own personal opinion.

## *B. Persons Involved in Criminal Proceedings*

### 1. The Judiciary

Criminal justice is administered not only by judicial officers (see above, Ch. 15, Section II A 2–3) but also by jurors. The jury system, which had been introduced in Greece in 1834 for certain offenses, was abolished in 1968 and replaced by the mixed courts. There are two types of such courts composed of four jurors and three judges each. They are competent to try felonies, the one as first and the other as second instance court. All members of the court decide jointly on all questions.

### 2. The Parties

As explained above, the prosecutor only in the formal sense is a party to the criminal proceedings; the only real parties in every respect are the defendant, the civil claimant and the third party with civil liability.

#### *(a) The Defendant* (κατηγορούμενος, katigoroumenos)

The defendant has a series of rights, some of which are guaranteed by the Constitution. The most important ones are:

(*i*) The general right to be heard (art. 20 Const.).

(*ii*) The right to appear with counsel and communicate with him both in the pretrial phase and during the trial (arts. 100 and 340 C. Crim. Proc.).

(*iii*) When the defendant appears before the investigating judge or before the court, he must be clearly notified of the charges, and his rights must be explained (arts. 103 and 273 II C. Crim. Proc.). In the pretrial phase, the defendant has the right to review the file and to receive copies of the documents contained in it (art. 101 C. Crim. Proc.).

(*iv*) When he is summoned to an investigation, he may ask for forty-eight hours (which may be extended) to prepare his defense, which he may submit in writing.

(*v*) The right to remain silent both in the pretrial phase and during the trial (arts. 273 II b and 366 II b C. Crim. Proc.).

(*vi*) The right to put questions to witnesses, experts etc., to make comments and applications and raise objections (arts. 99, 349, 126 C. Crim. Proc.).

(*vii*) The defendant is also entitled to defend himself at the end of the trial (art. 366 C. Crim. Proc.), and to speak last, either personally or through his counsel (art. 369 III C. Crim. Proc.).

(*viii*) Finally, he may appeal against the decisions of courts and councils.

#### *(b) The Civil Claimant* (πολιτικώς ενάγων, politikos enagon)

The civil claimant is the victim of the crime, the natural person or legal entity which has been directly damaged by it, e.g., the proprietor of a stolen object, he who suffered bodily harm, but also the survivors of a murdered person.

Such persons may participate in the criminal proceedings and pursue a civil claim for (i) reparation of the damages, or (ii) an indemnity for non-pecuniary damage, for example to their reputation, or pain and suffering (art. 63 C. Crim. Proc.). They must announce their appearance in the proceedings either during the pretrial phase or at the trial (art. 82 C. Crim. Proc.). If the claims as presented are not founded on the law, the other parties may ask that they be dismissed. The civil claimant has in many respects the same rights as the defendant, but his right to appeal is limited.

#### *(c) The Third Party with Civil Liability* (αστικώς υπεύθυνος, astikos ypeuthynos)

This is a person who, although not criminally liable for the offense, is bound to pay damages or indemnities or the pecuniary penalties and expenses; for example, if the defendant is a civil servant and the offense constitutes a serious violation of his duties, then the state may be summoned in the proceedings as third party with civil liability. That party has the same rights as the civil claimant. However, the participation of such a party is rather rare in practice.

## *C. Outline of the Procedure*

### 1. The Stages and the Principles

The criminal proceedings begin when charges are pressed and end always by a decision of a court or a judicial council. The proceedings are distinguished into the pretrial stage and the trial. Since each stage has a different goal, it is also governed by different principles. However, there are certain basic principles which are common to all stages of the procedure. These are:

(*a*) The aim of all stages is the search for the substantive truth. In criminal proceedings no 'presumed' or 'formal' truths exist (as they exist in civil proceedings, for example the full proof based on the confession of a party, the presumptions based on the absence of a party from the hearings, etc.).

(*b*) Thus, the search for the truth is made *ex officio*. Both the investigating officials (art. 239 II C. Crim. Proc.) and the court (art. 352 IV C. Crim. Proc.) have the power and the duty to seek the truth by all adequate means.

## 2. The Pretrial Stage

The pretrial stage aims at finding and securing the necessary evidence, so that it may be decided whether a person must be brought to trial for a certain crime (art. 239 C. Crim. Proc.). The principles governing it are the secrecy and the written procedure. No public hearings take place, but all investigating acts occur in the office of the competent official, written documents are submitted and records are kept. The public prosecutor of the first instance court is competent to press charges after receiving information about a criminal offense. The usual sources of such information are a complaint of the victim, a denunciation by a citizen, a report from another authority, etc. If the information included in the above documents is based on the law and not manifestly unfounded as to the facts, the public prosecutor is bound to press charges. The principle governing his activity is the mandatory prosecution (or principle of legality).

The initiation of criminal proceedings is effected by ordering one of the following procedures: (i) a summary investigation by a magistrate or a police officer under the supervision of the prosecutor, (ii) an 'ordinary' investigation carried out by a regular judge, or (iii) referring the case directly to trial. The last mentioned procedure is followed when the offenses are not severe and the facts clear. The ordinary investigation is mandatory when the offense is a felony, when the offender must be arrested and detained, or when the summary investigation needs completion. In all other cases, the summary investigation procedure is followed.

During the investigation (procedures under (i) and (ii)), witnesses are examined, expertises made, house search and local inspections effected, etc. Of particular importance is the possibility to detain temporarily the defendant, or to impose on him various conditions restricting his freedom of movement, for example the prohibition to go to or leave a certain place. Detention or the other restrictions are only ordered with respect to serious offenses, when sufficient grounds of suspicion exist, and provided that one of the following conditions is fulfilled: the defendant is suspect of fleeing, or especially dangerous, or in general there is a danger that more crimes will be committed. Especially the temporary detention of the defendant must be used only when it is absolutely necessary, i.e. as a last resort. The duration of such a detention cannot exceed eighteen months in cases of felonies and nine months in cases of misdemeanors.

### 3. Procedure Before the Judicial Councils

When the summary investigation procedures are completed, the prosecutor either refers the case to trial or to an ordinary investigation or, if he believes that there is not sufficient evidence for a trial, he refers the case to the judicial council (δικαστικό συμβούλιο, dikastiko symvoulio) with a motion to acquit without trial. When the ordinary investigation is completed, the case must be referred to the judicial council with a motion either to refer the case to trial or to acquit for various reasons.

The judicial council is a panel of judges deciding *in camera*. Their decisions must be reasoned like the decisions in public trials. The further procedure before the judicial councils is similar to the one before courts: appeals from the first instance council lie to the judicial council of appeal. Against the decisions in both instances an appeal for error of law before the Supreme Court is possible.

### 4. The Main Proceedings

#### *(a) The Preparatory Stage*

In this stage the defendant must be served with either a copy of the judicial council's decision referring him to trial or a special document of the prosecutor describing the act he is accused of and the legal provisions governing it. In addition, the defendant is notified in advance by both the prosecutor and the civil claimant of the names of witnesses to be examined, except in cases of minor importance. The defendant, however, is not bound to disclose the witnesses he is going to examine.

#### *(b) The Trial*

In the initial phase, the parties are identified. The defendant in minor cases need not be present but may be represented by his counsel. In misdemeanors, if the defendant is absent he is tried as if he were present, i.e. the court searches *ex officio* for the truth. In felonies, however, as a rule, if the defendant does not appear, the court adjourns and suspends the proceedings until he appears or is arrested.

At first, the prosecutor summarizes the charges. Then the president of the court asks the defendant if he wants to give general information to the court about these charges, reminding him that he will state his defenses himself after the taking of evidence is completed. Then the witnesses are examined. They are asked to say whatever they know on the subject, and then questions are put to them by the president of the court, the other judges, the prosecutor, counsel for the civil claimant, for the third party with civil liability and for the defendant, in that order (art. 357 C. Crim. Proc.). Then the experts' reports are read and the experts may be asked to give certain clarifications. All documents taken into consideration by the court must be read out aloud. The prosecutor and the parties may comment on the evidence, after the latter has been taken (art. 358 C. Crim. Proc.). Finally, the defendant may speak and defend himself. The president, the judges and the prosecutor may ask him questions. The parties may only put questions through the president. The prosecutor and counsel for the parties make their presentations summing up their case. The defendant and his counsel are always granted the last word (art. 369 III C. Crim. Proc.)

When all this is completed, the court retires and deliberates. First is the guilt issue. If the decision is 'guilty', then it is communicated in public and a discussion on the penal sanctions and on the claims of the civil claimant follows. The civil claimant and the third party with civil liability are not allowed to express their opinion on the penal sanctions but only on the claims. The sentence is communicated in public and must be drawn up in writing within eight days after the hearing.

### *(c) Appeals*

There are two kinds of appeals:

(*i*) The appeal *de novo* from the decisions of first instance courts and for any ground related to the law or to the facts; it lies to the courts of second instance. They retry the case, whereby the same procedure as before the former ones applies, with few exceptions. One of them is the prohibition of the *reformatio in peius*: if the appeal has been lodged only by the defendant or by the prosecutor in his favor, then it is not permitted to worsen his position; the decision on appeal must either be more favorable to the defendant or leave the decision of the first instance unchanged. But if the prosecutor or another party had lodged an appeal against the defendant, the court is not bound by this principle.

(*ii*) The appeals for error of law from all criminal courts lie to the Supreme Court. Such appeals are permitted only against certain kinds of decisions and only for a limited number of grounds provided by the law, consisting in errors of the decision or violations of law during the trial (arts. 484 and 510 C. Crim. Proc.). Among them, the wrong interpretation and application of a substantive criminal provision and the lack of the reasons, which reasons are mandatory under the Constitution (art. 93), are of particular importance. If the appeal is sustained, the Supreme Court vacates the decision and then either applies the law properly itself or remands the case for retrial to another court of the same level as the one which had rendered the vacated decision.

### *(d) Double Jeopardy*

If a person was convicted or acquitted through a non-appealable judgment, he may not be prosecuted again for the same acts, even if the latter are now qualified as a different offense (art. 57 C. Crim Proc.); for example if the defendant has been convicted for deadly bodily harm, he may not be prosecuted again for murder. It should be noted, however, that in exceptional cases (such as subsequent discovery that the evidence in the trial was false, or discovery of new evidence) the law provides for the possibility of reopening the case.

## Basic Bibliography

*A. In English*:

The Greek Penal Code, translated by N. B. Lolis with an introduction by G. Mangakis (F. R. Rothman & Co., South Hackensack, N.J., Sweet and Maxwell, London) 1973.

*B. In Greek*:

N. Androulakis, *Penal Law. General Part* (Textbook), fasc. 1–3 (Athens, 1985–1986).

N. Androulakis, *Penal Law. Special Part*, vol. I (Athens, 1974).

N. Androulakis, *Basic Concepts of the Penal Process*, fasc. 1–3 (Athens-Komotini, 1972–1979).

A. Bouropoulos, *Commentary of the Penal Code*, vols. I–III (Athens, 1959–1964).

A. Bouropoulos, *Commentary of the Code of Penal Procedure*, vols. I–II, 2d ed. (Athens, 1957).

N. Chorafas, *Penal Law*, vol. I, 9th ed. (by K. Stamatis) (Athens, 1978).

Ch. Dedes, *Penal Law. Special Part*, fasc. 1–6 (1976–1983).

Ch. Dedes, *Penal Procedure*, 6th ed. (Athens, 1983).

I. Gafos, *Penal Law. General Part*, vols. I–III (Athens, 1978).

I. Gafos, *Penal Law. Special Part*, fasc. 1–7 (Athens, 1957–1969).

I. Gafos, *Penal Procedure*, vols. I–III, 5th–6th ed. (Athens, 1966–1967).

I. Georgakis, *Penal Law. General Part* (*A Coursebook*) (1960).

D. Karanikas, *Manual of Penal Law*, vols. I–III (Thessaloniki, 1954–1961).

A. Karras, *Lectures on Penal Procedural Law*, fasc. 1–3 (Athens-Komotini, 1986).

G. A. Mangakis, *Penal Law. An Outline of the General Part*, 2d ed. (Athens, 1982).

I. Manoledakis, *General Theory of the Penal Law*, vols. I–III (Thessaloniki-Athens, 1976–1981).

I. Manoledakis, *Penal Law. General Part* (Thessaloniki, 1985).

I. Manoledakis, *Penal Law. Special Part: Introduction, Offenses Against Property*, new ed. (Thessaloniki, 1982).

T. Philippidis, *Lectures on Penal Law. Special Part*, fasc. 1–2 (1979–1981).

D. Spinellis, *Introduction to the Penal and Criminological Sciences* (Athens-Komotini, 1984).

D. Spinellis, *Penal Law. Special Part: Offenses Against Honor (Libel and Slander)*, 2d ed. (Athens-Komotini, 1982).

D. Spinellis, *Penal Law. Special Part: Offenses Against Property*, fasc. 1–2, (Athens-Komotini, 1984–1985).
A. Toussis-A. Gheorgiou, *Commentary of the Penal Code*, 3d ed. (Athens, 1967).
K. Vouyoukas, *Penal Procedural Law*, vols. I–II, 6th ed. (Thessaloniki, 1984).
I. Zissiadis, *Penal Law. General Part*, vols. I–III, 2d ed. (Thessaloniki, 1971).
I. Zissiadis, *Penal Procedure*, vols. I–III, 3d ed. (Thessaloniki-Athens, 1976–1977).

# Index*


| | |
|---|---|
| Abandonment of a ship | 12 E |
| | 12 N |
| Abortion | 18 II E 2 |
| Absence, as ground for divorce | 8 III A |
| Absent person, curatorship for | 8 VII D |
| *Absentia* | 4 II C |
| | 15 XI B |
| Absolute nullities | 4 V H |
| Absolute rights | 5 III A |
| Abstract contracts | 5 II H 1 |
| Abstract juridical acts | 4 V F |
| Abstract promise | 4 V F |
| | 5 II H |
| Abuse of dominant position | 10 VI |
| Abuse of right | 4 IV B |
| | 4 VII B |
| | 8 II E |
| in labor law | 13 II A |
| | 13 II B 2 |
| | 13 III D |
| Acceptance | 4 V D |
| | 4 V E |
| Access to courts | 3 IV D 6 |
| | 15 I |
| | 15 VIII A |
| Accessory | |
| criminal law | 18 II C 2 |
| property law | 6 II B |
| Accomplice | 18 II C |
| | 18 II C 2 |
| | 18 II E 1 d |
| Accounting | 17 II A 4 |
| Accumulated offenses | 18 II D 3 |
| Acknowledgment of child | 8 IV B |
| Acquisitive prescription | 4 VIII A 2 |
| | 6 IV B |
| Act | 18 II B 2 |
| | 18 II B 3 |
| Act of Parliament | 3 II B 6 |
| | 3 VI C |
| | 3 II B |
| Action | |
| commencement of | 15 VI A |
| for accounting | 15 X B |


* References are made to chapters with their subdivisions

| | |
|---|---|
| for declaratory judgment | 15 IV B |
| for judicial modification of legal relationships | 15 IV B |
| for partition | 15 IV A |
| for performance | 15 IV B |
| forms of | 15 IX C |
| inadmissible | 15 IV A |
| interrupting prescription | 4 VIII B 3 |
| possessory | 6 III |
| principal | 15 X D |
| to set aside the award | 15 XII E |
| types of | 15 IV B |
| *Actio negatoria* | 6 IV D |
| *Actio popularis* | 15 IV A |
| *Actio publiciana* | 6 IV D |
| Activity, private economic | 3 VI B 2 |
| Ademption | 9 II H 1 |
| Administration | |
| of the state | 3 IV |
| public | 3 IV D 1 |
| | 15 XI A |
| control of | 3 V A |
| Administrative acts | 3 IV D 3, 4 |
| | 14 III A |
| | 14 IV A |
| revocability | 3 IV D 6 |
| void and voidable | 3 IV D 5 |
| Administrative authorities | 3 IV A 2 |
| | 3 IV D 1, 2 |
| Administrative contracts | 3 IV D 7 |
| Administrative courts | 3 II B 6 |
| | 3 IV D 7 |
| | 3 IV D 8 |
| | 3 V C 1 |
| | 10 IV B 5 |
| | 10 VI |
| | 11 II A 3 |
| | 15 II C |
| | 15 III A |
| *see* also Council of State | |
| Administrative self-control | 3 V A |
| Administrative supervision | 3 V A 3 |
| | 9 II E |
| | 10 II |
| | 11 III D |
| Administrator | 15 III D 5 |
| | 15 IX D |
| | 15 XIII D |
| Adoption | 8 V |
| | 16 I D |
| | 16 II A |
| conditions | 8 V B |
| effects | 8 V C |
| termination | 8 V C |
| Adverse possession | 6 IV B |
| Affidavit | 4 V D |

| | |
|---|---|
| Affreightment, contract of | |
| cancellation | 12 II F 5 |
| carrier's liability | 12 II F 3 |
| contents | 12 II F 1 |
| demurrage | 12 II F 2 |
| form | 12 II F 1 |
| freight | 12 II F 1 |
| impossibility of performance | 12 II F 5 |
| laytime | 12 II F 1 |
| obligations of the parties | 12 II F 2 |
| | 12 II F 3 |
| | 12 II F 4 |
| rescission | 12 II F 5 |
| Agency | 4 VII |
| | 16 I C |
| by estoppel | 4 VII B |
| partially disclosed | 4 VII C |
| undisclosed | 4 VII C |
| *see* also representation and mandate | |
| Agricultural Code | 2 I |
| Aliens | 3 I C |
| | 16 I H 6 |
| criminals | 18 II D 2 b |
| seamen | 12 I D |
| Alimony | 8 III C |
| Allowances, tax | 17 II B |
| Alternative obligation | 5 I B 2 f |
| | 5 I G 2 b |
| Amnesty | 18 II B 7 b |
| Ancient Greek law | 1 II |
| Annuity | 5 II |
| | 10 VII B 2 |
| Antitrust law | 10 VI |
| agreements | 10 VI |
| prohibited | 10 VI |
| Committee for the Protection of Competition | 10 VI |
| dominant position | 10 VI |
| EEC law | 10 VI |
| negative clearance | 10 VI |
| register of cartels | 10 VI |
| Apparent authority | 4 VII B |
| Appeal | 1 II C |
| | 15 II B |
| | 15 III A |
| | 15 V A 2 |
| | 15 VIII |
| | 15 XI C |
| | 18 III C 4 c |
| as of right | 15 VIII A |
| constitutional guaranty | 15 VIII A |
| *de novo* | 18 III C 4 c |
| discretionary | 15 VIII A |
| extraordinary | 15 VIII A |
| for error of law | 18 III C 4 c |
| on the record | 15 VIII C |

| | |
|---|---|
| ordinary | 15 VIII A |
| | 15 IX B |
| | 15 XIII A |
| proceedings | 15 V A 3 |
| | 15 V B |
| regular | 15 VIII A |
| | 15 VIII C |
| | 15 IX B |
| | 15 XI C |
| Appellation of origin | 10 IV C |
| Application for annulment | 3 V C 2 |
| Arbitration | 13 II A 4 |
| | 13 III C |
| | 15 XII |
| | 16 IV |
| agreement | 15 XII B |
| constitutional status | 15 XII A |
| procedure | 15 XII C |
| Arbitration tribunal | 13 III C |
| Arbitrator | 1 II C |
| | 15 XII C |
| | 15 XII E |
| Assignment of claims | 4 V F |
| | 5 I K |
| Assignment of future interests | 4 VII C |
| Assignment of property | 5 I C |
| Association | 4 III A |
| | 11 I |
| freedom of | 13 I A |
| | 13 III A |
| | 13 III C |
| of enterprises | 10 VI |
| Assumption of debt | 5 I L |
| Athens, judicial system | 1 II C |
| Attachment | 15 X D |
| | 15 XIII D |
| Attempt | 18 II C |
| | 18 II C 1 |
| abandonment of | 18 II C 1 |
| Attorney | 15 II E |
| | 15 V D |
| | 15 VI F |
| | 15 X C |
| Code on Practicing Attorneys | 2 I |
| fees | 15 VI G |
| power of | 15 IV A |
| | 15 VI E |
| | 15 VIII D |
| | 16 I B 1 |
| Auction | 10 I |
| | 10 II |
| | 10 VII B 5 |
| | 12 II I |
| Audit | 11 II F |
| Auditors | 11 II H |
| | 11 III D |

| | |
|---|---|
| Auditors' Court | 3 II B 6 |
| | 3 VI C |
| Authorities | |
| local | 3 IV A 2 |
| regional | 3 IV A 2 |
| Autonomy of the parties | 16 I B 1 |
| Award | 15 XII D |
| | 15 XII E |
| | 15 XIII A |
| | 16 IV |
| Balance sheet | 11 II D |
| | 11 II H |
| Bank | 5 I B 2 c |
| | 10 VII |
| | 13 III B |
| capital | 10 VII A |
| credit contracts | 10 VII B 4 |
| credit control | 10 VII A |
| deposits of cash | 10 VII B 1 |
| deposits of securities | 10 VII B 1 |
| joint accounts | 10 VII B 3 |
| mortgages | 10 VII B 4 |
| | 10 VII B 5 |
| private transactions | 10 VII B |
| saving | 5 I B 2 c |
| savings accounts | 10 VII B 3 |
| statutory definition | 10 VII A |
| supervision | 10 VII A |
| unalienable deposits | 10 VII B 2 |
| Bank of Greece | 10 VII A |
| | 17 VII G |
| Banking activities | 10 I |
| | 10 VII A |
| Banking tax | *17 IV A 2* |
| Bankruptcy | 8 II F |
| | 10 III C |
| | 10 IV A |
| | 11 I |
| | 11 III F |
| | 11 IV |
| | 15 XI C |
| administrator | 10 II |
| claims of creditors | 10 II |
| compromise | 10 II |
| declaration | 10 II |
| fraudulent | 10 II |
| judge rapporteur | 10 II |
| legal effects | 10 II |
| of insurance companies | 10 VIII E 1 |
| of insurer | 10 VII B |
| persons subject to | 10 II |
| termination | 10 II |
| *Basilica* | 1 III B |
| Benefits (social insurance) | |

| | |
|---|---|
| basic substance | 14 IV A |
| categories | 14 IV A<br>14 IV B |
| imposition of ceiling on | 14 III B |
| legal nature | 14 IV A |
| prerequisites | 14 IV B |
| *see* also social insurance | |
| Bern Convention on protection of literary and artistic works | 10 V |
| Bill of exchange | 10 I<br>10 III<br>16 I B 1<br>16 I H 1 |
| acceptance | 10 III A 1 |
| contents | 10 III A 1 |
| definition | 10 III A 1 |
| endorsement | 10 III A 1 |
| guaranty of | 10 III A 1 |
| payment | 10 III A 1 |
| Bill of lading | 10 III<br>10 VII B 4<br>10 VII B 5 |
| contents | 12 II F 2 |
| Hague Rules | 12 II F 1 |
| issue | 12 II F 6 |
| Black economy | 17 I |
| Bonds | 10 III |
| bearer | 5 II |
| *see* also debentures | |
| Breach of contract | 5 I E 4 |
| Brokers | 10 I |
| Lloyd's | 10 VIII E |
| Brussels Convention on bills of lading | 12 II F 1 |
| Brussels Convention on maritime liens and mortgages | 12 II I |
| Brussels Convention on registration of rights on vessels under construction | 12 II A |
| Brussels International Convention on arrest of ships | 12 II J |
| Budget | 2 I<br>3 II B 4 |
| municipal | 3 IV B 4 |
| Building | |
| General Code | 7 VIII |
| illegal construction of | 7 VIII |
| municipal | 6 II E |
| ownership on | 6 IV B |
| permits | 7 VII<br>7 VIII |
| real rights on | 6 II B |
| regulations | 7 III<br>7 IV<br>7 VII |
| Burden of proof | 5 I I 1<br>5 I E 2 a<br>5 II H 2<br>5 III B |

| | |
|---|---|
| | 5 IV F 2 |
| | 6 IV D 2 |
| | 12 II F 3 |
| Business confidentiality | *see* disclosure |
| Business judgment | 11 II E |
| Byzantine law | 1 III B |
| | 1 IV B |
| Cabinet committees | 3 III C 3 |
| Canon law | 1 III B |
| Capacity | |
| for juridical acts | 4 V B |
| in conflict of laws | 16 I B 1 |
| limited | 4 V B |
| to appreciate and conform | 18 III B 6 a |
| to hold rights | 4 II A |
| to sue | 15 IV A |
| | 15 VII C |
| Capital | 10 II C |
| decrease | 11 II C |
| increase | 11 II C |
| of close corporation | 11 III B |
| subscription | 11 II A |
| Capital aids | 17 VII A |
| | 17 VII C |
| | 17 VII D |
| Capital concentration tax | 17 IV A 5 |
| Capital gain tax | 17 III D |
| Capital Market Committee | 11 II A |
| | 11 II C |
| Capital punishment | 18 II D 1 |
| Capodistrias | 1 IV A |
| | 1 IV B |
| | 10 I |
| Cargoworthiness | 12 II F 2 |
| | 12 II F 3 |
| Carriage of goods by sea | 10 I |
| | 12 II F 1 |
| | 12 II F 2 |
| | 12 II F 5 |
| Carriage of passengers | 12 II F 7 |
| Carrier | |
| liability | 12 II F 3 |
| | 12 II F 7 |
| *see* also affreighment | |
| Cash grants | 17 VII C 2 |
| Cassation | 15 VIII A |
| | 15 VIII D |
| | 15 VIII E |
| | 15 XI C |
| Cause | 4 V F |
| | 5 II H 1 |
| | 5 II H 2 |
| | 6 IV C |
| Cause of action | 15 III D 6 |

| | |
|---|---|
| | 15 IV A |
| | 15 VI B |
| | 15 VI E |
| | 15 VII A |
| | 15 IX C |
| Certificate of inheritance | 9 II F |
| | 15 XI B |
| | 16 I E |
| Chamber of Commerce | 11 II C |
| | 11 IV |
| Charter | 4 III B 1 |
| | 4 III B 4 |
| demise | 12 II F 1 |
| of close corporation | 11 III A |
| of corporation | 11 II B |
| | 11 II I |
| time | 12 II F 4 |
| Chattel mortgages | 6 VIII |
| | 10 VII B 5 |
| Checks | 10 I |
| | 10 III |
| conflict of laws | 16 I B 1 |
| | 16 I H 1 |
| crossed | 10 III B |
| definition | 10 III B |
| differences from bills of exchange | 10 III B |
| revocation | 10 III B |
| Child | |
| accountability for torts | 4 II A |
| acknowledgment of | 8 IV B |
| *see* also legitimation | |
| administration of property | 8 VII A |
| born in marriage | 8 IV A |
| born out of wedlock | 8 IV B |
| | 8 V B |
| | 8 VI A |
| | 8 VI C |
| | 8 VII A |
| | 9 IV E |
| conflict of laws | 16 I D |
| domicile | 8 VI A |
| name | 8 VI A |
| nationality | 8 VI A |
| *see* also minor | |
| Church | |
| and family law | 8 I |
| | 8 II C |
| and State | 3 II B 7 |
| statutory charter of | 3 II C |
| Civil claimant | 18 III B 2 b |
| Civil Code | 2 I |
| | 1 IV B |
| Civil law | 1 IV A |
| codification of | 1 IV B |
| Civil liability | 18 III B 2 c |
| Civil procedure, ancient Athens | 1 II C |

Civil servants 2 I
3 III A 1
3 V B

Claim
acknowledgment 15 V A 1
assignment of 4 V F
5 I K
auxiliary 15 III D
counter 15 III D
15 VI D 3
15 VII C
new 15 VIII C
preclusion 15 IX C
prescription 4 VIII A 1
small 15 VIII A
15 X B
subsidiary 15 VI B
Class action 15 IV A
Classical Greek law 1 II C
Close corporation 11 III
16 I F
bankruptcy 11 III F
capital 11 III B
charter 11 IIIA
dissolution 11 III F
distribution of profits 11 III E
formation 11 III A
liquidation 11 III F
management 11 III D
meeting of members 11 III C
merger 11 III F
parts 11 III B
taxation 17 II C 4
Code
definition 2 I
enactment 3 III A 4
of modern Greek law 2 I
Code of Civil Procedure 2 I
French 15 V
15 VIII A
15 VIII D
15 XIII D
old 15 I
15 X A
Code of Civil Servants 2 I
Code of Criminal Procedure 2 I
Code of Greek nationality 2 I
Code of Market Regulation 18 I
Code of Mines 16 I H 6
Code of Notaries 2 I
Code of Private Maritime Law 2 I
12 II
16 I G
16 III
Code of Public Maritime Law 12 II
Code of Traffic Regulations 18 I

Code on Customs 2 I
Codification 2 I
10 I
13 I
  Justinian's 1 III B
  of ancient law 1 II B
  of civil law 1 IV B
  of criminal law 18 I
  of modern Greek law 1 IV B
Coefficient of building surface 7 VII
Collateral relationship 8 II B
Collections
  of cases 2 V A
  of legislation 2 V B
Collective agreements 13 I A
13 II A
13 II A 4
13 III B
Collective labor law 13 I
13 III
13 III B
Collision of ships 12 II A
12 II L
12 II N
16 III
Commercial activities 10 I
Commercial Code 2 I
11 I
  project of 1981 11 VII
Commercial courts 10 I
Commercial IOU'S 10 III D
Commercial law
  application of general principles of Civil Code 4 1
  characteristics of 10 I
  history of 10 I
  in ancient Greece 1 II C
  reform of 10 I
11 VII
Commercial paper, forms 10 III
Common Customs Tariff 17 IV D
Common law
  Classical Greek law 1 II C
  Hellenistic law 1 III A
Company 3 IV C 2
11 VII
  compulsory participation in 3 IV D
  definition of II I
  expropriation 3 IV D 9
Compensation
  for damages
    future 5 IV H
    in the cargo 12 II F 3
  for death 5 IV H
  for dismissal of employee 13 II B 1
  for personal injury 5 IV H
    *see* also damages, reparations

| | |
|---|---|
| Competence | 15 III A |
| functional | 15 III A |
| subject matter | 15 III A |
| | 15 III B |
| | 15 III D |
| | 15 III F |
| | 15 VI B |
| | 15 VI F |
| | 15 IX C |
| | 15 XI C |
| territorial | 15 III A |
| | 15 III C |
| | 15 VI B |
| Complaint | |
| against enforcement | 15 XIII B |
| contents of | 15 VI B |
| | 15 VI E |
| new | 15 IX C |
| of appeal | 15 VIII A |
| withdrawal | 15 V A 1 |
| Component part | 6 II B |
| Compromise | 5 II |
| Concentration principle | 15 V B |
| Conciliation | 15 VI F |
| Condition | 4 VI |
| Confession | 15 VI D 1 |
| | 15 VI E |
| | 15 VII D |
| | 15 VII G |
| | 15 X C |
| Confessory action | 6 V |
| Confiscation | |
| of dangerous objects | 18 II D 2 v |
| of instruments or products of crime | 18 II D 1 d |
| Consanguinity | 8 II B |
| Consent | |
| of the victim | 18 II B 4 e |
| | 18 II E 1 c |
| *see* vices of consent | 18 II E 3 |
| vices of | |
| Consideration | 4 V F |
| Consolidation | 11 II I |
| | 11 III F |
| *Constitutio Antoniniana* | 1 III A |
| Constitution | |
| and EEC law | 3 I D |
| and international law | 2 I |
| | 3 I C |
| | 3 I D |
| and labor law | 13 I A |
| | 13 III A |
| | 13 III C |
| | 13 III D |
| Consumables | 6 II D |
| | 6 V |
| Consumption tax | 17 IV B |

*Contra non valentem* 4 VIII B 2
Contract
  abstract 5 II H 1
  action based on 5 II H 2
  administrative 3 IV D 7
  as a source of obligation 5 I A 1
  breach of 5 I E 4
  burdening third parties 5 I H
  cause 4 V F
  conclusion of 4 V E
  consideration 4 V F
  EEC Convention 16 I B 1
  for services 5 II C
  for the benefit of third parties 5 I H
  for the engagement of seamen 12 II D
  for work 5 II D
  form 4 V D
    16 I B 1
  frustration 5 I E 2 c
  fulfillment 5 I I 1
  interpretation of 4 V I
  mixed 5 II
  place of performance 16 I B 1
  proper law of 16 I B 1
  rescission 4 V C
  specific 5 II
  termination of long term 5 I E 2 d
  two-sided 5 I D
    delay 5 I E 3
    non-performance 5 I E 3 b
    rescission of 5 I F
Contributions
  of land 7 IV
  maritime law 12 II K
  social insurance 14 III A
    17 II B
Control
  administrative 3 V A 1
  financial 3 V A 4
  hierarchical 3 V A 1
  judicial 3 V C 1
  parliamentary 3 III A 4
    3 V B
Convention against torture and other cruel treatment (UN) 18 II E 4
Convention for the protection of literary and artistic products 4 II E
Conventional mores or usages 4 V C
    4 V E
    4 V I
Conveyance 5 I K 2
    6 VI
    16 I B 1
Cooperatives 17 II C 3
Copyright 5 III A
    15 XIII D

| | |
|---|---|
| Corporation | 11 II |
| annual reserves | 17 VII F |
| bancruptcy | 10 II |
| | 11 II I |
| bylaws | 11 II B |
| capital | 11 II C |
| | 17 VII C |
| *see* also capital | |
| charter | 11 II B |
| | 11 II I |
| contracts with directors | 11 II E |
| depreciation of asssets | 17 VII F |
| dissolution | 11 II I |
| EEC harmonization | 11 I |
| | 11 II B |
| | 16 I F |
| establishment in Greece | 16 I F |
| foreign | 16 I F |
| formation of | 11 II A |
| founders | 11 II A |
| | 11 II C |
| governmental supervision | 10 I |
| | 11 II D 3 |
| | 11 II F |
| law reform | 11 I |
| local government | 3 IV B 1 |
| name | 11 II B |
| officers | 11 II E |
| participation of foreigners | 16 I H 6 |
| preemptive rights | 11 II C |
| purpose | 11 II B |
| representation | 11 II E |
| seat | 16 I F |
| tax | 17 II C 1 |
| transformation | 11 II 1 |
| US comparison | 11 II I |
| Corporeal | 6 II |
| Council of State | 2 V B |
| | 3 II B 3 |
| | 3 II B 6 |
| | 3 IV B 4 |
| | 3 IV D 1 |
| | 3 V C 1, 2 |
| | 17 VI |
| Courts | |
| and Constitution | 3 II B 6 |
| | 3 VI C |
| categories | 3 II B 6 |
| civil | 3 II B 6 |
| | 15 II B |
| | 15 XI A |
| | 15 XI B |
| | 15 XII A |
| | 15 XII E |
| commercial | 10 I |
| division of | 15 III A |

| | |
|---|---|
| | 15 III G |
| extraordinary | 3 I |
| hierarchies of | 15 II A 1 |
| higher | 15 VIII A |
| intermediate appellate | 15 II B |
| | 15 VIII B |
| | 15 VIII C |
| juvenile | 18 III A 1 d |
| of appeal | 18 III A 1 a ii |
| one-member | 15 II A 4 |
| | 15 VII A |
| | 15 VII F |
| | 15 IX B |
| | 15 X B |
| | 15 X A |
| one-member district | 15 II B |
| | 15 III B |
| | 15 V C |
| | 15 VI C |
| | 15 X D |
| | 15 XI C |
| | 15 XII C |
| | 15 XII E |
| | 15 XIII B |
| panels | 15 II A 4 |
| | 15 VII F |
| | 15 VIII E |
| | 15 IX A |
| special courts | 3 II B 6 |
| | 3 III B |
| three-member district | 15 II B |
| | 15 III B |
| | 15 X A |
| | 15 XI C |
| | 15 XII E |
| *see* also administrative courts, criminal courts, second instance courts, Supreme Court, Supreme Special Court | |
| Counterclaim | 15 III D |
| | 15 VI D 3 |
| | 15 VII C |
| Counterproof | 15 VII E |
| Covenant on Civil and Political Rights (UN) | 3 VI 2 |
| Covenant on Economic, Social and Cultural Rights (UN) | 3 VI A 2 |
| Credit institutions | 5 I B 2 d |
| Credit tax | 17 II A 8 |
| | 17 II B |
| Creditor | 5 I A 2 a |
| | 5 I B 4 |
| co-creditors | 5 I M 3 |
| default of | 5 I E 5 |
| defrauding of | 5 II |
| preferential satisfaction | 6 VII |
| Crew | 12 II A |
| | 12 II C |

| | |
|---|---|
| | 12 II D |
| | 12 II E |
| | 12 II F 3 |
| | 12 II I |
| | 12 II L |
| | 12 II M |
| | 12 II N |
| Crime | 13 II B 2 |
| | 18 II A 2 |
| | 18 II D 1 |
| as a cause of disinherison | 9 VI |
| parties to | 18 II C 2 |
| special forms of | 18 II C |
| Criminal courts | 18 II A 1 |
| | 18 II A 2 |
| Criminal liability | 18 II A 2 |
| Criminal offense | *see* offense |
| Criminal proceedings | |
| Criminal punishment | *see* punishment |
| Cross-appeal | 15 VIII C |
| *Culpa in contrahendo* | 4 V E |
| Culpability | 5 IV E |
| | 18 II B 6 b |
| | 18 II B 6 b i |
| Curator | 6 IV |
| Curatorship, for absent persons | 8 VII D |
| Currency | 5 I A2 b |
| | 5 I B 2 b |
| Committee | 10 VII A |
| Custom | |
| as a source of law | 2 II |
| created by judicial decisions | 2 III |
| in criminal law | 18 II A 2 |
| Customs, Code on | 2 I |
| | |
| Damage | |
| caused by the fall of building | 5 IV F 2 |
| caused by the state | 3 IV D 8 |
| delictual | 5 IV B |
| future | 5 IV H |
| in the cargo | 12 II F 3 |
| non-material | 5 I B 2 d ii |
| positive | 5 I B 2 d i |
| Damages | 5 I B 2 d |
| | 5 IV I 2 |
| claimed by the dispossessed owner | 6 IV D |
| claimed by the possessor | 6 III |
| during the negotiating stage | 4 V D |
| for breach of the promise of marry | 8 II A |
| for delay of performance | 5 I E 3 |
| for moral harm | 5 IV I 2 a |
| for non-performance | 5 I E 1 2 |
| for personal injury | 5 IV H |
| interest rate | 5 I B 2 C |
| liability for | 4 VI |

*see* also compensation, reparations
Deactivation of rights 4 IV C
4 V H
Death 6 II A
benefits 14 IV C
compensation for 5 IV H
of employee 5 II C 2 d
presumption for 4 II B
protection of memory of deceased 4 II E
*see* also succession, descent
Death penalty 18 II E 1
Debentures 10 III
10 III D
10 VII A
*see* also bonds
Debt
abstract promise of 4 V F
acknowledgment of 5 II H
assumption of 5 I L
described by class 5 I B 2 a
5 I E 2 b
5 II A 2 b ii
in foreign currency 5 I B 2 b
recognition of 5 II H
Debt securities 11 II C
Debtor 5 I A 2 a
5 I B 2 a
5 I B 2 f
5 I B 4
5 I B 5
default of 5 I B 6
liability of 5 I B 7
5 I B 8
5 I E 2 a, b, c
5 I E 3 a
5 I E 4
solvency of 5 I K 4
Decentralization, principle of 3 IV B 1
Declaration of will 4 V A
4 V E
Decree
Presidential 2 I
3 II B 3
urgent 3 II B 3
Defamation 5 IV C
18 II B 4 e
Default
judgment obtained by 15 VI E
of creditor *see* creditor
of debtor *see* debtor
of parties in civil proceedings 15 X C
Defendant 18 III B 2 a
rights of 18 III C 4 b
Defense
excusable excess of limits of 18 II B 6 c ii aa
in civil proceedings 15 IV D

| | |
|---|---|
| affirmative | 15 VII C |
| self or of another | 4 IV D |
| | 18 II B 3 |
| | 18 II B 4 b |
| Delegation | |
| of claims | 10 III C |
| statutory for issue of decrees | 3 II B 3 |
| Delictual liability | *see* tort |
| Democracy | 3 II A 2 |
| parliamentary | 3 II A 4 |
| representative | 3 II A 3 |
| Demosthenes | 1 II C |
| Demurrage | 12 I F 2 |
| Deposit | 5 II |
| *see* also bank | |
| Depreciation | 17 II A 4 |
| | 17 III F 2 |
| Derivative action | 11 II E |
| Descent and distribution | 16 I E |
| Detention | 6 III |
| Development area | 7 VI |
| Diplomatic immunity | 16 III |
| Direct taxes | 17 III A |
| capital gain tax | 17 III D |
| on gifts | 17 III A |
| on property | 17 III B |
| on ships and shipping enterprises | 17 III C |
| on succession | 17 III A |
| Directors | |
| board of | 11 II E |
| compensation | 11 II E |
| conflict of interests | 11 II E |
| | 11 III D |
| delegation of powers | 11 II E |
| duties of | 11 II E |
| managing | 11 II E |
| Disclosure | 11 II F |
| | 11 III C |
| of business secrets | 10 IV A |
| Discovery | 15 VII A |
| Disinherison | 9 VI B |
| Dismissal of employee | 13 II B 1, 2 |
| Dissenting opinion | 15 IX A |
| Distinctive signs | 10 IV B 3 |
| | 10 IV B 4 |
| | 10 IV B 5 |
| Disturbance of conscience | 18 II B 6 a ii |
| Dividends | 11 II E |
| | 11 II G |
| withholding tax on | 17 II C 2 |
| Divorce | 8 III |
| | 16 I D d |
| by consensus | 8 III B |
| effects of | 8 III C |
| grounds for | 8 III A |
| | 8 II B |

| | |
|---|---|
| judgment | 8 III B |
| petition | 8 III B |
| procedure | 8 III B |
| Doctrine, legal | 2 IV |
| Documentary credit | 10 VII B 4 |
| Domicile | 4 II D |
| | 5 I B 2 b |
| | 8 II E |
| | 8 VI A |
| | 15 III C |
| | 15 III D |
| | 15 VI B |
| | 16 I E |
| | 16 I H 4 |
| | 16 II A |
| | 17 II A 1 |
| | 17 III A |
| *see* also *lex domicilii* | |
| Donation | |
| *causa mortis* | 9 II H 4 |
| | 16 I E |
| detrimental to forced heirs | 9 V B |
| *inter vivos* | 5 II |
| | 5 II H 3 |
| taxes on | 17 III A |
| Double jeopardy | 18 III C 4 d |
| Dowry | 8 II F |
| | 8 III C |
| Duress | 4 V C |
| | |
| Earnest | 5 I G 1 |
| Educative measures | 18 II B 6 a i |
| EEC | |
| accession of Greece | 2 I |
| | 3 I D |
| antitrust law | 10 VI |
| capital movements | 17 VII G |
| corporations | 11 I |
| | 11 II B |
| | 16 I F |
| employment law | 13 II A 4 |
| national | 16 I H 5 |
| | 16 I H 6 |
| taxation | 17 IV D |
| EEC Convention on contracts | 16 I B 1 |
| EEC Convention on jurisdiction and enforcement of judgments | 16 III |
| | 16 IV |
| Electoral system | 3 III A 1 |
| Embezzlement | 18 II E 6 |
| Emergency | |
| act | 3 II B 3 |
| law | 3 I B |
| | 3 IV D 1 |
| | 12 II A |

| | |
|---|---|
| powers | 3 II A 4 |
| | 3 II B 5 |
| state of | 3 II B 1 |
| | 3 II B 3 |
| in criminal law | 18 II E 4 |
| Employee | |
| dismissal of | 13 II B 1, 2 |
| responsibility for | 5 I B 8 |
| social insurance | 14 III A |
| *see* also employment, work | |
| Employers' association | 13 I A |
| | 13 III B |
| | 13 III C |
| Employment | |
| as a source of taxable income | 17 II A 3 |
| | 17 II A 5 |
| contract of | 5 II C |
| | 13 I |
| | 13 II A |
| | 16 I G |
| of definite duration | 13 II B 1 |
| of indefinite term | 13 II B 2 |
| EEC law | 13 I b 13 II A 4 |
| right to | 13 I A |
| working hours | 13 II A 1 |
| Energy | 6 II A |
| Enforcement proceedings | 15 II E |
| | 15 IV B |
| | 15 XIII |
| direct | 15 XIII C |
| distribution | 15 XIII D |
| for specific performance | 15 XIII C |
| indirect | 15 XIII C |
| of tax laws | 17 VI |
| provisional | 15 VIII A |
| | 15 XIII A |
| stay of | 15 VIII A |
| | 15 XIII A |
| to satisfy a money claim | 15 XIII D |
| Engagement to marry | 8 II A |
| Environment, protection of | 7 II |
| Equality of payment | 13 I A |
| | 13 I B |
| | 13 II A 9 |
| Equality of sexes | 4 II 5 |
| | 8 I |
| | 8 II E |
| | 8 II F |
| | 8 VII A |
| | 13 I A |
| | 16 I D |
| Equity | 1 III B |
| Establishment | 17 II A 2 |
| Estate | 9 II A |
| action for delivery | 9 II G |
| partition of | 9 VII B |

sale of 9 VII C
Estoppel
agency by 4 VII B
collateral 15 IX C
direct 15 IX C
equitable 4 IV C
16 IV
European Convention for the protection of human rights 3 VI A 2
3 VI B 3
15 VIII A
European Convention on information on foreign law 16 I H 5
European Court of Human Rights 3 VI C
European Social Charter 3 VI A 2
Evidence 15 V A
15 V A 2
15 VI C
15 VII
administration 15 VII F
admissibility 15 VII D
15 X C
burden 15 VII C
conclusive 15 VII E
15 X C
direct 15 VII D
documentary 15 VII D
15 VII E
15 VII F
15 VIII D
15 VIII E
15 X B
evaluation 15 VII A
15 VII G
15 VIII C
exclusionary rules 15 VII D
means 15 VII D
15 VII F
15 VII G
15 X C
subject matter 15 VII B
subsidiary 15 VII D
Exception 15 VI D 1
Exchange 5 II A 1
Exchange control 5 I B 2 b
Excuse, grounds of 18 II B 6 c ii
Executor 9 IV
15 IX D
Exemption clauses 5 I B 7 b
5 I B 8
Exequatur 15 XIII A
16 IV
*Ex parte* 15 X D
15 XI A
16 IV
Expenses 17 II B
Expert reports 15 VII D

| | |
|---|---|
| | 15 VII F |
| | 15 VII G |
| Export credits, insurance of | 10 VIII C |
| Expropriation | 3 IV D 9 |
| | 3 VI B 2 |
| | 6 IV B |
| Extinction of obligations | 5 I I |
| Fair administration, principle of | 3 IV D 2 |
| Family | |
| council | 8 VII B |
| disputes | 15 III B |
| | 15 III E |
| | 15 IV B |
| | 15 X B |
| | 15 X C |
| | 15 XII B |
| law | 8 I |
| Byzantine | 1 III B |
| church influence | 8 I |
| | 8 II C |
| mandatory character | 8 I |
| reform of | 8 I |
| Fault | 5 I B 7 a |
| | 5 IV D,E,F |
| Fees | 17 1 |
| Felonies | 4 V B C |
| | 18 III A 1 a |
| | 18 III C 4 b |
| *Fideicommissum* | 6 IV |
| | 9 II H 2 |
| | 9 IV E |
| | 9 IV G |
| Finance | |
| of local government | 3 IV B 4 |
| public | 3 II B 4 |
| Financial statements | 11 II H |
| | 11 III D |
| Fine | 15 V D |
| | 15 XIII C |
| First hearing | 15 III F |
| | 15 V B |
| | 15 VI A |
| | 15 VI C |
| | 15 VI D 3 |
| | 15 VI E |
| | 15 VII B |
| | 15 IX B |
| Flag, law of | 12 II A |
| | 12 II B |
| | 12 II M |
| | 16 I B 2 |
| | 16 I G |
| Forced share | 9 V B |
| Foreign law | 15 V A 2 |

| | |
|---|---|
| | 16 I H 5 |
| Foreign Policy and National Defense Council | 3 III C 3 |
| Forest Code | 2 I |
| Forfeit | 5 I G 2 b |
| Forty Archons | 1 II C |
| Forum choice | 16 III |
| *Forum non conveniens* | 15 III G |
| Fraud | 18 II E 7 |
| as a vice of consent | 4 V C |
| Freedom of association | 13 I A |
| | 13 III A |
| | 13 III C |
| Freight | 12 II E |
| | 12 II F 2 |
| | 12 II F 4 |
| | 12 II F 5 |
| | 12 II K |
| French influence | |
| on Greek law | 1 IV B |
| Fruits | 6 II F |
| Fund-raising committees | 4 III A |
| Fungibles | 6 II D |
| | |
| Gaming | 5 II |
| Garnishment | 15 XIII D |
| General average | 12 II K |
| | 12 II N |
| General elections | 3 III A 1 |
| Geneva Convention on negotiable instruments | 16 I B 1 |
| German Civil Code | 4 I |
| German influence on Greek law | 1 IV B |
| German Pandectists | 1 IV B |
| Gifts tax | 17 A III |
| *see* also donation | |
| Good faith | 2 III C |
| | 4 IV B |
| | 4 IV C |
| | 4 V C |
| | 4 V E |
| | 4 V H |
| | 4 V I |
| | 4 VI |
| | 4 VII B |
| | 5 I B 1 |
| | 5 I E 2 c |
| | 5 II B 3 |
| | 6 IV A |
| | 6 IV B |
| | 8 II D |
| | 10 IV B 5 |
| | 10 IV D |
| | 10 VIII B |
| | 12 II N |
| | 15 V D |
| | 15 VIII E |

| | |
|---|---|
| Good morals | 2 III<br>4 IV B<br>4 V H<br>4 V G |
| Government | |
| acts of | 3 V C 1 |
| and parliament | 3 III C 1 |
| central | 3 IV A 1<br>3 IV B 2 |
| composition of | 3 III C 2 |
| constitutional status | 3 III C 1 |
| executive powers | 3 II B 5 |
| local | 3 IV B 1<br>3 IV B 2 |
| Code | 3 IV B 1 |
| committee | 3 IV B 5 |
| finance | 3 IV B 4 |
| supervision | 3 IV B 5 |
| self-government | 3 IV C |
| system of | 3 II A |
| Government Gazette | *see* Official Gazette |
| Grants | 17 VII A<br>17 VII C 2 |
| Guaranty | 5 I I 2<br>5 I L 3<br>5 II G |
| Guardianship | 4 VIII B 2<br>8 VII B<br>15 XI B<br>16 I D |
| judicial | 4 V B |
| of interdicted persons | |
| of minors | 8 VII B |
| Guilt | 18 II B 5 |
| Habitation | 6 V |
| Hague Convention applicable to child support obligations | 16 I D |
| Hague Convention on the conflicts of laws relating to the form of testamentary dispositions | 16 I E |
| Hague Convention on the law applicable to traffic accidents | 16 I B 2 |
| Hague Convention on the recognition and execution of judgments relating to child support obligations | 16 I D |
| Hague Rules | 12 II F 1 |
| Harmenopoulos | 1 III B<br>1 IV B |
| Heirs | 9 II<br>9 III<br>9 IV<br>9 V<br>10 VII B 1<br>10 VII B 3<br>15 III D |

| | |
|---|---|
| | 15 IX D |
| | 16 I E |
| classes of | 9 III A |
| community among | 9 VII B |
| creditors of | 9 VII |
| disinherison | 9 VI B |
| forçed | 9 V A |
| | 9 IV F |
| intestate | 9 III A |
| minor | 10 VII B 2 |
| substitution of | 9 IV G |
| taxation of | 17 III A |
| unworthy | 9 II D |
| | 9 III B |
| Hellenistic law | 1 III A |
| Hexabiblos | 1 III B |
| | 1 IV B |
| | 8 I |
| Hierarchical control in public administration | 3 V A 1 |
| Hierarchical subordination | 18 III A 2 b |
| High Council for Economic Policy | 3 III C 3 |
| Homicide | 18 II E 1 |
| | 18 II E 3 e |
| *see* also murder | |
| Human rights | 3 VI |
| | 3 II A 5 |
| | 3 II B 3 |
| | 3 IV C 2 |
| protection of | 3 IV A 1 |
| | 3 VI B |
| | 3 VI B 3 |
| Immovables | 6 II B |
| | 6 IV |
| acquisition by foreigners | 16 I H 6 |
| possession in good faith | 6 IV B |
| Immunities (criminal law) | 18 II B 7 a |
| Impleader | 15 IV A |
| Import duties | 17 IV D |
| Imprisonment for debt | 15 XIII C |
| | 15 XIII D |
| Imputability | 5 IV E |
| | 18 II B 5 |
| | 18 II B 6 |
| | 18 II B 6 c i |
| Inalienable deposits | |
| Income | |
| negative | 17 II B |
| source of | 17 II A 3 |
| Income tax | |
| exemptions from | 17 II A 3, 4, 5 |
| of close corporation | 17 II C 4 |
| of cooperatives | 17 II C 2 |
| of corporations | 17 II C 1 |
| of foreign | |

| | |
|---|---|
| legal persons | 17 II C |
| residents | 17 II A 2 |
| | 17 II A 4 |
| | 17 II A 7 |
| of insurance companies | 10 VIII E 2 |
| of legal persons | 17 II C |
| of natural persons | 17 II B |
| of partnerships | 17 II C 4 |
| paid in foreign countries | 17 II A 8 |
| persons subject to | 17 II A 1 2 |
| presumed income | 17 II A 6 |
| taxable income | 17 II A 3, 4 |
| withholding of | 17 II A7 |
| | 17 II C 2 |
| Incorporeals | 6 II |
| | 6 VII |
| Indications of source | 10 IV C |
| Indirect taxes | 14 III B |
| | 17 1 |
| | 17 IV |
| Industrial property rights | 4 II E |
| Infanticide | 18 II E 1 e |
| Inheritance | |
| accretion | 9 III B |
| agreement of | 9 II H 5 |
| collation of | 9 III C |
| conflict of laws | 16 I E |
| partition | 9 VII B |
| Injury | |
| at work | 12 II D |
| | 13 II A 2 |
| bodily | 18 II B 4 e |
| | 18 II E 3 |
| pecuniary | 5 IV I 2 |
| personal | 5 IV H |
| verbal | 18 II B 4 e |
| Instigating principal | 18 II C 2 |
| Instrument | |
| authentic | 15 VII E |
| | 15 VII G |
| enforceable | 15 XIII A |
| | 15 XIII B |
| in writing | 15 XII B |
| notarial | 11 III B |
| | 15 II E |
| | 15 VII E |
| | 15 VII G |
| | 15 XIII A |
| | 16 I B 1 |
| private | 15 VII E |
| | 15 X C |
| *see* also evidence documentary | |
| Insurance (private) | 10 VIII |
| | 16 I B 1 |
| against property loss | 10 VIII B |
| | 10 VIII C |

| | |
|---|---|
| aircraft insurance | 10 VIII E 2 |
| contract of | 10 VIII A |
| | 10 VIII B |
| crop | 10 VIII C |
| export credits | 10 VIII C |
| fire | 10 VIII C |
| indemnity | 10 VIII B |
| insolvency | 10 VII C |
| insured interest | 10 VIII A |
| | 10 VIII B |
| life | 10 VIII D |
| | 17 II B |
| mutual | 10 VIII |
| over-insurance | 10 VIII B |
| reinsurance | 10 VIII A |
| risks | 10 VIII A |
| | 10 VIII B |
| | 10 VIII C |
| | 10 VIII D |
| *see* also private insurance business | |
| Insurance agent | 10 VIII E 1 |
| Insurance association | 10 VIII E 1 |
| | 10 VIII E 2 |
| Insurance benefits | 12 II E |
| | 12 II I |
| Insurance companies | 10 VIII E 1 |
| | 10 VIII E 2 |
| foreign | 10 III E 1 |
| taxation | 17 IV A 3 |
| Insurance policy | 10 III |
| | 10 VII B 4 |
| | 10 VIII C |
| | 10 VIII E |
| | 16 I B |
| Intellectual propert | 16 I C |
| industrial designs | 10 IV E |
| protection of | 10 V |
| rights | 4 II E |
| | 10 V |
| *see* also copyright | |
| Intention | 18 II B 6 b i |
| Interdiction | 8 VII C |
| | 15 XI B |
| Interest | 5 I B 2 C |
| | 5 I B 6 |
| | 5 I E 5 b |
| | 12 II G 2 |
| legal | 15 IV A |
| | 15 IV B |
| moratory | 5 I B 2 C ii |
| | 5 II F 2 |
| on bank accounts | 10 VII B 3 |
| on interest | 5 I B 2 C iii |
| International law | 2 I |
| generally accepted rules of | 3 I C |
| | 2 I |

| | |
|---|---|
| International treaties | 2 I |
| | 3 I C |
| | 3 II B 6 |
| | 17 II D |
| Interpretation | |
| of contracts | 5 II |
| of juridical acts | 4 V I |
| of legislation | 2 III |
| Intervention | 15 IV A |
| Inventory, benefit of | 9 II B |
| | 9 VII C |
| Investigation | 18 III B 2 a |
| | 18 III C 2 |
| | 18 III C 3 |
| Investment | |
| aids to | 17 VII B 2 |
| foreign | 3 IV D 9 |
| | 15 XII A |
| | 17 VII G |
| incentives | 17 VII A |
| | 17 VII G |
| productive | 17 VII B 2 |
| Issue preclusion | 15 IX C |
| *Iurisdictio* | |
| *contentiosa* | 15 XI A |
| | 15 XI C |
| *voluntaria* | 15 XI A |
| *Ius Greco-Romanum* | I III A |
| *Ius novit curia* | 15 V A |
| | 15 V A 2 |
| | 15 VI B |
| Jettison | 12 II K |
| Job security | 13 I |
| | 13 II B |
| Joinder | |
| of claims | 15 VI B |
| of parties | 15 IV A |
| Joint and several liability | 5 I M 2 |
| | 5 IV G |
| | 9 VII B |
| | 12 II D |
| Joint debtors | 5 I L 1 b |
| Judge | |
| administrative duties | 3 II B 1 |
| ancient Greek law | 1 II C |
| assigned by law | 15 XII A |
| post-Byzantine law | 1 III C |
| power | 15 V A |
| | 15 VIII C |
| | 15 X A |
| | 15 XI C |
| right to strike | 13 I A |
| seniority | 15 IX A |
| *see* also judiciary | |

| | |
|---|---|
| Judgment | |
| ancient Greek law | 1 II C |
| contested | 15 VIII D |
| declaratory | 15 IV B |
| default | 15 VI E |
| | 15 VIII B |
| drafting | 15 IX A |
| effects | 15 IX B-E |
| enforceability | 15 VIII A |
| final | 15 VIII C |
| | 15 IX B |
| | 15 XI C |
| | 15 XIII A |
| foreign | 15 XIII A |
| | 16 IV |
| inconsistent | 15 IV A |
| | 15 VIII D |
| non-final | 15 IX B |
| null and void | 15 IX B |
| on the merits | 15 IV A |
| | 15 VI D 1 |
| | 15 VI E |
| | 15 VIII C |
| | 15 IX C |
| operative part | 15 IX A |
| reports | 15 IX A |
| Judicial | |
| costs | 15 VI G |
| council | 18 III C 3 |
| decisions | 2 III |
| | 2 IV |
| | 3 II B 6 |
| independence | 3 II B 6 |
| | 15 II D |
| notice | 15 V A 2 |
| | 15 VII B |
| | 15 VII D |
| | 15 XII C |
| officer | 15 II A 2 |
| | 15 II A 3 |
| | 15 II D |
| precedent | 1 II C |
| | 2 III |
| | 15 II D |
| | 15 VIII E |
| protection | 3 V C 1 |
| | 4 VI |
| | 4 VIII B 4 |
| review | 3 II B 6 |
| | 3 IV D 3 |
| | 3 V C 1 |
| | 15 II D |
| staff | 15 II E |
| supervision | 15 XI B |
| Judiciary | 3 II A 5 |
| | 3 II B 1 |

| | |
|---|---|
| | 3 II B 6 |
| | 18 III B 1 |
| *see* also judge | |
| *Juge rapporteur* | 15 IX A |
| Juridical act | 4 IV B |
| | 4 V |
| | 4 VIII B 4 |
| | 16 I B 1 |
| | 16 I C |
| abstract | 4 V F |
| affected by vices of consent | 4 V C |
| capacity to conclude | 4 V B |
| contents | 4 V G |
| creating real rights | 6 I |
| | 6 II B |
| definition of | 4 V A |
| form of | 4 V D |
| immoral | 4 V G |
| | 4 V H |
| interpretation of | 4 V I |
| non-causal | 4 V F |
| nullity of | 4 V B |
| | 4 V C |
| | 4 V D |
| | 4 V G |
| | 4 V H |
| | 4 VI |
| | 4 VIII B 4 |
| obligations from | 5 I C |
| representation for | 4 VII A |
| | 4 VII B |
| rescission | 4 V H |
| simulation | 4 V C |
| unlawful | 4 V F |
| voidable | 4 V C |
| | 4 V H |
| *see* also contract | |
| Juridical persons | 4 III |
| categories of | 4 III A |
| law applicable | 4 III B |
| liability of | 4 III B 4, 5 |
| of public law | 3 IV C 1 |
| personality of | 4 III B |
| protection of name | 4 II E |
| representative organs | 4 III B 5 |
| seat | 4 III B 3 |
| taxation | 17 II A 2 |
| | 17 II C |
| Jurisdiction | 15 III A |
| concurrent | 15 III E |
| exclusive | 15 III D |
| general | 15 note 4 |
| *in rem* | 15 III E |
| international | 12 II L |
| | 15 III A |
| | 15 X C |

| | |
|---|---|
| | 16 III |
| lack of | 15 III G |
| | 15 VI D 1 |
| | 15 VIII C |
| | 15 IX A |
| *quasi-in-rem* | 15 III E |
| special | 15 III D |
| subject matter | 15 note 3 |
| transfer | 15 III G |
| Juror | 15 II A 3 |
| | 18 III B 1 |
| Justice of the peace | 15 II B |
| | 15 III B |
| | 15 IV A |
| | 15 V C |
| | 15 VI C |
| | 15 VI F |
| Justification | |
| | 18 II B 3 |
| | 18 II B 4 |
| Justinian legislation | 1 III B |
| Labor cases | 15 VI F |
| | 15 X A |
| | 15 X B |
| | 15 X C |
| | 15 XII B |
| Labor exchange | 14 IV C |
| Land use | 7 VI |
| Law | |
| enacted | 2 I |
| modern Greek | I IV A |
| passed *in pleno* | 3 II B 3 |
| private | 2 I |
| public | 2 I |
| unconstitutionality of | 2 I |
| | 3 VI C |
| *see* also legislation | |
| Lawgivers | 1 II B 2 |
| Law school | 15 II E |
| Lawyers, in ancient Greece | 1 II C |
| Lease | 5 II B |
| obligations of the lessor | 5 II A 1 |
| of living accomodation | 5 II B 7 a |
| of professional accomodation | 5 II B 7 b |
| rent | 5 II B 2 |
| termination | 5 II B 4 |
| | 5 II B 6 |
| usufructuary | 5 II |
| Legacy | 9 II H 1 |
| | 9 IV E |
| *see* also legatee | |
| Legal aid | 15 VI G |
| Legal duty | 18 II B 4 a |
| Legal interest | 15 IV A |

| | |
|---|---|
| | 15 IV B |
| Legal periodicals | 2 V B |
| Legal persons | *see* juridical persons |
| Legal writing | 2 IV |
| Legatee | 6 IV |
| | 17 III A |
| *see* also legacy | |
| Legislation | |
| as a source of law | 2 I |
| collections of | 2 V |
| delegated | 3 II B 1 |
| | 3 II B 3 |
| | 3 II B 6 |
| hierarchy between legal rules | 3 I C |
| power of Parliament on | 3 II B 3 |
| retroactive effect | 2 I |
| | 3 II B 4 |
| | 18 II A 2 |
| *see* also law | |
| Legislative | 3 II B 1 |
| | 3 VI B 2 |
| acts | 3 II B 3 |
| Legitimation | 16 I D |
| | 16 II A 2 |
| | 16 II B |
| *see* also acknowledgment of child | |
| Letters of credit | 10 III C |
| *Lex causae* | 16 I B 1 |
| | 16 I H 3 |
| *Lex celebrationis* | 16 I D |
| *Lex domicilii* | 16 I B 1 |
| | 16 I D |
| | 16 I E |
| *Lex fori* | 16 I B 1 |
| | 16 I B 2 |
| | 16 I E |
| | 16 I H 2 |
| *Lex loci* | |
| *contractus* | 16 I B 1 |
| | 16 I F |
| *delicti commissi* | 16 I B 2 |
| *Lex nationalis* | 16 I B 1 |
| | 16 I D |
| | 16 I E |
| | 16 I G |
| | 16 III |
| *Lex rei sitae* | 16 I C |
| | 16 I E |
| *Lex solutionis* | 16 I B 1 |
| | 16 I B 1 |
| Liability | |
| and obligation | 5 I A 3 |
| for animals | 5 IV F 1, 2 |
| for employees | 5 IV F 1 |
| from unjust enrichment | 5 III D |
| of civil servants | 3 IV D 8 |

| | |
|---|---|
| of innkeepers | 5 II |
| of juridical persons | 4 III B 4, 5 |
| of shipowner | 12 II E |
| state | 3 IV D 8 |
| Lien | 10 VIII E 1 |
| | 12 II I |
| Limitation | |
| of actions in maritime law | 12 II N |
| statutes of | 15 VI A |
| | 15 VII C |
| | 16 I H 3 |
| | 18 II B 7 |
| *see* also prescription | |
| Limited liability company | *see* close corporation, corporation, company |
| Limited partner | 11 V |
| Liquidation | |
| close corporation | 11 III F |
| corporation | 11 II I |
| general partnership | 11 IV |
| Liquidator | 15 IX D |
| *Lis pendens* | 15 VI A |
| Litigation | |
| ancient Greek law | 1 II C |
| taxation law | 17 VI |
| Lloyd's brokers | 10 VIII E |
| Loan | 5 II F |
| | 15 II |
| gratuitous loan for use | 5 II B 8 |
| subsidies | 17 VII A |
| | 17 VII C |
| Local government | *see* government |
| Lockout | 13 III D |
| *Logographoi* | 1 II C |
| *Loi-cadre* | 3 II B 3 |
| | 3 II B 4 |
| Lottery gains tax | 17 III A |
| Luxury tax | 17 IV B |
| Lycurgus | 1 II B |
| Maintenance | 8 III C |
| | 8 VI C |
| | 15 III B |
| | 15 VI G |
| | 15 IX E |
| | 15 X B |
| Mandate | 5 II C 2 c |
| | 5 II C |
| | 5 II E 1 |
| | 5 II G 7 |
| | 6 IV |
| | 8 II F |
| *Manque de base légale* | 15 VIII E |
| Marine insurance | 10 I |
| | 10 VIII |

| | |
|---|---|
| | 10 VIII B |
| | 10 VIII E |
| | 10 VIII E 2 |
| | 12 II A |
| | 12 II N |
| | 17 III C |
| Maritime | |
| assistance | *see* salvage |
| companies | 16 I F |
| law | 16 I G |
| privileges | 12 I I |
| Marriage | 8 II |
| by proxy | 8 II C |
| capacity to marry | 8 II B |
| celebration of | 8 II C |
| civil ceremony | 8 I |
| | 8 II C |
| conflict of laws | 16 I D |
| engagement to marry | 8 II A |
| interruption of | 8 II G |
| licence | 8 II C |
| non-existent | 4 V H |
| nullity of | 4 V C |
| | 8 II D |
| personal effects | 8 II E |
| | 8 VI B |
| | 8 VI C |
| religious ceremony | 8 II C |
| requirements and impediments | 8 II B |
| Marshal | 15 II E |
| | 15 XIII B |
| Master | 12 II A |
| | 12 II B |
| | 12 II C |
| | 12 II D |
| | 12 II E |
| | 12 II F 3 |
| | 12 II F 5 |
| | 12 II G |
| | 12 II I |
| | 12 II M |
| | 12 II N |
| | 12 II L |
| Matrimonial | |
| agreement | 8 II F |
| home | 8 II G |
| property | |
| autonomy of parties | 8 II F |
| common | 8 II F |
| presumptions | 8 II F |
| Maurer | 1 IV B |
| Mayor | 3 IV B 3 |
| Measures | |
| educative | 18 II B 6 a i |
| of security | 18 II D 2 |
| therapeutic | 18 II B 6 a i |

| | |
|---|---|
| Medium enterprises | 17 II A 4 |
| Mental insanity | 18 II B 6 a ii |
| Merchant | 10 I |
| | 10 IV B 1 |
| | 10 IV B 4 |
| | 15 XIII D |
| | 16 I F |
| Mergers, control of | 10 VI |
| *see* also close corporation, corporation | |
| Military Penal Code | 2 I |
| | 18 I |
| Mines | 16 I H 6 |
| Minister | 2 I |
| | 3 II B 3 |
| | 3 III C 1 |
| | 3 III C 2 |
| | 3 IV A 2 |
| | 3 IV A 1 |
| | 3 V B |
| deputy | 3 III C 2 |
| | 3 IV A 1 |
| of state | 3 IV A 1 |
| without portfolio | 3 III C 2 |
| Ministry of Agriculture | 3 IV A 1 |
| | 7 V |
| | 10 VI |
| Ministry of Commerce | 10 IV A |
| | 10 VIII E 1 |
| | 10 VI |
| | 11 II A 3 |
| | 11 II C |
| | 11 II I |
| | 11 II H |
| | 16 I F |
| Ministry of Culture | 3 IV A 1 |
| | 7 V |
| Ministry of Industry | 3 IV A 1 |
| | 7 V |
| Ministry of Interior | 3 IV A 1 |
| | 7 V |
| | 16 II A |
| | 16 II B |
| | 16 II B |
| Ministry of Justice | 3 IV A 1 |
| | 18 III A 2 |
| | 3 IV A 1 |
| Ministry of Labor | 13 III C |
| Ministry of National Economy | 3 III C 3 d |
| | 3 IV A 1 |
| | 7 V C |
| | 10 VI |
| | 10 VII |
| | 10 VII B 3 |
| | 17 II A 2 |
| | 17 VII D |
| | 17 VII F |

| | |
|---|---|
| | 17 VII G |
| Ministry of Public Works | 3 IV A 1<br>7 V |
| Ministry of Regional Planning | 3 IV A 1<br>7 V |
| Minor | |
| adoption of | 8 V A |
| capacity | |
| to enter into juridical acts | 4 V B a |
| to make a will | 9 IV A |
| to marry | 8 II B |
| commercial activities of | 10 I |
| criminal liability | 18 II B 6 a i |
| domicile | 4 II D |
| emancipation | 8 VII B |
| guardianship | 8 VII B |
| heir | 10 VII B 2 |
| protection | 8 VII |
| *see* also child | |
| Misdemeanor | 18 II D 1<br>18 III A 1 b<br>18 III C 4 b |
| Misrepresentation | 10 IV A<br>10 IV C<br>10 VIII B |
| Mistake | |
| as a vice of consent | 4 V C |
| in marriage | 4 V C<br>8 II D |
| of fact | 18 II B 6 b i<br>18 II B 6 b iii |
| of law | 18 II B 6 c i<br>18 II C 2 d |
| *Modus* | 9 II H 3 |
| Monarchy | 3 II A 1 |
| Monetary benefits | 14 IV C |
| Money | |
| exchange | 10 I |
| orders | 10 III |
| commercial | 10 III C |
| *see* also delegation | |
| Monks | 9 IV A |
| Moral harm | |
| indemnity for | 5 IV I 2 a |
| Mortgage | 5 I L 3<br>6 VII<br>12 II I<br>15 XIII D |
| acquired by bank | 10 VII B 4<br>10 VII B 5<br>10 VII B 6 |
| on a ship | 6 VII<br>12 II B<br>12 II H |
| preferred | 12 II<br>12 II G 2 |

registration 12 II G 1
simple 12 II G 1
on component parts 6 II B
on industrial machinery 6 II B
Movables 4 V F
6 II B
ownership on 6 IV A
6 IV B
6 IV C
proof of 6 IV D
possession in good faith 6 IV B
transfer of 4 V F
Municipal taxes 17 V A
Murder 18 II B 2
18 III A 1 a i
*see* also homicide
Mutuality rule 15 IX D

Name
of children 8 VI A
of partnership 10 IV B 1
10 IV B 4
of spouses 8 II E
protection of 4 II E
Napoleonic Code of Commerce 10 I
National Bank of Greece 10 VII B 2
National General Collective Agreement of 1984
13 II A 1
National Health System 14 IV C
National Insurance System 14 I
Nationality 16 I H 4
as the basis of jurisdiction 16 III
Greek
acquisition of 16 II A
Code of 2 I
loss 16 II B
of children 8 VI A
of spouses 8 II E
*see* also *lex nationalis*
Natural persons 4 II A
17 II A 2
Nationalization 16 II A
Necessity
as an excuse 18 II B 6 c ii aa
justifying the act 18 II B 4 c
Negatory action 6 IV D
Negligence 5 I B 7 a
5 I E 5 b iii
5 IV E
18 II B 4 b
18 II B 6 b ii
18 II B 6 b iii
18 II C 1
bodily injury by 18 II E
homicide by 18 II E 1 f

| | |
|---|---|
| Negotiable instruments | 6 VII |
| | 10 III |
| | 15 X B |
| | 15 XI B |
| | 16 I B 1 |
| *Negotiorum gestio* | 5 II |
| | 5 II E |
| | 6 IV |
| | 8 II F |
| | 16 I B 1 |
| New York Convention on arbitration | 15 XII A |
| Nomarch | 3 IV A 2 |
| | 3 IV B 4 |
| | 3 IV B 5 |
| Nomos council | 3 IV A 2 |
| Notarial | |
| act | 4 III B 1 |
| | 4 V D |
| | 4 V E |
| | 8 II F |
| | 12 II G 1 |
| | 12 II G 2 |
| form | 4 V D, 5 II B 6 b, 6 IV C |
| | 16 I G |
| instrument | *see* instrument notarial |
| Notary | 2 I |
| | 8 IV B, 8 VII B |
| | 9 IV C 2 |
| | 9 IV C 3 |
| | 9 IV I |
| | 10 III A 1 |
| | 10 VII B 5 |
| | 15 II E |
| | 15 IV A |
| | 15 VII E |
| | 15 VII F |
| | 15 VII G |
| | 15 XII B, 16 I B 1, 17 IV A 1 |
| Nullities | 4 V H |
| 'Nullum crimen' principle | 18 II A 2 |
| | |
| Object | 6 II |
| Obligation | 5 I A |
| | 5 I B |
| | 6 II B |
| alternative | 5 I G 2 b |
| | 5 I B 2 f |
| and liability | 5 I A 3 |
| contractual | 5 I C |
| definition | 5 I A 2 |
| divided | 5 I M |
| extinction of | 5 I I |
| fulfillment of | 5 I I 1 a |
| joint | 5 I M 3 |
| joint and several | 5 I L 1 |

| | |
|---|---|
| | 5 I M 3 |
| non-performance of | 5 I E |
| relativity of | 5 I A 4 |
| sources of | 5 I A 1 |
| to perform | 5 I B 1 |
| Obligor | |
| joint | 15 III E |
| Offenses | |
| accumulated | 18 II D 3 |
| definition of | 18 II B 3 |
| distinction of | 18 II D 1 |
| Offer and acceptance | 4 V D |
| | 4 V E |
| Officers, corporate | 11 II E |
| Official Gazette | 2 V A |
| | 3 III A 4 |
| | 10 IV D |
| | 11 II |
| | 11 II H |
| | 11 III D |
| | 17 VII D |
| Offshore activities | 17 II A 2 |
| | 17 II A 6 |
| | 17 III C |
| Omission | 18 II B 2 |
| | 18 II B 3 |
| Order | |
| interlocutory | 15 VIII C |
| of a superior | 18 II B 4 d |
| to enforce | 15 XIII B |
| to pay or deliver | 15 II |
| Otho, King | 1 IV B |
| Ownership | 6 I |
| | 6 II A |
| | 6 IV |
| acquisition of | 6 IV A |
| derivative | 6 IV C |
| original | 6 IV B |
| and estate | 6 IV |
| on movables | 6 IV A |
| | 6 IV B |
| | 6 IV C |
| | 6 IV D |
| presumptions | 6 IV D |
| private | 3 VI B 2 |
| protection | 6 IV D |
| recordation | 6 IV |
| right of | 6 IV |
| | |
| Par value | 11 II C |
| Parentage | |
| establishment of | 8 IV A |
| legal effects of | 8 VI |
| Parental care | 8 II C |

8 VII A
8 III C
Paris International Convention on protection of industrial property 10 IV
Parliament 2 I
3 II B 1
3 II B 3
3 II B 4
3 III A 2
3 IV A 1
acts of 3 I C
3 II B 3
and government 3 III C 1
composition of 3 III A 1
dissolution of 3 III A 5
during the Greek revolution 1 IV A
election of 3 III A 1
members of 3 III A 3
immunity 18 II B 7 a
legal status 3 III A 3
powers of 3 II A 4
3 II A 5
relating to public finance 3 II B 4
to amend Constitution 3 I B
to legislate 3 II B 3
Parliamentary control 3 III A 4
3 V B
Partnership 5 II
10 II
10 VII A
11 III C
11 III E
by shares 11 V
civil 11 IV
11 VII
general 11 IV
limited 11 V
name 10 IV B 1
10 IV B 4
non-commercial 4 III A
silent 11 VI
Party 15 IV A
15 XI C
dominant position 15 V A
equality 15 XII C
15 XII E
examination 15 VII D
initiative 15 V A 1
15 V A 3
15 XIII B
necessary and indispensable 15 IV A
non-existing 15 IX B
oath 15 VII D
15 VII G
15 X C

Patent 10 IV D
15 XIII D
  additional 10 IV D
  office 10 IV D
  protection of 10 IV D
  requirements for granting 10 IV D
  rights 10 IV D
  to inventions by employees 10 IV D
  transfer of 10 IV D
  use in good faith 10 IV D
  void 10 IV D
Paternity 8 IV A
8 IV B
Patrimonial rights 6 II A
Penal Code 2 I
Penal sanctions 18 II D
  *see* also punishment, penalty criminal
Penalty
  clause 5 I G 2
  criminal
    conversion of 18 II D 3
    custodial 18 II D 1 b
    death 18 II D 2
    for breach of tax laws 17 VI
    measures in substitution of 18 II D 2
    pecuniary 18 II D 1 c
    supplementary 18 II D 1 d
    suspension of 18 II D 3
Pension 14 IV C
  *see* also benefits
Peremption 4 VIII A 3
Performance 5 I A 2
5 I A 3
  by third parties 5 I B 4
  claim to performance in kind 5 I E 1
  constructive 5 I E 1 b
5 I E 3 b
  delay of 5 I E 3
  determined by a third party 5 I C 2
  determined by one party 5 I C 2
  fulfillment 5 I I 1
  future 15 V B
  illegality of 5 I E 2 a
  impossibility of 5 I E 2.a, b, c
  in good faith 5 I B 1
  kinds of 5 I B 2
  of two-sided contracts 5 I D
  partial 5 I B 3
  periodic 15 IX E
  place for 5 I B 5
  specific 15 IV B
15 XIII A
15 XIII C
  time for 5 I B 6
  voluntary 15 VIII B
Personal servitudes *see* servitudes

| | |
|---|---|
| Personality | 4 II A |
| | 4 II B |
| | 8 II E |
| definition | 4 II E |
| of juridical persons | 4 III B 2 |
| protection of | 6 II |
| right of | 6 I C |
| | 6 footnote 5 |
| Persuasion | 15 VII C |
| | 15 VII G |
| Petition | |
| action-like petition | 3 V A 2 |
| for declaration of absentia | 4 II C |
| formal | 3 V A 2 |
| Petty violations | 18 II D 1 |
| | 18 III A 1 c |
| Place of business | 5 I B 5 |
| Plan | |
| city | 7 VI, 7 VII |
| master | 7 VI |
| urban | 7 VI |
| Planning | |
| constitutional frame of | 7 II |
| legislation | 7 I |
| | 7 III |
| | 7 IV |
| operational urban | 7 II |
| | 7 III |
| | 7 VI |
| organs and agencies of | 7 V |
| protection of | 7 IV |
| regional | 7 II |
| | 7 III |
| rules of | 7 I |
| | 7 III |
| study | 7 III |
| | 7 IV |
| urban | 7 II |
| | 7 III |
| | 7 VI |
| Plea | |
| of unperformed contract | 5 I E 1 a |
| Pleadings | 15 V C |
| | 15 VI B |
| | 15 VI C |
| | 15 VI D |
| | 15 VI E |
| Pledge | 5 I L 3 |
| | 6 VII |
| | 15 XI B |
| | 15 XIII D |
| Plots, rearrangement of | 7 VI |
| Political parties | 3 III A 1 |
| | 3 III A 2 |
| Possession | 6 III |
| adverse | 6 IV B |

| | |
|---|---|
| in good faith | 6 IV B |
| protection of | 6 III |
| Possessory action | 6 III |
| Post-Byzantine law | 1 III C |
| Power | |
| discretionary | 3 IV D 2 |
| political | 3 II B 2 |
| separation of powers | 3 II A 4 |
| | 3 II B 1 |
| state | 3 II B |
| Power of attorney | *see* attorney |
| Predial servitudes | *see* servitudes |
| Preemptive rights | 11 II C |
| Preferred stock | 11 II C |
| Prematurity | 15 note 6 |
| Prescription | 4 VIII A 1 |
| accrual | 4 VIII B 5 |
| acquisitive | 4 VIII A 2 |
| | 6 IV B |
| commencement of | 4 VIII B 1 |
| extension of | 4 VIII B 4 |
| interruption of | 4 VIII B 3 |
| of non-use | 4 VIII A 2 |
| period of | 4 VIII B 5 |
| plead in the court | 4 VIII B 5 |
| reduction | 4 VIII B 4 |
| renunciation | 4 VIII B 4 |
| suspension | 4 VIII B 2 |
| *see* also limitation | |
| President of the Republic | 2 I |
| | 3 I B |
| | 3 II A |
| | 3 II A 3 |
| | 3 II B 1 |
| | 3 III B |
| | 3 IV D 1 |
| | 3 III C 2 |
| | 18 II B 7 a |
| and church | 3 II B 7 |
| decisions of | 3 III C 1 |
| powers of | 3 II B 2 |
| | 3 II B 3 |
| | 3 II B 5 |
| | 3 III A 5 |
| Presidential Decree | 2 I |
| | 3 II B 3 |
| Presumption | 8 II f |
| | 9 II F |
| | 15 VII B |
| | 15 VII D |
| | 18 III C 1 |
| for the proof of ownership | 6 IV D |
| for the property of the spouses | 8 II F |
| in relation to divorce | 8 III A |
| of paternity | 8 IV A |
| | 8 IV B |

| | |
|---|---|
| of taxable income | 17 II A 6 |
| Pretrial, in criminal proceedings | 18 III C 2 |
| Prices and Income Committee | 3 III C 3 |
| Prime Minister | 3 I B |
| | 3 III A 2 |
| | 3 III C 1 |
| | 3 III C 3 |
| | 3 IV A 1 |
| powers of | 3 II A |
| | 3 II B 2 |
| | 3 III C 2 |
| Priority | |
| specific | 15 XIII D |
| Private economic activity | 3 VI B 2 |
| Private insurance business | |
| inspection | 10 VIII E 1 |
| investments | 10 VIII E 1 |
| licence | 10 VIII E 1 |
| *see* also insurance | |
| Private law | 2 I |
| Probability | 15 VII C |
| | 15 X D |
| Procedural | |
| prerequisites | 15 IV A, 15 VI E |
| | 15 IX C |
| principles | 15 V |
| | 15 XIII B |
| Proceedings | |
| non-contentious | 15 XI |
| oral | 15 V C |
| | 15 VI C |
| ordinary | 15 VI |
| | 15 X A |
| | 15 X B |
| | 15 X D |
| special | 15 X A-C |
| written | 15 V C |
| Procuration | 4 VII B |
| Production of things and documents | 5 II |
| Productive investments | 17 VII F |
| Profession | 17 II A 3 |
| Professional orientation | 14 IV C |
| Profit | 6 II F |
| lost | 5 I B 2 d i |
| Promissory note | 10 I |
| | 10 III |
| | 10 III A |
| | 10 III A 2 |
| | 16 I B 1 |
| | 16 I H 1 |
| Proper law, contracts | 16 I B 1 |
| Property | 6 I |
| acquisition of | 6 IV A |
| | 16 I H 6 |
| assignment of | 5 I C |
| Byzantine law | 1 III B |

damage to 18 II B 4 e
immovable 7 VII
of children 8 VII A
personal 6 II B
private 3 IV D
real 6 II B
rights, conflict of laws 16 I C
rural
development of 7 III
redistribution of 7 II
separation of 8 II F
taxation on 17 III B
*see* also real rights
Proportionality, principle of 3 IV D 2
Prorogation 15 III F
Proxy 11 II D 1
11 II D 2
11 II E
Public audience 15 IX A
15 IX B
Public enterprises 3 IV C 2
Public law 2 I
legal persons of 3 IV C 1
Public order
rules of 4 IV B
Public policy 15 XII D
15 XII E
16 I H 2
16 III
16 IV
Public prosecutor 15 IX A 2
15 X C
15 XI C
18 III A 2
18 III B 2
Public servants 3 IV D 7
4 II D
14 III A
Publician action 6 IV D
Publicity 1 II C
Punishment 18 II A 1
18 II B 7
*see* also penal sanctions, penalty
Purchase of goods 10 I
*see* also sale
Purpose, corporate 11 II B

Quasi-contract 16 I B 1
Quorum 11 II D 2

Rape 18 II B 4 e
18 III A 1
Ratification
of international treaties 3 I C

| | |
|---|---|
| of void juridical acts | 4 V H |
| Real rights | 3 IV D 9 |
| | 6 I |
| | 6 II B |
| | 6 III |
| protection of | 6 IV D |
| | 6 VI |
| | 6 VII |
| security rights | 6 VII |
| taxation | 17 IV C |
| *see* also property | |
| Recidivists | 18 II D 3 |
| Reciprocity | 3 I C |
| Recordation | 6 IV C |
| | 6 VI |
| | 6 VII |
| | 9 II A |
| Referendum | 3 II A 3 |
| *Reformatio in peius* | 18 II C 4 c i |
| Regions (investments) | 17 VII B |
| Register | 15 VI A |
| Regulatory tax | 17 IV D |
| Relative nullities | 4 V H |
| Relativity | |
| of contract | 5 I H |
| of obligation | 5 I A 4 |
| Relief | 15 IV B |
| | 15 V A |
| | 15 V A 1 |
| | 15 VI B |
| | 15 VII A |
| | 15 VIII C |
| | 15 X D |
| Remand | 15 VIII C |
| | 15 VIII E |
| Remedy | |
| preventive | 15 IV B |
| provisional | 15 X D |
| | 15 XII D |
| repressive | 15 IV B |
| Renunciation | 4 V C |
| | 9 II B, C |
| *Renvoi* | 16 I H 1 |
| Reopening | |
| of contested judgments | 15 VIII A |
| | 15 VIII B |
| | 15 VIII D |
| | 15 IX B |
| | 15 X C |
| | 15 XI D |
| | 15 XII E |
| Reparations | 5 I B 2 d |
| | 5 IV |
| | 18 III B 2 b |
| for non-performance | 5 I E 3 |
| for tortious liability | 5 IV H |

5 IV I 2
5 IV I 3
*see* also compensation, damages
Representation 4 III B 4
4 V H
4 VII A
15 IV A
15 V D
15 VIII D
15 IX A
indirect 4 VII C
tacit 4 VII C
Republic 3 II A 1
*Res judicata* 3 V C 2
6 III
6 IV D
11 IV D
15 IV B
15 VIII A
15 VIII C
15 VIII D
15 IX B-E
15 X D
15 XII E
15 note 6
16 IV
as to non-parties 15 IX D
time limits 15 IX E
15 X C
*Res nullius* 6 IV B
Rescission 5 I E 2 c
5 I E 3 b
5 I E 4 b
contractual 5 I E 3 b
5 I F
of juridical acts 4 V H
Reservation of law 3 VI B 2
4 II D
5 I B 5
15 III C
15 III E 5, 6
16 I H 4
Resolutory condition 4 VI
Responsibility
for employees 5 I B 8
for one's own conduct 5 I B 7
Restitution 5 I B 2 d
5 III B, C, D
Retention of title 5 II A 4
Retirement 13 II A
Retroactive effect of legislation 2 I
3 II B 4
18 II A 2
Revendicatory action 6 IV D
Right
absolute 5 III A
abuse of *see* abuse of right

| | |
|---|---|
| civil, deprivation of | 18 II D 1 d i |
| deactivation of | 4 IV C |
| | 4 V H |
| definition of | 4 IV A |
| exercise of | 18 II B 4 a |
| fair use in labor law | 13 II A |
| | 13 II B 2 |
| | 13 III D |
| Right of access to courts | 3 IV D 6 |
| | 15 I |
| | 15 VIII A |
| Right to social insurance | 14 I |
| | 14 IV A |
| Right to hearing | 3 IV D 4 |
| | 15 VIII B |
| | 15 XII C |
| | 15 XII E |
| Rule of law | 3 II A 5 |
| | 3 IV D 1 |
| Sale | 4 I |
| | 5 II A |
| commercial | 10 I |
| of goods | 10 I |
| | 10 IV A |
| on approval | 5 II A 5 |
| passing of the risk | 5 II A 2 b |
| | 5 II A 3 |
| | 5 II A 4 |
| retention of title | 5 II A 4 |
| taxes on | 17 IV B |
| warrants | 4 VIII B 3 |
| Salvage | 12 II A |
| | 12 II E |
| | 12 II I |
| | 12 II M |
| | 12 II N |
| Saving banks | 5 I B 2 c |
| Seat | 15 note 5 |
| of corporation | 16 I F |
| Seaworthiness | 12 II C |
| | 12 II D |
| | 12 II F 2 |
| | 12 II F 3 |
| | 12 II F 5 |
| Second instance courts | 18 III A 1 d |
| | 18 III C 4 c |
| Secretary | 3 IV A 1 |
| General | 3 IV A 1 |
| Special | 3 IV A 1 |
| Securities | 10 VII B 1 |
| | 10 VII B 2 |
| | 10 VII B 5 |
| | 17 II A 3 |

*see* also commercial paper, debentures, shares

| | |
|---|---|
| Security rights | 6 VII |
| measures for protection of possession | 6 III |
| Self-defense | 4 IV D |
| | 18 II B 3 |
| | 18 II B 4 b |
| Self-governmental bodies | 3 IV C |
| Self-help | 4 IV D |
| to protect possession | 6 III |
| Sentence | 18 II D 3 |
| Separation of powers | 3 II A 4 |
| | 3 II B 1 |
| Service | |
| of judgments | 15 V A 3 |
| | 15 VIII B |
| | 15 VIII C |
| of summons | 15 VI A |
| | 15 VI E |
| | 15 VIII A |
| | 15 VIII D |
| Services, contract for | 5 II C |
| Servitudes | 6 V |
| personal | 6 V |
| predial | 6 II B |
| | 6 V |
| Set-off | 5 I I 2 |
| | 5 I L 2 |
| | 5 I M 2 |
| | 5 II C 1 |
| | 15 VI D 1 |
| | 15 XIII B |
| Settlement area | 7 IV |
| | 7 VI |
| Severance pay | 13 II B 1, 2 |
| Shareholders | |
| meeting | 11 II D |
| | 11 III C |
| authority of | 11 II D 3 |
| extraordinary | 11 II D 2 |
| quorum | 11 II D 2 |
| minority | 11 II F |
| Shares | 10 III |
| | 10 VII A |
| | 11 II C |
| no-par value | 11 II C |
| restrictions in the acquisition | 11 II C |
| subscription of | 11 II A 2 |
| | 11 II C |
| treasury | 11 II C |
| Ship | 12 II A |
| | 16 II H 6 |
| abandonment of | 12 II E |
| | 12 II N |
| arrest | 12 II J |
| collision | 12 II A |
| | 12 II L |
| | 12 II N |

| | |
|---|---|
| | 16 III |
| construction | 12 II A |
| | 12 II N |
| co-ownership | 12 II A |
| | 12 II B |
| | 12 II N |
| | 16 III |
| definition | 12 II A |
| foreclosure | 12 II J |
| jurisdiction | 16 III |
| mortgage | *see* mortgage |
| operator of | 12 II E |
| ownership | 12 II A |
| | 12 II E |
| | 12 F II 2 |
| transfer of, fiduciary | 12 II G |
| registration | 12 II A |
| | 12 II E |
| taxes on | 17 III C |
| Shipowner | 12 II E |
| | 12 II G |
| *see* also ship | |
| Shipping enterprises | 17 II A 2 |
| | 17 III C |
| Shipwreck | 12 I C |
| Signature | 4 V D |
| Signs | |
| as trade marks | 10 IV B 5 |
| distinctive on goods | 10 IV B 3 |
| | 10 IV B 4 |
| | 10 IV B 5 |
| Simulation | 4 V E |
| | 4 V C |
| Social insurance | 13 II A 2 |
| | 13 III D |
| | 14 I |
| benefits | *see* benefits |
| consecutive | 14 III B |
| contributions | 14 III A |
| | 14 III B |
| | 17 II B |
| duration | 14 IV B |
| fictional | 14 IV B |
| formal | 14 IV B |
| foundation | 14 III B |
| institutions | 14 II A |
| | 14 III A |
| resources | 14 II B |
| self-governance | 14 II B |
| insured risks | 14 IV B |
| permissive | 14 IV B |
| right to | 14 I |
| | 14 IV A |
| system | 14 I |
| | 14 II A |
| | 14 IV B |

Social policy 14 I
14 IV C
Solon 1 II B
Sources
of Greek law
ancient 1 II A
civil 1 IV B
criminal 18 I
modern 2 I
of Hellenistic law 1 III A
of post-Byzantine law 1 III C
social 14 III B
Sovereign immunity 16 III
Sovereignty
of the people 3 I B
restrictions on 3 I D
Spouse 9 III A
Stamp tax 17 IV A 1
17 IV A 2
Code on 17 IV A 2
Standing to sue 15 IV A
15 VI D 1
15 VIII C
15 X C
*Stare decisis* 3 II B 6, 15 VIII E
State
administration 3 IV
and Church 3 II C
economic support 14 III B
liability 3 IV D 8
organs of 3 III
powers of 3 II
social insurance contribution 14 III B
welfare 3 II A 6
Statutes
formal 2 I
substantive 2 I
Stock Exchange 10 I
11 II A 2
11 II C
17 II C 2
Strict liability 5 IV A
5 IV F 1
5 IV F 2
18 II B 5
Strike 13 I A
13 III C
13 III D
Subsidiary 11 II C
Subsidies 17 VII C 3
Substantive truth 18 III C 1
Substitution of legatee 6 IV
Succession 9 I
acceptance 9 II A
9 II B
forced 9 V A,B

| | |
|---|---|
| intestate | 9 III |
| liquidation of | 9 VII A |
| renunciation of | 9 II B, C |
| tax | 17 III A |
| testate | 9 IV |
| vacant | 9 II E |
| Suicide | |
| accomplice to | 18 II E 1 d |
| Supervision | |
| administrative | 3 V A 3 |
| Supplementary penalties | 18 II D 1 d |
| Support | |
| of ascendants | 8 VI C |
| of descendants | 8 VI C |
| of weaker spouse | 8 II G |
| Supreme Court | 2 I |
| | 15 II A 2, 3 |
| | 15 II B |
| | 15 II D |
| | 15 V A 2 |
| | 15 VI B |
| | 15 VIII E |
| | 15 IX A |
| | 15 XII E |
| | 15 XIII B |
| | 18 III A 1 d |
| | 18 III C 3 |
| | 18 III C 4 c ii |
| *see* also cassation | |
| Supreme Judicial Council | 15 II D |
| Supreme Special Court | 3 II B 6 |
| | 3 III A 1 |
| | 3 IV C |
| Suspensive condition | 4 VI |
| Tax | 3 II B 4 |
| | 10 VII B 3 |
| | 17 I |
| as maritime privilege | 12 II |
| deductible expenses | 17 II A 4 |
| definition | 17 I |
| direct | 17 III A |
| *see* also direct taxes | |
| double taxation, treaties for the avoidance of | 17 II A 2 |
| | 17 II A 7 |
| | 17 II C 2 |
| | 17 II D |
| | 17 III A |
| enforcement | 17 VI |
| free reserves | 17 VII F |
| imposition of | 3 II B 3 |
| | 17 I |
| in favor of third parties | 17 V B |
| indirect | 14 III B |
| | 17 I |

| | |
|---|---|
| | 17 IV |
| penalties | 17 VI |
| reduced rates | 17 VII E |
| system | 17 I |
| Tax Data Code | 17 II A 4 |
| Technical counsel | 15 VII D |
| Terms | 4 VI |
| implied | 5 I B 1 |
| | 5 II |
| Testator, capacity of | 9 IV A |
| *see* also succession | |
| Theft | 18 II B 6 b iii |
| | 18 II E 5 |
| | 18 II V 4 e |
| Theories of punishment | 18 II A 1 |
| Therapeutic measures | 18 II B 6 a i |
| Things | 6 II |
| | 16 I C |
| consumable | 6 II D |
| dedicated to public purpose | 6 II E |
| fungible | 6 II C |
| immovable | 6 II B |
| movable | 6 II B |
| out of commerce | 6 II E |
| subject to public use | 6 II E |
| Threat | *see* duress |
| Tort | |
| accountability for | 4 II A |
| as a source of obligation | 5 I A 1 |
| committed by the crew | 12 I E |
| conflict of laws | 16 I B 2 |
| liability from | 5 IV A |
| Torture | 18 II E 4 |
| Town council | 3 IV B 1 |
| | 3 IV B 3 |
| Trade disputes | 13 III C |
| Trade mark | 10 IV A |
| definition | 10 IV B 5 |
| deletion | 10 IV B 5 |
| foreign | 10 IV B 5 |
| protection | 10 IV B 4 |
| | 10 IV B 5 |
| | 10 IV C |
| registration | 10 IV B 5 |
| right for exclusive use of | 10 IV B 5 |
| Trade name | 10 IV B 1 |
| | 10 IV B 4 |
| Trade unions | 13 I A |
| | 13 III A |
| | 13 III B |
| | 13 III C |
| | 13 III D |
| | 15 X C |
| Transfer of movables | 4 V F |
| Transfer tax | 17 IV C |
| Traveller's checks | 10 III C |

| | |
|---|---|
| Treasury shares | 11 II C |
| Trial | |
| *de novo* | 15 VIII C |
| in criminal proceedings | 18 III C 2 |
| | 18 III C 4 b |
| Trust | 6 IV |
| | 16 I C |
| business | 11 VI |
| constructive | 11 II E |
| Turnover tax | 17 IV A 1 |
| | 17 IV A 3 |
| Tutor | 6 IV |
| *Ultra vires* | 11 II B |
| Unfair competition | 10 IV A |
| | 10 IV B 4 |
| | 10 IV C |
| | 10 IV E |
| | 10 VI |
| Unfair trading | *see* antitrust law, unfair competition |
| Unincorporated association | 4 III A |
| Unjust enrichment | 4 V F |
| | 5 III |
| as a source of obligation | 5 I A 1 |
| | 5 II H 2 |
| directness of transfer | 5 III C |
| general clause | 5 III A |
| Unlawful acts | 5 IV A |
| | 5 IV D |
| *see* also offenses, torts | |
| Unseaworthiness | *see* seaworthiness |
| Urban land consolidation | 7 VI |
| U.S. Second Restatement, Conflict of Laws | 16 I F |
| U.S. – Greece Treaty of friendship, commerce and navigation | 16 I F |
| Usufruct | 6 II B |
| | 6 V |
| | 6 VII |
| Utility models | 10 IV E |
| Value-added tax | 17 IV A 1 |
| | 17 IV A 3 |
| | 17 IV C |
| | 17 IV D |
| Venue | 15 III A |
| Vice-minister | 3 III C 2 |
| Vices of consent | 4 V C |
| | 4 V H |
| Vienna Convention on consular relations | 16 III |
| Vienna Convention on diplomatic relations | 16 III |
| Village council | 3 IV B 3 |
| Voters | 3 III A 1 |

| | |
|---|---|
| Wages | 13 I A<br>13 III B<br>13 III D |
| automatic adjustment | 13 II A 4 |
| of crew members | 12 II D |
| Warehouse operations | 10 I |
| Warehouse receipts | 10 III<br>10 III G<br>10 VII B 4 |
| Welfare | 13 II A 2 |
| Welfare state | 3 II A 6 |
| Wilful conduct | 5 I B 7 a<br>5 IV E |
| Will | |
| capacity to make | 9 IV A |
| conflict of laws | 16 I B 1<br>16 I E |
| contents of | 9 IV E |
| defects of | 9 IV C 1<br>9 IV F |
| extraordinary | 9 IV B<br>9 IV D |
| form of | 9 IV B |
| holographic | 4 V D<br>9 IV A<br>9 IV B<br>9 IV C 1<br>9 IV C 3 |
| interpretation | 9 IV E |
| loss of | 9 IV H |
| made at sea | 9 IV B<br>9 IV D 1 |
| made during blockade | 9 IV B<br>9 IV D 3 |
| military | 9 IV B<br>9 IV D 2<br>9 IV A |
| mystic (secret) | 9 IV B<br>9 IV C 3 |
| nullity of | 9 IV B<br>9 IV F |
| ordinary | 9 IV B<br>9 IV C |
| public | 9 IV A<br>9 IV B |
| publication of | 9 IV I |
| revocation of | 9 IV H |
| validity of | 9 IV F |
| Withholding taxes | 17 II A 7<br>17 II C 2 |
| Witness | |
| in civil procedure | 15 VII D<br>15 VII F<br>15 X C<br>15 XII C |
| in criminal procedure | 18 III A 2 |

| | |
|---|---|
| | 18 III C 4 a |
| | 18 III C 4 b |
| proof of commercial transactions | 15 VII D |
| | 10 I |
| Work | |
| conditions | 13 II A 2 |
| | 13 III B |
| contract for | 5 II C 2 a |
| | 5 II D |
| hours | 13 II A 1 |
| injury at | 13 II A 2 |
| leave | 13 II A 3 |
| Workers' confederation | 13 III A |
| York-Antwerp Rules | 12 I K |
| Zone | |
| of special aid | 7 VI |
| of special incentives | 7 VI |

# Index of Greek Words

A


| | |
|---|---|
| αγωγή | 15 VI A |
| ακυρώσεως διαιτητικής αποφάσεως | 15 XII E |
| αναγνωριστική | 15 IV B |
| αρνητική | 6 IV D |
| διαπλαστική | 15 IV B |
| διεκδικητική | 6 IV D |
| καταψηφιστική | 15 IV B |
| άδεια | 13 II A 3 |
| αδικαιολόγητος πλουτισμός | 5 III |
| αδικοπραξία | 5 IV A |
| αδυναμία παροχής | 5 I E 2 |
| αθέμιτος ανταγωνισμός | 12 II F 5 |
| αίρεση | 4 VI |
| αναβλητική | 4 VI |
| διαλυτική | 4 VI |
| αιτία | 4 V F |
| αιτιώδης σύνδεσμος | 5 IV B |
| άμβλωση | 18 II E 2 |
| αμέλεια | 5 I B 7 |
| αναγγελία | 15 XIII D |
| αναγκαστική διαχείριση | 15 XIII D |
| αναγκαστική εκτέλεση | 15 XIII B |
| επί πλοίων | 12 II J |
| αναδοχή χρέους | 5 I L |
| αναίρεση | 15 VIII E |
| amajopg[ (ejseke[rex) | 15 XIII B |
| ανακοπή ερημοδικίας | 15 VIII B |
| αναπαλλοτρίωτη κατάθεση | 10 VII B 2 |
| αναψηλάφηση | 15 VIII D |
| ανθρωποκτονία | 18 II E 1 |
| ανταγωγή | 15 VI D 3 |
| ανταλλαγή | 5 II A 1 |
| ανταπεργία | 13 III D |
| αντικείμενο | 6 II A |
| αντιπροσώπευση | 4 VII A |
| Ανώτατο Δικαστικό Ευμβούλιο | 15 II D |
| Ανώτατο Ειδικό Δικαστήριο | 3 II B 6 |
| αξιόγραφο | 10 III |
| αξίωση | 4 VIII A |
| απαράδεκτο | 15 IV A |
| απάτη | 18 II E 7 |
| απεργία | 13 III D |
| απόγραφο | 15 XIII B |

απόδειξη 15 VII A
συντηρητική 15 VII A
αποδοχή 4 V E
αποζημίωση 5 I B 2
αποθεματικά 14 II B
αποθετήριο 10 III D
αποκλήρωση 9 VI
απόλυση 13 II B 2
απόπειρα 18 II C 1
αποποίηση κληρονομίας 9 II C
απόσβεση των ενοχών 5 I 1
απόφαση 15 IX A
διαιτητική 15 XII E
αρραβών 5 I C 1
Άρειος Πάγος 3 II B 6
15 II B
18 III A 1
αρμοδιότητα 15 III A
καθ'ύλη 15 III A
κατά τόπο 15 III A
λειτουργική 15 III A
άρνηση της βάσεως της αγωγής 15 VI D 2
ΑΣΟΠ 3 III B 3
αστικώς υπεύθυνος 18 III B 2
ασφάλεια 13 II A 2
ασφάλεια ζωής 10 VIII D
ασφάλεια θέσεως 13 II B
ασφαλιστικά μέτρα 15 X D
ασφαλιστική εισφορά 14 III A
ασφαλιστική παροχή 14 IV A
ασφαλιστική περίοδος 14 IV B
ασφαλιστικός κίνδυνος 14 IV B
ασφαλιστικός φορέας 14. II A
αυξημένες αποσβέσεις 17 VII F
αυτουργός 18 II C 2
αυτοφία 15 VII D
αφάνεια 4 II C
αφορολόγητα αποθεματικά 17 VII F
αχρησία 4 VIII A

B

βασανιστήρια 18 II E 4
βιομηχανικά υποδείγματα και σχεδιάσματα 10 IV E
βιομηχανική ιδιοκτησία 10 IV

Γ

γάμος 8 II
γενική συνέλευση μετόχων 11 II D
γενικός διευθυντής 11 II E
γονική μέριμνα 8 VII A
γραμματείς (δικαστηρίων) 15 II E
γραμμάτιο εις διαταγή 10 III A

Δ


δάνειο 5 II F
δασμός 17 IV D
δεδικασμένο 15 IX B
δήλωση βουλήσεως 4 V A
3 II A 1
δημοκρατία 4 V C
δήμος 3 IV B 1
διαδικαστική προϋπόθεση 15 IV A
διαζύγιο 8 III
διαιτησία 15 XII A
  μόνιμη 15 XII C
  στο εργατικό δίκαιο 13 III C
διακριτικός τίτλος 10 IV B 2
10 IV B 4
διαμαρτυρικό 10 III A1
διασχηματισμός 10 IV B 4
διατακτικό 15 IX A
διαφυγόν κέρδος 5 I B 2
διαχειριστής 11 III D
διευθύνων σύμβουλος 11 II E
δικαιοδοσία 15 III A
δικαιοπραξία 4 V
  αιτιώδης 5 II H 1
  αφηρημένη 5 II H 1
δικαίωμα 4 IV
4 IV A
  αποδυνάμωση 4 IV C
  κατάχρηση 4 IV B
δικαστήριο
  διοικητικό 15 II A 1
  ποινικό 15 II A 1
  πολιτικό 15 II A 1
δικαστική αντίληψη 8 VII E
δικαστική δαπάνη 15 VI G
δικαστικό συμβούλιο 18 III C 3
δικαστικός επιμελητής 15 II E
δικηγορικός σύλλογος 15 II E
δικηγόρος 15 II E
διοίκηση 3 IV A 1
διοίκηση αλλοτρίων 5 II E 3
διοικητικό συμβούλιο 11 II E
δίπλωμα ευρεσιτεχνίας 10 IV D
δόλος 5 I B 7
δουλεία
  πραγματική 6 V
  προσωπική 6 V
δωρεά αιτία θανάτου 9 II H 4


Ε


έγγραφο 15 VII D
εγγύηση 15 II G
Εθνικό Σύστημα Υγείας 14 IV B

| | |
|---|---|
| ειδικές διαδικασίες | 15 X A |
| ειδικές διατάξεις | 15 X B |
| ειδικές δωσιδικίες | 15 III D |
| εικονικότητα | 4 V C |
| ειρηνοδικείο | 15 II B |
| εισαγγελέας | 15 II A 2 |
| | 18 III A 2 |
| εισηγητής | 15 IX A |
| εισφορά | 17 I |
| εκκαθάριση | 11 II 1 |
| εκκρεμοδικία | 15 VI A |
| Εκλογή | 1 III B |
| εκναυλωτής | 12 II F 2 |
| έκταξη | 10 III C |
| εκτασσόμενος | 10 III C |
| εκτάσσων | 10 III C |
| εκτελεστός τίτλος | 15 XIII A |
| εκχώρηση | 5 I K |
| ελεγκτής | 11 II H |
| Ελεγκτικό Συνέδριο | 3 II B 6 |
| έμβλημα | 10 IV B 2 |
| εμπορική εντολή πληρωμής | 10 IIIC |
| εμπορική επωνυμία | 10 IV B 1 |
| έμπορος | 10 I |
| εμπράγματη ασφάλεια | 6 VII |
| εναγόμενος | 15 IV A |
| ενάγων | 15 IV A |
| ένδειξη προελεύσεως | 10 IV |
| ένδικα μέσα | 15 VIII A |
| ενέγγυος τραπεζική πίστωση | 10 VII B 4 |
| ενέχυρο | 6 VII |
| τραπεζικό | 10 VII B 5 |
| ενεχυρόγραφο | 10 III D |
| ενοχή | 5 I A 2 |
| εις ολόκληρον | 5 I M |
| ενοχή (ποινικό δίκαιο) | 18 II A 5 |
| ενοχικό δίκαιο | 5 I A 1 |
| ένσταση | 15 VI D 1 |
| εντεταλμένος σύμβουλος | 11 II E |
| εντολή | 5 II E 1 |
| εντολή προς εκτέλεση | 15 XIII B |
| ένωση πιστωτών | 10 II |
| Εξάβιβλος | 1 III B |
| | 1 III C |
| | 1 IV B |
| εξέταση των διαδίκων | 15 VII D |
| Επαναγωγή | 1 III B |
| επίδομα | 14 IV B |
| επιδότηση επιτοκίου | 17 VII C |
| επιθαλάσσια αρωγή και διάσωση | 12 II M |
| επιταγή (εκτελέσεως) | 15 XIII B |
| επιτροπεία ανηλίκων | 8 VII B |
| επιχορήγηση | 17 VII C |
| εργαζόμενος | 13 II A 2 |
| εργατικό ατύχημα | 13 II A 2 |
| εργοδότης | 13 II A 2 |

ερημοδικία 14 III A; 15 VI E
εταιρία 11 I
  ανώνυμη 10 IV B 1; 11 II
  αστική 11 VII
  αφανής 11 VI
  ετερόρρυθμη 10 IV B 1; 11 V
  λύση 11 II 1
  ομόρρυθμη 10 IV B 1; 11 IV
  περιορισμένης ευθύνης 10 IV B 1; 11 III
εταίρος 11 III B
ευεργέτημα πενίας 15 VI G
ευθύνη 5 I A 2
  πλοιοκτήτη 12 II E; 12 II F 3
έφεση 15 VIII C
εφετείο 15 II B
εφοπλιστής 12 II E

Z

ζημία 5 IV B

H

ηθικός αυτουργός 18 II C 2

Θ

θεμιστές 1 II A
θετική ζημία 5 I B 2

I

Ίδρυμα Κοινωνικών Ασφαλίσεων 14 III A

J

Ιδρυτής 11 II A 1
ικανοποίηση ηθικής βλάβης 5 IV 1
ικανότητα
  διαδίκου 15 IV A
  δικαιοπραξίας 4 V B
  δικαίου 4 II A
  δικαστικής παραστάσεως 15 IV A
ισολογισμός 11 II D 1

K

κακούργημα 18 II D 1
καλή πίστη 5 I B 1
καρπός 6 II F

| | |
|---|---|
| καταλογισμός | 18 II A 5 |
| καταπίστευμα | 9 II Θ 2 |
| καταστατικό | 4 III B 1 |
| | 11 II B |
| κατάσχεση | 15 ΩIII Δ |
| πλοίου | 12 II 1 |
| κατηγορούμενος | 18 III B 2 |
| κατοικία | 4 II Δ |
| κατοχή | 6 III |
| κεφάλαιο | 11 II Γ |
| κληροδότημα | 9 II Θ 1 |
| κληρονομητήριο | 9 II Z |
| | 16 I E |
| κληρονομική αναξιότητα | 9 II Δ |
| κλοπή | 18 II Θ 1 |
| κοινή αβαρία | 12 II Λ |
| κοινός λογαριασμός | 10 XII B 3 |
| κοινότητα | 3 IX B 1 |
| κοινωνική ασφάλεια | 14 I |
| κοινωνική μέριμνα | 14 I |
| κοινωνικός πόρος | 14 III A |
| κράτος | |
| δικαίου | 3 II A 5 |
| κοινωνικό | 3 II A 6 |
| κυβέρνηση | 3 III B 2 |
| κύριος του πλοίου | 12 II E |
| κυριότητα | 6 IX |
| ΚΥΣΕΑ | 3 III B 3 |
| ΚΥΣΥΜ | 3 III B 3 |

Λ

| | |
|---|---|
| λήπτης | 10 III Γ |
| λογογράφος | 1 II Γ |

M

| | |
|---|---|
| μάρτυρας | 15 XII Δ |
| μέρισμα | 11 II H |
| μεταβίβαση κυριότητας πλοίου για εξασφάλιση απαιτήσεως | Ch.12 II G |
| μεταγραφή | 6 XI |
| μετατροπή | 11 II 1 |
| μετοχή | 11 II Γ |
| μέτρα ασφαλείας | 18 II Δ 2 |
| μητρόπολη | 1 III Γ |
| μισθός | 13 II A 4 |
| μίσθωση | |
| έργου | 5 II B |
| πράγματος | 5 II.B |
| μνηστεία | 8 II A |

N

| | |
|---|---|
| ναύλωση | 12 II Z |
| νομάρχης | 3 IX A 2 |

| | |
|---|---|
| νομή | 6 III |
| νόμιμη μοίρα | 9 X |
| νομιμοποίηση | 15 IX A |
| νομοκάνονας | 1 III B |
| νομός | 3 IX A 2 |
| | 15 II B |

O

| | |
|---|---|
| ολομέλεια | 15 II B |
| ομοδικία | 15 IX A |
| ομολογία | 15 XII Δ |
| ομολογίες | 11 II C |
| ανωνύμων εταιριών | 10 III D |
| Οργανισμός Απασχόλησης Εργατικού Δυναμικού (ΟΑΕΔ) | 14 IV C |
| όρκος | 15 VII D |

Π

| | |
|---|---|
| παραγραφή | 4 VIII A |
| αξιώσεως | 12 II N |
| παρανομία | 5 IV B |
| παράρτημα | 6 II B |
| παρέκταση | 15 III F |
| παρέμβαση | 15 IV A |
| παροχή | 5 I A 2 |
| εφάπαξ | 14 IV C |
| κατά γένος | 5 I B 2 |
| σε είδος | 14 IV B |
| Πείρα | 1 III B |
| πινάκιο | 15 VI A |
| πλαστογραφία | 15 VII E |
| πλημμέλημα | 18 II D 1 |
| πληρεξουσιότητα | 4 VII B |
| πλήρωμα | 12 II D |
| πληρωτέα εις λογαριασμόν | 10 III B |
| πλοίαρχος | 12 II C |
| πλοιοκτήτης | 12 II E |
| πνευματική ιδιοκτησία | 10 V |
| ποινή | 18 II D 1 |
| ποινική ρήτρα | 5 I G 2 |
| πολιτικώς ενάγων | 18 III B 2 |
| πράγμα | 6 II A |
| ακίνητο | 6 II B |
| αναλωτό | 6 II D |
| αντικαταστατό | 6 II C |
| εκτός συναλλαγής | 6 II E |
| κινητό | 6 II B |
| πραγματογνωμοσύνη | 15 VII D |
| προεδρικό διάταγμα | 3 II B 3 |
| προθεσμία | 4 VI |
| αποσβεστική | 4 VIII B |
| προίκα | 8 II F |
| πρόνοια | 13 II A 2 |
| προνόμια | 15 XIII D |

ναυτικά 12 II 1
προσαύξηση 9 III B
προσεπίκληση 15 IV A
προσφυγή 17 VI
ενδικοφανής 3 V A 2
πρόσωπο
νομικό 4 III
φυσικό 4 II
προσωπική κράτηση 15 XIII D
προσωρινή εκτέλεση 15 VIII A
προσωρινός τίτλος μετατρέψιμων ομολογιών 10 III D
πρόταση 4 V E
Πρόχειρος Νόμος 1 III B
πρωθυπουργός 3 III B 2
πρωτοδικείο
μονομελές 15 II B
πολυμελές 15 II B
πταίσμα 18 II D 1
πτώχευση 10 II
πώληση 5 II A

Σ

σήμα 10 IV B 5
σύγκρουση πλοίων 12 II L
συγχώνευση 11 II 1
συλλογική διαπραγμάτευση 13 III B
συλλογική σύμβαση 13 III B
συλλογικό εργατικό δίκαιο 13 III
σύμβαση 4 V E
αμφοτεροβαρής 5 I D
υπέρ τρίτου 5 I H 1
σύμβαση εργασίας 13 II A
αορίστου χρόνου 13 II B 2
λήξη 13 II B
ορισμένου χρόνου 13 II B 1
σύμβαση μεταφοράς επιβατών 12 II F 7
συμβιβασμός 15 VI F
συμβολαιογράφος 15 II E
Συμβούλιο της Επικρατείας 3 II B 6
συμπλοιοκτησία 12 II B
συμφωνία περί διαιτησίας 15 XII B
συμψηφισμός 5 I 1 2
συναλλαγματική 10 III A
συνδικαλιστική ελευθερία 13 III A
σύνδικος πτωχεύσεως 10 II
συνεισφορά 9 III C
στο ναυτικό δίκαιο 12 II K
συνεργός
άμεσος 18 II C 2
απλός 18 II C 2
συνεταιρισμός 17 II C3
συνήγορος 1 II C
σύνταγμα 3 I A
'σύνταγμα' 1 III B

σύνταξη 14 IV B
συστατικά 6 II B
σύστημα κοινωνικής ασφαλίσεως 14 I
σύστημα συγκεντρώσεως 15 V B
σωματική βλάβη 18 II E 3

T

τακτικός δικαστής 15 II A 2
τεκμήριο 15 VII D
τέλη 17 I
  καθαριότητας και φωτισμού 17 V A
τεχνικός σύμβουλος 15 VII D
τίτλος ισόβιας προσόδου 10 III D
τμήμα 15 II B
τόκος 5 I B 2
τραπεζική επιταγή 10 III B
τριμερής σχέση εργασίας 14 III A
τρόπος 9 II H 3

Y

υγεία 13 II A 2
υιοθεσία 8 V
υπαιτιότητα 5 IV B
υπαναχώρηση 5 I F
υπεξαίρεση 12 II F 5
18 II E 6
υπερημερία
  δανειστή 5 I E 5
  οφειλέτη 5 I E 3
υπόθεση εκουσίας δικαιοδοσίας 15 XI A
υποθήκη 6 VII
  απλή 12 II H 1
  προτιμώμενη 12 II H 2
  σε πλοία 12 II H
  τραπεζική 10 VII B 6
υπουργός 3 III B 2
υποχρεώσεις εκναυλωτή 12 II F 2
υποχρεώσεις ναυλωτή 12 II F 4
υφυπουργός 3 III B 2

Φ

φόρος 17 I
  δημοτικός 17 V A
  εισαγωγής 17 IV D
  εισοδήματος 17 II
  καταναλώσεως 17 IV B
  κύκλου εργασιών 17 IV A 3
  μεταβιβάσεως 17 IV C
  προστιθέμενης αξίας (Φ.Π.Α.) 17 IV A 1
  υπέρ τρίτων 17 V B
φορτωτική 12 II F 6
φύλλο ελέγχου 17 VI

X

χαρτόσημο 17 IV A 2
χρεωστικό ομόλογο εμπόρου 10 III D
χρησιδάνειο 5 II B 8
χρησικτησία 4 VIII A

Ω

ώρες εργασίας 13 II A 1
ωφελήματα 6 II F